Tough Man
The Greg Haugen Story

Anthony "Zute" George
Foreword by Jeff Fenech

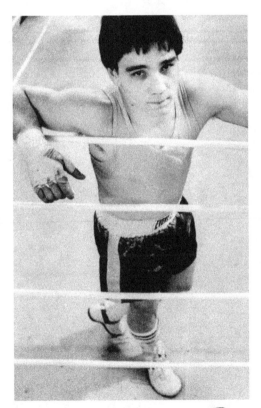

Thank you for
the support,
Zute

Dinner For Breakfast Productions—Bronx, NY
ISBN: 978-0-578-68611-0
Library of Congress Control Number: 2020908229
Title: Tough Man
Author: Anthony George
Digital distribution | 2020
Paperback | 2020

Published in the United States by New Book Authors Publishing

Dedication

I would like to dedicate this book to my lovely wife, Dawn George. She is my life, and my light.

Greg Haugen dedicates this book to Billy Bacon. Billy passed away during the making of this book. Greg met Billy in Canastota, and describes him as a great friend, huge boxing fan, and even bigger Greg Haugen fan. I never had the pleasure of meeting Billy, but I knew he and I would have gotten along just grand.

Greg also dedicates this book to his dad, Lee Haugen. Greg said that Lee was a proud marine and was responsible for his start in boxing. I had the pleasure to interview Lee on a few occasions for this book. He was terminally ill when I contacted him but was always generous with his time. He will be missed.

Zute

Go vegan. Because it will not kill anybody.

Table of Contents

Foreword by Jeff Fenech vii
Chapter One: Mexico's Favorite Son 1
Chapter Two: Three Words 3
Chapter Three: Life In Auburn Washington................................. 6
Chapter Four: Amateur Career & Alaskan Toughman................. 12
Chapter Five: Turning Pro 24
Chapter Six: 1986: Hello ESPN 29
Chapter Seven: Facing Chris Calvin.. 50
Chapter Eight: Rolling In '86 69
Chapter Nine: Fighting For The NABF 83
Chapter Ten: The Championship Level.. 98
Chapter Eleven: Beating Kronk Gold.. 112
Chapter Twelve: Fighting Paz: Facing The Devil In His Den..... 135
Chapter Thirteen: Olympic Gold... 169
Chapter Fourteen: Meeting The Devil A Third Time................... 186
Chapter Fifteen: The Comeback Trail: Back On ESPN 196
Chapter Sixteen: Macho Time.. 212
Chapter Seventeen: Sparring A Legend.. 238
Chapter Eighteen: Battle Of The Tough Guys............................. 242
Chapter Nineteen: An Arduous Tune Up: Or Was It?................. 253
Chapter Twenty: Mexico City 268
Chapter Twenty-One: Fighting With No Gloves.......................... 282
Chapter Twenty-Two: Trying To Tame A Tiger........................... 287
Chapter Twenty-Three: The Twilight Is Here 298
Chapter Twenty-Four: Retirement... 315
Chapter Twenty-Five: Rubbing Elbows 323
About the Author 335
Acknowledgements.. 337
References... 340

Foreword

Greg Haugen, born August 31st, 1960. Turned professional in 1982. Winning the IBF world Lightweight Championship against the heavily favored Jimmy Paul in his 20th fight at the Mecca of Boxing Venue, Caesar's Palace. Well, what can I say about this man who accepted all challengers. First and foremost, I am very happy to call Greg my friend, as his loyalty and honesty is his priority. I would like to acknowledge Greg as a fighter. I totally respect him as he helped me prepare for my first clash with Azumah Nelson. He gave me some great, hard rounds, so thank you my friend. But more importantly, as a fighter he feared no man. Greg fought the best of the best in a really tough period of the 80's and 90's. Names like Jimmy Paul, Ray Mancini, Pernell Whitaker, Julio Caesar Chavez, Hector Camacho and Vinny Paz. Wow, what more can you say? He won a second world title in 1991 in the super lightweight division in a tough battle with Hector Camacho. Greg always took to a challenge like a bull seeing a red flag. Greg was a real character outside the ring, and I remember one day in particular when we were on the golf course and a rattlesnake came out of the rocks. Well, all of us Aussie's stood very still and were petrified, but of course, not crazy Greg. Yes, he had to prove how crazy he was and grabbed the rattlesnake around the neck and chased us all with it. CRAZY. That's our Greg. But as a fighter he will always be remembered as one tough man who rose and took all challengers. Greg Haugen 40-10-1 (19, KO's). Three-time world champion! Take a bow.

—Jeff Fenech, June 25th, 2019

John Chemeres, on the left, raises Greg Haugen, (above) who rejoices after regaining the IBF title belt by hammering archrival Vinny Pazienza for 15 grueling roundes and capturing a unanimous decision (right).

(Courtesy of John Chemeres).

Chapter One
Mexico's Favorite Son

Mexico breeds boxers. It is just that simple. You can take it a step further and say Mexico produces warriors, as Mexican boxers have a brawling, yet scientific approach to their craft; lateral movement is not in their vocabulary, no more than it is for them to quit throwing punches. The Mexican boxing fans are just as intense and insatiable for violence. As Jorge Acre once said, "People do not pay to see dancing, they pay to see punches." Such an aggressive style has created a love affair between Mexican fighters and their fans like no other in the sport.

Ruben Olivares, Pipino Cuevas, Vicente Saldivar, Erik Morales, Marco Antonio Barrera, Salvador Sanchez, Miguel Canto, Juan Manuel Marquez, Chucho Castillo, Saul Alvarez, Gilberto Roman, Carlos Zarate, and countless others have captured the hearts of Mexican fans, and have satisfied their bloodthirst for violence as a spectator sport. But no Mexican fighter has been admired more than Julio Cesar Chavez, Sr. Don King eloquently called J.C. Superstar as the "idol of Mexico." Therefore, when Greg Haugen, a white guy from the highbrow United States of America, insulted their idol, they wanted his hide. A pound of flesh would not be nearly enough as redemption. They wanted their hero to beat and humiliate him, and they want to devour the scraps of the man who was called 'Mutt.'

As a result, when Greg Haugen was preparing to take on Chavez in Mexico City, he experienced hostility that perhaps no other man who has laced up the boxing gloves had. Not in the same capacity anyway. It is not a stretch to say that Greg Haugen would have been dead if not for heavy protection from Mexican soldiers both before and after the fight.

What could have brought on such a penchant for hostility?

Indeed, a question that most boxing fans of that time know the answer to. But the answer should not define who Greg Haugen was as a boxer, and who he is as a man. To get the unabridged version of

Greg is to peel the onion of one of the most exciting pugilists of his time. While Mexico City is a significant part of the Greg Haugen story, it is a mere smidgeon of the overall composite of a kid who had a rough, poor upbringing, who was a proverbial sponge for boxing and would always try and give his best, even when he was at his worst.

Greg Haugen may have not been as popular as Mexico's favorite son, but he was a product of the often-forgotten Auburn, Washington, and made that city proud. Greg Haugen touched everyone he ever met in an impactful way. Many were inspired by him, while some wish they never met him, most loved him, while others hate him. But even the biggest Haugen adversary would never question his toughness, as well his ability as a boxer. If you only know the story of Mexico City, you might not know about Greg.

Chapter Two
Three Words

"I always thought there was a deep, dark side, to Greg Haugen."
—Al Bernstein

Greg Haugen caught the ire of Chavez and all of Mexico by uttering three daggering words. "Tijuana cab drivers..." three words that were uttered by Greg, delivered with his classic, impish smirk. Indeed, Greg Haugen could fight, but he could also throw daggers with his words. Bob Jarvis, a boxing mainstay in the Washington area and the owner of the Hillman City Boxing Gym, said this of Greg, "I promoted Greg when he was an amateur...Greg was probably the king of the trash talkers, He would figure out some way to mess with you." Main Events promoter Kathy Duva added, "He was always up to something. His taunts were not just schoolyard taunts, there was thought put into it." With that said, it is unlikely that Greg Haugen thought his rhetoric towards J.C. Superstar would have had the repercussions that it did. But Greg did have to say *something* to spice up the fight.

Kathy Duva, who was a publicist for Main Events during Greg's heyday, explains, "There was no Twitter then. So, you had to find a way to get these reporters' attention to write something. Guys like Greg made my job a lot easier. He was so much fun." As usual, Don King probably verbalized Greg's gift of gab the best, "Greg was great at talking as well as fighting, I saw something in Greg, he was a great instigator, a great talker, and he had ability. That made him great and very promotable," Such qualities in Greg helped King and the boxing world cash in on the biggest live gate in boxing history.

Way before Mexico City, Haugen was a great success story that was cloaked in mystery and misunderstanding. A career that consisted of a decorative amateur career, an unbelievable run in a tough man competition, and a professional boxing career that saw Greg compete with the best boxers of the time. Capturing the lightweight, super lightweight and welterweight championship along the way. Despite these impressive credentials, an analysis of Greg Haugen, the pugilist, is similar to the blind man's elephant. He is the excellent counterpuncher to some, a boxer who likes to control distance to others, an immensely strong inside brawler to other observers, a defensive wizard to still others and a rugged, tough man to others. Very few boxers have been described in such an eclectic manner. As with the elephant, if you chose one attribute to describe Greg Haugen, you neglect what else made this complete fighter. Boxing historian Lee Groves painted a poignant picture of Greg the boxer, "He was a good counter puncher, had a very good, darting jab, he used movement, was very nimble on his feet, he used hand, foot, and shoulder feints. If you knew what to watch for, Greg was a joy to watch." John Chemeres adds, "Greg had one of the best jabs in boxing."

However, even these descriptions of Greg do not tell the complete picture. The thought process between his ears was not as conventional as his darting jab, but it dictated a lot of his career. Al Bernstein said of Greg, "I always thought that there was a deep, dark side to Greg Haugen." Like with many of his pre-fight analysis, Al hit the nail right on the head. Greg was the ultimate contradiction. Greg was always serious about boxing, but often, his passion for the sport was not congruent with his training habits. Jim Montgomery stated "I had one fight with him where he did not train one day…it was in California, and he won" Trainer Victor Machado talks about how Greg could have had an even better career if he was more disciplined. "Sometimes, Greg just didn't give a shit," explained Victor. Which is a scary concept because Haugen's boxing career was exceptional as is.

Before we peel the Haugen onion, let us take a look at a little warm-up activity.
In hopes of suppressing the Tijuana cab drivers stigma, those who were interviewed for this book were asked to define Greg Haugen in three words. The responses given supports the claim that quite a few people still overlook his significant boxing skills.

Victor Machado (Trainer and longtime friend): "A solid fighter."

Jeff Bumpus (Opponent and now friend): "A throwback fighter."

Vinny Paz (Opponent, still hated foe): "Douchebag, douchebag, douchebag." Indeed, Vinny still has a passionate dislike for Haugen, but he also described him as "A tough kid."

Jimmy Paul (Opponent, IBF Lightweight Champion): "Tough, rugged fighter."

Grover Wiley (Opponent, Greg's last victory): "Sledgehammer right hand."

Craig Houx (Boxer and self-proclaimed Haugen Doppelganger: "Heart, Courage, Balls."

Al Bernstein (Hall of Fame Broadcaster): "Mysterious, provocative, sardonic."

Lee Groves (Boxing Historian): "Confident, tough, resilient."

Edwin Curet (Opponent, ESPN Lightweight Champion): "Tough, awkward, nice."

Tony Lopez (Opponent, Multiple World Champion): "He's fucking crazy."

Bill MacDonald (Boxing Historian): "Tricky, smooth, consistent."

Pernell Whitaker (Opponent, Hall of Fame Legend): "A good gentleman."

Jeff Fenech (Sparring Partner, Friend, Hall of Fame Legend): "All time champion."

Paul Nave (Opponent three fight): "Tough, arrogant, genuine."

Kathy Duva (Main Events Promotor): "Impish, gritty, clever."

Livingstone Bramble, WBA World Champion: "He is crazy (laughing)."

Joe Belinc (Amateur Rival): "Cocky, super-tough, lucky."

Bret Summers (Amateur Rival): Bad attitude, funny."

Freddie Roach (Opponent): "Cocky, tough, good."

Don King (Promotor): "Great, promotable fighter."

Juan Carlos Alvarado (Opponent): "Strong, Warrior, Brave."

Joe Hipp (Former heavyweight, friend): "Intense, tough fighter."

What are your three words?

Indeed, an eclectic mixture of descriptions. None of which tells the true story of Greg Haugen, but all add to its narrative. Greg Haugen is no doubt a one of a kind special pugilist. This book is an attempt to illuminate Greg Haugen in a way that has never been done before. Through his voice, and the voice of others who fought him and knew him well.

Chapter Three
Life in Auburn Washington

"Greg took to boxing like a duck to water, when he was five years old, he would do everything right."

—Jim Montgomery.

Greg Haugen was born on August 31st, 1960, in Auburn, Washington. Greg was the second oldest of six kids. Greg's dad, Lee Haugen, was Norwegian, and his mother was Sioux Indian. Greg's last name is pronounced, How-Gun. Greg was born during the year of the rat. Fitting because Greg Haugen has the survival skills of a rat. When cornered, a rat can be most dangerous, whenever Greg Haugen felt cornered by an opponent or in life, he also had a huge bite. At the same time, as seen in films like Willard and Ben, when trust is earned, a rat can be tender, loving, and your best friend. A misunderstood creature. Just like Greg Haugen as a boxer.

There is even a misunderstanding about Greg's nickname, Mutt, which was given to him by his father. The narrative attached to the Mutt nickname is presented as if Lee was detrimentally addressing his son. The real story behind the nickname is that Lee Haugen was very fond of the comic strip, Mutt, and Jeff; the comic was well known for having a very tall and a very short man. Lee Haugen might not have been a stickler for details, however, as he labeled his vertically challenged son Mutt, who was indeed the taller man. "I had mistakenly identified Mutt as the shorter character in the comic strip. I found out years later that Mutt was the tall guy, and Jeff was the little guy, but that was how I named him Mutt," Lee explained. One could say that the mistaken identity was an efficacious one because it would be far-fetched to imagine Jeff as a captivating nickname. "My dad had told me about the Mutt and Jeff thing, and I didn't mind it. I grew up in the town of Auburn, and everybody knew me as 'Mutt,' I didn't think of it as derogatory," Greg said of the name. Lee Haugen also had pride in naming his son, and perhaps a little foreshadowing of the fighter in him, by naming Greg after

Gregory 'Pappy' Boyington, the famous combat fighter in the United States Marines. Lee also said he was, "very proud" of Greg and all that he accomplished. He did not think of his son as a Mutt, which has been the narrative in some circles over the years.

The year Greg was born was as captivating as his boxing career. The Cold War between the United States and the Soviet Union was in full swing, the United States also announced that 3,500 troops would be sent to Vietnam. John F. Kennedy was elected President, defeating Richard M. Nixon by a razor-thin margin.

In pop culture, Elvis Presley returned from the Army and recorded a bunch of hits, but the top song of 1960 was Theme from a Summer Place, by Percy Faith, the epic western Gunsmoke dominated the television ratings and the epic drama Ben Hur won a bunch of Academy Awards.

In sports, the Philadelphia Eagles won the NFL Championship, Bill Mazeroski and the Pittsburgh Pirates upset the New York Yankees in the World Series, the Montreal Canadians captured Lords Stanley Cup, the Boston Celtics were the NBA Champions, and Arnold Palmer won the Masters.

Cassius Clay (one of Greg Haugen's favorite boxers) won an Olympic Gold Medal in the Light-Heavyweight division. Gabriel Flash Elorde won the World Junior Lightweight title by beating Harold Gomes, Eder Jofre won his first world title by knocking out Eloy Sanchez, and Gene Fullmer had had an iconic year when he fought both Joey Giardello and Sugar Ray Robinson to 15-round draws and knocked out Carmen Basillio in 12 rounds. In the Fight of the Year, Floyd Patterson became the first fighter to regain the world heavyweight title by knocking out Ingemar Johansson in the fifth round. Like Floyd, Greg Haugen also regained the World Title from the man who he lost it from, Vinny Paz.

Greg shares the same birth year as Bono from U2, Sean Penn, John Elway, who was also born in Washington, Damon Wayans, Oscar winner Tilda Swinton, Cal Ripken Jr. and Rapper Chuck D. Those of note who were also born on August 31st, but in different years, include, singer Van Morrison, comedian Chris Tucker, NFL superstar Larry Fitzgerald, NFL Superbowl winning coach Tom Coughlin and singer Deborah Gibson.

While John Elway is probably the most famous athlete who was born in Washington, there is no doubt that Greg Haugen is one of the most successful fighters to be born in the state that Pinklon Thomas said in his book, Back from the Edge of Hell, was the Siberia of boxing. Trainer Victor Machado said, "Greg Haugen represented the state of Washington better than the Seattle Mariners. He won four world titles, and the Mariners still have not won a World Series." To add to Victor's quip, the Mariners have yet to compete in a World Series at the time of this writing.

However, there were other fighters born in Washington who had success on the professional level, Freddie Steele, Boone Kirkman, Rocky Lockridge, and Sugar Ray Seales lead the pack of these fighters. Of this bunch, Freddie Steele can be the only fighter that can claim a better career than Greg.

Greg also had some contemporaries who was born in Washington that excelled on the amateur circuit. Joe Belinc, Robert Shannon, and Brett Summers are amongst that group.

However, unlike those men, Greg came from Auburn, Washington, which former boxer and current referee Bob Howard, described as "the shithole of Washington." "It was a melting pot of sorts, but one thing everyone had in common was poverty. It is dirty, filthy. (There were) Houses that you think were knocked down, and they had two or three families living in them. Auburn is a horrible place. If I had to raise kids, there I would go live in the woods first. And that is where Greg grew up," declared Bob Howard.

Indeed, Greg was from a poor home, but he also had other, more pertinent problems as a youngster. Greg was a victim of class warfare in his neighborhood and was being picked on as a result. "It was a rough town. We were poor kids, so we got picked on a lot. I was part Indian, and the rich kids would make fun of me, they called me wagon burner," explained Greg. Greg was picked on at a young age and was the subject of racist rants.

Greg was also getting "beat up," was how he described. This abuse was happening to Greg at a time when Bullying Awareness and Social Media was not even a blip on the radar. As a young kid would do, Greg turned to his family for help. "He was about five, he was having trouble with bigger kids in the neighborhood picking on him. He came to me and asked me if I would do something about it. I told him I could not fight his battles for him," explained Lee Haugen, Greg's father. Not only was Greg a victim of bullying, the one person he felt he could protect, refused to do so. Greg always had a complicated relationship with his father. So many other parents would have intervened.

Lee Haugen had a different plan. Besides providing Greg with his unique nickname, which was more carefree in nature than depicted in the past, Lee provided his son with the most significant lifeline he ever had. "My barber, Jim Montgomery, was running an Elks Club sponsored boxing club for the boys in town, I took Greg there."

Jim Montgomery was a diamond in the rough in Auburn. He had a great mind for boxing and could fight a little bit, "Jim was a much better boxer than I was," Lee stated. When Greg first laced up the boxing gloves, there was foreshadowing that he would be better than both Jim and Lee. "Greg took to boxing like a duck to water; when he was five years old, he would do everything right'" said Jim of his young pupil. The bullying dissipated quickly after Greg opened up his lifelong toolbox. "Shortly after that, when he knew how to throw a punch, he didn't have too much trouble with the neighborhood kids," Lee Haugen stated. "The word got out that I could kick some ass if you'd mess with me, so nobody really messed with me after that," Greg added. In this case, Father knew best. However, by no means did Lee Haugen try and take credit for his sons' success, "Most of what happened with Greg was a result of Jim's efforts," Lee declared.

What happened with Greg was something to behold. At the age of five, Greg Haugen won the State Tournament at the Wallingford Boys Club, a 50-pound division. Greg followed up this dominance by winning the 55-pound division the next year. At six years old, Greg Haugen was already a two-time champion. Greg's success at such a young age had an impact in Washington, as the boys club implemented a rule stating that you had to be at least seven years old to compete in the boxing tournament. "By the time Greg was eight or nine, he weighed fifty-five pounds. No place in Washington, nor Oregon, could they find a kid to match him who weighed less than seventy-five pounds. Kids his size didn't want to get in the ring with him, and their coaches didn't want to put their kids in with him," added Lee Haugen.

Greg's success at a young age made it apparent that boxing was going to be part of his life for quite some time. But the state of Washington was not exactly the ideal stomping grounds for a young pugilist with aspirations for the professional ranks. Mainly when it came to sparring, which is an essential part of a boxer's success. For an inspiring young pugilist looking to excel as a professional, sparring was as elusive as Hector Macho Camacho was in his prime. "I couldn't get sparring in Washington. I would be lucky to get three or four rounds a day, and none of the fighters were as good as the guys I sparred in Vegas," Greg explains. Having said that, Greg did make a significant mark on Washington before he traveled for greener pastures.

Greg Haugen Five Years Old, 1965. He just started
boxing with Jim Montgomery (Courtesy of Greg Haugen)

Chapter Four
Amateur Career & Alaskan Tough Man

"Greg and I had the right idea, get out of Washington and go where
the boxing mecca capitals are and fight."
—Bret Summers.

Greg might have been flourishing as a young pugilist, solving his
bullying problem for all time in the process. But that did not mean
Greg Haugen was not without drama. Trouble arose at home. "My
dad left when I was nine years old. He and my mom divorced, and
he met another gal and just split," explained Greg. Lee stated that he
left Washington to pursue a law career. Greg's mother, Sandy
Berntsen, was the center of his universe, "I was a momma's boy if
you want to know. I miss the hell out of her. She could never really
come to watch my fights because she had to be half-loaded to watch
the fights. And nobody wanted to sit next to her because she would
elbow the shit out of you as I was fighting. She would beat the hell
out of you," Greg said of his mother.

Greg's father disappearing meant financial heartache for the
Haugen household. This is where Jim Montgomery's diamond status
grew exponentially in the Haugen household. Meeting Jim
Montgomery meant so much more to Greg and his family than just
self-defense. "If it wasn't for Jimmy, I would not have been able to
do anything in boxing he paid my way when we went to
tournaments. Jim would pay for everything out of pocket because
my mom couldn't afford to. I owe him a lot, he took me under his
wing and taught me how to fight," Greg described.

On the back of Generous Jim, Greg's early days as an amateur
opened his eyes up to a world, he had zero knowledge of. "I was a
small-town kid and really didn't know anything different from
Auburn. I got to see other towns when we went to boxing
tournaments," Haugen offered.

When Greg traveled and fought as an amateur, he got to witness
more than just eye-popping scenery. Bill McDonald, who was a

formidable amateur boxer, as well as an astute boxing historian explained, "The boxing scene in the pacific northwest during the seventies and eighties was pretty thick with amateur talent." McDonald also described boxing as a "wrong side of the track sport."

Joe Belinc, who was at the head of that thick talent and considered to be a defensive wizard, "If you can land one punch on him in three rounds, consider yourself lucky," said Bill McDonald of Joe Belinc's defensive skills.

Belinc spoke of a tight knit crop of amateur boxers who was just about an hour away from where Greg Haugen trained, "We had a little gym out of Marysville, Washington underneath the basement of a bingo parlor and we had some of the best fighters in the whole pacific northwest…and we had some the best battle of our career down in that gym. Between Bret Summers, Robert Shannon, and Darryl Stubblefield, we battled harder than most of those big fights (both amateur and professional) we had." A bold statement considering Joe Belinc gave Pernell Whitaker all he can handle on the amateur circuit; some would argue he bested Sweet Pea. If you ever watched film of Belinc as an amateur, you would know that this claim is no exaggeration. Greg fought Joe on the amateur circuit and stated, "I thought out of all the guys, Joey was the best in the area because he was a defensive southpaw. Joey just outboxed me," Greg explained of their encounter in the amateurs. Indeed, outboxing Greg Haugen, as well as arguably beating Sweet Pea Whitaker, are credentials that are not cut from the average cloth.

Given the tremendous amateur talent in Washington, you have to wonder why the professional scene was so bleak for these promising amateurs. Bill McDonald explained, "Guys like Johnny Bumphus and Rocky Lockridge got taken away right out the amateurs and went to the east coast with the Duva's." Bret Summers, a very decorated amateur from Washington, also corroborates why leaving Washington was a must decision, "We had a lot of great fighters, we had Johnny Bumphus, Sugar Ray Seales, Rocky Lockridge…but to get a fight and get it lined up locally, we had nothing close to that. Greg and I had the right idea, get out of Washington and go where the boxing mecca capitals are and fight." Greg went to Las Vegas, while Bret ventured off to Detroit and joined the famed Kronk Gym.

Joe Belinc added, "Boxing was great for us in Washington as far as the amateurs go, as a professional not so much, we had to travel to do anything. So, it was much, much harder to get the fights we needed." This narrative remained in Washington for many years. Joe Hipp, the heavyweight contender, also fought out of Washington and talked about the anemic transition with amateurs to the pros, "I had a really great amateur career, and I did not even know how to turn pro. I did not turn pro until I was twenty-three. There was nobody trying to recruit you to the pros back then. I did not see a lot of promoters out of Washington."

Washington was not always a dead zone for boxing. "Seattle has always been a pretty decent fight town. If you go back to the '50s and '60s, there used to be some good fighters, Boone Kirkman and guys like that. And they used to have some big fights in the Seattle Center Coliseum," said Bill McDonald. Bob Jarvis added, "Boone Kirkman was the first franchise of Seattle. Before the Sonics and the Seahawks, he was filling up the Coliseum every time he fought." In fact, Kirkman was featured on the cover of the June 1968 issue of The Ring Magazine, which was, erroneously, an honor never bestowed upon Greg Haugen. The article on Kirkman included Jack Hurley boasting that Kirkman was a new version of sliced bread. "That Jack Hurley was a great promoter. A lot of Boone's success had to do with him," added Jarvis. Hurley was well known for promoting the high-octane Tony Zale/Rocky Graziano fights. But perhaps his best sales job was turning Boone Kirkman into a cash cow.

Kirkman possessed rugged good looks and, with tremendous assistance from Hurley, was indeed an immense ticket seller in the Seattle area. Boone's biggest wins in the Seattle Center Coliseum were a third-round stoppage over Eddie Machen, "When he fought Eddie Machen, that was a big deal," Bob Jarvis indicated, and a sixth-round technical knockout over Doug Jones, Jones stooped Kirkman in seven rounds in their previous fight at the same venue. But Kirkman never fought for the title.

Other notable fights in Seattle include: Ezzard Charles fought and lost to, Harry Matthews, in 1956. This fight occurred when The Cincinnati Cobra was considered past his prime. Pete Rademacher, a pacific northwest talent, challenged for Floyd Patterson's heavyweight title in 1957. It was Rademacher's professional debut.

Boxing manager George Chemeres, who was also elemental in Greg's career, had a direct impact on the making of this improbable match up. Bobby Howard tells the story, "George and Pete Radamacher walk into the office of Jack Hurley, declaring that Pete wants to fight as a professional. Jack likes the idea and says he will get Pete started with some six rounders, then some eight rounders, and work his way up. George informs Jack that Pete is fixing to get a shot at the heavyweight title first go around. Jack laughs and shows them the door. Well, Pete opens this suitcase he was carrying and shows Jack that it has one-hundred thousand dollars in it, at least that is the amount I heard, it was money from a bee-bee gun company Pete was involved with. So, Jack goes, do you have a date in mind?" That date was the twenty-second of August in 1957. Pete proved game, he even floored Patterson early but was too outgunned to make his great heart a prominent voice in the fight.

In 1960, Sonny Liston fought Eddie Machen in a historic battle that went the distance, between two of the more mysterious men who ever laced up the boxing gloves. Eddie Cotton, a fantastic light-heavyweight contender, fought many times in Seattle during his underrated career. And Sugar Ray Seales- a Tacoma, Washington Olympic Gold Medalist- fought to a draw with Marvelous Marvin Hagler in 1974, in an often-discussed battle. Hagler upset Seales in their first meeting. The second time around, these fighters battled in the friendly confines (for Seales) of The Seattle Center Coliseum. The fact that there does not appear to be any film on this fight limit the discussions one can have. Bill McDonald stated that he was too young at the time but said: "I do know a lot of guys who did see it, and they all told me Marvin deserved the decision."

So why did the professional scene become depleted in Washington? Bill McDonald explained his theory, "During Greg's time, for whatever reason, there were no big promoters around. I think it is because there weren't any headline names anymore. Sugar Ray Seales was done by then, so all these young fighters had no marquees names to fight under. I would say that was probably the biggest reason."

McDonald also added, "Seattle was finally getting a football and baseball team, and I think the interest in sports shifted." With the franchise of Boone Kirkman also long gone, it appeared that the interest in boxing never shifted back to boxing, as Greg Haugen said, "there is nothing here," today.

There is no question Greg Haugen's amateur career was lengthy and bore fruit; however, the consensus is scattered regarding just how successful Greg was in the amateur ranks.

On the one hand, there is evidence that Greg Haugen was something of a prodigy as an amateur boxer. He was so good at a young age that the rules needed to be changed to level the playing played. On the other hand, there is a different narrative with some tangible evidence, "I went to the nationals eleven times, Greg Haugen went to the nationals zero times. Because he could not get out of the regionals, he could not beat guys like me or Joe Belinc," Bret Summers declared.

It is worth mentioning that the relationship between Bret Summers and Greg Haugen is not stable, "Greg and I do not get along. Greg has always had a chip on his shoulder. I would see him, and he would be like, fuck you Summers (chuckles), that was just Greg" explained Bret. Although turbulent, Greg and Bret's relationship is long in the tooth. "We fought each other for the first time, I believe when I was nine years old. I believe we fought eight or nine times. For the most part, I had the better of him. The last time I fought him was in 1982 in the regionals, to go to the nationals, and I beat him then also." Bret says he likes Greg and wishes that someday they could shake hands and be friends. What was Greg's response to Bret's Olive Branch? "Why would I? He was a rival, there is no reason to be friends."

Joe Belinc provides a more detailed, less flattering description of Greg as an amateur boxer, "He just wasn't that great an amateur. I was the last person to fight Greg as an amateur. I was much more of a counter puncher, so Greg was easy to fight for me. He was more of a puncher, brawler, and that was easy for me...but he was tough as nails."

Bill McDonald provides a more balanced description of Haugen's amateur career. "Greg came out of Auburn Elks. Greg probably had three hundred plus amateur fights. He was always tough. Greg was a very solid amateur."

John Chemeres, son of George Chemeres, recalls seeing Greg fight as an amateur when he was a "little kid." "He was a good amateur fighter. Greg did not back down from anybody. But he was never able to get over that hump. They were only three-round fights, and a lot of fighters do not blossom that way. Greg was one of those fighters," John explained. Having said that, John Chemeres stated that he and his father had a feeling about Greg, "Our impression was that he would be a good professional. There was something about him, he had confidence and he was crude."

How the fights went down between Greg and Bret Summers in the amateurs is also leveled by McDonald, "I think he and Bret had eleven amateur fights, Bret probably won six of those." McDonald's numbers do not back Summers' claim of getting the better of Greg by a large margin. Bill McDonald's declaration is telling because he and Bret Summers describe each other as "best friends," which makes McDonalds' claims more believable; at the very least, there is no bias there. Greg's version of his fights with Bret is much different, however, "I only fought Summers three times." John Chemeres also remembers Bret usually got the better of Greg, "Bret Summers could box, and Greg was not the same guy in the amateurs as he was a professional. He did not have all the tricks and moves that my father had taught him yet. But he held his own against Bret, and even won a few fights," John added.

Bob Jarvis also suggest that Greg was a very good amateur. "It was great to have Greg in the gym because he would spar with everyone. Greg also participated in many smoker fights at Bob Jarvis's boxing gym. "There would be like eight to ten fights a night, people would pay about five dollars to watch the fights, and the expenses would go to gloves and other things that the gym needed," Greg explained.

Bob Jarvis spoke about a specific smoker fight Greg was set to have with a 'Cuban kid' that was a "real bad dude." That bad dude's name was Francisco Rocche from Havana, Cuba, who relocated to Seattle. "He and Haugen fought, and we sold the place out. And man was it a war. Greg won," Jarvis said.

Greg said of Rocche, "We would see each other in the gym, and he would give me the evil eye. We didn't like each other. But I never exchanged words with him or anything, I didn't know him. But one day, we sparred, and this fucker was trying to knock me out. Time went by, and he kept coming to the gym, so I decided to start fucking with him, saying, 'drift on back to Cuba, you lily pad motherfucker,' that used to piss him off." Indeed, more than just schoolyard trash talk.

Getting Roche mad, who Jarvis said people called, "The Crazy Cuban," might not have been wise of Greg. According to Greg, Joe Toro, the highly regarded boxing manager, who handled Roche, would say, 'Haugen, you have to quit doing that, this guy is fucking crazy, and you keep pissing him off. He is going to go into a rage.' At first, Greg laughed off Toro's warnings. After all, Greg had a reputation of being a little loco himself, "I rather have Greg next to me in a fight than someone my size. He would never take shit from nobody, I don't care how big they were," offered Joe Hipp. Then he found a little bit about Mr. Roche. "He had these big numbers on his arms, I guess he was in prison and went free when they released them." Greg was referring to the Mariel boatlift emigration process of 1980, which Bob Jarvis corroborated that Roche was a part of.

Greg soon found out why 'The Crazy Cuban' was imprisoned, "I find out he was in prison for fucking eight years. He and his mom were walking home from the store. His mom has a bag of groceries under both arms. Well, it was crowded, and his mom accidentally stepped on this pimp's shoe. Well, the pimp smacked her and started ordering her to clean his shoe. So, Francisco smacked the pimp and knocked him out. Then he ran into his house, grabbed a machete, and whacked off both of the pimp's arm." That was the story Joe Toro told, according to Greg. Even Greg had to be a bit apprehensive about busting Roche's chops. A machete-wielding madman is an entirely different animal compared to a fistfight.

Such a fascinating story might be labeled an Urban legend, but there is no questioning that Roche was a Mariel boatlift prisoner and an outstanding fighter. "He was a southpaw and very good. These Cuban's are well-schooled. When you fight a Cuban (as an amateur), you are basically fighting a professional because they are taught from an early age, and that is all they do," Greg explained. Francisco Roche was no exception, when he was not defending his mother's honor, he was honing his craft in the boxing gym. "We ended up fighting in a smoker. I ended up beating him, but it was a tough, tough fight. We were going at it. I was the only guy he lost to. Which made him hate me even more. He would always curse me out in Spanish," Greg said. Indeed Greg, heard and believed the stories of Roche making his best impression of Jason Vorhees and took precaution, "I started watching my back coming in and out of the gym because he was a whack job and would always tell me, 'I'll knock you out motherfucker,' who knew how far he would take it," explained Greg.

Greg and Francisco never squared off again in any capacity. Roche turned pro in 1981 and compiled a modest record of 10-10-1, 2 KO's. He won five of his first six bouts, with the other contest being a draw against boxers without much experience but did not perform well when he stepped up in competition. Roche died in 2009 at the age of fifty-two. Greg was not aware of that fact, but was not overly shocked, figuring his taste for carnage probably got him killed. I could not find out how Roche died.

Indeed, Roche is another example of a boxer who was on par with Greg as an amateur, but who Greg clearly distanced himself from when he turned professional. Rival Bret Summers probably said it best, "When he got to the pros, he had a better career than all of us." Bret had some good moments as a pro, but as John Chemeres explains, "Bret was big around Washington as an amateur. But even when he went to Kronk Gym, he never blossomed as a pro. I was kind of surprised by that." Joe Belinc added, "As a pro, Greg did great because he was a battler. He did transition into a terrific counter puncher, but as an amateur, he was more forward, more of a puncher style." Belinc's assertion provides credibility to John Chemeres's claim that Greg really blossomed as a pro thanks to the seasoning of George Chemeres.

Greg Haugen explained how this somewhat sketchy, yet very active amateur career helped him in the famed ToughMan contests in Alaska.

Much has been said about Greg's time in Alaska, participating in the now famous ToughMan contests. Greg's undefeated record in those fights is where many people link his origin as a pugilist. "Everyone thought I learned how to fight in the ToughMan fights in Alaska," Greg explains, "Most people don't realize I had over three hundred amateur fights," he continues. Greg cites that amateur pedigree, to help him succeed against much bigger men who "wanted to take my head off."

Greg participated in these Alaskan tough men fight in the Pines Club, as well as Gussie L'Amour, two hot spots along the Alaska circuit where patrons were famished for alcohol and good old-fashioned violence. "They would rope off some rope in the bar and start matching guys against each other." The payout for the tough men combatants where a bit different in these places, "The Pines Club would pay 50 dollars for the winner, 20 dollars for the loser. Gussie L'Amour would pay 50 dollars for the winner, and the loser would get nothing but an ass whopping."

If there was very little science behind most of the participants who fought, the matchmaking for these fights was just as primitive. Greg describes a situation where drunken patrons were coerced by their equally ossified friends, to give their best impersonation of Philo Beddoe, "That fucking alcohol makes them brave. They would get that liquid courage, and their buddies would talk them into getting in there," Greg explained. Greg looked at these drunken fellows as an excellent opportunity to make some coin. However, like any pugilist who is worth their salt, Greg still respected these men, "Most of the guys I fought were tough, rugged guys. They didn't have any boxing experience." Knowing this, Greg would put on his thinking cap, where even back then, his boxing IQ was off the charts, indeed, at least three standard deviations above the average. "I would use my experience to outsmart them for the first round. By the time the second round came around, they were dead tired, huffing, and puffing. So, all they could do was quit or let me beat them up. It was a game plan that worked 24 out of 24 times."

It was a game plan that helped build on the Haugen legend, as his fights were in the highest demand, "People would come to the door and ask, 'Hey is Haugen fightin' If they said no they would turn around. If they said yes, people would pay 20 dollars to get it in, when it was usually like 5 dollars to watch," Greg said. It opened the doors for the witty Haugen to capitalize on his popularity, and Greg was becoming immensely popular, "Those tough guy fights were perfect for Greg. He had a big reputation up and down the coast because of them," Bob Jarvis said.

Greg added, "It got to the point where I was like, 'you want me to fight, especially these bigger dudes, you got to pay me 1,000 bucks a fight.'" The response he got was, 'oh fuck you, I don't pay nobody that.' "I said, okay then well I ain't fightin.' Well, I didn't fight for a few weeks, so it got to the point where they would be a small crowd every night. So, I had to get paid; otherwise, nobody was showing up." Greg kept showing up, kept winning and kept getting paid,

"Towards the end, I was getting them to pay me 1,000 dollars a fight. Because everyone was showing up to see me. They either hated me because I was from the lower 48, or they liked me. Most of them hated me because I was beating up local guys."

There is always that one fight that the fans crave for. If that match gets made, the fans go ballistic over it. Often in boxing, these fights go by the boards, and in the ToughMan lure, Greg thought his financial demands would have prevented his most anticipated Alaskan tough man contest. "I think his name was Jeff Rush, but they called him the Yukon Crusher. This guy was like 225 pounds about an inch taller than me, but he was rock-solid muscle." The Yukon Crusher was the only man on the tough man circuit who was respected that Greg did not fight. Knowing taking on this man would be a tall order, Greg decided to price himself out, they asked me, 'How much do you want to fight him,' I said, 'well he outweighs me by 100 pounds', they were like, 'Yeah so,' so I said 2,500 bucks. I didn't think they were going to pay me. I said an amount that was pretty high and figured there was no way they were going to give that to me that, but he said okay I'll give you that."

Never one to back out of a fight, ever, Greg now had to prepare for this massive challenger. For Greg, some good 'ol boxing history, sprinkled in with some Occam's Razor, helped him win the fight, "I just went out there and gave him the old rope-a-dope in the first round. He was swinging for the fences, trying to load up," Greg explained, he proceeded to "beat up" the Yukon Crusher for the final two rounds. As when Muhammad Ali felt outgunned against the stronger George Foreman, Greg used the elements around him, and a superior boxing IQ, to tire out his opponent. Also, tiring out his inexperienced opponents worked like a charm in his previous barroom brawls, so why abandoned this simple, but effective approach?

Indeed, the Yukon Crusher was bitter in defeat, "After the fight, he was like, 'It's a no-win situation, I look bad if I win because I am beating up a little guy, but I look bad if I lose because I got beat up by a little guy'. I was like, oh well, you made more money in one fight than you did in all the other fights."

Greg's success in Alaska was lucrative, but at the same time, it was not something he planned on making a career out of. Indeed, Greg had his sights set on boxing as a career choice. He was determined to find out if his early success would translate to beyond the amateurs and the bars of Alaska. The latter was what got Greg's foot in the door as a fighter to keep an eye on, After that everybody was like, "Oh you fought in the ToughMan fights, and no one bothered to ask me about my amateur fights." When Greg would correct them and say he did not get his start in the tough guy fights, they did not seem interested. Greg did not seem to be bothered about the total disregard of his boxing roots. After all, he was getting recognition, and getting paid to fight. In Alaska is also were Greg teamed up with Team Chemeres.

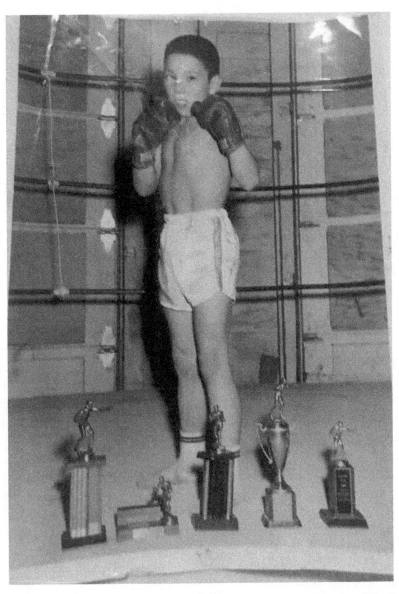

Greg at age seven in 1967. His impressive hardware fighting out of the Auburn Elks Gym
(Courtesy of Greg Haugen).

Chapter Five
Turning Pro

"I never went 10 rounds before, I did in the gym, but that's is in the gym, there is gym fighting and there is real fighting."

—Greg Haugen.

Greg Haugen's professional boxing career began on November 4th, 1982. At this time, future Hall of Famer Ray Boom Boom Mancini was the WBA Lightweight Champion, whom Haugen would later conquer. Meanwhile, the WBC Lightweight Champion was soon to be vacated by the legendary Alexis Arguello, who failed to capture the Super Lightweight title against Hall of Famer Aaron Pryor, a fight that occurred just eight days after Haugen's professional debut. Haugen fought Noel Arriesgado at the Tudor Club in Anchorage, Alaska. Noel came from the Philippines at had a record of 13-3-1, with 4 KO's. Noel was a fighter with great experience, as Ring Magazine had him as the number seventh-ranked featherweight in 1980.

It is unusual for a boxer making his debut to face an opponent with as many fights as Arriesgado had. A clear indication that Greg Haugen did not begin his career the way a protected cash cow would. Boxing historian Lee Groves compared Haugen's debut with the likes of Paul Gonzalez, Ray Leonard, Evander Holyfield and, Vasily Lomenchenko in the sense that it was a very ambitious start of a boxing career. Like Greg Haugen, all these pugilists had extensive amateur careers. Were Greg differed drastically from these men, "Greg wasn't thought to be one of these blue-chip guys. He wasn't an Olympian; he was coming out of the ToughMan in Alaska. No one really heard of him, I guess they just threw him into the woods because they thought maybe he was that good. And he was," explained Lee Groves.

Greg may not have made it to the Olympics, but his amateur career taught him plenty. "I thought I was better suited for longer distances because the fights I lost as an amateur were short fights, I would always take a couple rounds to warm up...I really didn't care who they put in front of me, I thought I was a good fighter and wanted to prove that. You don't see many fighters, especially nowadays, starting out fighting ten rounds, and in my third fight, I went ten rounds." Greg also had the mental makeup to persevere when perhaps he was not supposed to, "His inner strength makes him one of those special guys," added Jeff Fenech. Indeed, Greg's career got off to an extraordinary start.

Haugen won debut on a three-round decision, which is what the tough man fights were scheduled for. In his second fight, Haugen was already exposed to the concept of the rematch, as he faced Noel Arriesgado again, this time stopping him in seven rounds. When asked about Arriesgado, and the need for a rematch, Greg Haugen said, "When I beat him in three rounds, they said, 'oh that was lucky, how about a rematch for ten rounds' I said sure no problem. I wanted to fight these trial horses, tough guys who have been in there with some good fighters, I was just looking to get experience and get rounds." The Alaskan lightweight title was also at stake for this second fight, a serious battle that was not without a little comic relief. "When I fought Arriegasdo for the Alaska lightweight title, half the place was full of Filipino's, half the place was filled with my guys, and they all bet each other. As soon as they stopped the fight (in the 7th round), you see about half the crowd just dash to the door because they didn't want to pay the bet." A comical scene that was something to behold, and probably upstaged the fact that Greg now beat a much more experienced fighter than him on two occasions. These fights with the seasoned and successful Arriegasdo made for some excellent foreshadowing for Greg's career. Victories that a mere brawler could not have pulled off. Only great boxing skills could have. Greg's early and successful start in boxing helped shape great fundamentals, as Victor Machado described, "Greg had good boxing fundamentals. He was great at setting you up, staying on his toes, he had a great jab." A boxer with much more professional rounds under his belt just found that out.

For his third fight, on January 13th, 1983, Haugen returned to Washington, fighting at the Paramount Theater in Seattle. Greg described the Paramount Theater as a place for "mainly just rock shows, comedy shows." "It was the kind of venue where everyone was sitting on one side of the ring, the ring was on the stage...what I

25

remember most was that the main crowd was out in the seats, like a theater setting, it was different." Greg faced another fighter with a lot of experience Joe Perez, who sported a record of 4-12-3, 2 KO's. Greg said Joe was a "tough Mexican," the kind of fighter his management team felt would be great experiences for Greg.

When asked about going the ten-round distance for the first time as a professional, Greg said, "I never went ten rounds before, I did in the gym, but that is in the gym, there is gym fighting, and there is real fighting, I knew I was in good shape to go ten rounds it was just a matter of if the guy was going to put me threw ten rounds. The guy was tough, and I believe he had a lot more experience than me, Joe was one of those old trial horses who knew how to survive, he would lock you up when he got hurt, and he knew how to fight. It was good for me to go the ten rounds because I got the experience that I needed... I was just getting started. I was a good amateur, but I knew that I was a better pro and was looking forward to the long-distance fights. I was happy to go ten rounds and prove to myself I could do it. Until you do it you really don't know, it is a different setting than the gym because when you are in front of people you get the adrenaline going…there is more of a chance of you getting tired with the adrenaline draining you. After I went the ten rounds, I know I belonged and just wanted to keep fighting."

Greg won a unanimous decision and fought on a card that featured notable fighters, Dale Grant, who fought the like of Matthew Saad Muhammed, Marvin Camel, Jerry Martin, Jessie Burnett, and Eddie Davis. Heavyweight Larry Frazier was also on the card. He shared the squared circle with Pinklon Thomas, Floyd "Jumbo" Cummings, of Smokin Joe Frazier fame, Pierre Coetzer, and Frank Bruno.

Indeed, Grant and Frazier are further examples of Washington products who fought as professionals but came nowhere near the success of a Greg Haugen. Where the fans of Seattle aware that they were witnessing a future World Champion when they watched Greg Haugen in his third fight?

After the Paramount experience, Greg Haugen fought three straight times at The Red Lion Inn, in SeaTac, Washington. Max Cervantes, Larry Yazzie, and Chuck Peralta were the victims. The move to the Red Lion Inn was due to numbers. Greg explained that the Paramount was small, "We had to turn people away. We decided we were going to start promoting at the Red Lion. The Red Lion had a venue that you could open the walls up and make room for 10,000 people. I was drawing some good people, so we kept going bigger and better." "Greg had a good following when he fought in Washington, people would come in trucks to see him," Victor Machado corroborated.

Greg made quick work of Cervantes and Yazzie and won a 10-round unanimous decision against Peralta. While all three of these fighters had more experience as a professional than Greg, nobody would have mistaken these fighters as world-beaters. All three had losing records. In 1987, Chuck Peralta's inadequacies as a professional fighter were so apparent, the New Jersey State Athletic Commission banned him from the ring because it was ruled that any further action as a professional boxer could impede Peralta's health exponentially. As is often the case, incompetence is at the root of many State Athletic Commissions, and Peralta did manage to fight three more times after this ruling, twice in Arizona and once in New Mexico. But when Greg fought Peralta, he still had enough in the tank to take the future World Champion the 10-round distance. "He had fought a lot of big names, I wanted to test myself and see where I was at. He had been in there with some good fighters, better fighters than I was at the time, I realized I could fight, I could hang with these guys, Chuck taught me a lot because he was a seasoned veteran, he knew a lot of tricks, and he made me learn things in there. I was either going to get better or go by the waist side." Indeed, Greg Haugen was developing his skills and progressing as a boxer.

For his last fight of 1983, Greg Haugen changed scenery and went to Fort Lauderdale, Florida, fighting at the Galt Ocean Mile Hotel. Greg's opponent was Roosevelt Booth, 0-1, and Greg earned a four-round unanimous decision. Greg explained the reason for the odd change from a ten-round fight to a four-round fight was "Because the fact was I was fighting on somebody else's card and all that was available were 4-rounders, and I just wanted to fight. He was a veteran of the Ft. Lauderdale area. I was in Ft. Lauderdale to train with George Chemeres' friend, Lou Gross, George felt it was better for me to get all this experience from different people. After that fight, a lot of people had a chance to see me." The card Greg fought on featured an undefeated middleweight name Kenny Snow, 11-0, 8 KO's. A fighter who went on to have 67 professional fights, winning the ESPN Middleweight title in 1986, stopping Daryl Spain in the 10th round. Snow also fought John Mugabi in 1988, The Beast stopped Kenny in four rounds.

When asked about fighting outside of the Washington area for the first time as a professional, Greg said, "It was different, I didn't have the crowd support, but it didn't bother me. I kind of had blinders on...I knew that I was ready, I was stepping up in competition and that I could fight with the best of them and wanted to keep proving that." It should be noted that when speaking with Greg, he thought he stopped Roosevelt Booth, but the record indicates it went the four-round distance. Greg could not say for sure that the decision on record is an error. It was Greg Haugen's last fight in 1983. Greg's hard work and unconventional approach to the start of his career paid dividends and brought new challenges in 1984.

Chapter Six
Hello ESPN

"I particularly didn't like him that much when I first met him. When we finally fought, I wanted to beat him badly, it didn't work out that way."
— Freddie Roach on Greg Haugen.

1984 was a breakout year for Greg. It was a monumental year in the United States of America as well. Ronald Regan was re-elected President by destroying Vice-President Walter Mondale, the nominee for the Democrats. In music, American artists dominated the charts. Lionel Richie's Can't Slow Down Prince's Purple Rain, Cyndi Lauper's She's So Unusual, Tina Turner's Private Dancer and Bruce Springsteen's Born in the U.S.A.; which would have a direct link to Greg later in his career, all made a historic impact on pop culture that still stands the test of time. At the Box Office, the timeless comedies Beverly Hills Cop and Ghostbusters topped the charts, Gremlins terrified, as well as tickled fans, The Terminator franchise got underway, Captain Kirk Search for Spock, and The Karate Kid was the feel-good movie of the year. A film about a kid who was raised by a single mother and had a father figure that was not his biological father, who taught him how to fight. The fact that The Karate Kid came out the same year Greg Haugen made his television debut is symbolic.

1984 was also a very magical year in the world of sports. Dan Marino was breaking NFL records. The Detroit Tigers enjoyed one of the most dominant seasons in Major League Baseball history. The Celtics beat the Lakers to win the NBA championship in a rare 7 game series. And the Edmonton Oilers won Lord Stanley's Cup, putting an end to the New York Islanders' Dynasty, introducing a young kid named Wayne Gretzky to the world.

In boxing, Thomas Hearns knocked Roberto Duran out cold in two rounds, Julio Caesar Chavez Sr. beat Mario Martinez to capture his first world title, and Marvelous Marvin Hagler had his first fight in the famed Madison Square Garden in New York City, stopping the rugged Mustafa Hamsho in three rounds. In the Fight of the Year, Jose Luis Ramirez avenged his controversial loss over Edwin Rosario by knocking Chapo out in four rounds.

While 1984 was a solid year for professional boxing, it will be a year that will forever be remembered for the United States Olympic Team. A team that produced world champions like Virgil Hill, Evander Holyfield, Meldrick Taylor, Mark Breland, and Pernell Whitaker. Whitaker is a Hall of Famer and one of the best lightweights to ever lace up the boxing gloves. He and Greg were on a collision course to fight each other a few years later. But while Whitaker was becoming a household name in 1984, Haugen was honing his craft and paying his dues.

This process got off to a slow start for Greg in 1984, as he did not fight until September of that year. This was because Greg replaced George Chemeres with Wes Wolffe as his manager. "He (Chemeres) was so much older than me, I just really didn't appreciate what he was showing me, and I wanted to see other things," Greg said. "He (Chemeres) was in boxing 40 or 50 years and never had a world champion," added Greg. According to Greg, the split resulted in "bad blood," which would become a significant variable in Greg's development. John Chemeres said that George sold Greg's contract to Wes Wolffe because, "My father was tired of Greg and sold his contract. They were both hard-headed guys and I was in the middle of it." The spilt with George also contributed to a long layoff when all Greg wanted to do was fight.

Bobby Howard described George as a grandiose figure who made sure anyone who was in the same room would hear what he had to say. Bobby said George was a "street guy" who acted like a pimp and "treated fighters like whores." George Chemeres demanded that you looked into his eyes when he spoke to you, and you treat every word he spoke as gospel. Not the kind of guy you want to have against you. According to Bob Howard, the split had something to do with the crass approach that Chemeres used to get his points across, George Chemeres was a "polarizing figure," added Bill MacDonald. One unconventional belief that George had was that fighters were lacking anything of substance between the ears, "George also felt that fighters couldn't think, and he had to think for them," explained Bob Howard. Part of George's thought process for his fighters was offering advice about relationships. According to Bob Howard, this might have been what caused Greg to spilt with George, "It had something to do with Greg's girl, George said something to the effect that Greg could not bring his whores around. Greg warned him not to say that again, but of course, George did," explained Howard.

With George now in Greg's rearview mirror, no doubt flipping him the middle finger, Greg had to get the rust off that was building because of the layoff. Greg agreed to fight the respectable Ted Michaliszyn, who was 11-1-1 with 5 KO's going into the fight. Ted tested the waters of the amateur boxing scene in his hometown of Pittsburgh for three years before moving to Las Vegas and turning professional. Ted's fought four rounds against the infamous Chuck Peralta in his debut. The result of that bout was a draw. A local newspaper, however, described the fight as 'a spirited four-rounder' that 'many ringsiders saw Teddy as the winner.' Ted explained that he "knocked Chuck down, but it did not count as a knockdown. When I asked Ted if he thought the non-call was blatant, he said, "Maybe, I hit him, he fell, and they counted it as a slip." The trials and tribulations occur inside a boxing ring that gets underreported. In particular, when such an act happens on a smaller scale.

This grievance did not detract Ted from his goal, however. Ted had an active 1984 and was enjoying a three-fight winning streak going into his fight with Greg. It was Greg's first fight in Las Vegas. Greg felt moving and fighting in Vegas was necessary for his survival, as well as his appetite. "I was starving and knew I had to get out of the Northwest," explained Greg. It would also be Greg's first televised fight on the Entertainment and Sports Programming Network (ESPN).

ESPN first aired sports for cable subscribers on September 7th, 1979. The younger ESPN viewers might not realize just how paltry the number of live sports that was aired in the channel' infant stages. Boxing was not just ESPN's bread and butter in the early days, it was virtually the entire meal. In 1984, ESPN did not air live football, baseball, hockey, or basketball. Top Rank Boxing, the promotional giant, provided the boxing action for the network. So, not only was Greg having his first fight in Las Vegas and his first fight on television, but he was also fighting for Top Rank Boxing. Fighting Ted Michaliszyn was a major opportunity for Greg. With great opportunity comes tremendous pressure. Nobody can say they do not feel pressure; it is how the pressure is managed that typically makes or breaks you.

This was Greg's first fight after his breakup with manager George Chemeres. According to Greg, George put a big bullseye on his back. A bullseye that was painted with the help of Mel Greb, a Top Rank Boxing matchmaker at the time. According to Greg's story, both men conspired to match Greg with tough competition. "He (George) was set on getting me beat… so he told Mel Greb to put me in tough." It is worth mentioning that John Chemeres disputes Greg's assertion that George and Mel put a 'bounty' out on Greg, "My father was not that way. He and Greg had mutual respect. Mel was just trying to make good fights." Greg insists that the bounty is real, and perception is often truth. Believing in this bounty fueled Greg's fire, so, when in doubt, print the legend.

George has been depicted as a savvy guy, who has had his fair share of brushes with controversy. But he was as sharp as a tack. George Chemeres learned from masterminds like Ray Arcel, and Eddie Fucth. He became a mastermind of his own. "When we had John Palaki, Floyd Mayweather Jr. would come to the gym and Floyd loved working with my father," John Chemeres said. George was always thinking and looking for an advantage. Bob Howard tells one story of how George was always on his toes. Fight manager Mike 'Motormouth' Morton managed fighters such as Thad Spencer, Jesus Pimentel, Mike Colbert, Miguel Arrozal, Ray Lampkin, and Andy Kendall. To give you an idea of how impressive a talker Mike was, Don King provided Mike Morton with his descriptive nickname, Motormouth.

According to Bob Howard, "Mike and George were grandiose characters, so they did not like each other. One guy is always trying to steal the other guy's thunder." On one particular night, Bob tells a story of how they set out to hand one of their fighters a loss. George had John John Palaki, while Mike handled Miguel Arrozal. Bob Howard was the referee for this grudge match. "The night of the fight, Mike comes up to me and kisses me on both cheeks and says, 'I love you, Bobby, you are all right. You got my fight tonight; I know you are going to do the right thing.' So, George sees this, and when I go over to him, he gives me that Italian slap on the face and says, 'Hey pal, I saw that. He's got nothing on us, we go way back.'

And he gives me a hug and kisses me on one cheek. He knew Mike was looking," remembered Howard. One could only imagine just how many kisses took place on the cheek when George and Mel Greb began to conspire against Greg. And who kissed whom?

Ted Michalizsyn was thought to be good enough to get the job done. "I was supposed to lose against Ted because he was more experienced," Haugen said. As typical of Greg Haugen, the plan backfired.

Michaliszyn enjoyed a height and reach advantage against Greg. In the first round, Haugen showed us why he was so special. It was his shorter left jab that controlled the action. Greg double-upped on the jab, feinted with it, and followed it up with left hooks. Greg took Michaliszyn's height away from him by closing distance with his jab and working inside. Greg's impressive work with his jab was enough to win the round on judges Daily Shirley and Dave Moretti's scorecards. Haugen lost round one on judge Chuck Minker's scorecard, however.

The second round saw Greg come out like a house on fire, yet in complete control. Nothing wild. Ted was eager to meet Greg in the center of the ring and Greg's face exuded with confidence and he went to work right away. He picked Michaliszyn's shots with his gloves and saw Ted retreat. Greg, a master at cutting off the ring, did just that, and began to deliver, and place shots perfectly. Trapping Ted into the corner, Greg scored with stiff jabs, a thudding right to the body, and a short left hook that moved Ted against the ropes. Ted bounced off the ropes and tried to close the distance, but Haugen caught him with an even harder left hook as he was coming in. It was the kind of shot that exemplified what Greg Haugen was as a boxer when he was going well. Always in a position to deliver a telling blow.

That left hook backed Ted up more effectively than the previous shot, and Greg was able to score as Ted's back was against the ropes. Ted, however, was a confident pugilist who was no stranger to the spotlight. Greg's success did not discourage Ted, it made him more aggressive. But even at this early stage of his career, Greg was a crafty veteran, and he let his eager opponent come forward. Greg slipped every meaningful punch Michaliszyn threw and countered with his majestic jab. With his rhythm bothered and off-balance, Ted found himself once again, against the ropes with Haugen scoring.

When Ted managed to get off the ropes, Greg dug a hard left hook to the body, and once again, Ted Michaliszyn's was on his way to having a severe case of rope burn.

As is the case with most boxers, laying with your back on the ropes is no place to be. Even if you are doing well, the perceptions are always that you are losing when your opponent has you pinned against the ropes, unless you are Floyd Mayweather Jr., who was the ultimate master of fighting off the ropes, see the Miguel Cotto fight. Ted knew how detrimental it was to be on the ropes. So, he tried to fight with Greg in the middle of the ring for the rest of the second round. The results proved futile, as Greg landed the much harder shots. Indeed, Michaliszyn threw plenty of punches in that round. He even had Greg against the ropes momentarily, however, Greg was always in such a position that the blows intended for him often overreached its target. When this happened, Greg made Ted pay each time. The second round ended with Greg scoring a right uppercut, left-hook combination in the center of the ring. Astonishingly, Greg lost the second round on all three judges' scorecards.

The rest of this six-round fight was more of the same, as Greg swept the remaining rounds on Minker's card; after dropping the first two, and only lost round four on Shirley and Moretti's card the rest of the way. Greg Haugen was awarded a unanimous decision, with all three judges scoring the fight 58-56 in his favor. One can assume it took the judges a couple of rounds to get acclimated with Greg's mastery. Ted had some good moments landing uppercuts in round three but did not appear to do much damage, but Greg scored more often and showcased a more eclectic attack. He hurt Ted with a short, left hook, right-cross combination towards the end of round five, and was more accurate than the very busy, but often missing, Michaliszyn in the sixth round.

The Ted Michaliszyn fight should have put all on notice about Greg Haugen. It was a situation where Greg was coming off a long layoff and facing a guy in Ted, who was active and showed plenty of promise. According to Ted, he sparred with Ray Mancini, and Mancini told him he felt he would be a world champion one day. Ted had his sights set on major horizons in the lightweight division, and Greg Haugen, The ToughMan from Alaska, was supposed to just be a formidable roadblock to knock over on his way to the stars.

34

Ted even left his regular job to concentrate on his boxing career in an infinite manner. Ted also had a potential fight with the veteran Frankie Baltazar brewing if he defeated Greg.

There was no doubt Ted was prepared and ready to flash his skills for the Showboat crowd and the ESPN audience. But he was not preparing for a skilled amateur with such subtle skills most people still overlook today. Ted Michaliszyn even missed the memo on Greg's ToughMan stature. When I asked Ted what he knew about Greg going into their fight, "I didn't know anything about him, I just knew he was a white guy...a white guy can't be that tough," Ted chuckles.

While Ted admits Greg beat him fair and square, he downplays his skills to a certain degree. "I know I could have beat the guy...I just ran out of gas." Even when you see Greg's skills firsthand, you still have trouble believing it. In this fight, Greg doubled, and sometimes tripled-up his jab, he led and countered with great success. Greg fought the entire fight in the pocket, yet made his opponent miss time and time again. Stamina was low on the totem pole of reasons why Greg Haugen defeated Ted Michaliszyn.

Indeed, if an individual can develop such skills just by fighting in a bar, then boxing would not be considered the ultimate, grueling sport that it is, where only a select few have the skills and mental capacity to succeed on the highest professional level. You do not play boxing, and you do not showcase the kinds of skills Greg Haugen displayed in his first television fight if you are just a ToughMan. The evidence was there to prove, beyond a reasonable doubt, that Greg Haugen possessed world championship-caliber skills. Yet very few people held that sentiment at the time.

Instead of Greg suffering a significant setback, as was the plan for George Chemeres, it was Ted Michaliiszyn that suffered. Ted was considered a major talent who also had high marketability for television. ESPN, as well as Top Rank Boxing, shared this belief and were all in on selling Ted to the boxing public. "I was a pretty boy with blonde hair, curly hair, and they (ESPN) liked it," Ted said. After losing to Haugen, Ted explained that "Haugen took my TV time away from me." As a result, Ted was no longer given what we refer to today as A-side treatment.

Michaliszyn explained that he now had to face stiff competition "on the road." Ted did not perform well in this scenario. He retired

35

with a record of 11-7-2, 6 KO's, a record that took a major turn for the worse after losing to Greg. It is often believed that one loss in boxing is overstated, and it should not have the negative effect it usually has on pugilists. Thanks to Greg Haugen, Ted Michaliszyn experienced firsthand how one loss could be so detrimental to a fighter's career. Even though Ted had one loss prior to the Haugen fight, this loss proved to be unforgivable and came with damaging consequences.

ESPN now had an *undefeated* white guy, with rugged good looks to take Michaliszyn's place. For Greg, the Ted Michaliszyn fight was just what he needed. "It gave me the opportunity to be on TV and show that I can fight too," Greg said. Besides that, fighters benefit more when matched tough. As do the fans. As J. Russel Peltz once told me, "If you want to get out of the warehouses and the catering halls, you have to make the fights the fans want to see."

Indeed, George Chemeres and Mel Greb did Greg Haugen an immense favor. Greg embraced fierce competition, and he was more than accommodated by the dynamic duo.

Greg was also very realistic about what happened inside a boxing ring. While he won soundly, Greg knew how tough that first fight with Ted was, "He kept coming, kept coming, kept coming, which made me more hell-bent on breaking him down and getting to him, but I never really could because he was more seasoned than me."

At the same time, confidence was oozing out of Greg at this point in his career, "That wasn't the first time they expected some guy with more experience to beat me… the fact that I was fighting guys with more experienced really didn't bother me because I knew if I could get in there and fight my fight, and was in shape, it was going to be hard to beat me," Greg added.

Before Greg continued his impressive run as public enemy number one on ESPN, he faced Tony Villa, who lost to the likes of Bret Summers, Ted Michaliszyn and Roberto Juarez, Greg stopped Tony in the 2nd round. This fight took place in Las Vegas on September 27th, 1984. The main event featured Luis Santana, who went on to face world champions Milton McCrory, Darren Van Horn, Aaron Davis, Simon Brown Vinny Paz. and Terry Norris. It was Greg's last fight in 1984. A year that will go down in history and a year that jump-started Greg Haugen's career.

When the calendar changed to 1985, it left behind a historic year that would be tough to top. In the world of sports, 1985 had a great start. Superbowl XIX was anticipated to be one of the best in NFL history. Quarterback juggernauts Joe Montana and Dan Marino were set to square off in a can't miss thriller. Their teams combined for a record of 29-3 during the regular season. In the end, the game was a letdown, as Super Joe's 49ers proved to be too good for young Marino and his Dolphins. As the Superbowl was taking shape, Greg was getting ready for a rematch with Ted Michaliszyn.

This time around, the fight took place at Mountaineers Building in Seattle. A clear home-field advantage for Haugen. Indeed, Ted was asked to become a Road Warrior from the onset. While this fight was not televised, both fighters give a similar account of the fight, with Greg stopping Ted in seven rounds. "We went at it," Ted said, explaining that he doubled his punch output from the first fight. Greg claimed they threw more punches in their seven rounds than most fighters throw over a twelve-round fight.

"I knew I had to be in shape," Haugen said of the rematch. "I wanted to keep pressuring him the whole fight, I knew in the first fight I was close to getting to him, and I just needed to keep pressure on him, stay in the pocket, keep slipping and banging him. But Ted was tough, he didn't want to quit." When I asked Greg to describe the finish, Greg said, "It was a barrage of punches that I kept coming at him, the referee stopped it, didn't want him to get hurt, I just remember throwing massive shots at him… I kept throwing punches, and luckily it was enough to stop him."

Greg's next fight was also in the Mountaineers Building and made possible by Matchmaker Promotions. Greg's opponent was Juan Del Toro, who sported a record of 3-5., 1 KO. Juan is another fighter who might not be impressive on the surface, but he already had a twelve-round victory over Cristobel Pena and fought the twelve-round distance in a losing effort. The fight with Greg was scheduled for eight rounds, but never really got going. A clash of heads opened a cut on Del Toro's right eye in the very first round. The bout was a no contest. It was the kind of fight Greg craved at the time, a long battle against a tough, experienced Mexican fighter, but it was never to be.

After that fight, Greg traveled to the East Coast for the first time and was set to fight at the Resorts International in Atlantic City. It

37

would be Greg's return to ESPN, and the Chemeres/Greb tag team served up an even tougher opponent than Ted Michaliszyn. The fighter that was picked to defeat Greg was John Wesley Meekins, a 140-pound pugilist who was undefeated and on the rise. Meekins pulled out of the fight just one day before it was scheduled, however. Greg expressed that he was never given an explanation for the cancelation. Meekins was replaced by Jeff Bumpus, who was 19-1, 12 KO's.

In stature, Bumpus was the antithesis to Meekins. "I was training for a tall, lanky right-hander, now I had to face this stubby little left-hander," Haugen explained.

But Jeff Bumpus was not a pushover. Vinny Paz, who was called the Pazmanian Devil, described Jeff as being "tough as nails...the first tough fighter I faced." Bumpus' nickname was the Tazmanian Devil.

Going into the bout with Greg, Jeff's record was an impressive 19-1, 13 KO's. The Tazmanian Devil's only loss was a split decision to Paul Graham in his second professional fight. Graham was a resident of Indianapolis, which is where the fight took place. You do the math.

When I asked Jeff about being a replacement for Meekins, he said, "I got a call a couple of days before the fight...nobody really knows what the guy's name is, and they really couldn't tell me anything about him, other than he was the Alaskan State ToughMan Champion. That doesn't tell you a whole lot. When I get there (Atlantic City), Al Bernstein (the ESPN commentator at the time) asked me If I heard anything about Greg, I said no. Then Al said, well, he had 300 amateur fights. I go oh (and chuckles) I had about 20." Jeff explained he was thrown off because he thought he was set to fight an Alaskan tough man; instead, Bumpus agreed to fight a decorated amateur on short notice. Jeff knew he was giving up a lot against Greg in the experience department, "The first time I put on the boxing gloves was three years before I fought Greg Haugen."

Not that it would matter, Jeff would have taken the fight, nonetheless. But he felt it was a marketing ploy by Greg and his team to blanket his amateur record and publicize his tough man success instead. When I asked Greg why his amateur career was treated as classified information much of his career, he answered. "They never asked me about it."

Greg Haugen had a surprise of his own about Jeff Bumpus before their fight. Jeff explains that "Someone om my side of the camp was playing games with information." The information that was being withheld was that Jeff was a southpaw, Greg was under the impression that Taz was a right-handed fighter. Therefore, when the bell rang on July 17th, 1985, both Greg Haugen and Jeff Bumpus were dealing with, dare I say it, fake news.

Greg was not happy about it. "I wasn't real happy about having to fight him (Bumpus), I had been training for a right-hander, and all of a sudden, I am fighting a southpaw," Greg explained.

I asked Greg what made southpaws so different, he said, "Southpaws are hard. Everything you have been taught about boxing doesn't really work against southpaws. A jab doesn't work well against southpaws. It is more right hands and left hooks and keeping your left foot outside of his right foot and making him go to your right. This way, he cannot control you by going to his left. I fought a lot of southpaws in the amateurs, but this was basically my first time facing one as a pro. It really threw me off."

Perhaps Al Bernstein, as well as anyone else who downgrades Greg's performance against Jeff, should rethink their opinion based on Greg's description of the circumstances of this fight.

Even though both fighters were provided with an unpleasant surprise about each other, Jeff described a light-hearted moment shared between He and Greg before the fight. According to Jeff, he almost laughed uncontrollably when the fighters posed for the prefight stare down for the ESPN cameras, and Greg found this to be humorous. "If you gonna be scared of a mean look, you do not belong in a professional fight," Jeff Bumpus explained.

The fight enunciated what each fighter did well.

"At the start of the fight it was very obvious he is experienced, very sharp jab, he clearly had a lot of sparring, his timing was good, and he was very cagey about getting his distance down. I was used to guys being right in front of me. I hadn't fought anybody with his experience level at that point," Jeff Bumpus said.

Greg Haugen described Jeff as being "very tough…he made me work for it."

Jeff, who is a great boxing mind and should be a boxing analyst for television, peeled the Greg Haugen onion even deeper. "When I think about the fight now, it is clear to me Greg is a throwback fighter. His other opponents, as well as spectators, like to call him awkward. There is nothing awkward about his jab or anything he did."

I asked the Tazmanian Devil if he can name a fighter of the past that Greg did remind him of, he said, without hesitation, "Fritzie Zivic. Not for the dirty stuff, which is all anyone talks about. Watch Zivic' films and watch guys get a ramrod jab in their face over and over and an aggressive swarming style once he pokes that jab. It will remind you of Greg vs. Jimmy Paul."

This fight also showed off Greg's superior defensive skills. "I was pretty frustrated, I could not catch him cleanly, he had me pretty well figured out," Jeff said. Jeff did catch Greg with one great shot early in the fight, but that success was few and far between.

Jeff Bumpus also expressed frustration with ESPN analyst Al Bernstein's summation of the fight. "Al Bernstein said Greg looked terrible, which really pisses me off." Jeff explains, "I think Greg wasn't used to guys coming after to him the way I did…he won the fight, there was not much doubt about that, but I think they missed my ability to press the issue," Jeff said. Jeff feels his constant aggression helped Greg prepare on a new wrinkle. "His ability to counter improved after our fight… they worked on catching somebody coming at him with a left hook (after our fight) and it worked for him against top competition."

At the time, based on his performance against Jeff, Al Bernstein felt had Greg fought Meekins, he would have lost. A point that irritated Jeff when it was said, and it still does. When I asked Al Bernstein what he felt about that fight now, he still sticks by his summation. "I think had Greg fpoght that same kind of performance against Chris Calvin and Freddie Roach, he would have lost," explained Al.

It goes to show you that boxing can be the ultimate Rorschach test. But there should be no doubt how Greg Haugen looked on July 17th, 1985, had everything to do with the caliber of fighter Jeff Bumpus was.

Al Bernstein suggests that, since Haugen stopped both Calvin and Roach, he could have done the same to Bumpus had he been as sharp as he was against those fighters. While I always respect Mr. Bernstein's boxing insight, he is one of the pundits who coorectly felt Marvelous Marvin Hagler should have gotten the decision against Ray Leonard, which is the only thought any sound boxing mind should have. But here I think he has undervalued Jeff Bumpus as a fighter. On his best day, Greg Haugen would have had trouble stopping Jeff Bumpus, not even the great Julio Caser Chavez could stop Jeff. JC superstar, Vinny Paz, Greg, and anyone else who laced 'em up against Bumpus shows nothing but respect for him. That should speak volumes for everyone.

Jeff's ability to take a punch created another tongue in cheek moment both fighters remember to this day. "At the end of the fight I stuck my chin out and tapped it, he hit me with a solid right hand, at that stage of my career you could hit me over the head with just about anything, and it wouldn't shake me up, I was in great shape and had a very good chin. Greg and I had a laugh about that at the California Hall of Fame in 2015," Jeff said. But the fight was no laughing matter, and Greg had trouble against Jeff and the ESPN crew was not impressed with him, "I gave Greg a hard time because I was giving him a hard time of mastering his distance. Greg was all about distance. By jumping in, and being all over him, he had trouble," explained Jeff Bumpus.

One thing that cannot be disputed, Greg Haugen, had arguably his most impressive KO streak of his career after the Jeff Bumpus fight. Al Bernstein said that throughout his career, Greg "won with more guile than power." While this is probably true holistically, that was not the case during the stretch of ESPN fights Greg had after the Bumpus fight. Greg not only thanked Jeff for taking the fight on short noticed and being a hell of a tough customer. It was the kind of fight that showcased Greg's vast abilities, but it also taught Greg that he needed to improve his craft.

Because big fights were still looming and the George Chemeres 'put him in tough' bounty still had sharp, piercing teeth, Greg knew in each contest he would be put to the test. Greg Haugen fought next on August 22, 1985. Freddie Roach was next up.

Before he became a world-class trainer, Roach was a solid professional fighter and an ESPN staple. Roach's fight with Tommy Cordova in 1984, in which he lost a 12-round split decision, is still considered one of the best bouts ESPN has ever aired. Going into the fight with Greg, Freddie was 39-8. Freddie shared the ring with formidable competition such as Rafael Lopez, Lenny Valdez, Louis

Burke, Reynaldo Zaragoza, Delio Palacios, Efrain Nieves, Cordova, Joe Ruelas, Richie Foster, Bobby Chacon, and Jaime Balboa.

Going into the fight with Haugen, Roach was riding a three-fight winning streak and was looking to improve his place in the standings by defeating Haugen. Before the fight, Greg and Freddie knew each other well. They sparred and trained with each other. Greg said, "I had sparred with Freddie, a bunch of times in Johnny Tocco's gym…I had been handling him pretty easy, I was a lot stronger than him. I would just bully him around and have my way with him."

"When Haugen first came from Las Vegas, he was well-known for his tough man contests. I particularly didn't like him that much when I first met him. When we finally fought, I wanted to beat him badly, it didn't work out that way," Freddie Roach said. On their sparring sessions, Roach explained, "Sparring with him was very tough, he was a very awkward opponent. He had a big right hand, a really good left hook, and he was strong. Everybody that sparred with him as hard they could because he was very, very cocky," Freddie said.

Perhaps the results of these sparring sessions were not made public because most observers felt Roach would prevail. Al Bernstein said, "Greg was fighting someone who was more well-known and had an excellent skill set. His performance against Jeff Bumpus was workmen like, and it wasn't his best effort," therefore the consensus was that Freddie Roach would defeat Greg Haugen.

But Freddie Roach knew it was going to be a tough fight. In fact, Freddie's initial response was not to take the fight. Freddie Roach was supposed to fight Bret Summers instead of Greg. However, that fight fell through, and Greg was named as a replacement. Much to the displeasure of Freddie. "I told the promoters I am not fighting because I wanted to fight the other guy. I wasn't ready for Haugen…so I stopped training, as the fight got closer, I realized I needed the money to pay the rent, and I took the fight when I wasn't 100 percent prepared," Freddie explained. "I was pissed the promoter picked the opponent; usually they give you a chance to pick one of three choices, they didn't here, they wanted me to fight Haugen. Why do I have to fight this guy? Bret Summers, I fought in the amateurs before, and I didn't have any problems, I thought I could beat Summers. He was a good opponent, yes, but he wasn't as tough or strong as Haugen."

Bret Summers explained that he did not know why the fight with Freddie Roach was called off and was never given an explanation. Troy Summers, Bret's dad, who was instrumental in Bret's career, explained, "You never know why in boxing. Boxing was pretty well controlled by the likes of the Duva's, King, Arum, and Emmanuel Steward so, a lot of stuff happened that those who were not in that circle did not know about, it was happening behind the scenes. They always came up with some non-real reason, and you sort of just went with it. That is just how boxing was and still is today."

Going into the fight, Greg's confidence was high, but he knew that this was another example of the Chemeres-Greb bounty. "They were saying he was going to beat me because of his experience he had I think over 30 more fights than me…but people can say what they want, actions mean more."

The actions in the ring suggested that Haugen was the much more experienced pugilist.

Before the start of round one, referee Davey Pearl provided in-depth instructions to Roach and Haugen. During Davey's soliloquy, the body language of both fighters was telling. Haugen was stoic and steady, focused on his opponent. Roach appeared to have ants in his pants, with a wandering eye. Who was the seasoned veteran here?

As round one began, Freddie and Greg were caught up in a clinch. Haugen threw a right hand off the break, and Freddie Roach was visibly bothered by this action. Greg tried to offer his glove as an apologetic gesture, but Roach was having none of it. The remainder of round one played out as more of a feeling-out process than a high-octane affair. Both fighters were feinting and trying to set traps. At the same time, they were both throwing punches with mean intentions. Most of the punches were either slipped or blocked. Haugen appeared to win the round by landing the cleaner, harder blows, Freddie Roach seemed to be the worse for wear after a clash of heads in round one. On the official scorecards, judges Paul Smith and Hal Miller agreed and awarded Greg the round; Hall of Fame judge Jerry Roth, however, somehow awarded the round to Freddie Roach.

Early in round two, Greg landed a good left hook upstairs, followed by a sharp right to the body. Roach appeared to be outclassed as he threw a wide, telegraphed left hook that Greg blocked with ease, but he did not counter the amateurish blow by

Roach. Later in the round, however, Greg was not as kind and delivered a short, stiff left to the face of Freddie Roach, after slipping a Roach jab. At 1:15 of round two, the tide appeared to change. Roach landed the best punch of the fight up to that point. A thudding, straight right hand found its mark and woke up the crowd. Haugen appeared to take the punch well, but it was a shot that provided a thundercrack sound, sure to produce ewws and awws from spectators, both in the crowd and on television. Roach parlayed his success by showcasing a consistent jab the rest of the round. Slipping most of Haugen's leather in the process. Indeed, at the end of round two, it appeared that the Chemeres- Greb Bounty might be carried out. Haugen lost the round on all three official scorecards

Greg got off to a fast start in round three with two body shots that backed Freddie up. Just like Greg said, when he sparred with Freddie, it was clear Greg was the stronger fighter. Haugen then doubled up his jab and started to let his hands go with more speed and fluidity. For the rest of the round, Greg was first and working his jab with great success. A stiff Haugen, left hook, right-hand combination with under 10 seconds to go in the round left no doubt that Greg Haugen won round three.

Dominating round three in this fight was a watershed moment for Greg Haugen's career. Since Greg has had so many great moments, this one might have gone unnoticed until now. Whatever confidence Roach gained in that second round; Greg took it away with a resounding performance. The ordinarily patient, counterpunching, 'ToughMan,'switched up his game plan and took the play away from Freddie. While Haugen turned to the aggressor, he was never reckless in his pursuit of the veteran Roach. It was a round that showed how Greg responded to adversity, and he was a boxer with great diversity. Greg was awarded the round on all three official scorecards.

Greg Haugen was confident with his left hook upstairs and showcased this punch throughout round four. But Freddie Roach was no novice, and he began to time the Haugen left hook, which created clinches. Once again, it was apparent Haugen was the stronger fighter when the two pugilists were in the clinch. As in the earlier rounds, Freddie Roach telegraphed a wild left hook that Greg countered with a beautiful left hook, right cross combinations to the side of Roach's face. The power punches, as well as the rounds, were piling up for the Washington prodigy. Another standout of round four was Haugen's superior balance. It was he, not the more experienced Roach, who was always in a great position to punch. Freddie, the more experienced professional, was lunging and off-balance throughout round four. Judges Jerry Roth, Paul Smith, and Hal Miller recognized Haugen's superior work and gave him the round.

Round five saw another change of pace from Greg Haugen. Greg opted to work his jab and control distance. At distance, Greg landed a powerful right hand to Roach's body. The blow caused Freddie to wince. In a defensive mode, Freddie tried to tie up Greg, but the crafty Haugen managed to keep both of his hands free. Like any sound offensive fighter would, Haugen teed off on his desperate opponent and scored well both to the body and upstairs. At the center of the ring, Greg slipped a Roach jab and countered with a jab of his own. Haugen followed up his counter left jab with a left hook to the body and a right upstairs. It was vintage Haugen.

Greg Haugen's clinic in round five of this fight should be required viewing for all inspiring boxers. His ability to stay in the pocket, slip punches while in the pocket, and remaining in a superior position to land something hard, are skills that may go unnoticed but are yearned for by anyone who has ever laced up the boxing gloves. For all his experience, grit, and boxing knowledge, these were skills that Freddie Roach did not possess. Such skills are not easy to learn or maintain. Such skills seemed to come naturally to Greg Haugen. Somehow, two of the three judges scored round five for Roach. Only Paul Smith understood what he was watching.

Watching Greg at his best, and this fight with Freddie is a perfect example of such, despite what Jerry Roth and Hal Miller appeared to miss, reminds me of the great Salvador Sanchez. Sanchez lived in the pocket but was patient. His great jab was an overlooked equalizer for most of his fights, and he was always in a position to land a good shot. Like Haugen, Sanchez used slight movement to get out of harm's way of his opponents flying leather. Sometimes this superior skill can prove to be cumbersome. I say this because spectators from far away may think a Salvador Sanchez or a Greg Haugen is getting hit because they are not using exaggerated head movement or backing up to avoid their opponent's blows.

The classic fight between Salvador Sanchez and Juan LaPorte is a compelling example of this dynamic. LaPorte's aggressive style appeared to fool some spectators into thinking Sanchez was getting hit. And you did not even have to be far away to be fooled this way. Howard Cosell, who called this classic featherweight fight, consistently stated that LaPorte was landing when indeed, Sanchez was using his subtle movement to escape the intended bad intentions of LaPorte. Cosell was not far away from the action, so it is unclear why *he* kept making this error.

Another trait that Haugen shared with Sanchez was his killer instinct. Salvador Sanchez utilized his killer instinct in his most important fights, Danny Lopez twice, Wilfredo Gomez, Azumah Nelson. For Greg, his vicious streak came during his crucial time on ESPN, and for his big Pay Per View showcase against Ray Mancini.

Like Danny Lopez, Wilfredo Gomez and Azumah Nelson against Sanchez, Freddie Roach did not succumb to Haugen's killer instinct without a fight. In round six, Roach was determined to be the aggressor and stay in the fight. As blood emerged from his nose, Roach came forward with bad intentions. This was all Freddie can do, but in played right in the young matador's hands. Being the stronger, more skilled boxer with the superior jab leaves little room for success for a desperate fighter who feels he is down on the scorecards of a ten-round fight. Indeed, Roach had very little success, being the aggressor in round six. In fact, at around the 1:22 mark of the round, Haugen was coming forward and getting off first. More than enough to win him the round. This time, all three judges credited Haugen with the round.

Round seven began in the center of the ring. It was obvious that Greg was setting traps for his left hook to the body and upstairs, punches that worked well for him throughout this fight. It was not long after that Greg was backing up, hurting Freddie both to the body and head with his dreaded left hook. At this point, Roach was just fighting on pure will, and it was just a matter of survival.

But Freddie Roach was not the kind of fighter that was going to run or look for a way out. His brand of survival mode was to throw punches, tie up, and throw some more. Maybe something will land with enough significance that will stop this freight train that has been infringing upon me and making my life miserable. What we must understand is that up until this point, Freddie Roach had not been

46

beaten in such a manner. Most of his loses were close decisions. The one fight he was not in at all was a technical knockout loss to Lenny Valdez in two rounds, and that fight took place in 1982.

This fight with Haugen was a different kind of defeat for Freddie that he was not willing to accept without emptying his tank. As Freddie tried in vain, he continued to eat jabs from the composed Haugen. Greg knew he had his man, and he did not panic, another trait in boxing shared only by the select few. In round seven, Greg mad Joe Cool look like Hudson from the movie *Aliens.*

It must have been frustrating for Freddie Roach, a consummate professional, to have a guy standing right in front of him and yet be so hard to hit. To add to the frustration, as Greg became harder to hit, he could not miss his foe. Round seven became target practice for Greg Haugen, and his left hook was his favorite weapon. Frustrated and tired, Roach walked right into a short Greg Haugen left hook late in the seventh round and went down. Davey Pearl picked up his count with about 30 seconds remaining in the round. The never say die Roach beat the count, and convinced Pearl that he had enough of his bearings to continue to fight. Haugen wasted no time, and like a panther on the prowl, he closed distance on Roach and delivered a perfect left hook threw the guard of Roach. A stunned Roach could not keep his feet from under him and fell for a second time. This time Davey Pearl did not bother to count and opted to protect a beaten fighter from any further damage. Freddie Roach did not object to the stoppage, and Greg Haugen was as joyous as you would ever see him. "He had a very good counter left hook over a right hand, I should have learned from training not to throw that punch. I threw the right hand, I had a pretty good right hand, he countered over the top with a left hook, I did that twice, and he knocked me down twice, the referee said that's enough for tonight, I couldn't argue," Freddie said of the ending.

Greg did take time out to check on Freddie, who was being looked at in his corner. So often, Greg has been a fighter who has been said to get under the skin of others. But here, in his most significant win to date, Greg was the consummate professional. After the fight, Greg pointed out that he was given very little chance to beat Freddie Roach, but he knew that he could. As time has passed, Freddie Roach has found respect for Greg Hauge, "I respect him. He was sure of himself, I kind of like that because if you don't believe in yourself who the fuck is," Roach said.

A satisfying win, to say the least. It is an ideal dynamic when the odds are stacked against you. When virtually nobody gives you a chance. When all you want is support, but all you receive is doubt. Such a dynamic creates self-doubt. So much so that you can question yourself right out of your goals. But, for personality's like Greg Haugen, such doubt can fuel the fire, be that boost that hits the spot. When you add into the equation, you are entering a ring, all by yourself, and on the other side is a man who is going to try and hurt you, bad, self-doubt can create all kinds of dangerous scenarios.

Greg Haugen beat Freddie Roach not just because he was the better-skilled boxer. But because he took all that doubt and turned it into motivation. All his experience, as well as Eddie Futch's tutelage, and Freddie Roach was still handicapped in a severe way against the rising lightweight. Greg's win over Roach opened eyes. One inspiring young pugilist the win got the attention of was Craig Houk, "That is when I knew he was the real deal," Craig said of Greg. Craig went on to face legends such as Meldrick Taylor, Julio Cesar Chavez, and Hector Camacho. He also has a quirky attachment to Greg, "A lot of people get us mixed up. They ask, 'Are you Greg Haugen,' and I say, 'Yeah I am Greg Haugen,' because he was twice as good as me," Craig joked.

Yankees owner George Steinbrenner destroyed a large screen television when his New York Yankees dropped the World Series against the Arizona Diamondbacks in 2001. While big screens televisions were not commonplace in 1985, I am sure there were a lot of broken appliances in the households of George Chemeres and Mel Greb after Haugen's great victory. As is turned out, George's grandiose demeanor and impressive knowledge of the sweet science did not equate to him always getting his way. Like with that Arrozal vs. Palaki fight, Bob Howard explains, "During the fight, Arrozal got mad because I warned him for a low blow, and he stormed out of the ring. I stopped the clock and told him to get back in the ring. He did, and the fight wound up being a draw. George was pissed at me, he felt I should have disqualified Arrozal for leaving the ring. That was the only time I remember George cussed me out. But I saw him a few months later, and he acted like it was nothing." It would take more than a few months to mend the fences of Chemeres and Haugen, however.

Knocking off Haugen proved to be a much more onerous task than expected. If a seasoned veteran with the best trainer in the business could not get the job done, who would Team Chemeres turn to next to defeat Greg? How about a fighter who was a killer puncher? Literally.

Chapter Seven
Facing Chris Calvin

"I was not all that sure I wanted Greg to take that fight. Calvin had a reputation of being a tough guy, and I didn't want Greg to get hurt or killed."

—Lee Haugen.

Boxing is a brutal sport. When a professional athlete laces up the boxing gloves for competition, it can indeed be the last act they ever execute in life. For this reason, we all appreciate and love boxers for putting their lives on the line for our entertainment. However, there is a flip side to that prestigious coin. A significant portion of the public cannot watch boxing because of its brutality. To take it a step further, a tremendous voice exists, which annunciates that boxing should be banned. As far back as 1917, when a fellow named Young McDonald lost his life in the squared circle, they have been outcries, and measures against the sweet science. When McDonald met his fate, prizefighting in a legalized manner was in its infancy stage in the United States of America. In fact, in many states, boxing was illegal and conducted on the black market if you will. After McDonald's death, boxing was once again illegal in New York until 1920.

Boxing resumed in 1920 in New York State, under the rules and regulations of the Walker Law, which was responsible for the classic eight weight classes. Ever since then, men like Tex Rickard, Bob Arum and Don King have made a fortune off the backs of professional athletes willing to risk their lives in the name of entertainment and competition. When it is done right, the fighters also build up a friendly bank account and a comfortable lifestyle, however that dynamic does not happen as often as it should.

With that said, boxing has been a source of income, a lifeline, for many human beings, like Greg Haugen. For every Young McDonald, there are thousands of immigrants and inner-city kids who would have been lost in the streets if not for the confines of a boxing gym. And when a fighter really makes it and gives back, Hollywood cannot draft a better script. Some of the stories of boxers making it are heartfelt to the core. Like when Marvelous Marvin Hagler donated a bunch of boxing gloves to an inner-city gym, or when Riddick Bowe was able to buy a house for his mother, his first gesture when his fistic prowess finally paid huge dividends. Greg Haugen was always the kind of person who gave back as well. Female fighter, Shelly 'Shelito's Way' Vincent declared that without boxing, she would be dead.

While all these stories are what makes boxing great, there is nothing worse than a fighter who succumbs in the ring. The first time I was introduced to this type of tragedy was when Johnny Owen lost his life after his battle with WBC bantamweight champion and Hall of Famer Lupe Pintor. I was very young then but was addicted to boxing. I remember watching the Pintor vs. Owen fight like it was yesterday. Owen did not pass right after the bout, but when the news hit the airwaves, it was a shock to my system. For these reasons, my family made sure I was always just a boxing spectator and never a participant. Part of me regrets that I listened to them, part of me is very glad I did.

There was a rash of boxing deaths in fights that were televised around the time of Johnny Owen's unfortunate fate, with lightweight Duk-Koo Kim dying after his grueling battle with Hall of Famer Ray Boom Boom Mancini at the forefront. Then there was Chris Calvin vs. Shawn Thomas, televised on ESPN's Top Rank Boxing Series.

Chris Calvin could fight. There was never going to be anyone who was going to say otherwise. Johnny Giansante, Calvin's first trainer, is on record saying Chris was one of the toughest kids that he has ever come across. But did Calvin ever want to be a boxer? "I just followed in my daddy's footsteps," Calvin explains. Chris did everything his father did; first, he enlisted in and boxed in the Navy, then he became a professional, then a firefighter. As an amateur, Chris won the Nashville Golden Gloves and won the all Navy championship three years in a row. Calvin presented the perfect image for the ESPN/Top Rank Boxing formula. He was a power puncher, white and good looking. Calvin looked like the prototypical soap opera star of the day; his perfect mustache was second to only Orlando Canizales's in the '80s.

Chris Calvin's professional debut was on the undercard of the Thomas Hearns vs. Sugar Ray Leonard welterweight unification extravaganza. Talk about starting out at the deep end of the pool, "Can't really ask for much better, to be on a special card like that," Calvin said of the experience. But such a spotlight could be a bit overwhelming for a young kid making his debut, "It throws your body and mind into a whole different game," was how Calvin described the atmosphere that night. Indeed, Chris did drop his pro debut to Darrell Cottrell via a four-round decision that night. Did the big atmosphere affect his performance? "I can't say if it did or not. I guess I was kind of scared," was Calvin's response.

Calvin persevered, and put some early disappointments in his rearview mirror. Soon enough, he was fighting on ESPN. "We signed some kind of contract with ESPN," Calvin explains. The returns on Calvin fights were exceptional, "Most of my fights had a lot of action, and they (ESPN/Top Rank) liked those kinds of fights, instead of a lot of running around," Calvin explained.

The first round of his fight with Anthony Murray was a poor man's version of Hagler vs. Hearns. After some contentious action, an electric Calvin straight right hand dropped Murray. Murray was out and looked to be in real danger. Instead of calling a halt to the action and attend to Murray's safety immediately, the referee Rudy Battle decided to count to ten. A sheer moment of incompetence. To see Murray's mouthpiece dangling out of his mouth, as Battle was wasting precious time, is a disturbing image.

When Calvin faced Forrest Winchester, a tall glass of water who was the brother of Kronk world champion Hilmer Kenty, he did a good job getting inside; as Winchester was intent on snaking his left jab in Calvin's direction to keep distance and working when he got there. Showing his diversity, Chris also scored at long range against the taller foe. In the closing seconds of round three, Calvin landed a crippling overhand right, followed by two short left-hooks, that put Winchester down. Forrest survived the round, but the end was near. At the start of round four, Winchester immediately hopped on his bicycle, but soon found himself at the end of a beautiful, straight Calvin right hand that once again put Winchester down. A game Winchester beat the count, he even protested to Tony Orlando that his trip to the canvas should have been ruled a slip. The replay gave some credence to Winchester's protest. There was no doubt about the next knockdown, however. As Calvin landed a short right cross on Winchester's jaw. A devastating punch that almost sent Forrest through the ropes. Tony Orlando stopped the fight immediately, and once again, Winchester protested Orlando's actions.

Perhaps the best display of power by The Southern Rebel was in his showdown against Bret Summers of the Kronk Gym. Another gem of a fight during the early days of ESPN. Calvin dropped Summers eight times in that bout, before stopping him in the tenth round. "I got in the best shape I ever been in for my boxing career when I fought Bret Summers, that was a great fight," Calvin stated. Bret Summers also speaks of the grueling pace of that fight, "The first two rounds I totally outboxed him. Halfway through the third round, I hit him with a hard shot and thought I hurt him a little bit, then I decided to slug with him, then SPLASH! I went down," Summers said.

Summers added about Calvin's punching power, "There are different kinds of feelings when you get hit. Calvin hit me with thudding shots, I don't know how to explain it, it was like THUD, then you go down." Summers said that every time he went away from his game plan of trying to box Calvin, he would go down. "It was frustrating," Summers said. "I was a little hardheaded, thinking he could not hurt me. Well, maybe a lot hardheaded," Summers admitted. The Bret Summers fight was telling because, according to Chris Calvin, "I was promised a title fight from Top Rank if I won the Summers fight, and that never happened." Instead, Calvin was matched against Shawn Thomas on ESPN for his next fight.

When asked why the title shot did not come, after all, it is hard to fathom not selling Chris Calvin after his run of fights on ESPN, Calvin stated, "I was never told anything about it." This declaration is not to suggest that Chris Calvin does not have a theory as to why he did not receive a title shot after the Summers fight, "They tried to get me to change my name (from the Southern Rebel) to the Fighting Fireman, and I never did. I think that might have had something to do with it, but I can't say for sure," Calvin offered. Indeed, pride in the Confederate Flag does not present well. But Calvin squelches that belief, "I was never prejudiced. I was the only white guy on the Navy boxing team, and those fellows put their pants on the same as I do. I just liked the flag, and I wanted to stand up for the South," Calvin explained.

Indeed, The Southern Rebel did not receive a warm welcome when he fought on the East coast, as he did quite a bit. However, Calvin's fighting style often changed their minds. One fight that turned out this way was Calvin's draw against Edwin Curet, which took place in Massachusetts, "When the fight started they booed me for like ten minutes straight, then around the sixth round they started hollering for me to win," Calvin explained of his real-life Rocky moment. When he dropped a controversial decision to Robin Blake in 1983, Calvin explained that "people came up to me from his hometown saying I won the fight." Blake was a world-class level fighter, "He was fast, a good mover, but he could not hit hard like Haugen," Calvin summarized.

While Chris Calvin had power and charisma, he lacked in one vital area of boxing, sparring. "Down in Nashville, I couldn't get much sparring, and they never sent no one to spar with. That was one of the downfalls of my career," Calvin said. Any boxer worth his salt knows the importance of sparring. Rocky Marciano benefited from his sparring with Cesar Brion, Robert Brant stated that his sparring sessions with Errol Spence Jr. were instrumental with his growth, and Greg was always at his best when he sparred with blue-chip talents such as Cubanito Perez, Roger Mayweather, and Hall of Famer Jeff Fenech. Calvin's inability to get good sparring was such a big story, it often came up as a topic of discussion during his televised fights on ESPN. Indeed, it even came up during the Shawn Thomas fight.

Chris Calvin and Shawn Thomas fought in a lightweight battle on May 29th, 1985. Thomas was a fighter out of Detroit, Michigan. A short, compact southpaw. Thomas described himself as a "boxing left-hander" Like Bret Summers, Shawn Thomas was never knocked down as a professional. Coming off a loss, Thomas was the clear B-side fighter but still considered a risk. The kinds of fights ESPN's Top Rank series was known for at the time. "They put you in wars every fight, that is what made ESPN. The promoters put everybody in with tough fights, it was very competitive. There were no one-sided fights," Freddie Roach, a frequent flyer on ESPN, explained.

The amazing thing about this fight is that it was a competitive contest up until the stoppage. If a narrative has been created that suggests the Chris Calvin vs. Shawn Thomas fight was a one-sided affair, that narrative is indeed a false one. Shawn was ahead on the

54

scorecards up until the tragic ending. Thomas took the fight to Calvin every round. Backing him up on several occasions and fighting well on the inside. There were moments in round six where Thomas was walking Calvin down, and finding The Southern Rebel's body. Interestingly enough, referee Stanley Berg took a point away from Thomas towards the end of round six for holding behind the head. An odd decision from Berg, who sported the worst comb-over known to mankind.

While Berg did warn Thomas for not holding behind the head at around the 1:12 second mark, the first time he did so demonstratively, he took a point away from Thomas the very next time he did it. Excessive, to say the least, predominately because Calvin was initiating a fair share of the clinches, and even mushed his foreman into Thomas's face during one of the breaks, and Berg did not say a word to him. Had this fight not ended in tragedy, Berg's questionable point deduction would have been the story of the battle.

In round seven, both men were still landing good shots, Calvin started to find the range with his right hand. But Thomas was giving as good as he got. He landed a showy one-two, right jab, straight left combination on Calvin's face. The real danger for Thomas came when Calvin started to trap him against the ropes, where Calvin was able to land hard shots with leverage, as Thomas did not showcase good defense when he was against the ropes. Calvin began to take over and was landing clean right hands when Thomas was off the ropes as well.

These hard shots appeared to start taking the starch out of Shawn, but he was not getting battered to the point where it would be a concern. It wasn't until Calvin once again backed Thomas into the ropes again where Shawn seemed vulnerable. The mouthpiece of Thomas came flying out, and Calvin's power almost sent Thomas through the ropes, allowing Calvin to tee off on a defenseless fighter. Calvin did not land clean punches when Thomas was in this posture, and Berg broke the fighters and let the action continue on.

Calvin immediately muscled Thomas into the ropes and did damage. Berg stepped in after about sixteen unanswered punches were thrown by Calvin, not every punch was hellacious, but it was enough to do permanent damage. Shawn Thomas did not go down under the barrage of punches, but soon slumped down when he was being looked at by the ringside doctors. Both the doctor and Stanley Berg tried to keep Thomas on his feet and walked him over to his stool. Doctor Albert Willets began to give him smelling salts to revive him. The doctor then administered an ice pack behind Thomas' head. Soon after, Thomas was taken out on a stretcher. Before the ESPN telecast went off the air, they announced that Shawn Thomas suffered from a cerebral concussion and exhaustion. Thomas died on July 3rd, 1985, after being in a coma since fight night.

Chris Calvin felt Berg did not step in early enough, "As far as I can remember I had Thomas pretty hurt on the ropes and I think I kind of looked at the referee and he didn't even move, so, I threw a few more punches, and he stopped it," Chris explained.

I asked Chris if this statement meant that he felt the referee was slow in reacting to protect Shawn, he replied, "In my opinion, he was." This moment has been played inside the head of Chris Calvin for many years. Chris also explains how he regrets never speaking with the Thomas family. "One of the things that really bothered me was that I never got to talk with the family. I want to tell them I am really sorry that it ended up like it did," Calvin said. Joe Smelley, Shawn Thomas's manager, also felt Berg was negligent and brought charges against him, the Indiana Boxing Commission cleared Berg of all wrongdoing.

A significant criticism of Berg that should be mentioned is that when Calvin was hurting Thomas, there was a point where not only was Calvin holding over the head, he was landing a punch while doing so, Stanley Berg did not say anything to him. How can he be so bold with Thomas, and deduct a point after only one warning, and not say anything to Calvin? Also, Berg could have ruled a knockdown when Thomas went through the ropes, this could have been an opportunity to evaluate Shawn's condition. When Berg instructed the fighters to resume fighting after Thomas was freed from the ropes, he did not even look at Shawn Thomas to examine his condition. Berg's attention to detail was as robust as the time he spent on his hair.

Calvin, like all fighters before and after him, should not be held responsible for what happened, assuming there is no foul play with the rules. Like a wolf who smells red meat, Chris jumped on Thomas when he had his man hurt and finished him with hellacious blows.

That is his job. No, it is not the everyday job duties known to most ordinary people. But combat sports participants should never be mistaken for everyday people. What boxers have to do to succeed does not allow them to be.

Of course, none of this makes it any easier when a fighter does lose his life on the job. Like Chris Calvin, Shawn Thomas was a fighter who was just trying to earn living. It has been reported that Thomas's last words were, "Is this the end of my career?" Even at his most desperate moment, a fighter always thinks about fighting. Soon after Shawn Thomas uttered these words, he fell into a coma and never regained consciousness.

Calvin's victory was supposed to be a moment of celebration. One next step to a lightweight title fight. Instead, it provided him with demons that boxers such as Sugar Ray Robinson, Emile Griffth, Joe Bugner, Ultimino Ramos, Jim Moore, Alan Minter, Wilfred Scypion, Lupe Pintor, Ray Mancini, Barry McGuigan, Albert Davila, Jorge Vaca, and Brian Mitchell can relate to.

Indeed, Chris Calvin had remorse, but he had a fight to prepare for. A big fight. Calvin was scheduled to fight Greg Haugen on November 6th, 1985. Calvin explained that he went about training camp the same as the others, and with what was at stake, could there be time for remorse? "Once again they said the winner would get a title shot," The way Chris presented in preparation for the Haugen fight gave some the impression that he was insensitive to the death of Thomas. When interviewed by Al Bernstein prior to the fight, Chris stated, "I tried to put it out of my mind" Despite Calvin's statements and demeanor, ESPN analyst Al Bernstein had a feeling what Chris was trying to sell was mere window dressing, "Chris was misinterpreted as this Southern Rebel. A raucous, crazy, violent kind of guy. That was not Chris Calvin. He was a thoughtful guy. I do believe after coming back from that kind of a situation (Shawn Thomas's death) was not easy for him," Al Bernstein said.

What other choice did Chris Calvin have but to try and put this tragic event behind him at the time? Chris stated that such a task is impossible, however. "It never really is behind you," Calvin told me.

Whatever demons that were lurking for Chris Calvin had to be put on hold for his own survival. There was business at hand in the name of Greg Haugen. When I asked Chris if he had any say in fighting Greg next, he said, "I had nothing to do with getting my opponents. I was tied with ESPN, so they had a big say." When asked what he knew about Greg going into the fight, Chris stated, "I didn't really know too much about him. Just like any other fight, I was trying to get in there to win."

Once again, going into the fight, Greg Haugen played the role of the underdog. "For a long time, Greg was not considered the favorite in his fights," Al Bernstein explained. It was only natural that he was not considered the favorite since going into the fight, Chris Calvin was perceived as this killer puncher, literally. Greg Haugen was a 7-1 underdog for his fight against The Southern Rebel.

After being burned from the Johnny Meekins cancelation, the tough southpaw in Jeff Bumpus and the veteran Freddie Roach, George Chemeres, and Mel Greb had to be thrilled to match Haugen up with Calvin. Like the iron Calvin had in his gloves, there must have thought their plan to make Greg lose was ironclad. Indeed, to suggest Chris Calvin was one of the hardest punchers in lightweight history is not an overstatement. And there is plenty of anecdotal evidence, apart from the Shawn Thomas tragedy, to back up such a claim. "I asked Greg once, when his career was over, who punched the hardest, he said, without hesitation, 'Chris Calvin," Bill McDonald stated. Edwin Curet was asked if Calvin was the hardest puncher he ever faced, he answered with an emphatic "Yes!" Curet also said that "He was a great puncher, but he had a style that fit mine. We fought to a draw."

Just because Chris never won a world title should not mean Chris should not be remembered as one of the hardest punchers in boxing history. A killer punch is not always in keeping with victories at boxing's world-class level. Earnie Shavers is widely regarded as the hardest heavyweight in boxing history, and *he* never won a world title either. In fact, Shavers lost to the majority of fighters who swear by his freakish power. But when a fighter possesses such power, it is a tangible factor that your opponent must respect and prepare for. Calvin enjoyed this same freakish power.

Nobody knew this better than Greg Haugen going into the Calvin fight. Greg would not ever say out loud he was scared to fight any man, but he did admit he knew what Chris was capable of, and he did not want to be another Shawn Thomas. "I was not all that sure I wanted Greg to take that fight. Calvin had a reputation of being a tough guy, and I didn't want Greg to get hurt or killed," added Lee Haugen.

Once again, referee Davey Pearl gave lengthy instructions to the fighters in the center of the ring. Unlike in the Freddie Roach, Greg's face showed a hint of distraction when listening to Pearl (maybe he was wondering if this guy was paid by the word). Perhaps Greg did not have the same stone-cold look in this fight because he did not have the same confidence that he did going into the Roach fight, a fight that he knew he was the stronger man. In this fight, he was about to mix it up with a man who had a 94 percent knockout percentage and killed a guy in his last fight. Sometimes a little fear goes a long way in a boxing match. When I asked Greg about this contrast of stare downs, he said, "Davey came in the dressing room before the fight and made it a point to let me know that he was in charge, whatever he said goes. I knew Davey was a good referee, we needed to listen to him...those guys can stop the fight and take points away from you. That is not something I wanted to have done, so I made sure I was concentrated on his instructions." Greg's comment may be interpreted as a deflection regarding his fear of Calvin. However, Greg said in no uncertain terms that Shawn Thomas's death weighed heavily in his mind, "I knew he punched hard; I tried not to get hit with those big shots, and he killed that guy before me, and I did not want to be the next guy. Even though he had good power in both hands, I tried to stay away from his right hand because that was his money punch."

When round one began, the fighters met at the center of the ring, missing with their jabs. Greg was determined to be the aggressor and landed a good right hand to the body while Chris was backing up. Calvin, however, countered with a better shot, a short, left hook. This punch spun Greg into a vulnerable position against the ropes. While Greg was backing into the ropes, he threw a lazy punch with his left, it was not quite a jab and Greg short-armed the punch. Chris Calvin took advantage of a rare technical error by Greg and delivered a pulverizing overhand right that landed flush on Haugen's left cheek. When recounting the blow, Haugen said, "He caught me better than I have ever been caught in my life, I was on my feet still, but I was out on my feet...I blacked out...but I knew that I got hit with a right hand, and I knew he was probably coming with a left hook, so I got down low."

And you can see Haugen time the big Chris Calvin left hook, not once, but twice during that sequence. Greg did not see the first left hook coming, it was boxing IQ and instinct that made that happen. When Greg ducked the second left hook, he tied up Calvin. Greg then tried to get his jab going again but continued to lock up Chris, as it was clear Greg was hell-bent on smothering the Southern Rebel's power. Greg proved strong enough to back Calvin up in the clinch. Calvin was surprised by these events, "He was tough, could take a punch, and man was he strong," Calvin said of Greg. Chatty Davey Pearl broke them up, and Greg had the fight once again in the center in the ring, where he needed it to be.

If the Freddie Roach fight proved that Greg Haugen had experience beyond his professional years, the Chris Calvin fight conveyed this point exponentially. How many professional fighters could get walloped, to the point that everything goes black, and still be aware of what the next punch will *probably* be, and get out of the way? Once the fight got back to the center of the ring, Greg's confidence was back. Calvin, however, was still throwing bombs. Greg, thinking things were getting too close for comfort, tied Calvin up again and walked him down back into the ropes. Pearl broke up the fighters, and the action pursued once again in Greg's comfort zone.

This sequence of the fight is telling because it showed that Greg could push around a big puncher in Calvin. In boxing, typically a bigger puncher is the stronger man. To get a better idea of how deceptively strong Greg Haugen was, Chris was also physically bigger than Greg as well. When I asked Greg if he was surprised by this dynamic, he said, "It didn't surprise me. Most of the guys I fought I was stronger than. I had a good base, big legs. I was not surprised I could walk him around. I wanted to establish to Chris I was the fucking stronger guy of the two and that I was going to be in control. Guys like that, you need to assert your domination early in the fight because they can make it miserable on you if you do not."

Calvin was not without boxing savvy as well, because when Greg did clinch, he did not waste his energy and waited for the break. As the rest of round one continued, Greg started working his jab more effectively, but Calvin hit Greg with another big right hand, which Greg appeared to take better. Again, Haugen crowded Calvin to smother his power and getting hit with the big right hand. Greg managed to avoid further punishment and did catch Chris with an excellent right hand towards the end of round one. All in all, it was a massive round for Chris Calvin, probably the most lopsided round in Greg Haugen's young career. But Greg was able to take Chris Calvin's best in the round, and he managed to finish the round well. Confidence was on the rise for the ToughMan from Auburn, Washington, even though judges Dalby Shirley, Hal Miller, and Lou Tabat all correctly scored round one for Chris Calvin.

In round two, Greg started off bouncing on his toes, that right hand did revive him and soon smothered Chris, walking him down into the ropes. It was clear that Greg wanted to avoid Chris's long-range power and was strong enough to walk him down. Haugen would score with a jab and close distance once more. When Haugen forced Chris into the ropes this time, Davey Pearl warned Greg to watch his head. There was a lot of clinching in this round. Pearl was once again earning his money as he kept having to break the fighters up. Greg was forcing most of the clinches, but he was also scoring with short shots in close. Calvin was much better at long range and Haugen knew this. Haugen began to score well in the last part of the round. He hit Chris with some effective one-twos and landed a thudding right hand while Calvin's back was against the ropes. By the end of the round Haugen was in rhythm with his defense as well, slipping most of Calvin's shots. A sloppy round indeed, but a Haugen round for sure. Greg won the round on all three of the official scorecards.

The action started off rough in round three. Greg tried to triple off his jab, but there were more clinches than effective punches at the start of the round. Soon after, Greg was in full matador mode, and Chris could not touch him. Greg either slipped Chris's big shots or used his clever movement to avoid the brunt of Calvin's blows. At the same time, Haugen's accuracy went up in round three. Greg tripled up on his jab once more, this time landing, and followed this sequence up with a beautiful right hand. While the punches landed were not devasting, they scored. More importantly, they frustrated Calvin, forcing him to lunge at Greg. Greg managed to tie Calvin up and waited for Davey Pearl to break them up. In these clinches, however, Chris Calvin started to waste energy by trying to break out of Haugen's vice-like grip.

Haugen was in full confident mode now. His jab was in rhythm, and it kept Chris off balance. Greg became brave enough to start throwing and scoring to the body as well in round three. Calvin was becoming tired and frustrated, while Greg was moving well, reminiscent of the Roach fight. Haugen secured another round, but not in the eyes of the ESPN announcers. They gave Calvin round two, and shockingly round three. Round three was another sweep on the official scorecards for Greg.

Chris Calvin was more aggressive at the start of round four and landed well to the body and upstairs. He threw a telegraphed left hook that Greg ducked and subsequently tied up Chris. This sequence seemed to disturb the excellent rhythm Calvin was building. But Greg was not exactly setting the world on fire either in this round. Save for his jab, Greg seemed very reluctant to let his hands go for much of the round. Greg was still able to clinch and walk Calvin down, which appeared to tire Calvin even more than he was. Haugen landed a good, short right hand with under 20 seconds to go. Greg did enough with his left jab, as well as his ring generalship to edge out round four. The three officials scoring the fight also had the same sentiments.

Like in round four, Calvin started off round five quick. Firing off one-two's that did not find its mark flush but woke up the crowd. Greg crowded Chris to alleviate the attack. Calvin, however, was getting the better of the exchanges early in the round. The Haugen clinches started to become excessive. While this is a tactic that will tire out your opponent, and provide you with a breather, it is not conducive to winning rounds. At least it should not be. But Greg's clinching was more about strategy than not being willing to engage. He tasted Calvin's power from long-range, more than he ever wanted to in round one. But he also discovered early how easy it was to grab Chris and walk him down. As he continued to do this in round five, you could see he was setting Calvin up for a big shot. That big shot did not come in round five. The round ended with Chris Calvin gaining confidence and momentum, as he swept his first round on the scorecards since round one.

Haugen came out more urgent in round six and was firing his jab with purpose. Haugen then slid to the right and fired off short left and rights in close. This sequence of punches forced Calvin to back off. In pursuit, Haugen ripped a right hand to Calvin's body. This punch took some starch out of Calvin and he looked for salvage against the ropes. Realizing Calvin was looking for a breather, Haugen back off and forced Calvin off the ropes. This is another savvy move by Greg that might have gone unnoticed. Most fighters probably would have attacked Calvin on the ropes. But Greg knew Calvin would have braced himself to absorb whatever attack Greg launched, and it probably would have led to a clinch. Instead, realizing Calvin's legs were not quite steady, Greg took a little step back that made Chris come to him. Brilliant. Greg said of this tactic, "I could feel as the fight went on, he was getting weaker, from round three on he was not able to bull me around and he felt weaker in the clinches. I could tell he was losing strength, my philosophy was I was going to wear you down from walking you down…around the fourth round, he wasn't really resisting when I pushed him around, so I knew it was working and wanted to keep tiring him out."

Once the action resumed in the center of the ring, Haugen started working his jab again, but another clinch ensued, and Greg walked Calvin back into the ropes. Just like before, Haugen stepped back and let Chris come to him. Haugen was trying to dig to the body more, but both fighters were doing a lot of wrestling. After Davey Pearl broke the fighters, Haugen used a beautiful head and shoulder feint to land a strong left hook. This was the punch I believe Greg was setting Calvin up for out of the clinches. Calvin responded with a hook of his own, but Greg blocked it well. Greg landed another stiff left hook upstairs that forced another clinch; in round six, it was Chris Calvin that was forcing the clinches.

Haugen was now intent on throwing his hands, but an exhausted Calvin was tying Greg up. The big difference, though, was Chris did not have the strength to walk Greg into the ropes. In fact, when Pearl broke up the fighters, Calvin did not use the veteran move of sliding behind the referee to buy more time. Instead, Calvin slid right in front of Greg after the breaks (a tactical mistake many of today's fighters make). With Calvin right in front of him after the break, Greg closed distance with his jab and began to work upstairs with short little uppercuts. With a tired Calvin in front of him and his confidence brewing, Haugen began to pop a championship-caliber jab in the face of the Southern Rebel.

At about the 1:20 mark of round six, Greg Haugen followed up one of these jabs with a thudding overhand right that landed close

Calvin's forehead. It forced a desperation clinch from Calvin. Coming out of the break, Haugen's body language changed. His posture was of a man who knew he had damaged goods in front of him. The killer instinct was in full swing. When I asked Greg to describe the sequence that ended this fight he said:

"I remember staggering him, and he went up against the ropes, I remembering knocking him through the ropes and the judge pushing him back in...he got up, and Davey Pearl asked him where he was, Chris told him, 'yes,' and he let him continue, so I jumped right on him and I didn't give that guy a chance to breathe...I just started throwing shots, nonstop, one after another...up until that point it was the biggest stoppage of my career, especially when they predicted me to lose, this was the third fight in a row. But that really didn't bother me. What bothered me was the fact that George was trying to get me beat all the time, but it kind of fueled my fire to just keep proving them wrong. I knew that I could fight, but I knew that these guys they were throwing me in with were supposed to be beating me, but I wasn't gonna have it. I just wanted to keep proving them wrong, luckily I did on that fight."

After studying the fight, Greg Haugen's victory had little to do with luck. It takes a special breed of fighter to keep his bearings and know when to duck a left hook with bad intentions, *after* being rocked by a right hand from what Bill McDonald describes as an "Ernie Shavers type puncher." It takes a special kind of fighter to be able to not only survive such a sequence but to bounce back and land heavy shots of your own. It takes a certain amount of patience, as well as a high boxing IQ, to back off and let your opponent come to you when he is looking for a breather on the ropes. It takes an exceptional fighter with a specific something to take his opponent out when he smells blood.

The sequence that took Chris Calvin out was exceptional. It began with Greg landing a hellacious left hook upstairs. This time Greg knew he had to attack, and he led with a superpower punch. A moment of the fight that should not be taken for granted. I have watched many boxing matches and have observed situations where one fighter has another fighter defenseless, and they miss their opponent with wild, telegraphed blows. In the epic fight between Marvelous Marvin Hagler and Ray Leonard, there was a moment in the fight where Hagler missed badly and was left wide open.

Leonard *tried* to take advantage of this situation, but instead, through a wild shot of his own that missed badly, Marvin covered up, responded with body shots, and Ray backed off. Now, Marvin was nowhere near hurt, but a world-class fighter like Ray Leonard missed a chance to land a big punch on a wide-open target. Legend has it, Ray's eyes were closed when he threw the punch!

Ernie Shavers' eyes were wide open when he landed possibly the most talked-about punch in boxing history, save for the Phantom Punch. The Acorn's missile right hand that dropped Larry Holmes in their 1979 rematch is so revered that it is sometimes overlooked that Shavers did not knock Larry out. Like Carlton Fisk game-winning home run in the 1975 World Series; an iconic sports moment that did *not* produce a title. What is not so often discussed is that Shavers lost his cool and missed a dazed Holmes, after getting off the deck, with perhaps the most telegraphed, wildest punches in boxing championship history. Amir 'Hard Core' Mansour had Dominick Breazeale out on his feet early in their fight. Mansour tried to take Dominick out but missed with every haymaker he threw. Mansour tired out as a result and was stopped later in the bout. That fight probably cost Mansour a title shot, as Breazeale secured a title fight against Anthony Joshua after his comeback win. There are countless other examples that anyone who has watched a ton of boxing matches can point to. Nevertheless, it was so impressive to see Greg do it in a fight he was supposed to lose. At a time when he was not supposed to have the kind of experience needed to execute such things in a boxing ring.

Was Greg Haugen lucky to demonstrate such ability? I do know we were lucky to watch him do it.

There have been some questions about whether Chris Calvin was in full throttle coming off the Thomas tragedy. Bill McDonald said, "Calvin was coming off elbow surgery and the Shawn Thomas fight... that being said, Chris Calvin, I think, was near the top of his game that night...he had the opportunity to land those big bombs on Greg, the same bombs that he landed on a lot of guys and put them out for the night. Greg was able to take those shots and have the perseverance and tenacity to be able to come back and wear Calvin down, because Calvin was in that fight up until the sixth round. If he would have knocked Greg out with some of those big bombs in the first round, we would not be having this conversation. The better man won that night."

Chris Calvin explains that he was not at his very best emotionally for this fight, however. "I knew I had him, but it was my first fight back after Shawn Thomas died on me, when I got him hurt, instead of getting on him I kind of backed off. Boxers always have an excuse when they lose, but that is what happened, I just did not have it in me to get on him after Thomas died. I thought I had Greg Haugen hurt, but I didn't get on him the way I normally would. To me, that is what lost my fight with him," said Calvin.

Bret Summers also saw some apprehension from Chris, "Calvin was starting to get to Greg, and it seemed to me Chris hit the brakes. My thinking was he was having flashbacks of killing a kid, and he let off," remembers Bret Summers.

But Chris Calvin did continue to fight and knockout six other opponents after the Haugen loss, "Greg had a little bit better chin than them other guys. I hit him with some pretty good shots that took those other guys out," Calvin explained. Calvin's statement is compelling. Exemplifying that Greg should get nothing but credit for this win.

A point Bret Summers, a bitter rival of Greg, corroborates, "You have to give Greg credit, he beat him pretty good, I didn't expect it at all."

One cannot help to wonder how Chris Calvin's career would have been different had he be given his promised title shot instead of fighting Shawn Thomas. Calvin has his own thoughts, "I think I could have been champ. I was upset at the time (that he felt the promise made to him was broken), but I do not hold grudges against anybody now, I had my peace with the good Lord up above, and I asked for forgiveness," Calvin summarized. This summarization does not suggest that Chris does not still feel the wounds of the tragedy, "I still think about it. Even when nobody brings it up. If someone brings it up… (paused and began to choke up) it is a tragic thing that happened. You wish it never happened and hope it does not happen to anyone else," Calvin finished.

Calvin has not turned his back on boxing completely "I have worked with kids in the gym. It is a good thing to teach. I think it helps kids with confidence, and it gives you respect for life," Calvin explained.

Greg Haugen's upset over the power hitter Chris Calvin was a great way to end a very productive 1985 for the man they called Mutt. "The Chris Calvin win was key," Bob Jarvis stated, "That was a big deal that catapulted him to where he needed to be. When Greg knocked out Calvin that pretty much ended the chance of a Bret Summers fight from happening," added Jarvis. Greg Haugen was now on track for the boxing limelight in 1986.

Greg's fight with Chris Calvin was intense. Greg said that Chris turned the lights out on him early in the fight. But 'Mutt' prevailed for a tremendous victory. Pictured is Greg going to a neutral corner after knocking Chris Calvin through the ropes. (Courtesy of Greg Haugen).

Chapter Eight
Rolling in '86

"I consider the fight I had Greg to be the hardest."
—Juan Carlos Alvarado

The 1980s, the decade of excess, was in full swing in 1986. It began year two of Ronald Reagan's second term as President. If you were not falling in love with material things, you were probably paranoid about the Cold War and the inevitable nuclear showdown with the Russkies; spoiler alert, that showdown never happened, because the Russians loved their children too! If you were not caught up in the world of politics in 1986, you might have been mourning the explosion of the Challenger Space Shuttle. That explosion killed seven human beings on January twenty-eighth of 1986. This horrific event enunciated how excess was in full swing, as the news outlets replayed the terrifying explosion on television for what seemed like 100,000 times. While space travel in 1986 was a disaster for the United States, it was very fruitful for the Soviet Union. So, yes, space travel was all about politics too. The excess of politics continued in 1986, as President Reagan's showdown with Mikhail Gorbachev was trumped in the news by the Iran-Contra fiasco. And if none of that scared you, the AIDS epidemic was killing people at an alarming rate, yet, President Reagan would not even acknowledge the disease by name.

In the world of pop culture, MTV played to a growing audience, Madonna, the Material Girl, and Michael Jackson's little sister, Janet, dominated the music charts. Top Gun, a high-octane popcorn movie that glorified naval aviation, crushed the competition at the box office and created a surge in naval recruitment. Mission Accomplished! Eddie Murphy became a cross over star, as his guilty pleasure song, Party All the Time, was one of the biggest singles of 1986. Oprah Winfrey's popular talkie went national, and Bill Cosby led a wave of successful sitcoms that competed with the television drama Dynasty, the greatest example of 80's excess on the idiot box in 1986.

The sports world was also doubling down on excess in 1986. Haley's Comet made a rare visit to our solar system shortly after the Chicago Bears were set to wrap up the most dominant season in NFL history. However, dominating the gridiron was not enough for the Bears, as their infamous music video, The Superbowl Shuffle was probably more memorable than the Superbowl itself. For all the wrong reasons. The New York Mets and the Boston Red Sox participated in a World Series for the ages. The Red Sox blew a breath-taking game six a via historic comeback by the Metsies. Years later, the Mets' bad boy image and epic partying are talked about more than even that classic game six. The excess continued in the NBA, as Larry Bird's Celtics captured their sixteenth world championship in a season which they dominated from start to finish. This team benefited in a significant way by landing Bill Walton, an all-time great center who many believed had seen his best days several years ago. But Walton rallied and gave a team that was already filthy rich in talent, the jolt they needed to put them over the top. To add to the excess, the Celtics also owned a lottery pick courtesy of a horrendous, one-sided trade with the now-extinct Seattle Supersonics. That lottery pick turned into the number two overall pick, where Boston selected the highly touted Maryland forward Len Bias. Unfortunately, the fans of Beantown were never able to witness Bias playing alongside the deep Celtics roster because he died of a drug overdose. Bias died in what was supposed to be a symbol of celebration, and probably the most unfortunate example of how detrimental the attitude of excess could be. Len Bias was given an expensive sports car and a line of cocaine before he even made one basket as a professional athlete. Let that sink in.

Boxing was probably the one sport where a working man's code prevailed over excess. It should be a surprise to no one that Greg Haugen's breakout year came during one of the most memorable years in boxing history. For starters, Marvelous Marvin Hagler, the ultimate hard hat pugilist, thrilled the boxing audience with a brutal title defense over John The Beast Mugabi. Mugabi, a working-class warrior who grew up on the streets of Uganda. Evander, The Real Deal, Holyfield won his first title in a fifteen-round classic over Dwight Muhammad Qawi. It was the first and only time Holyfield went the fifteen-round distance, and he narrowly escaped with a split decision. Holyfield was a blue-collar guy who fell victim to a bad call at the 1984 Olympics. Indeed, during a time where everyone seemed to be getting away with everything, Evander was called out for a minor infraction and paid dearly for it. Speaking of blue-collar, Dwight Muhammed Qawi was a man who never fought as an amateur and learned how to box in prison. Qawi probably deserved better on the scorecards in that fight, but it was Holyfield's time.

Both fights were sensational, but brutal fights. Your body parts ached for days just from watching the leather crush flesh in these fights. Imagine what it is like to actually be hit in these fights. James Hagler, Marvin's son, stated that the Mugabi fight was the only time his dad had to be carried back to the dressing room.

Yet, neither one of these fights was Ring Magazine's Fight of the Year. That honor belongs to Steve Cruz's title-winning effort over hall of fame featherweight champion Barry McGuigan. It was a fifteen round war that does not have to take a back seat to any fight in boxing history. Period. The elements alone make this fight special. Doing battle in the makeshift outdoor arena in Caesars Palace in Las Vegas, Nevada, the thermometer read a blistering 110 degrees. The sun, beating down on both fighters, was as intense as the excess the decade was so proud of. Cruz, as blue-collar and nice as could be, and McGuigan, a man who was raised in Ireland during the time of The Troubles, never stopped throwing punches.

The banner year in boxing did not stop there. Hector Macho Camacho's narrow escape against Edwin Rosario in Madison Square Garden is still debated today. While Hector's style might not be in keeping with a blue-collar mentality, Camacho was a poor kid from an area of the Bronx that was destitute and neglected by City Hall. Nobody gave the Macho Man anything. Meanwhile, Edwin grew up on the impoverished streets of Puerto Rico. Marvin Johnson, the old pro who was thought to have had his best years behind him, stopped both Leslie Stewart and Jean-Marie Emebe in classic fights that could have easily been named fights of the year, especially the Emebe fight. The fact that Marvin captured the light heavyweight title for the third time by beating Stewart put him on the shortlist for Fighter of the Year. Johnson was a unique fighter, as he was part of the USA Olympic team; capturing a bronze medal in 1972, he presented more like a lunch pail type fighter, who received zero breaks despite his Olympian status. A Haugen type fighter.

1986 also saw a fascinating heavyweight tournament play out on HBO, boxing's premium cable network. While dull and erratic at times, this tournament produced moments that were aesthetically pleasing to the boxing fans who were lucky enough to afford HBO in 1986; the rest had to read about it in those vastly popular boxing magazines. Such as Trevor Berbick's upset victory over Pinklon Thomas; the fight that proved to be the origin of Harold Ledermen (without the shtick voice by the way) as HBO's guest judge. But Berbick and Ledermen was just a backdrop for the historic year for Iron Mike Tyson.

When Tyson was coming up, his nickname was The Animal. Mike grew up on the disreputable, savage streets of Brooklyn, and taken in by Cus D'Mato, an aloof boxing genius who had a great disdain for the government, as well as the boxing powers that be. 'The Man,' as well as the '80s excess, were public enemy number one for Cus. Anyone who knew boxing realized Tyson was destined for greatness and would break the ceiling of boxing lure, but it was Cus who snatched this young man up and tantalized him. Cus's impact on Tyson was just as impactful as a Tyson uppercut.

By 1986 Cus D'Amato was gone, but Tyson was polished, put on a busy schedule, and ready to go. He crushed Trevor Berbick in two rounds and became the most exciting thing that boxing had ever seen. Even when Mike was passed his prime and getting knocked out, the world would appear to stop and gawk. If Tyson required a Kleenex it made the news cycle. While Greg Haugen could never rival Mike Tyson in terms of popularity, few fighters can, Haugen is the one fighter that can match Tyson's output in 1986. Indeed, Greg's 1986 resume was as impressive as the year itself.

Unlike Hagler, Holyfield, and Tyson, Greg Haugen was not supposed to be winning the boxing matches he participated in. Not in 1985 and not when the calendar turned to 1986. Which began with Greg facing Charlie White Lightning Brown. Brown was an Illinois product and considered a better than average puncher. He had victories over Alfredo Escalara, Frank Newton, Luke Leece, Arnie Wells, Remo DiCarlo, and Louis Burke. Brown also challenged Harry Arroyo for the IBF version of the lightweight title. Like Ted Michalizyn, Chris Calvin, and Haugen, Brown was a skilled pugilist with the right complexion for television. Greg Haugen vs. Charlie White Lightning Brown was another example of what Al Bernstein said was ESPN's formula in the early days, match guys up tough, and see who rises to the top.

In hindsight, it is erroneous that Brown was the favorite over Haugen. Going into the fight, Greg was enjoying a great stretch, stopping Freddie Roach and Chris Calvin, as well as besting the formidable Jeff Bumpus via a tough ten-round decision. Meanwhile, Brown's recent activity saw him getting stopped by Arroyo, as well as Harold Brazier. With that said, experience goes a long way in boxing. If all else is perceived to be even, the fighter who has 'paid their dues' will likely be favored. Lee Haugen stated that White Lightning Brown made sure everyone knew he was the more experienced pugilist, "Charlie was a pretty good contender, and he was bragging that he had more knockouts than Greg had fights."

Brown was riding a three-fight winning streak going into the Haugen fight, but the only opponent of merit was Ted Michaliszyn, who was coming off two straight losses to Greg Haugen. Successful boxer author and handicapper, Christian Guidice, once told me that when looking at predicting fights, it is much more relevant to look at the recent activity. Based on recent activity, it is challenging to justify Greg being an underdog against Brown. But that appears to be the minority opinion. Ted Michaliszyn, the first common opponent for Greg and Charlie, thought Charlie was going to best Greg. Why he felt Brown would win at the time, he explained, "I thought Greg was easier to fight, I guess I was wrong."

Other opinions did not matter much to Greg, as he was feeling something going into the Charlie Brown fight, "I thought '86 was going to be a good year, I was coming into the prime of my career, and I wanted it to be a productive one. Charlie was the start. I didn't have much tape on him, but I generally didn't watch a lot of tape because most of the time, what you are seeing on the tape you might not see when you fight him. I just look for the little tendencies that they have. In the first round with Charlie, the bell rang, I come out, and we meet in the middle in the ring, I go to duck down and bend in, and I see him cock his right hand back, so I jumped out of there. And I am telling myself, 'now go back in there and stay just a little bit longer and let him commit to that right hand.' So, I go back in there, and sure enough, he did the same thing, he cocked his right hand back, and I stayed a little longer, he threw that right hand, and I took a half-step back and hit him with a left hook, and the fight was over."

Even during his most fabulous display of power, Greg Haugen was cerebral. Setting traps. At his best, Greg was master of outthinking his opponent, and this was perhaps the most explosive reward for such great craft. Even with all his success, Greg Haugen does not do first-round, one-punch, knockouts. That was Mike Tyson's bag. Greg made this concession himself, "I wasn't known as a big puncher...I was the kind of puncher that was going to knock you out with a three or four-punch combination; I really didn't have one-punch power. Charlie was never knocked out like that, so I thought it was a good start to 86. I was twenty-six years old, and I felt I could have beaten any of the lightweight champions of that time. After knocking out Charlie, I knew I was well on my way."

The Charlie White Lightning Brown fight was also boxing historian Lee Groves' introduction to Greg Haugen. Lee is also the proud owner of an impressive boxing collection of boxing matches that began with Greg Haugen's banner 1986 year. "The first time I saw Greg fight on television is tape one, fight one, of my collection, when he fought Charlie White Lightning Brown. Of course, I didn't get to see much of Greg, because he knocked Charlie out in round one with a hook to the jaw. Right on the point of the chin. Brown falls forward, and he didn't give referee Carlos Padilla a very good answer when asked, 'how are you,' and the fight was over. Now I didn't know (at the time) that this was atypical of Greg," recalled Lee.

The one-punch knockout of Charlie White Lightning Brown obliterated the idea that Greg should be the underdog against more experienced pugilists. After all, when watching all of Greg's ESPN fights up until this point, it is evident that the sole advantage all his opponents had over him, Michaliszyn, Bumpus, Roach, Calvin, and Brown, was more professional experience. In the skills department, Greg proved to be superior in every other way against this very impressive lot of opponents. It also illuminated the question of Greg's power. White Lightning got to witness firsthand what Chris Calvin attested to, "Greg Haugen was the hardest hitter I fought," Calvin declared.

Greg's winning streak also helped establish a second home in Las Vegas for Greg. The Auburn, Washington native, was determined to plant his flag in Las Vegas, and he was succeeding with this quest. The Showboat Hotel & Casino was the backdrop for most of Greg's ESPN victories, and after the Brown win, he was a definite fan favorite. Just like his ToughMan days in Alaska.

After his big win over Brown, Haugen was featured in the highly regarded The Ring Magazine. Greg was chosen for the New Faces segment, written by Jack Welsh for the April 1986 issue. Mr. Welsh highlighted Greg's stoppage victories over Freddie Roach, Chris Calvin, and Charlie Brown, making him more than ready for the next step. Championship status. Welsh indicated that Haugen hardly broke a sweat against Brown and how impressive such a performance was since Brown had twice the experience. In the article, Brown explained that he got caught cold. Welsh's piece also indicated that Hector Camacho, the WBC lightweight champion, was the ultimate target for Team Haugen.

Being featured in a magazine such as The Ring was monumental at that time. Boxing magazines in print were immensely popular in the '80s and an essential outlet for fans to obtain information. There was no internet at the time. Also, Greg was fighting exclusively on ESPN, and at that time the Entertainment and Sports Programming Network did not reach nearly as many homes as it does today; which is why many of the early boxing matches are hard to find such as Johnny Davis vs. Yaqui Lopez and Greg's fights against Ted and Jeff, please Mr. Arum, open up your vault on ESPN Plus. The Ring Magazine was sure to garner Greg more recognition.

The scent of Greg's peak was strong and confident, so he wanted to stay busy. Greg was back in the ring on February 16th. His opponent was a journeymen Juan Carlos Alvarado and the MGM Grand Reno was the venue. It was the co-feature for the Livingstone Bramble vs. Tyrone Crawly WBA lightweight title fight and an important fight for Greg in the rankings. Greg described Juan as a fighter who was "tougher than his record." Indeed, Alvarado was battle-tested, he fought Julio Caesar Chavez and Rene Arredondo prior.

Regarding the Chavez fight, Juan explains, "The fight was in Culiacan, Sinaloa Mexico, and they were taking care of him too much. They didn't allow us to have a very physical fight, the fight

75

was stopped in the third round when we were barely warming up. The people got mad because they wanted to see more action. Julio Caesar Chavez was taken down from the ring, and people threw beverages at him, they put me on their shoulders."

In communicating with Juan, he spoke of Greg in more high regard than Julio, in fact, I got the impression Juan did not particularly like the great legend, so I asked him about my suspicion, Juan replied, "It is not that I don't like him it is just that he never gave me the opportunity for the rematch and I asked him twice. When I fought him, he wasn't famous yet, and he could have fought me again." Juan also explains that the fight, "I fought him on May 12th, 1982, not May 8th, like it says on the internet."

Juan fought Greg a little over three years later in 1986; by that time, Julio was on everyone's radar. But Juan did not know much about Greg Haugen. "I did not know much about him, I just knew that it (our fight) was an eliminating fight for the NABF championship," Juan explained. Which meant that Greg Haugen translated into a massive opportunity for the Mexican pugilist. An opportunity Juan tried his best to capitalize on. "He was a good fighter, tough, and he hurt me a lot on the inside, I was lucky to pull that one out," Haugen said of the fight.

Alvarado said of the fight, "I remember it was a hard fight, we hit each other a lot, and neither one was taken down. Both of us were really hurt. At the end of the fight, the people threw money at the ring, because they saw it was a great fight. It was a better match than the main event. Even the promoter gave us a little bonus." When I asked Greg if his account of the end of the fight, were the fans were throwing cash at them, was true, he said, "Oh yea, first time I saw something like that."

There are some accounts of the fight that Greg and Juan do not agree on, however. According to Juan, neither fighter went down. While Greg claims he put Juan down to end the fight, "I think it was a left hook to the liver that put him down," Greg detailed. Neither man's story is in keeping with what is described on the resource site BoxRec, which states Juan Carlos Alvarado was down in the sixth round, but does not indicate how the bout ended, other than it was a technical knockout in the ninth round. The official scorecards support Greg's claim, as all three official judges gave Greg a 10-8 round in round seven. The bout was stopped by referee Mills Lane at

39 seconds of the ninth round. Greg Haugen only lost one round, the third, on one of the judges' scorecards, Lillian Runningwolf, who was the first female boxing judge in the state of Nevada. Judges Doug Tucker and John MacSweeney awarded every round for Greg.

Numbers aside, both fighters have nothing but respect for each other. "Greg is a very strong person, and during the fight, I couldn't take him down. My hands got swollen from the strength I was using, and he still didn't fall. He surprised me how much he endured my punches and how strong he is. Both of us ended up really hurt from all the punches. Greg is one of the best boxers I have fought. I consider the fight I had Greg to be the hardest. He is one of the greatest champions in the world, made out of steel. Very polite and humble," Juan said of Greg.

Considering Alvarado took shots from JC Superstar, to name Greg Haugen as his hardest fight is all you should need to know about Greg Haugen when he was at his best.

With the victory, Greg was set to return to the Showboat for his biggest fight to date.

March twenty-sixth, 1986, was supposed to be an advancement in Greg Haugen's career. It was the day he was to face the grizzled veteran Edwin Curet for the North American Boxing Federation (NABF) lightweight title. The NABF was established in 1969 by the World Boxing Council (WBC) and served as their regional championship. If you capture the NABF title, it was the gateway to a WBC world title fight. Fighting for the NABF belt had other tangible ramifications, as it meant Greg would be fighting twelve rounds for the first time in his career. Greg indicated that he trained for five hard weeks, as he knew Edwin Curet was a "tough fighter."

As brutal as boxing can be, it can be just as bizarre at times. Some incidents and circumstances occur in boxing that you just do not witness in other sports. Thankfully, a fight falling apart the day before it is scheduled is one of the more obscure circumstances of boxing. However, that is precisely what happened the day of March twenty-sixth, 1986, when Edwin Curet turned up ill, canceling the NABF lightweight showdown. "It was kind of fishy to me; all of a sudden, he was sick at the morning at the weigh-in, so they were rushing to replace," said Greg.

That replacement was Ken Willis. A southpaw from Connecticut. Willis had a record of 6-12-6, (1 KO), but was well seasoned. Ken had laced 'em up against top competition such as Tyrone Crawley, Bobby Johnson, Freddie Pendleton, whom he fought to a draw, Jocko King; another draw, Tyrone Trice and Rodney Moore. Indeed, Greg would be making a mistake if he had the mindset that Ken Willis would be easy work. Greg, always the thinking man's fighter, knew better and was weary from the jump. "I didn't have any info on Willis…it was a fight I was supposed to win. Finally. But he was the kind of guy that makes you look bad. He was a survivor. I had to get through that fight to get to the next one. It was a last-minute thing…but you got to keep plugging," Greg detailed.

Greg's confidence level did not waver, however, just like with the Jeff Bumpus fight, he had to face a seasoned, hardened, southpaw with little preparation. But unlike that fight, everything was one the line against Ken Willis.

With so much on the line, I asked Greg if there was ever a discussion about not fighting on March twenty-sixth and just wait for Edwin to get healthy. "No, I am not that way. I put the work in. I didn't want to see five, six weeks of training go out the window. I did not want to disappoint the crowd, I knew a lot of people came to see me. It was onward and upward," Greg answered.

Indeed, the event was a big one for boxing. The bout was the main event on ESPN. The Showboat was buzzing as Chuck Hall, decked out in a lavish tuxedo, introduced the fighters. As Hall's golden tonsils began to speak of Greg's credentials, the cheers of the crowd rose. Greg had regularly been fighting on ESPN up until this point. He was becoming a household name in Las Vegas as a result of his activity. Many of the Auburn faithful made the trek to Vegas to witness their hometown hero shine as well. A last-minute replacement had no impact on the interest of this important event in Greg's life. A raucous crowd was waiting for their red meat.

When the two pugilists met inside the ring to listen to referee Carlos Padilla's instructions, Greg's eyes never wavered off Ken Willis. This replacement from Connecticut was the only thing that occupied the cerebral mind of Haugen. Ken Willis tried to keep his eye on his world-class opponent; after all, this is the kind of moment that rarely comes for a guy like Willis. Ken was also looking down at the canvas as Padilla spoke. Both fighters touched gloves and went back to their corners. Before the bell rang for action, Ken Willis looked to the skies and pumped his right glove in the air. No doubt, he was seeking inspiration from somewhere. An inspiration that would help him capitalize on this once in a lifetime moment. A touching moment that might have gone overlooked. However, once that bell rings it is just you and your opponent.

As the fight began, Greg circled to Willis' right and threw a right-hand lead, a common strategy against a southpaw. The punch made little impact, but it was an immediate indication that Greg was thinking about nobody but the man in front of him. Greg continued to fire the right-hand lead in round one and had mild success with that punch. The round was Greg's, however, as he mixed up his punches well, including his jab and a left hook to the body. Greg's exceptional defense was also on display in round one, as he consistently slipped Ken's right jab and rolled with any punches that did find its mark.

Ken Willis came out fighting right-handed in round two. No problem. Haugen began to double up his jab and hook off his jab. Willis, who's style just screamed herky-jerky, switched back to southpaw, so, Greg once again cranked up the right-hand leads, as well as sprinkling in lead left-hooks. A beautiful hybrid left jab/uppercut, right-hand combination backed Willis up at around the 1:19 mark of round two. Greg followed this success up with a right-hand lead and thudding right hook. While these punches did not appear to seriously hurt Willis, they were scoring. In fact, they were the only punches that were scoring. Aware of this, Willis tried to stand his ground and bull Haugen into the ropes. The tactic worked, and Willis dug two right hooks into Greg's body. Greg smothered Willis and walked him back, another demonstration of Greg being stronger than his opponent. The rest of the round took place primarily in the center of the ring. Where Greg Haugen was the boss.

Ken Willis came out of round three with more urgency and backed Haugen into the ropes. With his back to the ropes, Greg dug a compelling right hook to the body, then circled to his left, getting off the ropes. Both fighters opened up more in round three. The leather was flying, but Greg Haugen was the more accurate, as well as tactical, pugilist. What was so impressive about this sequence was how relaxed Greg appeared to be. Any fighter I ever spoke with, talks about how important it is to be relaxed in the ring. A dynamic not easily obtained when someone is trying to rearrange your face and move your organs to places that they have no business being.

Round three of Haugen v. Willis should also be standard viewing for the benefits of being relaxed inside the squared circle.

In round three, Haugen was doing a beautiful job of disarming Willis's attack and setting up his own punches at the same time. Haugen mixed up his lead punches-a left jab, that hybrid jab/hook, the right-hand lead, upstairs, downstairs-and it confused the heck out of Willis. Greg hit the jackpot with this attack by landing a thudding lead right hand that stunned Ken Willis. Willis' survival skills kicked in and managed to prevent any further severely damaging blows from Greg. But Greg continued to be first and diverse. While Ken Willis did not throw another meaningful punch the rest of the round.

Ken Willis was probably still worried about that right hand because he started round four using lateral movement, trying to keep Greg at distance. Round four was uneventful up until about the 1:19 mark, where Greg hurt Willis again with a right-hand lead and well-timed body shots. The last minute of the round saw both men try to establish superiority on the inside. Greg won this battle by landing the harder, more accurate shots on the inside.

Rounds five through eight saw Greg dominate Ken. Willis laid on the ropes, absorbing Haugen's combinations for much of rounds six and seven. Willis was berated by his corner to throw more punches in-between rounds. Towards the end of round eight, Willis upped his work rate, but all this accomplished was opening the door for Greg to show what a defensive master he could be, as he slipped virtually every one of Willis' punches on the inside. Judges Jerry Roth, Hal Miller, and Paul Smith all appeared to be fooled by the activity of Willis, however and gave him round eight, his first round of the fight.

Round nine took an odd turn, as Greg stopped throwing punches. For the first time in the bout, Willis was first during most of the round and landed some effective right hooks to the body. Perhaps Greg was just taking the round off, but he did appear to be out of gas. When I asked Greg if he ran out of gas or was just taking a round off, he replied, "A little bit of both. I was not expecting to go ten rounds with a trial horse, journeymen, southpaw." Ken Willis did not take full advantage of Greg's apparent fatigue because he threw very few combinations in his quest to get back in the fight. One punch at a time would never be enough to take out a Greg

Haugen. Hal Miller was the only judge to score round nine for Ken Willis, as Jerry Roth and Paul Smith both saw something that was not in keeping with reality and scored round nine for Greg.

In round ten, Greg appeared to get his second wind, as he was first throughout the round, however, with slightly less starch on his punches. Nonetheless, Greg dominated the round with right-hand leads, jabs, and accurate body punching, sweeping the final round on the official scorecards. When the bell sounded to end round ten, there was no doubt Greg Haugen would be the winner. The scorecards read 99-91, 98-92, 99-91 in favor of Haugen. Officials Jerry Roth and Paul Smith awarded Greg every round save round eight, while official Hal Miller gave Ken Wills rounds eight and nine. After the bout, Greg Haugen told Al Bernstein he hurt his right hand and might have to take some time off. He also appeared disgusted about the Edwin Curet cancellation and spoke as if he should not have to fight him since Edwin did not show up when he was scheduled to. But Greg knew the decision would be up to Top Rank Boxing, and he would abide by what the powerhouse promotion company decided.

While he won a sound decision against Ken Willis, Greg Haugen did not impress the ESPN telecast with his performance. In fact, Al Bernstein suggested that Greg was the product of luck because had he fought Edwin Curet on this night, instead of Willis, he would have suffered a major setback in his career. When I asked Greg about this belief, he added, "Well…yes and no. I mean, who knows if Curet would have been able to stand up to the kind of punishment that he would have been taking for nine or ten rounds. That would have been a lot different fight. Willis was a tough guy to hit with combinations, and I wasn't training for a southpaw, I was training for a right-hander. So, that kind of threw me off guard. But shit happens. I just had to win the fight, which I did, and move on to the next one."

In some ways, Greg's performance against Ken Willis is one my favorites. Yes, it was a fight that snapped his knockout streak, yes, it was a fight he was supposed to win handily. However, as with Greg's entire career, the onion has many more layers than that. The reason why I revere this performance so much is because it showcased Greg as a polished boxer and not just a tough man. Only a polished boxer could handle a Ken Willis the way Haugen did. He was first and diverse against a tricky southpaw and showed how good an inside fighter he is in this fight. He executed a thinking man's fight against a guy who specializes in getting in your head. Save for round nine, Haugen never wavered from his game plan and was in complete control.

This fight also showed just how big Greg's balls were. Not many guys would be willing to fight any southpaw on such short notice, and Ken Willis was a southpaw who had survival skills, taking many exceptional fighters the distance. Haugen never wavered on taking on such a challenge, while most in his place would have opted out.

I think the reason why Haugen's performance in this fight was more scrutinized than praised was because of the time the fight occurred. During an era of champions who took care of their business inside the distance more often than not-Marvelous Marvin Hagler, Thomas Hearns, Michael Spinks, Dwight Qawi, Wilfredo Gomez, Donald Curry, Julio Caesar Chavez, Mike Tyson- fighters who went the distance where not glorified at this time. Even the blazing skills of Hector Mach Camacho came under fire after the Edwin Rosario fight, as he started relying on the judges' scorecards more and more. Haugen's fight against Willis came long before fighters like Floyd Mayweather Jr. and Andre Ward received high praise for their defensive-minded, winner twelve results.

But nobody is going to tell me Haugen's performance against Ken Willis was not aesthetically pleasing. Haugen was a defensive genius against Willis, and he never stopped moving his hands. Thinking the whole time. In a match where he could have easily been dejected and distracted. True, Willis was not a championship level, but those kinds of fights were right around the corner for the Toughman from Alaska.

Chapter Nine
Fighting For The NABF

"On tape, he looks easy, but it is hard to get a good shot on his head, or even his body."

—Edwin Curet

Ruben Navarro became the first NABF lightweight champion. He failed to capture the WBC lightweight title from champion Ken Buchanan, who was the undisputed champion at the time. Jimmy Robertson was the next NBAF lightweight titleholder, and he was demolished by Roberto Duran in their WBC title fight. Proving the gateway from NABF to world championship status was cumbersome to enter once you arrived there. In fact, up until the Haugen v. Curet showdown, the only NABF lightweight champion to parlay his belt into a direct world championship was Hector Macho Camacho, although many people felt Jose Luis Ramirez should have earned this distinction when he faced Edwin Rosario in 1983. Would either Greg Haugen or Edwin Curet repeat the same faith as the Navaro's and the Robertson's of the world, or would they follow in the footsteps of the Macho Man? Questions that could only be answered after the combatants squared off.

If Greg Haugen needed to take some time off to heal his hand, he did not do so. He fought Edwin Curet for the NABF title less than two months after the Ken Willis fight. When I asked Greg if his hand was fully healed for the fight, he said, "Probably seventy-five percent. I had pain in it, I was more pissed off for the fact that Curet pulled a fast one on me. I was sparring a guy my height, who was right-handed, and they throw me with a left-hander."

Greg got in vivid detail as to what happened to his hand after the Ken Willis fight. "Over the years, my knuckle would bleed underneath in my right hand. There was like a blood clot, every time I would hit that part, it would bleed underneath my hand. So, over time, every time it bled, it would make this little piece of cartilage, and it would just get bigger. Eventually, it would push my

83

metacarpal, which is the protection of the knuckle, away from my knuckle. So, if I turned my hand a certain way and hit that one spot, oh man, it (the pain) would put me through the roof. But I found out it was only a certain position I put my hand in. After the Curet fight, I went and had it fixed." Greg might have waited until *after* the Curet fight to get his very problematic right hand fixed, but he would not wait to address another issue that surfaced in the Ken Willis fight.

"I wasn't in the best of shape going into the Willis fight, but after that fight, I went right back into the gym to continue to add to my conditioning. So, by the time I came around to the Curet fight, I was rock solid." Greg said.

Edwin Curet was not as confident with the shape he was in going into the rescheduled NABF lightweight title fight. Edwin proclaimed to me that he did not want to have the match postponed because of his cold and said of the postponement, "It didn't help me much." Unlike most observers, Edwin Curet was fully aware of the boxing skills Greg possessed. "I liked my chances against him, but I knew that he took a good punch, and he wasn't easy to hit. He had a good way of getting away from big punches," said Curet.

When facing such opposition, a boxer needs to be sharp. Because of the postponement, Edwin was worried that he lost some of this sharpness. Sharpness Curet felt he had going into the original date. "The worst enemy of a fighter is not being active, he (Haugen) was tuning, tuning, tuning, while I was just in the gym. But no excuses, I got over that fight a long time ago," added Edwin.

At the time, though, Edwin's inactivity-his last fight was a little over five months ago, a lifetime for a fighter in those days-was getting the best of him. Although Curet was aware of the challenge Haugen presented, his mind was not focused. "Going into the fight, I was a little anxious. I wanted to get it over with to get a title shot. But I never got a title shot," said Curet.

Indeed, mental focus was key to a fighter's success. Edwin Curet's mental focus was compromised, while Greg Haugen's, compliments of a stellar winning streak, was as mentally focused as a fighter could be.

For this NABF lightweight championship, Edwin Curet entered the ring first, wearing a light blue robe, accompanied by the Petronelli Brothers. Once Haugen got settled inside the squared circle, he appeared ready to go. Shadowboxing with a stone-cold stare. Focused and determined. Once again, Chuck Hall served as the ring announcer. Donning a perfect tuxedo, Hall first introduced Rockin' Robbie Simms-another fighter from the Petronelli stable- as he was getting ready to face the legendary Roberto Duran in June; Simms went on to beat the Hands of Stone in a close, entertaining scrap. Another gem of 1986.

When Hall introduced Edwin Curet, the crowd responded with more jeers than cheers. When it was Haugen's turn to be introduced by Hall's golden tonsils, the crowd responded with warm cheers. Indeed, the run the ToughMan from Alaska was on helped to mold a respected reputation and great fanfare. When referee Carlos Padilla gave instructions to Curet and Haugen, Greg knew none of those fans were going to help him against Edwin. "I knew Edwin was tough. He worked with the Petronelli brothers, with Marvin (Hagler), and he came to fight," Greg added.

As the action began for round one, the ESPN blow by blow man erroneously dubbed Edwin Curet as the slick boxer, and Greg Haugen as the power puncher, in this matchup. Indeed, Greg Haugen stopped four of his five opponents going into the Curet fight, however, to give the edge to anyone over Greg in terms of slick boxing skills up until now was a grave mistake. This point was accentuated right away in round one, as Haugen slipped a wild left-hook from Curet. Greg followed up this display of defensive prowess by tying Edwin up, walking him down, and digging a right hook to the body before the Padilla break.

The rest of round one saw Greg Haugen outslick Edwin Curet. As Edwin showcased substantial lateral movement, but Greg's subtle footwork, head movement, and feints parlayed into accurate body punches and a nice left hook upstairs to give Haugen the edge in a close, feeling out, opening round. The official judges saw it a different way. Both Dalby Shirley and Tenny Smith gave this close round to Edwin Curet, while Dave Moretti gave Haugen the edge on the scorecards.

In round two, the Haugen left hook upstairs proved to be the best weapon of the round. But, the true story of the round was Greg's undefeated defense, as Edwin Curet failed to land one effective punch on Greg. It was a superior display of ring generalship from Haugen, and, ironically, this display from Greg occurred in a round where the ESPN announcers questioned the ring generalship of Haugen, based on the Ken Willis fight. Sometimes what is right in front of you escapes the eye. Both Dave Moretti and Dalby Shirley also failed to see the better work from Greg, as they both gave the round to Curet. Tenny Smith disagreed and score round two for Greg.

Round three was not a good one for Greg in terms of work rate. Edwin Curet was the much busier pugilist, which is ironic because in between rounds, Stan Tischler, Haugen's trainer, asked for the Auburn native to be more active in round three. Greg's low work rate does not suggest he lost the round, however. As most of Curet's punches either missed or were defused by Greg's ring generalship. The most significant, effective, blows in round three came from Haugen, even though Curet threw many more punches. How do you score such a round? Indeed, it is effortless to criticize a judge- I have done my fair share- but round three of Haugen vs. Curet is one of those rounds where you would be just as effective choosing a winner by playing ini mini miney moe. Since Curet was trying to make the fight, he probably edged out round three. Proving to be a very difficult fight to score, once again, the judges were not in agreement on the third round. Moretti and Shirley scored it for Haugen, while Smith favored Curet.

Round four saw more roughhousing on the inside. Both fighters found their backs against the ropes and did some holding. Haugen won the round by landing the harder blows during the meaningful exchanges. Greg also showed us what a good inside fighter he can be during this pivotal round four. Al Bernstein had Curet up two rounds to one as round four began- Bernstein based his scorecard on the inactivity he observed from Greg. Greg upped his work rate slightly in round four and sat down on his punches more. As a result, Greg Haugen appeared to do enough to win the round. Tenny Smith did not agree and scored the round for Curet, disagreeing with his peers Moretti and Shirley in the process.

After round four, Goody Petronelli, Curet's trainer, urged Curet to box more, citing that Curet looked sloppy trying to slug with Greg. Sound council from the veteran trainer, but such advice overlooks the fact that Edwin was not the better boxer in this boxing match. Looking at Greg's career holistically, you can count on one hand the number of times he was outboxed, or his opponent showed superior ring generalship- the percentages became even lower when Greg trained hard for a fight. Edwin Curet was never going to be that guy who could beat a Greg Haugen by boxing, not even on Greg's worst day. But Edwin appeared outclassed during the roughhousing on the inside as well. This was not an easy fight to strategize for Team Petronelli.

Petronelli's advice did not pan out for his fighter in round five. Haugen took advantage of Curet's decision to be less aggressive. Greg still was not throwing enough punches for Al Bernstein's liking, but Greg was getting off first throughout the round, while Edwin was initiating all the clinches in round five, as well as being tamed by Greg's defense- Curet missed and missed the entire round badly. Round five was the first round where all three officials agreed with each other, scoring the round for Greg.

When round six began, Edwin Curet tried to keep the fight at distance. The diverse Haugen jumped on Curet right away. Greg dug an effective left hook to the body and followed this punch up with a hard right-left combination- a sequence of punches the ESPN announcers ignored. The rest of round six was a decent one for Curet, however. As the pugilist from Puerto Rico abandoned his corner's advice and let his hands go, throwing more power punches. This strategy paid dividends for Curet, as he landed his hardest punches of the fight; a hybrid left-hook uppercut that backed Greg up-the kind of punch Razor Ruddock made famous- was the highlight of round six. Edwin Curet won round six on both Moretti and Shirley's scorecard, Smith scored the round for Haugen. In five out of the first six rounds of this fight, the judges were in disagreement on the scoring.

While it appeared that Al Bernstein was overlooking a lot of the excellent work Greg Haugen was doing in this fight, in particular, his superior defense, one thing the Hall of Fame announcer was spot on about was Greg Haugen's work rate was lower than usual in the first six rounds. Haugen was hit more in round six and appeared to be getting tired. Would it feasible for Greg Haugen to throw more punches? Based on work rate alone, it could be argued that Edwin Curet could have been ahead going into round seven. A further argument can be made that round seven of this fight was the most crucial of Greg Haugen's career up until that point.

If round seven of the Edwin Curet fight was the most important of Greg Haugen's career from that point, he certainly did not fight with any sense of urgency. Once again, Greg was very economical with his punches. Greg's accuracy with his right hand probably won him the round, however. Stiff rights to the body and an excellent right hook upstairs from Haugen were the best punches of the round. Haugen fought like he was in control and did not feel like he had to do anything different. But Curet was still throwing a lot more punches than Greg. Such a circumstance can coax a judge into giving the busier fighter the round. To a keen observer, Greg was setting traps and making Edwin spend a lot of energy with little reward; virtually all of Edwin's punches were either missing or lessened by Greg's defensive prowess. Haugen's skills were not for not in round seven, as he swept the round on all three of the official scorecards.

Another noteworthy circumstance occurred in round seven. Referee Carlos Padilla warned Curet a few times for questionable tactics. In one instance, Greg's subtle footwork caused one of Curet's blows to land in the back of Haugen's head. After the warning, Greg offered Curet his left glove as a gesture of peace. Curet, probably fed up with all the warnings he was getting, as well as not being able to catch Haugen flush, did not offer his glove in peace back. The ever-savvy Haugen caught on right away that Curet had no interest in peace mode and covered up right away. A textbook example of 'protect yourself at all times' from Greg Haugen.

As the bell rang for round eight, it was believed that the fight was still in the balance. Al Bernstein was not impressed with either fighter's performance, and the Showboat crowd was not as energetic as it was at the start of the bout. Warnings for both fighters to pick up the pace. Greg's corner was indeed asking for more. The Petronelli Brothers told Curet that he won rounds six and seven and instructed him to stick with the current game plan. Obviously influenced by the fact that their fighter was much busier.

When the round began, Haugen began working his feints and seemed to be more committed to his left hand. Haugen also continued to dig that right hand to the body when the opportunity presented itself. Curet was still letting the leather fly but continued to be bested by the Haugen defense. In this round, on more than one occasion, Haugen would let Curet lead, slip the punch and counter with a compelling left hook. When Greg did lead, he worked the jab nicely and kept Curet off balance. In the last minute of the round, Haugen appeared to be angered by a low blow from Curet. Haugen took over the real estate in the ring and backed Curet into the ropes, landing stiff right hands when Curet's back was to the ropes. Curet managed to get off the ropes, Greg greeted him with a right hook to the body and came back with a left hook upstairs. Once again, the blow by blow announcer missed Greg's work and opted to point out a counter from Curet that did not score as well as Haugen's two-piece. As round eight ended, Haugen landed a straight right that turned Curet around, followed by another straight right that backed Curet up. There were punches landed by both men after the bell, but nothing that appeared to be damaging. Greg Haugen was the clear winner of round eight and was beginning to land with more authority. Round eight was another sweep on the scorecards for Haugen. His second in a row. Greg was now up 78-74, and 77-75, two times, going into round nine. This twelve-rounder was still anyone's fight. But Greg owned the momentum.

Greg controlled the first half of round nine with his jab. Like a maestro, he found a home with the left jab on Curet's face and made Edwin miss badly with his power punches. At about 1:20 of round nine, Greg landed a straight right; one of his best power punches of the fight, that hurt Edwin. Curet turned southpaw briefly after that blow but soon went back to the orthodox style. Haugen responded by stuffing four left jabs in Curet's face, followed by a straight right and another left upstairs. It was a sequence of punches that did not land with great force, but the punches landed enough to take its toll on a fighter who was frustrated and worn down with all the wild missing Greg was making happen. To his credit, Curet did not waver in terms of throwing power punches, but, save for a lunging right hand, Greg did a masterful job of slipping the punches coming his way. It would be hard to imagine Goody and Pat Petronelli thinking their fighter won round nine.

Greg's cornermen where elated when he walked back into the corner after round nine. It was almost as if they felt a Haugen victory was a foregone conclusion. After all, Greg padded his lead by once again sweeping the round on the official scorecards. But a fighter knows that they should never sell their opponent short. Indeed, not only is Greg Haugen a fighter, he is one of the smartest boxing minds you can ever know. Greg responded to the celebratory nature of the corner by saying, "He is still dangerous," almost gasping to get the words out. His head trainer responded by saying, "They are always dangerous, just stay on top of him, he's got nothing left."

Greg's facial expression suggested that he did not share the same enthusiasm that Curet was spent and would be a walk in the park from this moment on. But the fighter that he is, Haugen knew he had to go out there and finish the job. Before he went out for round ten, Haugen struggled to get some spit up. Hocking with his throat with minimal results of saliva. A symbolic indication of just how taxing this NABF title fight was.

Greg soon became a clairvoyant, as Curet came out with the most urgency of the fight at the start of round ten. Wailing away with four power punches that only a great defensive fighter such as Greg could weather. A good fighter is always most dangerous when they are on the brink of defeat, and Edwin Curet was no exception. Curet was not about to lay out the red carpet for Team Haugen. Haugen was able to keep his cool and worked his jab well after the initial onslaught from Edwin. Knowing the danger Curet still possessed, Haugen continued to tame Curet with his jab and avoided the power punches the pugilist from Puerto Rico never stooped throwing. Such a disciplined display of boxing was lost on Al Bernstein, as he accused both fighters of "not fighting well." That thought process changed a bit towards the end of round ten when Greg scored with a solid left to the jaw of Curet. Haugen followed this power punch up with a powerful left hook-right hand combination that appeared to stun Edwin at the very end of round ten. It was another shutout on the scorecards for the Mutt from Auburn.

As Edwin Curet walked back to his corner, the Petronelli Brothers met him with some honesty. Berating him for letting Haugen make him look like a fool and saying he looked "terrible." Perhaps a better choice of words could have been used, but the words were all true. Where Team Petronelli failed, however, was with the erroneous advice that Edwin had to "throw more punches." As if that was the answer to the problem. All Edwin was doing was throwing punches throughout the whole fight. Indeed, Haugen was giving Curet a boxing lesson, but it was not because of a low work rate from Curet.

If throwing more punches was the only advice the Petronelli Brothers had to improve their fighters' chances of winning, well then, they were the ones who were terrible. Or maybe they were just a victim of underestimating the ToughMan from Alaska, or was it Auburn, Washington? After all, the Petronelli's were sound cornermen who helped bring along Marvelous Marvin Hagler. No Team Petronelli was not incompetent. Edwin Curet said, "Goody Petronelli was the best trainer I ever had." Like many others, they failed to see the excellent boxing skills that stood there right in front of their eyes. The Greg Haugen magic trick was having one of its most beautiful moments in the championship rounds of this NABF championship fight. When talking to Edwin Curet, he was aware of the reality that was happening in the ring. "I missed a lot of big shots. If I landed some of these punches, I could have had a chance to stop him. On tape, he looks easy, but it is hard to get a good shot on his head, or even his body," Curet said.

The Magicianry of Haugen continued in round eleven as Greg morphed into the full-fledged aggressor. Throughout the round, Greg was first and diverse. Using his jab to perfection and backing Edwin Curet up on several occasions. Where he did not let his hands go like he should have in the first nine or so rounds, Haugen was now letting the leather fly with pinpoint accuracy and with bad intentions. Another sweep on the scorecards. In round twelve, Haugen chose to let Curet lead, as he was content to keep Edwin off balance with his jab and counter when the opportunity arose. Again, there was no lack of work rate from Edwin Curet, but very little of it was effective. Curet could have been given the round just on punch volume, and Dalby Shirley and Tenny Smith indeed did just that. It should have been obvious Greg was the boss in terms of boxing skills and ring generalship in this last round, as it was throughout most of the fight. Dave Moretti recognized this and scored round twelve for Greg.

When the final bell rang for this NABF championship fight. Greg Haugen and Edwin Curet embraced with the utmost respect for each other. It is that beautiful, contrasting moment that can only be produced by combat sports. When I see two fighters embrace at the end of a tough fight, it gives me chills every time. After the embrace, Haugen had an intense look on his face. He needed to hear the scorecards read. He knew he won the fight, but he needed to hear it.

When Chuck Hall indicated the fight was scored a unanimous decision, the tension from Greg Haugen's face dissipated. He knew they could not score a unanimous decision for Curet. The scores read in Haugen's favor, 118-110, 116-112, and 116-113. Greg Haugen was now the NABF lightweight champion. Dave Moretti handed in the lopsided scorecard of 118-110, scoring only rounds two and six for Curt. Edwin is still perplexed by the 118-110 scored card today. "He was probably paying a favor for Bob Arum," Edwin said of Dave Moretti's score. "I thought the fight could have went either way because I won a lot of rounds in the beginning. Just because a fighter wins the late rounds does not always mean he wins the fight," added Curet.

With all due respect to Edwin Curet, who was an excellent competitor in his day, an outcome where Greg Haugen's hand was not raised would have been heinous.

The joy on Haugen's face was a high contrast to the stone-cold stare we often see, or even the impish smile when he is trying to capture the ire of his opponent. No, this was sheer, unadulterated bliss, from a man who is known to always be calculated. With his guard constantly up. It is the kind of contrasting emotions only boxing could produce.

After the bout, Haugen proved once again he was a clairvoyant, as he donned a baseball cap that read: GREG HAUGEN N.A.B.F LIGHTWEIGHT CHAMPION. The white lettering over the blue cap was so 1980s. In his interview with Al Bernstein, Greg cited the issues with his right hand as the reason for being so economical for most of the bout. He also indicated that given Curet's reputation of having a great chin, he did not expect to knock out his opponent. Always thinking. Such a victory meant big things for Greg's future. With his string of victories on ESPN, Top Rank Boxing understood that Greg Haugen was ready for the next level of the sport.

Indeed, it was one of the best fights of Haugen's career, although, listening to Al Bernstein, Greg did next to nothing, compared to Curet's nothing. I think the reason why Al was so critical of Greg's performance on the Curet fight because, once again, it was the product of the times. Had Greg put on such a performance in the Floyd Mayweather Jr./Andre Ward era, social media would have praised Haugen's performance as the true art of boxing: hit and not get hit. But Greg toppled Edwin during a time where Mike Tyson was making headlines, and the boxing world was still having a hangover from the Marvelous Marvin Hagler vs. Thomas Hearns euphoria. If you were looking for a similar type of fight with Haugen and Curet, it would be understandable that you were let down.

But Greg did not let down his supporters. As NABF Lightweight Champion, a big fight, for big money, was soon on the horizon. Jack Welsh covered for the fight for The Ring Magazine, his fight report appeared in the August 1986 issue. In that report, Welsh stated that, while Greg did a good job handling Curet, he described the fight 'wasn't a pretty exercise to watch, 'it is a shame that Mr. Welsh seemed to have wasted his time, because he missed a great fight that had ebbs and flows, technique, grit, and superb boxings skills and defense from Haugen. I often wonder if writers get paid extra for disparaging narratives. Jack Welsh was aware enough to indicate that Greg Haugen was ready for 'better things,' was how he scribed it; I assume he meant the championship level. Greg would have to face another high-level trial horse before he moved on to 'better things.'

Winning the NABF light title had a lot of weight to it. Such an accomplishment meant a shot at a world championship was in reach for Greg Haugen. In those days, such an opportunity meant fighting the fifteen-round distance for the first time in their professional career. For Greg Haugen, a title shot was all he wanted. "I thought about it all the time," Greg explained.

Before such a dream can be reached. Greg was matched up against the tough Ernie Landeros. Ernie was a tough, up and coming fighter. "They were talking about a title fight, that didn't materialize, so I just wanted to stay busy, they asked me if I wanted to fight Ernie and I said sure...I didn't know a lot about him, there wasn't a lot of tape on him, but I knew he was a good fighter, he was going to come to fight so I had to be ready," added Greg. Ernie certainly did not consider himself a trial horse going into the fight.

Landeros sported a record of 13-2-2 (6 KOs). He had notable scraps against Loreto Garza, whom he fought to a draw, and back to back fights against Jimmy Jackson, where he avenged a split decision loss with a first-round KO. That victory came on the undercard of Haugen's first-round KO against Charlie White Lightning Brown. To underestimate Landeros would not be wise.

Going into his fight with Greg, Landeros had never been knocked out and had been the victim of bad decisions. Besides the controversial loss to Jackson, Landeros boxed the ears of off Martin Quiroz in Las Vegas, his reward was a split decision loss. Indeed, Landeros was no stranger to the politics of boxing, Las Vegas, or Greg Haugen, "You work so hard to get to that spot, and you have it taken away by a bunch of idiots who don't know what they are doing. It's frustrating to have to go in there and continue to do your thing and have some idiot take it away from you…you have to just keep doing your thing," is Greg's opinion on bad decisions in boxing.

Greg Haugen versus Ernie Landeros was once again on ESPN and promoted by Top Rank Boxing. The Sahara Hotel in Las Vegas was the venue. Las Vegas was the home for five of the last six fights Haugen had. The major difference this time around was Greg Haugen was the heavy favorite. How did it feel to be expected to win? "I knew that I was going to win every fight that I fought. Against Roach, Calvin, Charlie Brown, they underestimated me, and I knocked all three guys out, so I knew I was just going to continue to win and fight my fight," Greg said.

As referee Carlos Padilla gave instructions at the center of the ring to Haugen and Landeros, Haugen stood straight up like a peacock, ready for action. Haugen got started as soon as the bell rang for round one, firing a stiff lead right to the forearm of Landeros, followed up by three stiff jabs. Greg then tested the body of his opponent and followed that attack up with a double jab and straight right hand. Landeros seemed to keep his focus, but he was doing little throwing in return. The rest of round one saw Greg out work and outland Landeros by a significant margin. Throughout the round, Haugen was first and diverse in his attack. Mixing up his punches well but staying true to his stiff jab. It was vintage Greg Haugen. One of the best rounds he has ever boxed. This round is all the evidence that you need to show that Greg Haugen was so much more than a tough man. "I was pretty much dominating with my jab, he couldn't get close to me," Haugen said of his first-round performance. Judges Dalby Shirley, Art Lurie, and Pat Jarmin all scored the round for Greg.

In between rounds, Ricky Kauffman, Landeros' cornerman, spoke calmly and instructed Ernie to work his jab. But offered no advice on how to deal with the Haugen jab, the jab he was being schooled with. Landeros did come out better in the second round, however, although it was not due to his jab. Landeros decided to let the power punches fly instead. He dug a strong left hook to Haugen's body and landed a sharp overhand right that landed well. Haugen took the blows well and proceeded to try and establish his jab. Greg began to work his jab from different angles and varied its momentum- some jabs were of a flicking nature, while others were stiff, like in round one. The diverse use of his jab allowed Greg to set up Landeros with a strong left hook upstairs. Greg followed up this work with another solid jab and a thudding left hook to the body. Greg was once again the boss, but Ernie absorbed the punches well and kept coming forward. He even had some success backing Greg into the ropes and ripping 'Mutt' with body shots. Ernie Landeros was there to fight.

The Landeros jab even started to take shape in round two, and he once again forced Greg into the ropes and punished him with good body shots. Greg's facial expressions were not of despair, but he certainly knew he was now in a fight. Greg did not give up his jab, but he proceeded with more caution in round two. The much-touted Haugen defense decided to make an appearance, as Greg began to slip the Landeros jab with consistency, but Landeros was still landing thudding body shots with both hands. "He was hitting me with a few shots, but they really didn't bother me, I was getting frustrated that they were landing," explained Greg. Greg was tough to hit upstairs, but the hard body shots kept finding a home for Ernie Landeros, and probably winning the round for Ernie. Dalby Shirley and Art Lurie agreed and scored the round for Landeros while Jarmin scored round two for Haugen.

Round three began with Greg being busy with his jab. Greg was even able to sprinkle in straight rights and left hooks. But once again, Landeros was able to back Greg into the ropes early in round three and landed another series of stiff body shots. A strong left hook to the body from Ernie appeared to be the most damaging blow, Greg provided a facial expression that was sort of a hybrid grimace-smile, and nodded his head no, as he danced off the ropes and away from his opponent. Greg might have been hurt, such a reaction suggests as much, but he kept working his jab, mixing it up well. Greg kept throwing off the jab, and it was anyone's guess as to how he would attack Ernie; left hooks upstairs, rights to the body, Greg was at his diverse best. However, nothing could stop Ernie from coming forward and going to the body. Ernie had another good sequence when he doubled up his jab, backing Greg into a corner, Ernie then threw a nice straight right, right to the body, combination. Again, these were hard punches that appeared to take some starch out of Greg.

Haugen answered this sequence by forcing the fight back to the center of the ring. Greg was once again the boss, as he scored well from distance, as well as on the inside. Landeros tried to answer with a money left-hook, right-hand combination that Greg blocked, and responded back with a three-punch combination. The Haugen jab continued to control the pace, and Greg even began to minimize the damage of the Landeros's body shots with subtle movement that helped him block these punches. There was a telling moment at the end of round three. Greg backed Ernie into the ropes for the first time at around the thirty-second mark of round three. It was the first time Greg looked like the stronger fighter-a rarity in Greg's fight up until this point. But in two out of three rounds, Greg proved to be the superior boxer and slightly ahead. Both Shirley and Jarmin had Greg ahead 29-28 after three rounds, while Shirley favored the work of Landeros, and had him ahead after three rounds.

The rest of the fight saw Greg Haugen in control of a grueling, hard-nosed boxing match. Greg neutralized the successful Landeros body attack by using his jab overtime and working off that jab with a very diverse attack. During these rounds, there was some wonderful inside-fighting that Haugen controlled. For these reasons, Haugen swept the rest of the fight, save for round seven. This summation is not to suggest it was a walkover for Greg. Ernie was there the whole time and even had good moments, scoring with impressive straight rights and left hooks. It was a great display of pugilism by both men, as the leather never stopped flying. The number of clinches in the whole fight did not exceed the total that Muhammad Ali and Floyd Mayweather Jr. often have in one round. Another classic battle on ESPN that has all but been forgotten. Both Haugen and Landeros should be more celebrated for this great fight. Greg Haugen was just one step ahead of Ernie most of the fight.

The scorecards were all read in favor of 'Mutt.' Chuck Hall announced scores of 97-93, 98-93, and 98-92 for Greg Haugen. There was some sprinkling of boos after the decision. What was the issue? Perhaps they felt for Ernie based on past discrepancies. However, this was not the fight to look for retribution. As competitive as Landeros was, to suggest he won more than three rounds in this fight would be erroneous and far from in keeping with reality. "I thought I won the fight pretty handily, after about the fourth or fifth round I was able to keep him on the outside and work my jab when my jab is working, I am a tough guy to beat," was Greg's assessment of the fight.

Haugen delivered another fistic masterpiece, were his subtle adjustments took away what was working best for his opponent early in the fight. Haugen delivered when he was a prohibited favorite, and, thanks to the fact that he kept being matched tough, kept getting better.

In the post-fight interview, Greg spoke about injuring his right hand-an issue that has plagued him prior to this fight-and indicate that he felt the state of Nevada does not allow enough wrapping of a fighter's hand. "One roll of gauze is not sufficient," Greg told Al Bernstein after the fight.

Greg also talked about Terrence Ali, who was supposed to be Greg's next opponent. Ali was showcased as a boxer who possessed slick speed and movement, the kind of opponent Greg has yet to face. "He (Ali) had very fast hands, he loved to put on the proverbial show, especially for the Atlantic City fans, and he would go out and throw these huge flurries, he was a very good boxer," Jeff Bumpus, an opponent of Terence Ali, said of his style.

A fight with Terrence Ali was never to be. But that might have been a good thing for Ali. "Greg's mastery at distance would have prevailed over Terrence, Terrence was an arm puncher, and that is not going to get it done against Greg," Jeff Bumpus said.

A fighter like Terrence Ali would soon find himself in the rearview mirror of Greg because Greg had his sights set of much more turbulent, yet rewarding, roads. Indeed, Kronk fighter Jimmy Paul was considered a thoroughbred amongst thoroughbreds and was looking to cash in on some Christmas money at the expense of the fighter they called Mutt.

Chapter Ten
The Championship Level

I don't care who you are; if you have a world title, then you have a
target on your back.

—Leeonzer Barber

Jimmy Paul was the antithesis of Greg Haugen as an amateur boxer.
It was apparent to everyone that Paul was a blue-chipper, and his
treasure trove of trophies at the national level enunciated this point.
"I was a top amateur in 1980. I knocked out Frankie Randall, who
they said was the number two guy, So I knew I was going to go far
in the Olympics, next thing I know they decided to boycott, so I was
pissed off because I did not get a chance to win my gold medal,"
explained Jimmy. Gold medal or no gold medal, there was no
questioning just how great Paul was as an amateur.

Where Jimmy does have a lot in common with Greg is how they
were both introduced to boxing. "I got into a fight at school. He
started it, of course. He was a bully, and one day he decided to hit
me, and I decided to hit him back. He was one hundred twenty-five
pounds, I was only ninety pounds, I got kicked out of school for one
day," said Jimmy.

Jimmy Paul did what he felt he had to do, but he also knew
consequences were sure to follow from his home. "My dad was a
strict reverend, so I thought I was going to get whooped. But when I
explained to my dad, he did not whoop me," Jimmy said to his
surprise. Jimmy decided he wanted to investigate boxing to defend
himself better. "I went to the gym and begged the coach to teach me
to box," explained Jimmy.

Jimmy's persistence paid dividends, and not only was Paul
introduced to the sweet science of boxing, but he also flourished at it
from the beginning. Jimmy explains he won a boxing tournament
after only two weeks in the gym, and that was just for starters. "I
impressed the coaches, and I was winning. Because I was winning, I
was going all over the place, like Canada," Jimmy added.

Being able to compete and travel at the amateur level was so crucial to Greg Haugen's development as well. But Paul, based on his greater amateur success, discovered a more lucrative pipeline to pugilism. "I ended up being in the same gym with the likes of Duane Thomas, The McCrory Brothers, Percell Davis, we were all top guys in the amateurs," Jimmy said. This collection of talent laid its groundwork in Detroit, Michigan, where another legendary boxing story was just beginning its development. "I had a coach named Jack Farmer, and he decided to take us over to Kronk to meet Emanuel Steward, and we started training for Kronk," Jimmy explained.

Kronk Gym was a claustrophobic basement that served as a training facility since the 1920s for the inner-city kids of Detroit who inspired to be just like Joe Louis, the heavyweight king, and Detroit's adopted son. Despite its long history, Kronk Gym was not put on the map nationally but started to get recognition in the late '70s. Promising stars in the making like Hilmer Kenty, Micky Goodwin, and Thomas Hearns were getting noticed. At the helm of these young upstarts, was Emanuel Steward, a forceful leader who knew how to take fighters to the next level.

Leeonzer Barber, a Kronk fighter who won the world light heavyweight championship, described his first encounter with Kronk as "life-changing." "I have been around a lot of boxing gyms in the Detroit area, Detroit was known as a fight town. I had been to Brewster, Johnson, King Solomon's, Twenty-First Century, and a couple of other gyms (in Detroit), obscure places, but Kronk had a culture of excellence. At first, it was just a tough gym, but around '79, '80, you could see changes around there. Guys were developing beyond their years, they were at Kronk only a couple of years, and they looked like they had been there for five years. You couldn't come down there and be average. If you wanted to test yourself, if you came from another gym, you came down to Kronk to test yourself. I knew I was in a unique place. I must give Emmanuel credit for that; his obsession with boxing played out in the fighters," Leeonzer explained.

Despite the reputation, as well as the flashy gold trunks, Jimmy Paul was not too keen on fighting for Kronk at the start. "I didn't care for Kronk at the time because we were fighting against Kronk," Jimmy said.

It was during these competitions with Kronk fighters where Jimmy Paul first got a taste of the underbelly of boxing. Jimmy talked about this experience. "The McCrory Brothers and I made up a song...Kronk, they steal fights, it ain't right, oh no, no no...Milton McCrory fought someone from Kronk, and they stole the fight from him. Emanuel Steward knew they stole the fight, so he walked over and told him, 'you won the fight,'" Jimmy said.

This situation left a bad taste in the mouth of Jimmy regarding Kronk. "We were not comfortable with Kronk for a long time, but after a while we became Kronk," Paul said.

Jimmy Paul was comfortable as a professional boxer, however. He ran havoc through the lightweight division from 1980-1983. His long reach of seventy-two inches was unusual for his division. Such a physical attribute can allow a fighter to throw his jab in a variety of ways. It was the jab that caused some friction between Paul and Emanuel. "He didn't like the way I used my jab, I flicked it, and he didn't like that, but the jab was the keypunch in boxing," explained Jimmy. It is hard to argue with what Jimmy was doing because the results were there, "He beat some good guys in the Detroit area like Alvin "Too Sweet" Hayes, that was a big fight in Detroit," Leeonzer Barber explains.

Indeed, it is difficult to question a legend such as Steward, but it is equally hard to dispute the technique of Jimmy Paul early on, as he was piling up the wins. But a flicking jab was not the only thing Jimmy Paul brought to the table. Not by a country mile. Lee Groves explains that Paul was a "Big right-hand puncher." It was Paul's performance against Andy Ganigan, a formidable puncher in his own right, that really put Paul on the map.

Paul dropped the Hawaiian Punch six times on route to a sixth-round technical knockout. But with the impressive victory over Ganigan, Paul explains he was also frustrated because of that fight. The frustration was because Emanuel Steward called on his fighter to face Ganigan on just three days of notice. "I shouldn't have to do that, that guy can punch," Jimmy explained. Opinions are sure to differ on whether or not Jimmy has a legitimate gripe against Steward in this instance, but there is no question Paul answered the call impressively.

After the Ganigan victory, Jimmy Paul did suffer a setback, however. He dropped a close decision to Daryl Tyson. A fight that occurred after a four-month layoff, which was equivalent to being off a year in those days. "I finally got a fight with Daryll Tyson on five days' notice. I knew I wasn't ready, but I was so excited to get a fight. So, I took the fight when I shouldn't have," Jimmy said.

Jimmy Paul was already stewing because he thought a title shot was coming his way. The way he explains it, Emanuel Steward told Jimmy Paul that he had a very vested interest in the Edwin Rosario versus Jose Luis Ramirez lightweight championship fight. The way Jimmy explains it, Emanuel said to him, "If Rosario wins this fight, you will be number one and get a title shot. Two years go by, and I couldn't get a title shot, I was getting sick of it."

Through Jimmy Paul's lens, the Kronk Legend was failing him. First, Emmanuel could not get his fighter a title shot, but he was also calling on Jimmy to take fights on short notice against formidable opponents. This frustration never seemed to leave Jimmy. "Camacho wouldn't fight me, Bramble wouldn't fight me, I couldn't get the fight with Rosario. I could never get the big fight," Jimmy exclaimed.

Jimmy Paul is the poster boy of the boxing business. "Nobody wanted to fight him (Paul). He was the classic high risk, low reward guy. He was like Winky Wright, Tim Austin, Tom Boom Boom Johnson, Antonio Tarver, Cory Spinks…guys who were seen as outstanding fighters, but they can't, for whatever reason; whether it is outside influences or a lack of perceived charisma, they can't move the needle, and they can't draw enough money to warrant the risk. A fight with Jimmy Paul at that time was just not worth the risk," explained Lee Groves.

Leeonzer Barber corroborates Lee's comment, "You are a product out there, you have to be a draw. Manny (Emanuel Steward) was all about putting asses in the seats. At twenty-three, twenty-four, you don't understand that shit. You don't really get it. You are just trying to be a fighter, so, if all that talking and flare is not natural for you, it is hard to sustain," Leeonzer explained.

When I asked Livingstone Bramble about avoiding Jimmy, his answer sort of justified Lee Groves' explanation. "I never got the call to fight Jimmy Paul, we never got that call. I would have considered it if the money was right. But the money had to be right. I wasn't going to fight Jimmy for a little bit of money. But we never had the offer as far as I know," Bramble said.

It is not unrealistic to suggest that Jimmy Paul might have never been given a shot at the lightweight title if it were not for a newly minted boxing organization that manifested from the armpit of the sport.

For many years, the WBC and the WBA were the two boxing sanctioning bodies that produced recognized world champions. In some cases, fighters were undisputed champions, but there was also a good representation of two world champions in one weight class (today there could be as many as five). Circa 1982, the WBA was on the verge of voting for a new President, Gilberto Mendoza, the incumbent, was believed to have his days numbered. However, in boxing, you never know when the rug is going to be pulled from under you.

Lee Groves explains, "The defining moment for the IBF was at the WBA convention. Bob Lee was running against the incumbent. It looked like the perceived sentiment was that the American Lee would be the new WBA president. But, with considerable help from Bob Arum, there were some shenanigans. Some tactics that were not on the up and up. But, as is said, all is fair in love, war, and boxing. Bob Lee lost, and it was very controversial."

Like so many boxers who gave it their best effort inside the squared circle, only to have their efforts taken away from them by individuals wearing suits. But when a boxer gets robbed in the ring, apart from very few occasions, they just accept the thievery and move on. Bob Lee decided to be proactive about the manner and created the International Boxing Federation, also known as the IBF. It was initially called the USBAI, and eventually morphed into the IBF," Lee Groves added.

The IBF was perceived as legitimate almost right from the get-go. Part of the reason for this acceptance was probably because of the stench connected to Mendoza and the WBA. But there was also a tangible reason why the IBF was a welcomed addition to the sanctioning bodies. "One of the things I thought the IBF did that was really smart was in some cases they awarded their belts to existing champions," Lee Groves said. This act was a statement made by Bob Lee that spoke to the boxing world. It would have been foolish to suggest different world champions other than the likes of Marvelous Marvin Hagler, Donald Curry, and Aaron Pryor, and when there was not a clear-cut champion, they fought it out.

But where the IBF really paved the way for legitimacy was in the heavyweight division. Where boxing is often made or broken. Like the other juggernaut champions, Larry Holmes was given the IBF and, by 1984, since Holmes was very selective about who he defended his title against, the IBF was the only sanctioning body that recognized Larry Holmes as the heavyweight champion. Holmes was the sole big name in boxing that did not have either the WBC or the WBA title. This circumstance gave the IBF a very polished look of legitimacy.

Having said that, the Larry Holmes onion should have been peeled for further investigation. First, the IBF played right into Holmes' hands, he wanted nothing to do with the very talented Greg Page, who was the WBC mandatory at that time or any other perceived 'tough fight' at that time, the IBF just giving him the title, while not forcing his hand, was just what Larry Holmes needed. Also, according to Pinklon Thomas, Bob Lee promised him that he would not just award Holmes the title and would have Pinklon and Larry fight it out. But after Bob Lee realized Holmes was not going to fight Pinklon, he just awarded Holmes the title.

But the reality was that the IBF had a fresh coat of paint on it circa 1984 and moved the boxing needle in the right direction.

The lightweight division was a division that did not have one recognized champion. Hector Camacho held the WBC title, while Livingstone Bramble was the WBA champion. A need for a newly minted champion was decided by the IBF. On January 30th, 1984, Charlie Chu Chu Brown faced Melvin Paul for the vacant IBF lightweight title in Atlantic City. It was an odd choice, as Paul was stopped in six rounds by Robin Blake in his previous fight, and Brown had yet to face top-tier competition and already had two blemishes on his record. But it was a spirited fight nonetheless, as Charlie won a spilt decision over fifteen rounds of pugilism.

Charlie Brown's first title defense was against Harry Arroyo, a hard hat type of fellow from Youngstown, Ohio. Harry was an undefeated dynamo, who really defined what an 80's fighter was at the lower weight class; grit and the willingness commit to the pocket, oh yes and some solid, underrated boxing skills, especially in the area of counter punching. Sound familiar? Harry came in with some stiff competition under his belt. He defeated Arnie Wells, Joe Manley, Steve Hilliard and the aforementioned Robin Blake. The one checkmark in Charlie Brown's favor was going the full fifteen rounds already. Harry Arroyo fell just short of reaching the fifteenth round in his bid for the title as he stopped Brown in the fourteenth round to capture the crown.

Arroyo defended his title against Charlie Brown, then against Terrence Ali, both by stoppages. Harry Arroyo was a fighting champion, but he did not have the superstar status of a Camacho or a Bramble; therefore, there was no need to protect him against a Jimmy Paul. Nobody was in the 'Harry Arroyo business.' Also, Arroyo did not have one ounce of Prima Donna in him, as some might suggest of The Macho Man, so a fight against Jimmy Paul was easy for Arroyo to accept. But even this fight was not supposed to be for Jimmy Paul, as he was a fill-in for Robin Blake.

When Arroyo defended his title against Jimmy Paul on April 6th, 1985, it was anything but easy. Harry was dropped three times by Paul and given a standing eight-count on another occasion. This display of power was enough for Jimmy Paul to secure a unanimous decision over fifteen rounds. Two of the scorecards read for Paul by a wide margin, but, miraculously, Frank Cappuccino had Paul the winner by only one point, 142-141. You have to wonder the reason for such an erroneous score. It had nothing to do with the action produced inside the squared circle.

Nevertheless, Jimmy Paul was a world champion, and he was ready to be a fighting champion. Paul's performance against Arroyo to win the title should not be forgotten in boxing history. As Jimmy Paul excelled under the most cumbersome of circumstances for a boxer. "He took the fight on short notice. It is hard to win the title on short notice, but Jimmy did it. I was shocked," Leeonzer Barber explained.

Up first for Jimmy Paul was Robin Blake, a rugged, tricky southpaw. Blake had to pull out of the Harry Arroyo title fight. Paul stopped Blake in the fourteenth round. Paul was electric and dominate throughout the contest, knocking Blake down in the ninth and twelfth rounds before finishing him off in round fourteen with blistering combinations.

It was the fights against Harry Arroyo and Robin Blake that people point to as evidence to show just how great Jimmy Paul was. It showed that not only was Jimmy Paul the best lightweight in the world, but was one of the best fighters in the sport at the time. Paul was a pugilist who had tremendous balance and above-average defense, especially in the pocket. In that pocket, Paul would torture you with a pinpoint jab and bionic overhand right. When quarters got close, Jimmy could also cripple you with a thudding left hook. His seventy-two-inch reach advantage was freakish for the weight, which meant he can tag you even if you felt you were at a comfortable distance. The one asset Jimmy did not have was a chance at the big names.

After his destruction of Robin Blake, Paul spoke with CBS blow by blow man Tim Ryan and addressed his robust agenda to unify the lightweight title. Indeed, given all the champions' skill sets, there is no doubt these fights would garner fan appreciation, eyeballs, and dollars. But it was not meant to be. Jimmy Paul pointed out Ryan's response when he told him of his plans, "If you listen to what Tim said, he said, 'hopefully the boxing powers that be will allow that (unifying the title) to happen,' why would he say that?" Paul said.

One thing was certain, Jimmy Paul was not going to wait to unify the lightweight championship. After Robin Blake he fought in a non-title bought against Fred Pendleton, a fighter who has his own great story and is thought in high regard from Paul, "Pendleton was a tough fight, he could stop on a dime and knock you out," Paul said of the pugilist they called "Fearless." Paul then defended his title against Irlesis 'Cubantio' Perez, an accomplished professional who often sparred with Greg Haugen. Going into the fight with Paul, Cubanito's only loss was a ten-round decision to Hector Camacho, who was the WBC lightweight champion at the time. Paul defeated Cubantio by a tough, majority decision over fifteen rounds of boxing. Paul versus Perez is another fight that is not spoken about enough. It was a great, grueling fight and fit right in with the magical year of 1986.

Paul followed up this tough title defense with a rematch against Darryl Tyson, the only man to defeat Paul. This time around, Paul won a comfortable fifteen-round decision against Tyson. Paul pointed to the fact he now had a full camp to prepare for Tyson, "If I am in shape, I know what is going to happen." It was Paul's second title defense in 1986, with both fights going the full fifteen rounds. At this time, the IBF was the only sanctioning body that was still having their champions fighting the fifteen-round limit exclusively. There was no doubt Jimmy Paul had a full, grueling year of pugilism, now it was time for Emanuel Steward to award Jimmy with a 'soft touch.'

After the Darryl Tyson fight, Jimmy Paul was the best of the lightweight crop from the point of view of the keen boxing observer. Greg Haugen was among this group. "We felt Jimmy was the best of all the lightweight champions." But accolades only go so far. Paul still could not get the big paydays. "Jimmy was seen as the 'other guy.' You had Camacho, a charismatic champion and Bramble, the 'snake man,' with the Rastafarian persona, then, of course, Rosario upset Bramble, who was a monster puncher. Then you have Jimmy Paul, a fundamentally sound workman, but he did not have a lot of charisma, he didn't move the needle as a result," Lee Groves explained.

None of this meant Paul was not on par in terms of ability with the other champions. "Ability for ability, Jimmy was a talented guy," Lee Groves said. Emanuel Steward must have known these intangibles were frustrating to Jimmy, it was time to make his fighter feel better.

Victor Machado tells the story that Emanuel Steward was looking to get one last fight for Jimmy in 1986, in December. It was an attempt to get Jimmy some "bonus Christmas money," as Machado explains. Not having to fight his mandatory, Team Kronk could have picked any lower ranked fighter by the IBF. There stood Greg Haugen, a perfect Christmas bonus as far as Paul was concerned.

From the very start, Jimmy Paul had a blunt assessment of Greg Haugen as a boxer, "I got the height, reach, everything on him. He can't outbox me; his punches are not that sharp. I should knock this guy out by the 8th round," was Jimmy's assessment of Haugen. Greg knew he was not given much of a chance, as the 4-1 odds against him suggested, but he was not deterred by this, "I just laughed it off. I am not an easy fight for anyone when I am right," Haugen explained.

Leeonzer Barber did not have rave reviews for Greg Haugen when he first saw him fight but was not as disparaging as Paul was with his scouting report of 'Mutt,' "He did a lot of basic moves, in and out. I didn't see anything spectacular, but he was consistent, rugged. But he did not come with a lot of bells and whistles like Vinny Paz." Leeonzer said of Haugen.

Leeonzer also hinted at Jimmy Paul making one of the biggest mistakes a champion could make going into this fight, "I don't care who you are; if you have a world title, then you have a target on your back. You are going to get the best version of everybody you go up against, your opponent is going to be one-hundred percent ready for you. If you come in eighty, eighty-five percent, you are in for a rude awakening. If he took Greg light, that would be a problem," Leeonzer explained.

Leeonzer's description of the target on a champion's back is why no world title should ever be considered a 'trinket.' While it may be true that too many belts exist today, if you hold one around your waist, your opponent's radar, thirst, and focus on beating you rises exponentially. Therefore, if you are a fighting champion, as Jimmy Paul was, you should be given your due, regardless of lineage or illegitimate alphabet soup. Opposing fighters train for champions like a lion searching for red meat out in the wild.

Greg Haugen knew that fighting Paul for the belt meant more money and television exposure if he won, he also knew Jimmy Paul was by far the best fighter he was going to go up against, he was going to have to fight him for a scheduled fifteen-round fight, and some people think lineage takes precedent? Talk about no ability to peel the onion.

For this fight, Haugen was not going to leave any stones unturned. "I studied some tape of Jimmy, and I knew he had a hell of a jab, he set that right hand up with his jab, he put guys to sleep with his right hand, but he also had a good left hook. I wanted to go out there and put pressure on him. My philosophy for most fights was to go out there and mentally and physically wear guys down, round after round, just keep going. So, my game plan was to take that jab away from him, I did that by throwing short little hooks to the rib cage," Haugen explained.

Greg also knew he had to prepare for the fifteen-round distance and addressed that as well, "I was working with four different sparring partners, I never went fifteen rounds, if you never done it, it is a big thing to do. You have to know in your body you are able to do it. So, I sparred fifteen rounds with three or four different guys. I would go three or four rounds with one guy, and they would throw a fresh guy at me. Knowing you could go fifteen rounds is brain food, but until you go fifteen, you are not sure if you could do it," Haugen said.

Greg also explains he sparred with some high caliber opposition in preparation for the Jimmy Paul fight, "I sparred many rounds with Roger Mayweather, he had the same stature as Jimmy, tall and lanky. He used his jab a lot and had a big right hand. I sparred hundreds of rounds with Roger. I also sparred with Cubanito Perez."

Greg Haugen's approach to this fight, both tactically and physically, was impeccable. If Greg was going to lose to Jimmy, it was not going to be because of a lack of preparation and training.

The same could not be said of Jimmy Paul and his camp.

Since Jimmy held Haugen in very little regard, he did not take advantage of a clear ace in the hole walking around Kronk Gym. Bret Summers was an amateur rival of Greg Haugen and an adequate professional in Kronk Gym. Brett explained that he tried to be the voice of reason for Jimmy, "I was down there with Jimmy Paul, they were just laughing it away, saying 'that white boy ain't got nothing for us,' I was like okay. I kept telling him Greg Haugen can fight, he's got this herky-jerky style that is going to give you problems," Summers said.

Jimmy disputes, Bret's claims, "I don't remember Brett saying that."

But Bret was persistent in his claim, "They just wouldn't listen to me. I offered to show Jimmy what Greg does, I know his style, I seen him so many times, I grew up with him. They could have taken advantage of it, and they didn't," insisted Summers.

Jimmy Paul's lack of interest in tactical preparation for this fight might suggest he did not train hard for this fight. Jimmy reacted to this point by saying, "No way. I respect anyone who gets in the ring with me, I looked at Haugen and said I should knock this guy out, but everyone has a fighter's chance. I trained as hard as I always do."

Bret Summers does not dispute this claim but also suggests that being in shape is not all it takes, "I believed he trained okay. But psychologically, when going into a fight, if you think you are going to beat somebody easily, and when you thought what was going to happen doesn't happen, it is pretty hard to fight then. I think a serious Jimmy Paul with the right attitude could go in there and beat

Greg. But because of Jimmy's attitude, I felt Greg would give him a good going, and he did," Summers said.

It is also worth mentioning that Jimmy Paul and Bret Summers could be perceived to have had a somewhat sketchy relationship. The way Summers explained it when they sparred, "I was able to do pretty good with Jimmy in sparring." Troy Summers, Brett's dad and boxing coach, said, "the truth was when you saw Brett spar with Jimmy, you could see he was beatable."

Jimmy Paul tells the sparring sessions with Summers with more detail, "Bret was telling Emmanuel he should be champion instead of me because he was beating me up in the gym, but I was working on my defense against him. Well we fought again, and I beat him up that day, Emmanuel was there. Bret walked out of there, looking crazy. I can't miss Bret Summers," explained Jimmy.

Leeonzer Barber explained that he cannot comment on who's version of the story, Jimmy Paul or Brett Summers, is more accurate because he was not in Paul's camp, "I was in Washington preparing for my pro debut, so I cannot say if Jimmy took Greg light or night, but if he did that is the reason why he lost the fight," Leeonzer said.

Jimmy Paul adds further evidence that he was at his absolute best in preparation for the Haugen fight in with a story of handling Duane Thomas in the gym, who was training to fight John Mugabi as the main event of the Paul-Haugen fight. "Duane Thomas comes in early one day, and he comes in on my time and gets in the ring, so we sparred, and I handled him. If I could hurt the bigger Duane Thomas, what was I going to do to Greg Haugen? Emmanuel Steward comes up to me and says, 'Jimmy, I know you are really ready for this fight,'" explained Paul.

The confidence Jimmy Paul was feeling going into the fight with Greg Haugen was soon to change for the worst. Jimmy describes what perceives to be as peculiar circumstances that had an impact on his performance.

The anomalies began for Jimmy with Emanuel's handling of Stan Weaver, Jimmy's personal protégé, "Every time I fight, he comes to the gym to deal with me only. We are in Las Vegas (for the Haugen fight), and Stan tells me that 'Emanuel is trying to keep me away from you, he wants me to pick people up from the airport, but I am only supposed to deal with you,'" Paul explained.

Anyone who is a creature of habit could relate to Jimmy's concerns. Would anyone expect Wade Boggs not to eat chicken before he played baseball? The question is, why would Emmanuel do this?

Another disruption in routine is cited by Jimmy, "We usually have a doctor at all of our fights, Dr. Lorenz. For this particular fight, he didn't show up. I walked into the suite, you know when you walk into a room, and you feel everyone is talking about you, they look at you, and they look away like you are the topic of discussion. I got that feeling when I walked into this room," Paul explained.

What Jimmy was walking in the room for was a B-12 shot, which he would always get from Dr. Lorenz before a fight. "I get the shot from a different guy, and I get a feeling…I don't know about this guy," Paul said.

Troy Summers confirmed that all the Kronk fighters would get a B-12 shot before a fight, but he does not remember any specific doctor who would administer these shots. "There was no doctor that I knew of unless he was invisible," Troy explained. Troy also added that he felt the B-12 shot affected his son Brett Summers' performance against Chris Calvin. Leeonzer Barber does remember Dr. Lorenz, however, and explains that he also received B-12 shots from him. "Detroit had brutal winters. It is easy to catch a cold when you come out of this hot ass gym (Kronk). Your pores are still open, your immune system is still down because you just sweated the nutrients out of your body. You are constantly in a vulnerable position as far as catching viruses. When you are getting ready for a fight, that is when some shit will come down on you. You'll feel a twinge in your throat, or something in your nose, it happens more than people believe. Emmanuel Steward was a fighter, he knew what happened in these circumstances, so he would have guys go get hit up with a B-12 to fight any viral infections that might be coming on. B-12 shots kind of helped you out. Dr. Lorenz was the guy for that," Leeonzer detailed.

One has to make up their own mind as to why Leeonzer clearly remembers Dr. Lorens and Try Summers does not.

Now Jimmy Paul has two disruptions in his routine that are shrouded in mystery.

Going into the fight Greg Haugen was never better prepared, whereas Jimmy Paul was thrown two Sandy Koufax like curveballs.

Max Kellerman always asks what fighter he would rather be after a round, there is no doubt anyone would rather be Greg Haugen going into this fight.

Chapter Eleven
Beating Kronk Gold

"It is always good to see someone who beat you go on and win the championship."

—Chris Calvin

When Greg Haugen met Jimmy Paul in the center of the ring for prefight instructions, he was greeted by referee Davey Pearl, a familiar face to Greg. But that would be the only recognizable dynamic for Greg. Never had he fought 15 rounds, and never before did he test his skills against a pugilist as accomplished or as skilled as Jimmy Paul.

Greg was aware of how good Jimmy was, yet he seemed very comfortable at this stage because he did his homework. As Davey Pearl pontificated what he expected from these consummate professionals, Greg's facial expressions never wavered; in fact, he glared in defiance at Jimmy. Paul looked rather indifferent, business-like, just like he always was.

When the bell rang for round one action, the two fighters met at the center of the ring. Paul flicked his jab a few times in Greg's direction (the same kind of jab Emanuel Steward reportedly disliked), but they fell way short of landing. Greg bob and weaved, offered some feints, and tried a lead right hand that Jimmy blocked. Jimmy then ran off another series of jabs, with only one of these punches finding a home on Haugen's face. Greg's game plan seemed to include the abandonment of his formidable jab, as he threw very few jabs in this early stanza. Instead, Greg dug a hard-right hand to the body, and a solid lead left hook. While neither caused much damage, they were more impressive than Paul's jab early on. And it showed just how intelligent and diverse Greg Haugen was as a boxer.

Greg knew he had to put the pressure on a fighter like Paul, at the same time, he also knew Paul would pick him apart with his jab if he just bulled his way in. Greg was bouncing and feinting, and this seemed to confuse Paul. He did not know what Greg would throw.

For Jimmy's part, he tried to throw the jab in different ways and from different angles, but Greg was still avoiding most of these punches and kept getting hard, sneaky body shots in on Jimmy. Those short little hooks he worked on in camp.

Paul kept throwing his jab in round one but did little scoring with it. Even when Jimmy did get home with his jab, Haugen answered with a hard body shot. It was almost an exclusive jab fest on Paul's part in round one. He did try and throw a left hook to the body, and a lead right hand, both of which missed. The last punch was answered by a very stiff Haugen left jab to the face of Paul, a forceful blow that caused Paul to cover up. Haugen scored with a solid left hook to the body in the final seconds of round one. Haugen's work to the body and ability to make Paul miss the majority of his punches won the round for the big underdog. Judges Art Lurie, Robert Cox, and Ed Levine all agree in giving Greg round one 10-9.

Jimmy reports not feeling himself right away, "I come back to the stool, and I try to sit down and almost fall off, and I am like why am I feeling like this, this guy ain't landing no punches yet. I literally felt like I lost balance when I tried to sit on the stool," Jimmy explained.

If Jimmy looks back at the tape, he will see that Greg Haugen did indeed land punches, virtually the only scoring done in the round. With that said, it is hard to believe that Greg landed with anything that had the kind of force needed to make Jimmy feel the way he described.

When Jimmy did get squared away, Emanuel Steward covered him with a towel and instructed Jimmy to close the gap, as he was giving Haugen too much room.

In round two, Greg was first to get to the center of the ring and appeared to be the boss, "just keep going," was always Greg's approach when he was right. Greg proceeded to dodge the many jabs thrown by the champion, and even started to score with his own left jab. Greg was darting in and out and still looking for that left hook to the body. Bouncing and full of life, Greg's confidence was growing by the second, and he even started leading with his jab, doubling up on his jab and throwing a right hook behind it. Again, nothing was landing with thudding damage from Greg-at least that is how it appeared- but the only landing that was being done was from Greg, and it was clear he was in charge in there.

Paul still tried to throw the jab in vein, and ate a double jab from Haugen, causing Paul to tie up the Auburn, Washington native. Haugen then slipped a lethargic left jab and landed a straight right, Paul took this punch well, but it was another score from Haugen, nonetheless. Seconds later, Paul landed his best punch of the round, a solid left-hook that appeared to get Greg's attention, but did not stop his rhythm. Paul then missed with two jabs and threw a right to Haugen's body, which Greg backed off from to minimize the damage, Greg then jumped in with a hard right to the body that straightened Jimmy up and caused him to back off. The rest of the round saw both fighters trying to control the pace with their jab, Jimmy wanted to keep Greg at distance with his jab, while Greg was setting up his jab to land those hard body shots. Both fighters had mild success at different points in this round. The results of round two differed on the scorecards, both Lurie and Cox scored it for Paul 10-9, while Levine gave the round to Greg 10-9.

When Greg got back to his corner, Stan Tischler, Greg's trainer, asked for more pressure and assured his fighter that Jimmy Paul had nothing to beat him with. Tischler would not have agreed with two-thirds of the scoring in round two.

Round three saw Greg beat Jimmy to the center of the ring once again. Jimmy was flicking his jab, and Greg continued to want the body. He threw a thudding right hook to Paul's body early in round three and doubled down on his work with a left hook to the body that did some damage. Paul appeared to be getting sluggish and apprehensive and kept missing big with his jab. Greg tried to make Jimmy pay when he missed by throwing left hooks upstairs and hard rights to the body. None of these punches landing with super authority, but it was the better work being done. As round three continued, the Haugen body shots were finding more of a home, and the punches Jimmy Paul was offering became more peculiar. They were short, infective punches, the more he threw, the more unsure of himself he appeared to be. It was like listening to someone talk and constantly stop at mid-sentence. There was no punctuation on Jimmy Paul's punches.

Paul did manage to land an authoritative right hand behind a double jab, that appeared to wake up the Kronk Champion. As a result of that punch landing well, there was an immediate transformation in Paul's confidence and body language. Paul was now coming forward and throwing punches correctly. But at his best, Greg Haugen is a defensive wizard, and Paul barely landed a meaningful glove on him the rest of the round. The end of round three saw Greg Haugen once again in charge, with Jimmy Paul backing off and throwing a lazy jab.

When you talk about ring generalship, superior defense, and dictating the pace, Greg Haugen had all those checkmarks in round three. To go along with the hard body shots he landed, there should be no doubt as to who won that round. "Every time he jabbed, I just ducked under and threw that right hook to the ribcage, he would wince in pain when I hit him good to the ribcage," was how Greg described the action. Miraculously, however, only Art Lurie gave round three to Greg. Robert scored called it even, 10-10, and Ed Levine gave the round to Paul 10-9. It makes you wonder how Levine could score what appeared to be a closer round two for Greg, but not round three.

When Jimmy Paul went back to the corner, Emmanuel Steward urged his fighter to be more aggressive. 'This is not a game,' Steward urged, in a berating manner. It appeared as if Steward felt Haugen won round three. Now, there is no denying the greatness of Emanuel, as well as his impressive accomplishments and likability; however, it would be hard for anyone to identify what Jimmy Paul heard that was sound advice. First, Jimmy Paul knows better than anyone he is not playing a game. Also, Steward offered Paul no instructions as to how to deal with what was giving him trouble. Emmanuel simply pointed out that Paul had Haugen badly hurt but let Haugen off the hook.

Now, there is a long paper trail of Steward berating his fighter when he feels they let their opponent off the hook. Who could forget his tirade during Lennox Lewis' fight with Mike Tyson? Steward also urged Thomas Hearns to throw his right hand more often, and with force, throughout his rematch with Ray Leonard- 'throw the Goddam right hand' was said so often it was almost as if it was on a loop. Steward had also done this to Paul on many occasions in previous fights as well.

Brett Summers also describes how Emmanuel Steward could be salty with his fighters, "Emmanuel was pretty tough on guys. When I fought, he would scream at me in the corner. In one fight, he told me

I would have to get a job if I didn't get it going. We went back and forth, sometimes in the corner. He was pretty serious."

In this case, Emmanuel's rhetoric seemed ingenuine. In no way was there an opportunity for Jimmy Paul to stop Greg Haugen in this round. Emmanuel's advice became even more peculiar when he told Paul his lack of aggression cost him money. Instead of conjuring up a game plan on how to deal with a very frustrating style, the Kronk Gym leader was talking about dollar signs? Why? If Emmanuel Steward is indeed a top-class trainer, why does he not know that aggression was the worst possible approach against Greg Haugen when he was at his best? It plays right into his hands. Emmanuel would have been much more effective in this situation had he given the same cogent instructions he gave Paul late in his fight with Fred Pendleton. Where was that much-needed instruction?

Early in round four, Greg Haugen landed another compelling left hook to the body after a Paul jab. While not a particularly devasting body shot, it was a punch that did serve its purpose because Jimmy Paul proceeded to throw half-hearted jabs, that appeared to be shortened, at Greg. Later in the round, Paul seemed to be throwing an authoritative right-hand but pulled the punch back. It was not a feint from Jimmy, like the classic right-hand feint Evander Holyfield set up Buster Douglass with. No, this was a situation where Paul looked, dazed and confused and reluctant to throw. It was clear the Haugen body shots were not only finding its mark but dictating the pace of the fight. Jimmy Paul was a version of the champion we never saw before; he was confused and reluctant.

Greg continued to soften up the body of Jimmy Paul in round four-the blows appeared to be coming home even harder this round. Greg also began to score more often with headshots, courtesy of left and right hooks. Greg doubled up on his jab in the final seconds of the round. These punches were the most meaningful jabs in the round. In the second half of the round, Paul tried to be more aggressive with his jab, but it was finding air instead of the flesh of the man they call Mutt. As the bell rang to indicate the end of round four, Haugen glared at Paul, as if to say, 'I got ya,' and sauntered back to his corner, oozing with confidence. All three judges scored the round for Haugen 10-9.

Jimmy Paul landed his best punch of the fight, up until that point, in round five. A stiff, straight, right hand that pushed Haugen back.

It was the kind of punch only the best-conditioned fighter can stand up against. However, Haugen, the consummate professional he was when he was going well, did not waver, and continued to work the body. Greg even kicked up his defense a notch. But Paul was on top of Greg a lot more in this round and made it close. The hard body shots probably won Greg a very close round. As the case with most rounds that are close, the judges did not agree on the scoring in round five. Lurie scored it for Jimmy Paul, 10-9, while Cox and Levine favored Haugen's work rate in round five.

Greg was boasting with confidence at this point of the fight. "By the fourth or fifth round, he was afraid to jab. Jimmy's game plan was to control me with the jab, it didn't really work out for him. When you take away one of your opponent's best weapons, he is just an average fighter. After about the sixth or seventh round, he was hesitant about throwing the jab. If he did throw it, he kind of threw it with what we call his foot in the bucket, he was afraid to commit to it. He would throw this kind of jab where he would go to his side, he wasn't extending the jab," Greg explained.

Jimmy explains that after five rounds. "I started feeling so bad, sleepy...I thought there was something wrong with my water, I didn't' know what was going on," Jimmy explained. Jimmy's suspicions attached to this fight were heightened when he learned that Walter Smith, who worked his corner, was arguing with Stan Weaver about what water bottle to use. "Why did they want me to drink from a certain bottle," Paul wondered.

Haugen went right for the body at the start of round six, indicating he was still in control of the fight. Haugen then deflected a few of Jimmy's jab, following up with a stiff right to the body, and an even stiffer left hook upstairs. Jimmy Paul tried to dictate the pace, as he was often first with his jab. Doubling, and even tripling the punch that was the reason for Paul's success in so many other fights. But on this night, the jab could not land, and it created openings for Haugen to attack the body. A hard, overhand right landed upstairs for Haugen at around the sixteen-second mark of round six. Such a punch tells a spectator that a fighter is growing in confidence. Haugen knew he was in control and started to mix up his shots in round six. Haugen threw another authoritative right hand over a Paul jab with seconds remaining in round six, but this time the punch missed its mark, causing a clash of heads. Greg Haugen immediately checked his right eye. Opened flesh from a clash of heads would have been devasting for the challenger at this point.

Indeed, Haugen had a minor cut due to the clash of heads. Despite the cut, Haugen took round six on all three scorecards 10-9, but that did not mitigate the danger of opened flesh. For a spectator to suggest any cut is minor might be considered an error in judgment, in particular, for a fifteen-round fight against a world-class opponent. "Every time I had been cut in a fight, it was always from a head butt. The skin doesn't have much give when it is clashing with heads. He head-butted me, so I started worrying about that because my face could swell up or my eye could swell up, I had never been fifteen rounds, so I was worried, neither one of those things (from getting head-butted) is a good thing," Greg explained.

Jimmy Paul now had some momentum, even if he did not appear to be in control of this fight. After all, Jimmy Paul and his seventy-two-inch reach now had a target to concentrate on. Any fighter can tell you much of an advantage cutting your opponent can be. Can Jimmy Paul dig deep and take advantage of this opportunity? Jimmy Paul also had experience in his favor. The champion went the full fifteen rounds three times to Haugen's none, Paul also had a stoppage in the fourteenth round over Robin Blake. Few things that are as rare and special as a late-round stoppage during a fifteen-round fight in the sweet science.

Going into round seven, Greg also had an abrasion above his upper lip, so there were visible marks to give Paul confidence. But not much else changed in terms of the pattern of the fight early in round seven. Paul continued to snake out his jab, as Greg tried to land a variety of body punches over Paul's jab. Haugen dug a hard-right hand to Paul's midsection and followed it up with a stiff left hook on the inside to Paul's head in the first minute of round seven. Thudding, effective shots that backed Jimmy up into the ropes. Realizing he had his man hurt, Greg responded by opening up, but Greg threw wild, amateurish bombs that a fighter of Paul's caliber avoided with ease.

These power punches were one of the few times Greg looked inexperienced as a professional. Paul appeared to regroup, steady-legged, and flicking his jab in an attempt to control distance. Greg began to reach with his punches, never a good move, but Paul did little to make him pay for this mistake. At around the 1:25 mark, the sudden chaos seemed to vanish inside the ring, as Greg regrouped and was once again landing hard body shots over Paul's jab. The rest of the round was primarily fought at range. Providing the ToughMan from Alaska the chance to showcase his skills from distance. Jimmy Paul was three inches taller than Greg Haugen and enjoyed a five-inch reach advantage over him. Greg had no business out jabbing Paul, but this is what was happening late in round seven. Remarkable. Round seven was another three-way sweep for Greg on the scorecards.

Lee Groves told me that one of his criteria for voting for fighters for the International Hall of Fame is if that fighter' skill level is above that of his contemporizes. If beating Jimmy Paul from distance, even though he was at a significant disadvantage in the tale of the tape, does not show that the boxing skills of Greg Haugen were indeed a notch or two above the fighters of his day, I am not sure what will convince you.

Both fighters were listening to instructions from their corner before round eight. The crowd was becoming more vocal in the favor of Haugen at this point. They were sensing that something special was brewing, and they were thrilled to be a part of it. While boxing has high replay value, there is no substitute for being at a great fight live. Such circumstances meant little to Greg Haugen, however. He still had a cut to deal with, as well as having to potentially fight another twenty-four minutes in a fight were his work rate was already high. Greg must have heard the crowd, must have thought that he was ahead, but nothing could have been taken for granted at that point. In particular the scoring of the fight. It could be said that even Mister Magoo could see that Greg Haugen had a comfortable lead after seven rounds, however, Mister Magoo was never a boxing judge. Instead, the history of boxing shows judges who rendered such heinous scorecards that the only explanation for such actions was that there were no explanations. And often, no consequences. For every Jose Juan Guerra, judges who have been exiled because of their poor judgment, there are at least twenty Adalaide Byrd's. Greg Haugen had to keep the pressure on and position himself for an opportunity to stop Paul if he wanted to guarantee victory.

Gil Clancy commented on how Stan Tischler, who served as Haugen's cornerman, as well as head trainer for this fight, made the cut above Haugen's right eye a non-factor. The value of a great cut man cannot be downplayed. "Luckily, I always had good cut men; Stan was excellent. He knew how to stop cuts. When I fought back east, I had Eddie Aliano, they called him the clot, he was one of the best. Having a good cut man…those guys could keep you in a fight. So, I always made sure I paid a little extra for someone who knew what they were doing. Because if they keep me in a fight, I could get a big payday in the next fight," Greg explained.

Early in round eight, Greg continued to work from distance. Bouncing on his feet, scoring with a stiff jab, and digging a hard right to the body, all Jimmy Paul could do was tie his opponent up. This was the pattern for much of the round. Greg was growing with confidence, mixing up his punches, landing with short little power shots. Both upstairs and to the body, Greg even scored with a lead left hook. It was an absolute clinic by Haugen. For about two minutes and fifty seconds, Paul could not touch Greg, save for a straight right hand that momentarily backed Haugen up. In boxing, that is a minor consequence for staying in the pocket, "I don't care who you are, you are going to get hit if you commit to the pocket," Greg once said to me. This theory held most accurate at the very end of round eight, as Jimmy Paul scored with a beautiful straight right that hurt Haugen, backing him up to the ropes. Since that punch came at the end of the round, there this no telling how Jimmy could have capitalized. It was the best punch of the fight up until that point. Greg acknowledged that the Paul right hand was lethal, "Jimmy could punch."

Round eight of this fight is one of those rounds that make judging very cumbersome. While Haugen clearly won all but ten seconds of the round, Paul landed one punch that arguably did more damage than all of Greg's punches combined in that round. How does a judge score such a round? It was similar to round two of the classic Julio Caesar Chavez vs. Meldrick Taylor fight. It is what makes boxing the best sport to debate. Robert Cox favored the sledgehammer right hand of Paul, scoring round eight 10-9 for him, while Lurie and Levine awarded Greg the round, 10-9.

Emmanuel Steward felt Jimmy could have ended the fight had he pressed more after that telling shot. But with just seconds to do so, it is hard to say that as a certainty. Would it not have been more productive to encourage Paul to keep the momentum that right hand gave him going? Again, I know Emmanuel Steward is boxing royalty, but I think it is a legitimate question.

Greg Haugen appeared to weather the storm of the Paul right hand and went back to business in round nine. His legs seemed steady, and he was still bouncing with confidence. Greg kept popping his jab and scoring hard body shots over the Paul jab. Paul did seem to have more life to him but still could not touch Greg with his jab early on. Round nine was almost a carbon copy of round eight, save for two major contrasts. First, Greg was a tad more conservative with the punches he was throwing, while his work rate did not go down, he did not open up with the kind of power shots he did in round eight. Second, there was no big equalizer landed by Jimmy Paul. If you watch boxing long enough, you know that these two circumstances go hand-in-hand. It all amounted to another round for Greg Haugen. The three judges, however, all agreed on this being a Jimmy Paul round. The first round that the champion won unanimously, 10-9. Boxing, the ultimate Rorschach test.

If Emmanuel Steward made an error in judgment after round eight, he regrouped when his fighter went back to the corner after round nine. Steward provided Jimmy with salient instruction on how to set up Greg once again with that right hand. Would it work?

Nowadays, the bell rings for the tenth round in a championship fight, it is considered to be approaching the so-called 'championship rounds.' Back in 1986, the start of the tenth round meant you still have five more rounds to go. That is telling, changing the sport of boxing in a sensational way. A transformation that was already underway in '86, however, the IBF was still exercising the fifteen-round limit. The only major sanctioning body still doing so.

Knowing there was an abundance of time left in this fight, Stan Tischler still instructed Haugen to "let everything hang out" going into round ten. Stan knew there was still enough time to lose this fight on the scorecards; therefore, every round was precious. Tischler was also savvy enough to identify that when Greg was moving forward, he was the boss. It was when Greg was backing up and at distance when Paul landed his most telling blows.

Both of these world-class fighters received reliable counsel from their trainers going into this tenth round.

Round ten began with Greg still attacking the body after Jimmy's jabs missed their mark. But these punches did not have as much starch on them as in previous rounds. Was fatigue setting in for a fighter who has had his conditioning questioned in previous, much shorter fights? If Haugen did need a rest, his wish was granted when referee Davey Pearl stopped the action so the tape could be fixed on the left glove of Jimmy Paul. Shortly after this occurrence, Jimmy backed Greg into the ropes and scored well. Haugen managed to get the fight back in the middle of the ring, but Jimmy scored from distance there as well. But Greg was still doing a good job of avoiding most of Paul's jabs and kept going to the body as a result of the opening these misses created. Later in the round, Haugen scored well with a straight right upstairs, off a double jab. While Jimmy Paul seemed stronger than any other point of the fight, his legs were spry, and he was throwing with more purpose, he did not land enough punches to claim the round. By contrast, Haugen seemed to be tiring a bit but was still doing the best scoring of the round, as well as making his opponent miss a more significant percentage of punches. But Paul swept round ten on the scorecards. The champ was now closing the gap with questionable scoring.

Round eleven saw Haugen get off first with his jab, and score with a left hook to the body. As many times as Greg stepped into land body shots, Paul never figured out how to make him pay for this tactic. Haugen landed two more punches to the body- a left hook, followed by a right hook-and Paul offered nothing of substance back. Greg then slipped another jab and landed one of the harder right hands to the body out of the last few attempts. Paul then missed with another jab, and Greg countered with a double jab to the champion's face and followed up that work with a left hook to the body. Paul then flicked two half-hearted jabs in Haugen's direction.

Greg's title winning effort against Jimmy Paul was an epic battle of skill & attrition. Greg has always been perceived as a pugilist who likes to work from distance. Here he shows he is the Boss on the inside against Jimmy Paul. (Courtesy of Greg Haugen).

Haugen tried to counter with an overhand right, but the punch missed its mark. The overreach put Greg in an awkward position that caused Greg to slip. Throughout Greg Haugen's career, balance was virtually never an issue; this was one of the few times Greg's balance was compromised inside the squared circle. Davey Pearl wiped Haugen's gloves off, and the two pugilists went back to work.

Seeing his opponent on the floor must have triggered something in Paul because he teed off with a thunderous left-hook, but Haugen ducked the blow. Haugen continued to do the majority of the scoring, as he scored with short little body shots on the inside. Haugen's confidence must have been building because he tried to throw a lead left-look when the fighters were back at distance. But Jimmy Paul showed he can slip a telegraphed punch as well. Haugen decided to go back to the basics and scored with a left hook to the body the next time Paul missed with his jab. At the one minute and thirty second mark, both fighters missed with jabs at the center of the ring. Both men were letting their hands go more, with Greg doing most of the scoring. A nice one-two found its mark for Greg, the showiest punches of the sequence. For the rest of round eleven, Jimmy Paul dug down and threw more power punches, most of these punches missed. The only scoring was being done by the huge underdog. Yet, another round that appeared to be easy to score was with debate. Ed Levine disagreed with his peers, who both gave Greg the round 10-9. Paul now won three rounds in a row on the Levine card and was still very much in a fight he appeared to be getting outclassed in.

Jimmy Paul went back to his corner and had his desire questioned by Emmanuel Steward. Steward implored Paul to step it up because he now needed a knockout to win the fight.

The tactic from Steward worked, in the sense that Jimmy Paul increased his work rate and intensity exponentially in round twelve. For the first time in the fight, Paul's jab was finding its mark, and the champion's hands never stopped moving, even when the fighters were on the inside. It might have won him the round, but Greg continued his pace as well and scored well to the body throughout the round. A showy one-two landed for Greg at the very end of round twelve. Making it one of the few rounds that were a nightmare to score in this fight. But Jimmy Paul's work with his jab was probably the deciding factor, as all three judges awarded him round twelve.

Greg Haugen never had to continue his night when the bell rang for the twelfth round before this fight. As Haugen sat on his stool, his face was marked, and he was visibly tired, taking deep breaths to maintain stability. Even though it appeared as if he was winning the lion share of the rounds, there was no doubt he was in a fight. It speaks to how tough a nut Jimmy Paul was to crack. In a fifteen-round fight, there is a much larger opportunity for a fighter to come from behind. With three rounds left to go, and with his work rate increasing, Jimmy Paul still had a real chance of retaining his title. Haugen requested some water before Tischler shoved the mouthpiece into Greg's mouth for the thirteenth round.

You could not help but wonder what was going to Greg Haugen's mind when he answered the bell for round thirteen. "You are dead tired, but you know you have to keep going. By the fourteenth round, I was dragging. I was so tired," Greg explained.

Jimmy Paul came out with the same intensity as the previous round. This time he abandoned the jab and opted to wing left hooks at Haugen's head. None of the punches landed for power, but it was clear that Paul was going to be less predictable the rest of the fight. But Haugen was still able to step in and land hard shots to the body. Right hook, whack! Left-hook, whack! Just like that, Haugen took control of the round. Haugen was making Paul miss and was in a position to land something in return, Greg's body shots never failed him in this fight, and there were essential for this telling thirteenth round. Round thirteen was not a going away round for Greg Haugen, however. Save for Greg's bodywork, everything else appeared to be even in this round, resulting in another split round. Both Lurie and Cox favored Paul in round thirteen, while Ed Levine broke his streak of giving four consecutive rounds for Paul, scoring it 10-9 for Haugen.

Going into round fourteen, Art Lurie had Greg Haugen ahead 124-123, Robert Cox had the fight even 124-124, and Ed Levine's score read 125-122 in favor of the challenger. The fight was still in the balance, and a solid six minutes could have been enough for Jimmy Paul to successfully defend his title, even though head trainer Emanuel Steward all but gave up on his fighter.

Round fourteen was fought at a feverish pitch, as both men never stopped trying to sling leather at one another. Boxing is a great sport to debate, and everyone thinks they are the ultimate connoisseur when it comes to the sweet science. And while the curriculum of boxing has gone through many transitions-not just from the bare, knuckle era to the Queensbury Rules, the basic concept of boxing has never changed in the sense that the success of a boxer begins and ends with how well they can punch their opponent in the face. Or the body. The effort put out by both Greg Haugen and Jimmy Paul in the fourteenth to accomplish this simple act of carnage should not be taken for granted. The level you must be on to do what they did in the fourteenth round is not easily achieved. Only a small percentage of human beings have ever gotten there. Regardless of who you felt won this round.

With that said, I think Jimmy Paul won the round. He began to mix up his punches better, and Greg's bodywork was not as abundant. Paul even did some good work to the body himself. Paul responded well to the urgency that was presented in his corner. It was clear he had the desire to retain his championship. But Ed Levine was the only judge whose score was in keeping with that belief, as both Art Lurie and Robert Cox scored round fourteen for Greg.

Stan Tischler must have also scored round fourteen for Jimmy Paul because he told Greg he needed the last round to secure the victory. The Kronk corner, with a now silent Steward, also felt the fight could be won with a big fifteenth round, but preferred Paul ended the fight before the voice of the judges were heard. Up until this point, this fight produced more than most people expected. The official scores now read 134-132, 134-133, and 134-132, all for the challenger. These scorecards meant that even if Jimmy Paul won all three scorecards 10-9, he would lose a majority decision. Paul did need a colossal round to win. Greg did not, but with scorecards this close, against a Kronk champion, it is hard to fault Stan Tischler with urging Greg on for his own big round.

Round fifteen was boxing at its highest level. Both fighters stood in the pocket and never stopped throwing. Both fighters made their opponent miss a large quantity of punches, but also scored well. Again, Greg Haugen's bodywork was probably enough to win the round, but Paul did all he could to claim the round as well. But if you are going to be brutally honest, there was not enough of these rounds for Jimmy Paul to claim victory.

When the bell rang to end the fight, both fighters embraced. Haugen did not just raise his arms in victory but also took the arm of the champion to raise with pride. As both fighters awaited the decision, Greg looked confident, while Jimmy presented as if he had doubts. Paul looked for assurance from his corner, but he received little of it when his team was cutting off his gloves.

While waiting for the decision to be read, Greg Haugen sought out his opponent and raised his arm in the air for a second time, "It was just good sportsmanship. For one, I was happy I just went fifteen rounds. I knew in my heart I won the fight. I just beat the best lightweight there is, and I was pretty happy about it," Greg explained of his actions. "Jimmy was a master of his craft," Greg added.

The legendary Chuck Hall began to render the decision. He started by reading the score of one-hundred forty three for Greg Haugen, followed by Hall saying, "one-hundred forty...check that..." the crowd groaned as Hall stopped reading the scorecards mid-sentence, Haugen paced in agony. "The longer it takes for the judges, it is usually not a good thing. I was as nervous as hell. I knew I did enough to win the fight, but I have seen so many bad decisions, and shit happens in Vegas, you do not take anything for granted until you hear your name called. Some of the worst calls in the world have been done in Vegas because you have these idiots that they let score a fight, and most of them don't know a fucking jab from a straight right, who knows how they are scoring a fight. It tends to make me nervous, especially in Vegas," Greg explained. Hall's misstep was followed by a long pause. Boxing is never short on theatrics, but this was not the kind of drama anyone would embrace.

The delay was caused because Hall had to go back to the scorer's table for some kind of clarification. "I think he went over to make sure he was reading the score right, that was my impression, I just know it was taking a very long time," Greg said. Once again, Hall began to read the scorecards, the first score read for all even at 143 apiece. The crowd groaned in disapproval. The second scorecard read as 143-142, but Hall did not offer what fighter the winning score belonged to. If you have been watching boxing for a long time, you now know somebody has won a majority decision. But who? With scorecards this close, anything is possible. Chuck Hall's read the final scorecard of 144-141. Now with a wider scorecard, reality suggests that Greg Haugen is the only name that could be read, as I do not think anyone could claim Jimmy Paul won this fight by more than one round, while it is perfectly reasonable to think Haugen bested Paul by three rounds since he did build up a big lead. As if the fight did not produce enough drama, here we have one of the most gut-wrenching reading of the scorecards ever for a boxing match.

Indeed, reality trumped science fiction as Hall said those magic words every boxer yearns to hear, "And new...." The Showtime Network aired the fight and showed both, Paul and Haugen, on a split-screen during the decision. When it was clear who the winner was, the reaction of the fighters produced television magic. The jubilant Haugen and the indifferent, if not shocked, Paul, captured forever for the world to see. From start to finish, this fight produced the kind of high-stakes theater only combat sports can render. And to take nothing away from fighters today, there will never be anything like a fifteen-round boxing match. Ever. It is unfortunate all the great boxers from the 90s and beyond never got the chance to be a part of this unique dynamic.

Greg Haugen was now the lightweight champion of the world. He accomplished this feat by beating arguably the best 135-pound champion at the time, and throughout fifteen grueling rounds. It anyone wants to talk about lineage over substance, well, welcome to the world of foolery. The world belonged to Greg Haugen and was a legitimate world champion.

The mix up on the scorecards was not clarified, but the judges did disagree about the final round. Art Lurie scored round fifteen for Paul, but Haugen had the edge on the final score, 143-142. Robert Cox also scored the final round for the champion, making his final score level at 143-143. Ed Levine once again went against his peers and scored the last round for Greg Haugen, giving him a score of 144-141 over the champion, securing the majority decision win.

"It was the highlight of my career," Greg said.

During the post-fight interview, Tim Ryan asked Greg about his tough man fights, alluding to the fact that these contests were the primary source of skill-building for Haugen's career at this point. Haugen was kind and answered Ryan's question by stating that fighting the much larger men of the tough man contests certainly was a plus. But why no mention of Haugen's amateur experience, or his impressive run that earned him this title shot? Time after time, Greg was matched with someone who supposedly had more experience, and time after time, Greg outclassed these fighters. Yet, not one mention of these facts throughout the telecast.

Indeed, Greg Haugen was a world champion. He was finally being noticed and taken seriously. But just as evident was that he was still being misinterpreted.

"I think they thought that is where I got my start. Most people didn't realize I had been fighting since I was five years old, I had over three-hundred amateur fights. That is why I was able to beat all those guys in the tough man fights," Greg said.

Jimmy Paul's post-fight comments were in keeping with his story. He explained to Tim Ryan that he just felt so tired.

To understand Jimmy Paul's version of what happened in this fight, you first have to understand the mindset of Jimmy Paul. Jimmy is a guy who never felt he belonged. He thought he did not belong to the Kronk Gym, and he was not close to Emmanuel Steward. For Jimmy, Emmanuel was not this statue of virtue, but the guy who could not deliver on his promise of getting him the big fight. Instead, Emmanuel was the guy who kept getting him fights against fierce competition on short notice. Leeonzer Barber also explains he did not have the best relationship with Steward, "My issue with Emmanuel was that he was just too bogged down to be with me. I didn't know he had gyms in Arizona and overseas. And by the time I was fighting in world title fights, Emmanuel was sort of a hired hand for big-name fighters, and Emanuel didn't show up for my fights. The only thing I wanted was to stay active and get the most out of my years. Make that money, unify the title. I did not get all that I wanted to get. And Tommy Hearns was the focal point. He was the big moneymaker, and a lot of guys probably felt pushed aside. I did," Leeonzer said.

Jimmy Paul also felt that the boxing world thought of him as being in the way. That is why the Hector Camacho's and Livingstone Bramble's never fought him. Once you can understand and appreciate Jimmy's mindset, well, then you can look at his story through a critical lens.

What else is Jimmy Paul going to think when an array of odd circumstances rears its head before and after this fight? It was not just the bizarre doctor replacement or the sudden removal of Jimmy's right-hand man. Jimmy also explains that before the fight, his father and brother overheard two gentlemen in an elevator say, "We got to take this title from Jimmy Paul. Now, these men did not know that was my father and my brother, but why were they saying that? What does that mean, take the title from Jimmy Paul?" Jimmy said. Then the fight starts, and Jimmy feels fatigued when he should not be feeling this way, and then there is a debate about which water bottle to use.

It is after the fight where Jimmy really gets suspicious. He talks about his odd encounter with Emmanuel Steward right after the fight, "Emmanuel was looking everywhere except at me, looking at the walls. Normally he would look right at you and be like, 'motherfucker you didn't fight, it is just that simple,' he would say it like that, he would whack you. I didn't get whacked that night. Why?" Jimmy asked.

Perhaps the biggest thing that bothered Jimmy is a bit misconstrued. Jimmy Paul still believes that Emmanuel Steward should not have been anywhere near Greg Haugen's wedding "Emmanuel Steward was at Greg's wedding the next day. What is that? I am still being asked about that," Jimmy explains. Actually, it was two days after the fight, and Emmanuel was not invited to the wedding, according to Greg, "I fought on December the 5th and got married on the 7th at Caesars Palace. Pearl Harbor Day, that should have been a sign right there not to get married. Emmanuel Steward and Duane Thomas showed up at my suite and told me they had no idea who I was. Jimmy did not have to fight a mandatory, so he could have defended the title against anyone ranked. Emmanuel said they watched taped of me and thought I was just a slow white guy, so they said they would take that fight, not having any idea of who I really was," Greg explained.

Leeonzer Barber, a true insider of Kronk, as well as the character of Emmanuel Steward, indicates that Jimmy Paul's claim is unlikely because Steward was by Jimmy Paul's side during his fights, "If Emmanuel worked the corner, he wanted you to win. He was all in with you. He did not want to be associated with losers. Emmanuel Steward would take pots and pans overseas with him because he didn't like to go to restaurants or eat hotel food overseas. He would cook for us. That is how paranoid he was. If he was fixing for Jimmy to lose, he would have just not shown up," Barber detailed.

Leeonzer also presents evidence that suggests Jimmy Paul might have scrimped on his training regimen for Haugen, "My coach, Lou Deberges mentioned to me that Jimmy had trouble making weight for that fight. He was not on weight a couple of days before the fight. Jimmy was in the hotel room bathroom, with towels at the bottom of the doors to block all the crevices of the bathroom. They had the bathroom steamed up, trying to get that weight off for that fight. Wrapped up in towels thirty to forty minutes at a time. That is suffering," Leeonzer explained. "You take him (Greg) serious, you probably have no weight issues. If you think you are going to take a guy easy, you are not going to run as long, you are not going to train as hard," Leeonzer added.

If you peel the onion, a failure to make weight does not necessarily mean a fighter was lax in training camp. Leeonzer Barber also indicates that Paul was outgrowing the 135-pound lightweight limit for some time, "The weight was killing Jimmy, I felt he should have gone up to 140," Leeonzer said.

However, taking drastic measures to make weight can be a valid reason for Jimmy's sluggish body in the fight. A much more reasonable explanation than a diabolical plan to take Jimmy Paul out of the championship picture. However, in boxing, you cannot rule out the latter, however absurd as it may sound.

Leeonzer stresses that Jimmy's issues with weight before this fight is probably a product of taking Greg light, even though he stated that Jimmy would have been best served to move up.

Jimmy Paul suspects Emmanuel Steward might have cashed in on the long odds against Haugen, or at least someone did that had inside influence. "At one point (before the fight) I was lying in my bed and said, 'If I take 250,000 dollars and bet against myself I would make a million dollars, I could then go back and win my title…if I was saying this to myself, what would others think," Jimmy explained

Jimmy Paul confessed he never confronted Emmanuel about his suspicions, "I wanted to, but I never did," Jimmy said. I also asked why Jimmy has not made his suspicions, as well as the odd circumstances connected to this fight, public, he explained, "The average person is going to think this is an excuse you come up with for losing. So how do you talk about it? I am giving you the story that I believe."

Leeonzer Barber's reaction to Jimmy's story supports Jimmy's excuses theory. "I am sure Dr. Lorenz not being there would bother you if you lost, now if he won, that shit wouldn't have bothered him. But when you come up short, those little inconsistencies tend to wear on you," Leeonzer Barber said. "But I had issues making weight too, if you left a lot on the scale, when the fight gets deep, you are basically just a walking ragdoll," Leeonzer added.

Most fighters have what people call excuses when they lose, the window was left open in my hotel room, and I got sick from the draft, I did not have a good camp, I had marital problems…the list is long. What is different about Jimmy's story is he is putting his loss on outside influences with a vested interest in him losing, and suspects that the man who was supposed to be taking the best care of him might have had a hand in it, or, at the very least, was well aware of it. A bombshell, even for boxing's standards.

I present you with Jimmy's story, so you can make your own conclusion. It is not to disparage Emmanuel Steward, who was no doubt a great trainer, but he was not without flaws. He did not do a good job in the corner that night and we should be able to point it out. Is it likely that Emmanuel conspired to get Jimmy beat? Jimmy Paul definitely thinks so. His voice has a right to be heard, and Emmanuel showing up to Greg's wedding is not a good look.

One thing that should not change, however, is the fact that Greg Haugen fought a great fight, and his effort should not be taken away from him. One of the best performances in lightweight history. One thing that Jimmy Paul still gets wrong to this day is his analysis of Greg as a boxer, "All of the fighters I fought for the title before were better than Greg Haugen," Jimmy claims. He is wrong about that.

When Greg Haugen upset Jimmy Paul, the boxing world noticed and acknowledged.

Livingstone Bramble: "Major upset! I was very surprised. Greg beat him, and he beat him handily."

Joe Belinc: "He wasn't scared to go fight this guy, he wasn't like 'I can't beat Jimmy Paul,' he was like, 'I am going to kick his ass,' and he believes it."

Bill McDonald: "I knew Jimmy Paul wasn't going to knock Greg out, but I figured he would win a decision. I thought Jimmy had too much depth, too much experience. But once again, Greg proved everyone wrong. He is a Cinderella story."

Freddie Roach: "Jimmy Paul was a great champion. Nobody thought Haugen could beat Jimmy Paul. He fought a great fight."

Chris Calvin: "It is always good to see someone who beat you go on and win the championship."

There is no boxing scribe no more eloquent with their use of vocabulary than that of Lee Groves. Lee's summation of this fight was perfect, "In the Jimmy Paul fight, Greg was first, last and always."

While the boxing world was speculating and/or celebrating Haugen's victory, the loss for Jimmy Paul hurt even more than Greg's ripping body shots, "After the fight, I just felt so bad, I felt cheated by boxing. Losing the title was like breaking my heart," Jimmy said. Based on the fact that Jimmy could never fight his way back into contention speaks volumes. He was never able to put the pieces back together. Not only did he lose to Greg, but he felt beaten by boxing, betrayed by those who were supposed to have his best interest. Whether you believe Jimmy or not, there is no doubt that he really felt that way. Sometimes perception is so strong it takes over and becomes a reality.

The reality for Greg Haugen was that he was now champion and had to now defend the title he fought so long and hard to get.

Greg Haugen's upset over Jimmy Paul has enough nuggets attached to it to make up a book all on its own. First, the fight itself was spectacular. Boxing on its highest level. The contrast in corners is also a fascinating study. Stan Tischler did a masterful job as Greg's head trainer. He changed his rhetoric when he felt it was necessary and did a great job as Greg's cut man. Emmanuel Steward's work as Jimmy Paul's head trainer was a stark contrast. He failed to give his fighter confidence and offered little salient instructions to his fighter. Paul's last surge in the fight was in no way a reflection of Emmanuel Steward's skills as a confidence builder, which is not in keeping with the Hall of Fame trainer's career. In fact, it appeared that Paul performed better when the Kronk Legend went mute. Bizarre.

What was just as bizarre was the scoring of this fight. Ed Levine had the most significant gap in favor of Greg Haugen but was the only judge to score four straight rounds for the champion. All three judges agreed on seven of the fifteen rounds, 1,4,6,7,9,10, and 12. Yet, the judges were not in agreement in any of the last three rounds. Greg Haugen won on two of the three judges' scorecards, but only managed a sweep on four rounds in the fight.

Overall, it appeared that the judges missed the mark of Greg Haugen's dominance. A unanimous decision should have been rendered. While Compubox did not officially count the fight live, prominent punch counter Lee Groves counted the fight years later, similar to what he did in the book produced by Lee Groves and Bob Canobio, the founder of Compubox, Muhammad Ali: By the Numbers. The stats are in keeping with the round by round breakdown provided here. The finals stats saw Greg Haugen with a significant advantage in overall punches landed, jabs landed, and non-jabs landed, which are officially called power punches. Jimmy Paul only had an edge in punches landed in three rounds. While stats do not always reflect the winner of the fight, studies have shown Compubox numbers is a better than average measure of being in keeping with the perceived winner of the boxing match.

GREG HAUGEN MD 15 JIMMY PAUL
12/05/86 - LAS VEGAS

Total Punches Landed / Thrown

	1	2	3	4	5	6	7	8	9	10	11	12	13	14	15
HAUGEN	14/36	14/45	25/53	24/55	25/52	28/55	24/51	34/69	21/53	13/44	26/55	13/49	26/57	34/73	27/72
	38.9%	31.1%	47.2%	43.6%	48.1%	50.9%	47.1%		49.3%	39.6%	29.5%	47.3%	26.5%		37.5%
													45.6%	46.6%	
PAUL	13/80	12/71	11/75	14/76	18/76	16/10 0	11/75	15/74	13/81	16/70	17/61	21/79	28/10 4	25/88	21/88
	16.3%	16.9%	14.7%	18.4%	23.7%	15%	14.7%	20.3%	16%	22.9%	27.9%	26.6%	26.9%	28.4%	23.9%

Jab Landed / Thrown

	1	2	3	4	5	6	7	8	9	10	11	12	13	14	15
HAUGEN	9/26	7/31	8/21	8/28	5/16	9/23	7/19	10/29	6/28	3/26	5/20	2/25	10/27	8/27	2/19
	34.6%	22.6%	38.1%	28.6%	31.3%	39.1%	36.8%	34.5%	21.4%	11.5%	25%	8%	37%	29.6%	10.5%
PAUL	7/69	5/55	3/48	4/46	5/34	5/59	5/52	5/49	6/57	7/46	1/20	3/32	5/39	7/38	2/26
	10.1%	9.1%	6.3%	8.7%	14.7%	8.5%	9.6%	10.2%	10.5%	15.2%	5%	9.4%	12.8%	18.4%	7.7%

Power Punches Landed / Thrown

	1	2	3	4	5	6	7	8	9	10	11	12	13	14	15
HAUGEN	5/10	7/14	17/32	16/27	20/36	19/32	17/32	24/40	15/25	10/18	21/35	11/24	16/30	26/46	25/53
	50%	50%	53.1%	59.3%	55.6%	59.4%	53.1%	60%	60%	55.6%	60%	45.8%	53.3%	56.5%	47.2%
PAUL	6/11	7/16	8/27	10/30	13/42	10/41	6/23	10/25	7/24	9/24	16/41	19/47	23/65	18/50	19/62
	54.5%	43.8%	29.6%	33.3%	31%	24.4%	26.1%	40%	29.2%	37.5%	39%	38.3%	35.4%	36%	30.6%

Final Punch Stat Report

	Total Punches (Body Landed)	Total Jabs (Body Landed)	Power Punches (Body Landed)
HAUGEN	348 (235)/819	99 (24)/365	249 (211)/454
	42.5%	27.1%	54.8%
PAUL	250 (108)/1198	70 (3)/670	180 (105)/528
	20.9%	10.4%	34.1%

Note

Fighting as a 4-to-1 underdog challenger in his adopted hometown of Las Vegas, Haugen fought the fight of his life and scored a majority decision victory over Jimmy Paul to win the IBF lightweight title. Paul fought hard to retain his title (he averaged 79.9 punches per round to Haugen's 54.6) but he appeared stale for the first two-thirds of the fight, a combination of making weight but also

Haugen's tremendous sharpness (he led 42%-21% overall, 27%-10% jabs, 55%-34% power) and excellent body attack (235 of 348 overall connects, 67.5% of total). Haugen averaged 54.6 punches per round and out-jabbed the taller Paul (24.3 attempts/8.6 connects per round to Paul's 44.7/4.7), whose jabs often fell short of the mark. Haugen's in-and-out movement and depth perception was particularly outstanding. Haugen led 348-250 overall, 99-70 jabs and 249-180 power and prevailed 12-3 in the CompuBox round-by-round breakdown of overall connects, indicating the majority decision probably should have been unanimous. Scoring: 144-141, 143-142 H, 143-143.

Chapter Twelve
Fighting Paz
Facing the Devil In His Den

"The plan was always to have Vinny and Greg fight"

—Kathy Duva

It was 1987, and Greg Haugen was a world champion. 1987 was also the year where some of the luster was coming off the decade of excess. Ronald Reagan underwent prostate surgery in January, indeed a scare. The Gipper's surgery was a success; however, the conclusion of the Iran-Contra affair was not as favorable for the President, who was losing his popularity. The stock market crash in October of 1987 was an eerie symbol of just what grabbing with both hands could get you. Or was it? The man who spouted 'morning in America,' could not say the word AIDS, also took a hit in the courts, as his heinous Supreme Court nominee, Robert Bork, was voted down in the Senate. In that same year, we saw the first National Coming Out Day. Proud gay and lesbian individuals marched on Washington for their rights. A good year for progressives, not so much for conservatives and yuppies.

In movies, the film Wall Street annunciated the aspect and repercussions of greed. When Michael Douglas was not greedy he was unfaithful in the smash Fatal Attraction, Cher took on an Italian accent and won an Oscar; those years with Sonny paid off, Robert DeNiro became Al Capone, Jack Nicholson tortured three sexy witches; good luck getting that movie made now, and Arnold Schwarzenegger screamed at the top of his lungs while battling a Predator.

In television, Gene Roddenberry gave us Star Trek: The Generation. Captain Jean-Luc Picard was a revealing contrast to the womaninzing, cowboy-like, Captain James T. Kirk. A timeless classic, The Next Generation was ahead of its time, taking on subject matter such as the heinous nature of enslaving animals for food, and how the size of a personal portfolio is meaningless to the Prime Directive.

In music, the luster of excess was dissipating in music as well in 1987. Prince was playing more socially conscious music. Michael Jackson had a Bad follow up to his classic Thriller album, begging people to leave him alone. Bruce Springsteen told the world he had marital problems. Pink Floyd scrapped their legal battle with Roger Waters and had A Momentary Lapse of Reason. And U2, a politically conscious band, who for years fought for the release of Nelson Mandela, had a breakout year with their classic album The Joshua Tree.

The sports world saw the New York Football Giants finish off their great year with a Superbowl win in January. However, the NFL took a big hit later that year when the season was interrupted by a work stoppage. The NFL, in a sad disgrace, made matters even worse when they had replacement players replace the players who were negotiating for a fair collective bargaining deal. To add insult to injury, many NFL players crossed the picket line to play with the 'scabs.' Major League Baseball enjoyed a much better campaign as their season ended with a stellar seven-game World Series. The Minnesota Twins bested the St. Louis Cardinals in a series where home-field advantage was the difference in every game. Indeed, Cardinals manager Whitey Herzog should have sought out Greg Haugen for some road warrior advice. In the NHL, the Edmonton Oilers continued their dominance with a convincing win over the Philadelphia Flyers for Lords Stanley Cup. And once again, the NBA saw the powerhouse teams of the Los Angeles Lakers and the Boston Celtics duke it out for the championship. Magic Johnson was just too clutch for Larry's Celtics this time around.

The world of boxing saw an interesting, if not a peculiar year in 1987. The headline fight being Ray Leonard's 'upset' over Marvelous Marvin Hagler. A con job for sure. Indeed, while more competitive than perhaps many people thought, this fight is the robbery of the century. Greg Haugen said of this fight, "Hagler got flat out robbed. He didn't lose that fight, it is a joke to say Leonard won." Thomas Hearns, another Ray Leonard rival, had a good 1987, as he captured a world title in a third division when he dismantled light heavyweight champion Dennis Andries on national television. Hearns topped this feat by also adding the middleweight title to his collection when he knocked out Juan Roldan for the middleweight title, his fourth division title.

However, no boxer was more on display, or under the microscope, as Mike Tyson was in 1987. Tyson first captured the WBA heavyweight title by beating James Bonecrusher Smith in a twelve-round decision. Unfortunately, the only bones that were being crushed in this fight were the heads of people when they hit the pillow, as this was one of the dullest matches of all time. Smith won the title from Tim Witherspoon, in a fight where Spoon told me personally that he threw the fight on purpose because he did not want to fight Mike Tyson for the minuscule purse that Don King was offering, "I am not fighting no Mike Tyson for no five-hundred thousand dollars," Witherspoon explained. Tyson followed up this performance with a stellar knockout of Pinklon Thomas. Thomas was upset by Trevor Berbick in 1986, but many still considered him as the best chance to give Mike Tyson a fight. They were right for a few rounds, as Thomas controlled the pace with his piston-like jab until he didn't. It was the Tyson jab that made the difference in his next fight against Tony Tucker. Tyson controlled Tucker with his jab, a man who stood six foot five, with an eighty-two-inch reach, to capture the IBF version of the heavyweight title. Iron Mike was now the undisputed king of boxing. He finished out his 1987 by giving 1984 Olympian Tyrell Biggs a brutal beating. Looking at what Tyson did in 1987 is remarkable and will never be seen again. The idea of a fighter as big as Mike fighting four times in one year has gone the way of the eight-track tape.

Even with Mike Tyson's banner year, 1987 needed a jolt for boxing, as the established stars were just not getting it done. Aaron Pryor lost in his only fight. Hector Camacho only fought once. Macho won a forgettable fight against Howard Davis Jr. Both Ray Mancini and Larry Holmes was gone. Michael Spinks only fought once. Indeed, boxing needed an adrenaline shot, and Greg Haugen and Vinny Paz were prepared to provide it.

In boxing history, fighters who have won the title in big upsets then had to face the ultimate challenge in their first defense. After upsetting Max Baer, James Braddock had to defend his title against Joe Louis. Evander Holyfield was first up for James Buster Douglas after Buster shook up the world by beating Mike Tyson. After Lloyd Honeyghan upset Donald Curry, he had to defend his title against the accomplished Johnny Bumphus. While Vito Antuofermo's upset win over Hugo Corro was not on the same scale as the upsets mentioned above, nobody had a tougher first title defense than Vito, as he had to face Marvelous Marvin Hagler. Marvin was the number one ranked middleweight for a long time but was avoided by Corro, as well as Rodrigo Valdez, the man Corro dethroned for the title.

At the same time, there is also a narrative that shows fighters who faced what could be considered a soft touch for their first title defense. Floyd Patterson met the very underwhelming Tommy Jackson. George Foreman faced the barely recognizable Jose Roman. When Muhammad Ali upset Foreman, he first defended against Chuck Wepner, who was a 40-1 underdog. Larry Holmes met Alfredo Evangelista for his first title defense, a fighter many boxing scribes described as a human punching bag. After signing a multi-fight contract with HBO, Riddick Bowe chose Michael Dokes as his first title defense. Dokes was a shell of the fighter he was at the time, and his body was deprecated by substance abuse; who could forget the image of Dokes nursing a beer at Madison Square Garden during a Knicks game the week of the fight?

After Edwin Rosario controversially won his lightweight title fashion against Jose Luis Ramirez, he was given the softball toss of Robert Elizondo to hit out of the park for his first defense. Ray Leonard's first defense was against Davey 'Boy' Green, who at his best was a second-tier guy, and had seen his better days. Both Roberto Duran and Carlos Monzon fought three over the limit non-title bouts (albeit Duran was upset by Esteban DeJesus in one of these fights) before defending their title against soft touches Jimmy Robertson and Nino Benvenuti respectively. Now, some people may take issue with calling the Hall of Famer Benvenuti a soft touch. However, if you examine this fight through a critical lens, and take into account that Monzon overwhelmed Nino when he won the title from him and that Nino only fought once after losing to Carlos, a loss to Jose Roberto Chirino, getting knocked down twice in the process, the only way you can view Nino is as a soft touch at the time of this title defense.

For Greg Haugen, he would fall under the umbrella of an unprotected pugilist, as he had a very tough first title defense against Vinny Paz, The Pazmanian Devil. Vinny explains how that unique nickname came to be, "My mother used to tape everything on VHS tapes with me. I went home one day, and my mother says, 'Oh Vinny, there is so much nice stuff on you. Wait 'til you see. I taped everything. But Vinny, there is one thing, your friend Mike Rotay, why did he say your name wrong?' Mike was a newscaster and a friend of mine. I was like, 'Ma, what are you talking about Mike knows how to say my name? So, she goes let me show you,' and Mike says, 'Vinny Paz, the Pazmanian Devil' so I said, 'Oh my god, that is unbelievable' I didn't even have a pro fight yet. It stuck like glue, and it does until this day. The Pazmanian Devil still lives."

Vinny was named Vinny Pazienza back then, but he made an official name change, "I have been Vinny Paz since 1999. I did like a Muhammad Ali, Cassius Clay because he was my guy." Much like Greg Haugen, Paz was very fond of the young pugilist from Kentucky, "When I was five years old, and I fell in love with this guy Muhammad Ali, and that was it. My dad took me to the local boxing gym, and I never turned back since I was five years old." So, Greg and Vinny also have the fact that they began boxing at a very tender age in common.

Going into the fight with Greg, Paz was 22-1, with 17 KO's. Paz defeated fighters such as Jeff Bumpus, "Jeff could fight, he was a tough little white boy. I tried to get him out of there so bad, but he would not go down," Paz said of the Tazmanian Devil, not to be confused with Vinny's Pazmanian Devil nickname.

Paz also bested Melvin Paul, Joe Frazier Jr., Nelson Bolanos, Roberto Elizondo, and former world champion Harry Arroyo, "Harry was tough, a former world champion. That was one of my first big wins," Vinny explained. Most of Vinny's fights took place in either the friendly confides of Atlantic City or his home state of Rhode Island. The Civic Center in Providence was dubbed the Devil's Den when Paz fought there. The maniacal crowd supported Vinny with such great passion, it can be argued that the Civic Center was the most excellent sixth man boxing had ever seen in the United States.

When Vinny fought Bolanos, the bout was featured as a WBA lightweight title eliminator. Vinny talked about the importance of this fight, "I was really psyched to fight Balonos, he had a great record, 31-0-3. I was in shape, ready to go, and I gave him an ass whipping," Paz explains. However, a WBA title fight did not happen. Vinny explains, "I was ready to fight, I think Edwin Rosario was the champion at the time, but something happened...so then they got me the IBF fight against that little douche bag called Greg Haugen, I think his name is."

Kathy Duva, Hall of Fame Main Events Promoter, who was the Main Events publicist at the time, explains how Vinny was a big part of their plans from the get-go, "Vinny was signed at Main Events as soon as he turned pro," Kathy said. Kathy explains that Main Events was also interested in Greg Haugen, "Early in his career, he (Greg) was on all of those ESPN shows and we were becoming aware of him, we became very interested because he was in the same weight class as Vinny," Kathy explained.

What was not to be interested in? Two white fighters with intriguing personalities and serious boxing skills. A promoter's dream. "The plan was always to have Vinny and Greg fight," Kathy explained. But Greg had to win that fight with Jimmy Paul to have that happen," Kathy added.

Once Greg pulled off the upset, there was no stopping the inevitable. "You knew the styles and personalities meshed together. It was meant to be," Kathy Duva said.

Greg Haugen explains that there were other fights discussed before they settled on Paz, "We talked about a couple of different fights. Bob Arum wanted me to fight Cubanito Perez, but he was kind of a friend of mine, we trained a lot, sparred a lot, I really wasn't into fighting Cubanito. I wanted a little better fight than that," Greg explained.

When it was settled on Vinny, Greg said that he knew who Vinny was, but he did not see him much, "I really didn't watch much tape on Vinny. Personally, I thought I would knock Vinny out. I didn't think he could handle my pressure, but he withstood a lot," Greg said.

A war of words was exchanged between Greg and Vinny that indeed spiced up an already dream fight to promote. "The thing I remember the most was the pre-fight banter. Vinny is a tough guy; Greg is a tough guy. Tough knows tough," Lee Groves remembers. Greg Haugen felt he was so tough, he promised Paz he would rip off his pizza face. Proving Greg's mettle once again of being a class A trash talker. Vinny Paz was not Joe Frazier to Haugen's Ali, however, and he did his share of verbalizing, in an attempt to get under Greg's skin. Paz knew what buttons to hit as well, referring to

Greg as an ESPN club fighter. Paz was also brilliant at using props. At one press conference, Paz whipped out a doll that had a shirt which read IBF Chump, Paz took this doll and doused it with ketchup, promising that is what Haugen's face would look like. But Greg gave it back to Vinny just as good. Perhaps the best example of Haugen's wit appeared in the March 1987 issue of KO magazine, when he responded to Paz' drawing power in Providence, by stating, 'Big deal. You can get 10,000 people out there to watch the tide come in."

Dave Murphy also remembers that trainer Lou Duva had a significant stake in the pre-fight trash talk, "Most of the bad blood going into the first fight was Lou Duva agitating Haugen," Dave remembers. The pre-fight coverage on NBC corroborates this dynamic as the cameras capture Greg Haugen walking away from one of the press conferences in a huff after there were words exchanged with Lou. "He was trying to embarrass and insult me, so I wasn't going to have it. I told him to shut up, you pug bulldog looking mother fucker. I had enough and walked out. The press conference was between me and Vinny, it wasn't about me and Lou," Greg explained. "He was telling me he was going to take my belt. I said the only belt you were going to get was the one I am wearing around my waist. I got to Lou during the second fight with Vinny, telling him, 'Come on Lou, tell your fighter how to stop the jab, besides with his face' I would hear Lou tell Vinny, 'You got to stop getting hit with that jab,' but Lou never told him how, 'what do I need to do, besides not get hit by it?' Lou's job was to watch and give instructions, he sees what we don't get to see, he needs to tell you something (constructive) anybody can say 'don't get hit,'" Greg added.

Where the fight took place was also a big part of the story. The Providence Center was the selected venue for Greg Haugen's first title defense. So, not only was Greg matched up tough for his first defense, he had to travel east to fight in arguably the biggest home-field advantage of all time.

The way Kathy Duva explains it, it was the only choice from a business standpoint, "Vinny was drawing big crowds for fights that were not even meaningful, fighting for a world title fight, we knew that would sell out the Providence Civic Center, there was just no way Greg was going to be able to draw that kind of crowd in

Nevada. At that time, fights in Vegas were fought in front of crowds of three thousand people, a big fight like Salvador Sanchez and Wilfredo Gomez had a crowd of about four thousand people. There were no big 20,000 seat arenas in Nevada then. When you did do a big fight in Vegas, it was held in a parking lot arena, it was temporary and only for very, very, very, big fights, like Hagler vs. Hearns. This fight wasn't so big that they were going to build a big parking lot. It was a much bigger fight in Providence, and it had to go there. We broke the record set by Frank Sinatra in Providence," Kathy said.

As a champion, Greg Haugen was a victim of the times, "Today, if you have a fighter from Vegas who was champion and you had some fighter from somewhere else, *that* fighter would be stuck going to Vegas. But that did not happen for a very long time, even in the nineties, they were building arenas for fights like Holyfield vs. Bowe," Kathy Duva explained.

But you cannot help when you are born, and Greg Haugen was never afraid to face the toughest challenges.

The television networks also preferred smaller venues. They seek out that condensed, claustrophobic look of the crowd. Maniacal and salivating for their pound of flesh. Still the best and purest form of reality television. Of course, the Providence Civic Center holds way more than four thousand people. With that said, the fight report from Jay N. Miller of Ring Magazine indicates that the crowd at Providence were slightly below expectations, citing a Celtics playoff game and high-ticket prices as potential reasons for the turnout. In the November 1987 issue of KO magazine, Jeff Ryan fleshes out the attendance issue with more detail in his popular Fight Confidential segment. In that segment, Ryan also cites the high-ticket prices as a reason for the fight underperforming at the gate but stresses the point that the major problem was that the tickets for this fight were drastically higher than Paz's fights against Joe Frazier Jr. and Nelson Bolanos. In those fights, the hard-working base of Providence only had to pay twenty-five dollars and thirty dollars, respectively, for the top ticket, for the Haugen fight the top price rose to one-hundred dollars a ticket. Adjusted for inflation today, one-hundred dollars equates to close to two-hundred twenty-five dollars.

The reason for the significant increase in tickets was not an example of price gouging, but of necessity. As a world champion,

Greg had to get paid a much higher fee than Joe Frazier Jr. and Nelson Bolanos, thus the rise in ticket prices. But as far as the fans of Providence were concerned, Greg Haugen was as faceless and meaningless as Frazier Jr. and Bolanos. This fight was just like all the others, a Vinny Paz showcase that he would no doubt win. They wanted their bargain-basement prices just the same. In fact, in their minds, they must have felt that Greg Haugen should pay them for allowing him to be in the same presence as the Pazmanian Devil for one day.

Having said that, this crowd was much bigger than anything that could have been generated in Las Vegas. And it was a raucous crowd. 9,000 plus people felt like 20,000. A crowd, insatiable for the flesh of only one man. Greg Haugen. That, and the constant shots of Greg's mother and sister watching the action from a bar in Auburn that was filled to the brim with maniacal Haugen fans, waiting to see plasma drip from the 'Dago' on the East Coast, gave NBC the desired effect they always strive for. The fans that invested their time to watch, whether it was live, or on NBC television, were treated to forty-five minutes of ferocious pugilism and bravery that will never be forgotten.

Going into the fight, Vinny Paz had a lot of advantages. He had the crowd, and he had the drawing power. While Greg was on television quite a bit, his fights were on ESPN and Showtime, at the time, these networks were not in as many homes as today. That exposure could not compare to the numbers Paz was generating on NBC, a robust network.

Perhaps the biggest insult to Greg attached to this fight is the fact that only Vinny Paz appeared on the cover of the fight program. "It was Duva's doing. I really didn't worry about it too much. My thinking was on the fight, the fact that they tried to chump me on the program didn't really affect me too much," Greg explained.

Greg Haugen had some of his own advantages. He had the edge in experience; Greg had already been the fifteen-round distance. Also, his quality of opposition was slightly better than Vinny's. And Vinny Paz had some health issues.

Paz broke his nose, postponing the original date of the fight, and Vinny was ill going into the fight, "I was sick that day because I was killing myself to make the weight, I finally made the weight, 135, and then after that I just gorged myself, I was shoving everything down my throat, bananas, chocolate, pancakes, whatever it was I was just glomming it. So, I got sick as a dog, I was vomiting, diarrhea, it was crazy. I had to fight him at four-thirty in the afternoon," Paz said.

Kathy Duva explains, "We recognized that Vinny was very ill. Vinny was dehydrated. When you are dehydrated, you cannot hold food down. I remember after the weigh-in, he could not keep anything down. So, I told my husband (Main Events Promotor Dan Duva) to go to the store and buy Pedialyte. I knew it didn't have any sugar in it because I had little kids. He was able to get his strength back. The fact that he went fifteen rounds is absolutely miraculous."

It was excellent for Main Events that Kathy Duva was such a quick thinker. The way she explains, everything was on the line for Main Events in this fight, "I remember my husband telling me if Vinny lost, we would have to close down the company on Monday. We (Main Events) went from putting on little club fights to putting on Leonard Hearns in '81, Pryor Arguello in 83, we had signed the eighty-four Olympic fighters, but we had done this with investors. So, what money we made was going back to investors. It got to the point that we were way overextended...Holyfield and Whitaker had not reached their championship status. Everything was on the line for this fight," Kathy explained.

The judges that were selected for the fight suggested an even playing field, "They had one judge from Vinny's hometown (Clark Sammartino), they had one from Nevada (Keith MacDonald), and they had a neutral judge from Miami (Ric Bays)" Dave Murphy explained.

Lee Groves refers to Haugen vs. Paz, "An underrated trilogy, a terrific three-fight series." With the first fight serving as the anchor in the series. "The first fight is one of those fights you have to watch really close," Groves added.

Vinny Paz entered to the sound of a raucous Providence crowd, "Other than Stan Tischler and the rest of the corner, I do not think that anyone was rooting for Greg in Providence," Dave Murphy said. "Rhode Island was Guinea territory, nothing but gangsters," Victor Machado added. But Greg debunks that rumor by stating that quite a few Italian-Americans from Providence were on Greg's side, "When I was in Providence, I would be doing my roadwork in the morning, half of the Italian guys, the business owners, would say to me, 'kick his ass,' because they did not like loud-mouth Italian's like Vinny. And the other half was yelling to me, 'you are going down.'" It appeared as if the half that wanted to see Paz prevail were one hundred percent of the Providence Center.

Lee did have one special fan on his side. By the time this fight happened, Lee Haugen, Greg's dad, was once again a frequent flier in Greg's life. But Greg was not keen on how Lee appeared to be a half-hearted father. So, Greg did what he always does, he pulled no punches, "I told him I was tired of him coming in and out of my life, and if he wanted to be in my life he had to make an effort or he was gone, so, he made an effort and was part of my life," Greg explained. With that said, their relationship was not always a box of popcorn, but Greg said it was nice that he was involved. Greg also credits Lee immensely for his boxing career, "If it wasn't for my dad I would have never gotten into boxing."

For the first fight, Paz wore a vibrant red, white and green outfit, the decor of the Italian flag, that emphasized the Pazmanian Devil moniker. Even the spangles on Paz' boxing shoes were bouncing with confidence.

Greg Haugen entered the ring wearing a more traditional, hooded robe that bore the lettering, Greg Haugen IBF Lightweight Champion proudly on his back. ACDC's rock tune, Bad Boy Boogie, Greg's entrance song, was being drowned out by a chorus of boos. The kind of reception a left-wing liberal would receive at an NRA convention. All Greg could do was flash his boyish grin when the boos escalated upon his name being announced by ringside announcer Frank Carpano.

Greg and Vinny stood nose to nose during the prefight instructions from referee Waldemar Schmidt, one of the most epic stare downs in boxing history. All that was left to do was to fight. And fight they did.

Greg Haugen was the aggressor, as well as the more accurate puncher in round one. Paz expanded a lot of energy and flash, but Greg was making him miss. Save for a left jab in the middle of the round, as well as a nice left hook, in the last twenty seconds, Paz landed very few meaningful punches. Greg did well to the body and scored with his jab. A sharp left hand landed by Greg at about the thirty-one second mark of the round. It was the kind of round that was clearly influenced by the pro-Paz crowd. Anything that Vinny did resulted in big roars, while Greg's work was greeted with the sound of crickets. Compubox numbers suggest a close round, with Greg out landing Vinny thirteen punches to eleven. Greg had a crucial edge in power connects, nine to five, which are all punches that are not a jab.

Round two started with Greg trying to establish his jab, he offered feints, both with his jab, as well as a lead right, but Paz was now doing a good job of making the champion miss. At the 1:59 second mark, Paz landed a decent right hand over a Haugen jab. However, Haugen took the second minute of round two by landing the better punches, including a thudding left hook when he had Paz trapped in the corner. The round was still up for grabs in the final minute. Once again, Greg Haugen was the more accurate pugilist with his punches, while Paz was the showier boxer. A round that should not have been that tough to score, but with the crowd roaring at any move by Paz, it is understandable how people can be fooled into scoring it for the Pazmanian Devil. Compubox saw an edge in connects for Paz ten to seven, but the power connects were all even at six apiece.

The first minute of round three saw both men miss with a lot of punches. Paz showcased good lateral movement and fought from a more defensive stance. Vinny also landed the more meaningful shots in this first minute. The second minute of round three saw Paz display his best imitation of Willie Pep and made Greg miss a lot of punches. But Paz's work rate was low during this minute, making it tough to give either fighter the advantage in this second minute of the round. The last minute of round three was a nightmare to score. Paz landed the best punch during this sequence, a nice right uppercut that forced Greg's head upwards and backward. However, for the rest of the minute, Paz did not land with anything of significance, where Greg did do some scoring, but with nothing that authoritative. Overall, I would give Paz round three. Compubox numbers saw Greg edge Vinny twelve connects to eleven, with Greg having an edge in power punches eight to seven.

That uppercut must have provided Paz with more confidence as he started the first minute of round four more aggressively. However, neither fighter did much in this first minute, making the round even up until that point. Haugen took the second minute of round four, as he was the more accurate jabber. The final minute of round four saw Greg Haugen score and counter well. Both fighters did a lot of missing, but it should have been clear to most observers that Greg out landed Vinny in this last minute. Enough to win him the round. Greg Haugen out landed Paz once again, according to Compubox, twelve to eight, but once again, things were all even in the non-jabs department at six apiece.

The first minute of round five saw Greg become more accurate with his jab, while Paz was overreaching with his jab, and virtually every other punch he threw in the first minute. Greg also sprinkled in a good left hook during this stanza. The second minute of this round was more of the same. Greg even landed a good right to the body, where Vinny missed with virtually every punch he threw. Vinny managed to bull Greg into the ropes during the final minutes of this second minute, but Greg covered up well and blocked the Paz leather. In the final minute of this round, the action got back to the center of the ring, where both fighters scored well. But Paz had a slight edge. Here is a round that Greg won two out of the three minutes, more than enough to win the round. But if you listen to the crowd and only remember the final minute of the round, then you can score it for Vinny Paz, a dynamic that occurs in boxing more often than it should. Paz's strong last-minute saw him take the advantage in overall connects fifteen to ten, according to Compubox. Amazingly, power punches were once again all even, this time at eight connects apiece. Haugen is only given credit for landing two jabs in round five, it certainly appeared that he landed more than that.

After five rounds, realistically, Vinny Paz should have only won two rounds, but you could see how he could have been given four of the first five rounds. It would have been wrong to do so, but considering the setting, it is understandable how a judge could be fooled. Also, boxing judges have the absolute worst point of view from where they sit. Former world champion Donny LaLonde recently told me that he put on his judge's hat and was amazed to discover that you can only see about twenty-five percent of the action from where you sit as judge. You can argue that a judge depends on crowd noise for the vantage points that are impeded by their location. Why boxing insists on seating their judges in a position that impedes their vision so, is a big mystery.

Dave Murphy gave Paz the first three rounds. Citing Paz's speed as the main reason for the sweep, "Paz came out strong, and he was fast, which surprised me because they did talk about his diarrhea. I think Greg got off to a slow start," Dave Murphy explained.

Round six was the first round of the fight where we saw a dominant round. And that was from the champion. Greg boxed beautifully. He countered well, and pot shot Paz with a stiff jab and a thudding right hand. "Haugen had a very good sixth round," Dave Murphy concurred. Perhaps the most important aspect of round six was that Greg Haugen drew blood from Paz, smashing open that broken nose that delayed the fight in the first place. Fifteen rounds were cumbersome enough, "It was brutal," Vinny Paz said of training for and fighting fifteen round fights. Now he had to contend with a possible rebroken nose for the last nine rounds of the fight. Compubox numbers do not support a dominant round, however. Paz had the edge in overall connects, fifteen to fourteen, but Greg had the advantage in power punch connects, ten to eight.

After the good Haugen sixth-round, Lou Duva implored Paz to jab his way in, as he was giving the champion too much room. Lou also called for more body work.

Rounds seven through nine should have been clean rounds for the champion. Round eight would have been the only round up for debate in this sequence, as Paz got off to a good start in that round and landed some of his best power punches up until that point. However, the pace and tempo, were controlled by the champion and he was the more accurate puncher. By the end of round nine, Vinny Paz was markedly slower, his legs were going and there was virtually no starch on his punches. With that said, Compubox numbers once again contradicts this assessment. Round seven saw Paz with an advantage in overall connects, as well as power punches, in both cases by one connect. Round eight favored Greg in all three Compubox categories by a close margin. Round nine's statistics suggested more of an edge for Greg, as he had the edge in overall connects twelve to nine, as well as a big advantage in non-jabs, nine to three.

Vinny Paz upped the tempo in round ten. But once again, it was a round that was controlled by the Haugen jab. Paz did more missing, loading up on big shots. The kind of shots that look good despite the fact that they missed their mark. And while Greg dictated the action, he failed to land any showy punches in this round. Round ten and eleven were rounds you can see people getting fooled into scoring it for Paz. Compubox numbers give a small edge for Paz in all three connecting categories, which are total punches landed, total jabs landed, and total power punches landed, in both of these rounds.

Round twelve was the best round for Vinny up until now. He controlled the pace with disciplined aggression and landed the best punches of the round. However, even Vinny Paz knew this round was an anomaly up until now, "I was losing that fight after twelve rounds," Paz said. Copmubox numbers saw Paz out land Greg in overall connects fifteen to thirteen.

The championship rounds of this fight were a television network's dream.

The first minute of round thirteen saw both fighters try to score with their jabs. They both missed. Paz then tried to sprinkle in a wide left hook that Greg slipped and countered with his own short little left hook. Paz back off and circled his way back to the center of the ring and slung his jab at Greg once again. Greg slipped this punch and landed his own stiff jab on Paz's face. Paz came back with a good straight right, left- hand combination. Paz then backed off and circled around the ring, with Greg trying to reach him with his jab. Both fighters met in the center of the ring in the final seconds of this first minute, but neither man could muster up an advantage. The second minute of this round belonged to Haugen. He landed the harder shots and backed Paz into the ropes. Paz did a good job of slipping most of the Haugen attack, but his lack of work cost him the second minute of round thirteen. The final minute of round thirteen secured the round for Greg as he landed stiff jabs and right hands on Paz's face. Vinny's face was now resembling a horror movie, and he seemed totally out of gas when the bell rang to end the round. The decibel level from the raucous Providence Center crowd lowered exponentially during this sequence. According to Compubox, the number of punches thrown and landed rose significantly for Greg; he threw an astonishing ninety-two punches: his highest work rate being fifty-seven punches thrown prior, connecting on twenty-two of those punches, with fifteen of those punches being non-jabs. Conversely, Paz only threw fifty-five punches by Compubox's count, landing a mere eight of those punches. Compubox numbers are not always in keeping with the winner of a round, especially when the numbers are tight, as they have been in this fight; however, the numbers in round thirteen are so in favor of Greg, it is hard to imagine anyone giving Paz this round. Squelching Vinny's assessment that he won the last three rounds.

Round fourteen was boxing at its highest level. Both men had every right to be exhausted, yet they were both unloading punches as if the opening bell just sounded. Greg Haugen, as he was in most of the rounds, was the more accurate and authoritative puncher for most of the round and should have won the round. Compubox numbers disagree with this assessment, crediting Paz with more overall connects, twenty-six to twenty-two, and an edge in power punches, twenty-one to fifteen.

After the fourteenth round, Stan Tischler told Greg that he needed a knockout to win.

Round fifteen was more of the same as both fighters let it all hang out. But to watch this round with the keen eye that Lee Groves says is required, it was a round that should have been scored for Greg Haugen. Vinny threw the flashier punches, but as Greg Haugen said, "Vinny wasn't really hitting me." But a judge would not know that if their view of the fight was impeded and they were influenced by the crowd. In that dynamic, Vinny Paz's assessment of the fight is true, "I only won that fight because it was a fifteen round fight and I won those last three rounds," Paz explained. The Compubox numbers do not support this claim, as Paz is credited with landing only seventeen out of ninety-one punches thrown. Greg was credited with twenty-eight connects out of seventy-eight punches thrown. With twenty-three of those punches being non-jabs.

When the fight ended, the judge's scorecards read 144-141, 144-141 and, 144-142 in favor of Vinny Paz, the new IBF lightweight champion of the world. Greg Haugen's great effort was for not.

Ferdie Pacheco reported that most of the reporters at press row scored the fight for Greg Haugen. Dave Murphy did not see it that way, "I had Vinny by one point." As did Kathy Duva, "It was a great fight. Of course, I thought Vinny won," Kathy said.

However, Kathy Duva acknowledges the weight the crowd at the Providence Civic Center had, "It helps to have the crowd. There is no doubt that the crowd helps judges see a fight," Kathy conceded. "Home field advantage made a big difference. It mitigated all the blood spilled by Paz," Lee Groves added.

Of course, the Greg Haugen people had a major issue with the decision. "It was a robbery. Pat Putnam of Sports Illustrated told me that was one of the worst decisions he has ever seen," Jim Montgomery opined.

Greg Haugen maintains that he was robbed until this day. "It wasn't really a close fight," Haugen demanded.

Dave Murphy points out that these remarks are not in keeping with Greg's feelings right after the bout, "Haugen said that it was a close fight, he (Vinny) fought well. There was no outrage (right after the fight)." I asked Greg about the change of opinion regarding the decision, he stated, "I said that to make him not feel as bad as he should because I just kicked his ass. Even Ferdie Pacheco pointed out that most of the reporters scored the fight for me. And Vinny was their guy."

There are many well-respected boxing people who also felt Greg Haugen's hand should have been raised in victory in Providence:

Bill MacDonald: "I thought Greg won the first fight."

Joe BeLinc: "Greg clearly won."

Craig Houk: I thought it could have went either way, but since Greg was the champion he should have kept his title."

Zac Pomillio: "Going into the fight I didn't see much of Greg, I knew he beat Paul from reading the magazines. But I saw Vinny on NBC a lot. Going into the fight, I was a Vinny Pazienza fan, but when it was over, I was a Greg Haugen fan. I thought Greg won the fight."

Freddie Roach: "Paz is a friend of my family, we fought in a lot of tournaments together, but I thought Haugen won that fight."

Leoonzer Barber: "I thought Haugen outboxed him. That little funny move he did with his feet, where he would like feint the punch, step back, and he would counter your counter. He kept getting Paz with that same shit, he had Paz off balance, walking into shots. As flashy as he (Paz) was, I thought Greg did win that first fight."

Lee Groves: "It is not one of those fight you cannot casually watch. You have to really look closely. You have to know what you are seeing. It is that kind of fight. I do not think it was a dominating performance either way, but I think Greg did enough to win that first fight."

John Chemeres: "I thought Greg won. But it was a close fight. My father thought Greg could have done a lot better, he got hit with too many punches."

Mike Acri: "I thought Haugen won. Let's be honest, he ran, Vinny was a runner, at the lighter weights Paz was more flash than substance."

Vic de Wysocki: I had Haugen winning 10 rounds to 5, and a couple of the rounds for Pazienza were generous. Haugen was calm, cool, and collected (and precise with his punches) throughout the fight. His foot movement was compact and controlled, great head movement too. Pazienza bounced around ring awkwardly, recklessly flailed away with his punches, missing with many of them round after round, or they landed on Haugen's gloves/arms. Pazienza only scored in small flurries when he did land, but too little and too few. Haugen also methodically pressed most of the action while Pazienza danced around off-balance, missing with many of his punches., while often rough-housing Haugen instead.

I was a professional Judge for 3years before I began my current career as a referee and feel many Judges get caught up in the boxer who is flying around the ring constantly throwing punches (like Paz was vs. Haugen). They are basically convinced (or more like fooled) that the busier boxer is winning the rounds. When what they really should be doing is watching closely at how many punches the "busy" boxer is actually landing in each round!!!!

Jeff Ryan, who covered the fight for KO magazine in their October 1987 issue, scored the fight for Haugen by the slim margin of 143-142. Ryan also reported in that magazine that Sports Illustrated, The Philadelphia Daily News, The New York Post, and The New York Times all had Greg Haugen winning the fight. Ryan did indicate he felt the fight was razor close, mainly because Greg did not press in the last four rounds, which is in keeping with Paz's assessment of the fight. It is ironic that the synopsis of the fight, from some accounts, is that Greg made the fight closer than what it should be by playing the role of counter puncher down the stretch, a role that served him so well throughout his career.

KO magazine's 1987 issue published the opinion of the fans in their Between Rounds section of the magazine, a section that was usually about two pages long of mail from fight fans. There was overwhelming support for Greg in this section. One letter read:

152

Robbery!!!!

I am getting increasingly angry at what has become a normal practice in the world of televised boxing. There is a blatant favoritism and outright protectionism of elite boxing "heroes," and it is very bad for the great sport. I recently had the misfortune to watch another one of these horrible injustices.

Greg Haugen clearly beat Vinny Pazienza in their bout for Haugen's IBF lightweight title but was unfairly denied the decision. Haugen didn't have the appeal of the flashy Pazienza, so his title was neatly stolen away by the judges who had the nerve to give five of the last six rounds to Pazienza. Pazienza, who ran around like a boob throwing pitty-pat punches, was getting hit with solid punches throughout the fight. He had one eye closed and his nose broken.

Forgot about the old-time worries of the mob fixing fight; the network boys have cornered the market on corrupt dealings within the ring. Let's face the facts; The only way the fighter not favored by the networks can win is by knockout. Haugen's loss to Pazienza on NBC is a commentary of how hard-working fighters are being cheated.

-L. Bruce De Oilers
Dana Point, Ca

While there is no evidence that NBC could fix a fight, as this fan suggests, a Vinny Paz victory was indeed a favorable outcome for the network that is as proud as a peacock, "NBC was in the Vinny Paz business," explained Lee Groves. Lee's statement does not suggest he feels NBC influenced the scores in any way, it just annunciates the statement that the network benefited more from a Paz win.

Another fan letter, from John A. Serpe, of Kenosha, WI, called Paz' decision of Haugen "the greatest ring robbery since Jimmy Ellis was given a decision over Floyd Patterson in 1968." In addition to letters from the fans, the Between Rounds segment of this issue of KO also included an editor's note, indicating that they were "flooded" with fan letters regarding the Haugen-Paz fight and the vast majority of responses received felt that Greg Haugen deserved the decision.

KO magazine did not forget the outcry against the decision and apparently agreed with that sentiment, as they awarded that fight the

Billy Graham-Joey Giardello Highway Robbery Award in their 1987 year-end issue.

Robbery is the operative word when listening to Lee Haugen's take on the fight. Telling a tale that reminiscent of the film noir of the 1930s. "Greg allowed his manager (Wes Wolffe) to make bad decisions for him. Probably the worst one was fighting Vinny in his hometown. That town was run by the mob. Vinny's dad was a soldier in the mob. When we pulled up behind the arena, I saw dozens of black windowed limos. It was clear to me the mob was running that fight. Greg was in trouble." Greg was also aware of the alleged involvement of organized crime, but he was not focused on it "There was talk that I would not get out alive if I won the fight because all the mob had the money on it. But you never know what is real talk and what is bullshit. I did not worry about it. I was just focused on the fight. I knew if I fought my fight, it would be fine. I wasn't going to worry about getting out of there alive."

Lee's observations did not stop there, as he claims he and Stan Tischler observed the judges assigned for the fight having breakfast with Lou Duva fight week. Their chumminess convinced Lee that this fight was not on the up and up. Apparently, neither Lee nor Stan shared that information with Greg, "This is the first time I am hearing about it, but it doesn't surprise me," Greg offered.

Vinny Paz was not without his supporters in terms of winning the fight, albeit it is a much smaller representation based on the feedback that I received:

Billy Calogero, AKA Billy C: I thought Paz won it. Funny story, I had Greg on my show a few times and was talking to him several times off air for a bit. During an interview live on the show, I asked him the same thing about his fights with Paz, and his response was, "He's a fag."

Jim Trunzo, Straight Jab Media: Vinny Paz challenged Greg Haugen for the IBF Lightweight title. Haugen's camp worried prior to the fight about the fact that the setting for the bout was, for all intent and purpose, Paz's hometown. On top of that, one of the judges was also from Providence. After watching the fight several times (but I didn't see it live!), I scored the bout for Paz by 1 point in a bout that I felt could result in either a Paz win, a Haugen win, or perhaps what might have been the fairest, a draw.

I would argue against undue influence by the location in relation to the judges. Certainly, Sammartino could have been accused of favoritism because he was a hometown judge. However, Rick Bays was from Miami and Keith MacDonald from Nevada. Considering that the scoring was identical, I take that as weighing more on the side of no shenanigans as opposed to some type of collusion. Having sat ringside at many fights and all around the ring, I know the problems that arise, depending upon where you're sitting: at times, you simply can't see whether or not certain punches – especially body blows – hit or are blocked; you have tougher time determining the force of the blow; you fail to catch every counter unless the fighter's head snaps back. So, for identical scores to come in, with different rounds being scored 10-10 or 10-9 unless there was some type of pre-arranged system of scoring, I don't understand how the cards can be questioned.

That said, while collusion might not have occurred, poor judging certainly could. As I stated, this was a brutally difficult fight to score. I personally had far too many 10-10 rounds, for example. If I were to argue for Haugen getting the short end of the stick, I suppose my defense of the claim would focus on the fact that there was more of a likelihood that the scores should NOT have been identical. When rounds are so close – and throughout the fight, not just one here and there – you would think three different people (in this case the judges) would be more likely to see things differently (i.e., one scores it even, another for Haugen and the third for Paz.) On that basis, it would be one heck of a coincidence to come up with three identical scores.

My personal preference when scoring close rounds is to look at which fighter was more aggressive, although I try to balance that if the opponent counters exceptionally well and often. I think that Haugen was clearly superior when it comes to counterpunching. If the judges' bias leaned toward aggression, they would most likely give the nod to Paz.

Another factor that might have accounted for a Paz win would be his 'flash.' I hate the thought of that. I can't stand the gimmicks of guys like Paz, Camacho (after he became a runner!), or Naseem Hamed. But to the uninitiated, it has an effect, much like the effect of the crowd's support for a fighter.

Haugen is my type of fighter: blue-collar, comes to fight, respectful toward opponents (unless they push him too far), etc. But in spite of that, in spite of my bias against showing off, I still had Paz by the slimmest of margins. I wouldn't have been disappointed had the fight been won by Greg or had they called it a draw. But that's me, just one person.

Jay N. Miller covered the fight for Ring Magazine and scored the fight in favor of Vinny Paz, 145-142.

Wes Moon, another scribe from the Ring Magazine, wrote a piece that did not dispute the decision; however, it was not flattering of the new champion:

What writers share with aficionados is that constant search for that boxer who brings into the ring the something extra-that electrifying punch, or style, or speed or presence. Paz, in winning his one-third of a world championship, the IBF third, brought none of these things. His brash manner, red, white and green, sequined outfits, flashy combination of punches, needless posturing, are but a parody of ring greatness- Wes Moon.

Indeed, Moon's comments are condescending and unflattering towards Vinny Paz. Wes droned on about how Paz lacked the qualities of a Dempsey, a Marciano, or an Ali. As typical of boxing, the narrative by the people who watch and cover the sport bellyache about how it pales into comparison of yesteryear. I like to call it Old Man-idous.

It has gone on in boxing forever. And it is ridiculous. During Carlos Monzon's rematch with Emile Griffth, the narrative of the ABC broadcast was how both fighters did not compare to the days of Sugar Ray Robinson. While this particular fight between Monzon and Griffth was dreadful and had every right to be criticized, it was silly to dismiss both fighters in that way. Or does anyone not think that Monzon and Griffth are all-time greats? When Mike Tyson fought James Tillis on ABC, Jim Lampley suggested that Mike Tyson had an easy path to the championship because of the deficiencies of the heavyweight division. After Marvelous Marvin Hagler was robbed by two judges in Vegas, Steve Farhood actually questioned the greatness of the Marvelous One in a piece he wrote for KO magazine. Even Marvin was considered fair game as an active fighter. Bashing active fighters, because it is perceived that they are not as great as older fighters, is an ongoing issue in boxing that has snowballed into a dangerous boulder today. Even active fighters themselves sometimes do it. But I have a feeling it has always been that way, it is just more pronounced today because of social media.

Vinny Paz just went fifteen hard rounds facing dire circumstances, and for that, he should not have to hear how he does not compare to Jack Dempsey. A fighter, who, when he was champion, took three years off between title defenses. Of course, all Vinny Paz did was prove his great toughness and desire throughout his career. As did Greg Haugen. Their first fight was spectacular and right up there with all the great lightweight title fights in boxing history. Period.

Dave Murphy also felt Paz won a very close fight and points out that the big crowd was not the only disadvantage for Greg in this fight, "The referee (Waldemar Schmidt) seemed to break them a little quicker than I would have liked. Especially in that era. In the 80s they let you maul a little more. I think Haugen could have benefited from a different referee," Murphy explained.

Jim Montgomery maintains that Pat Putnam of Sports Illustrated told him that this fight was the worst robbery he had witnessed. When reading Putnam's article about the fight in the June 15th ,1987 issue of SI, he does not state explicitly that the decision was the worst injustice that his eyeballs had laid eyes on, but he does suggest the judges were influenced by the pro-Paz crowd, instead of the actual action in the ring. Putnam also focused on judge Clark Sammartino, writing, 'only a churl would suggest that a judge from Providence with an Italian surname (Clark Sammartino) would have given Haugen anything less than an honest count in his first defense of the IBF title.

Sammartino, Paz's paisain, read this article and responded with a letter that was published in the July 6th, 1987 issue of SI:

JUDGES VIEW

I was one of the judges at the Greg Haugen-Vincent Pazienza fight in Providence on June 7 (Local Boy Makes Good, June 15), and in response to your story I would offer the following comments. Ricardo Bays of North Miami, Fla., and Keith MacDonald of Carson City, Nev., (the other two judges) and I were a very experienced, professional group. We were not, as was suggested, influenced by crowd noise, because we are trained to concentrate only on the contestants for the full three minutes of each round. I was not then, nor would I ever be influenced by the race, color, creed, nationality or religion of any fighter.

Our main objective is to decide a winner in a fair, professional, honest, unbiased manner. We did this on June 7 and found—by identical scores—Pazienza to be a little better than Haugen and, therefore, a unanimous winner in a close, well-fought contest.

CLARK A. SAMMARTINO, D.M.D.

Providence

The cynic may suggest that Sammartino's rabbit ears suggest guilt. Clark continued to officiate fights until 2017. The first Haugen and Paz fight was his second fight as a judge; his first fight was Vinny Paz's important showdown against Roberto Elizondo. To be assigned such an important title fight with virtually no experience is alarming, to say the least. It is easy to believe that such an inexperienced judge would be influenced by the fans. It is equally alarming to believe that Team Haugen would approve of such an official. To be fair to Clark Sammartino, he went on to have a solid reputation as a judge, even though it appeared he got this one wrong.

Final Compubox numbers gave Greg Haugen the edge in total connects, two-hundred fourteen to one-hundred ninety-six, power punches, or non-jab connects, one-hundred fifty-five to one-hundred thirty-three. Paz had the edge in total jabs landed, sixty-three to fifty-nine, which is a bit ironic considering how much better Greg's jab is compared to Vinny's. Paz also had an edge in total punches thrown, nine-hundred ninety-one to nine-hundred twelve. The biggest advantage in this fight was the crowd noise in favor of Paz, however. The Compubox numbers, and the ebb and flow of the fight itself, provide for pleasurable conversation and analysis. But the simple fact still remains, after the fight, Greg Haugen was no longer the champion, regardless of what anyone thought. That is how boxing works.

Officially, Greg Haugen joined a long list of fighters who failed to defend their title in their first defense. While the fighters in this group are very talented, it is not a group any boxer wants to be in. Both James Braddock and James Buster Douglas failed to defend their title. Marvin Johnson failed to defend his title the first two times he captured the light heavyweight title. When Nino Benvenuti first captured the middleweight title, he lost his first defense against Emile Griffith, the man he won the title from. Roberto Duran had little time to celebrate after he won the welterweight title from Ray Leonard and gave the title back to the '76 Olympian just a few short months later. Indeed, Greg Haugen was dead set on emulating the feats of Griffith and Leonard. Greg began to get right to work.

Whatever the consensus was, and indeed it was overwhelmingly in agreement that Greg deserved to win, it was not going to help Greg get that tangible belt back. Greg and his team were well aware of this and became very proactive in their quest to be champion again.

The first action Greg Haugen took in the quest to win his title back was to bring back an old foe to his camp. "After I was robbed against Vinny, I decided to bring George Chemeres back. I had known George for a long time. I thought I'd give the old man a chance to work with a world champion. And George was smart, I learned a lot from him," Greg explained. When I asked Greg if any words were exchanged between him and George, considering George was on a mission to get him beat, Greg said, "There were some things I said to George about trying to get me beat. But it made me a better fight, and George knew his shit. I chose to give him another chance." John Chemeres stated that Greg assured his father that he would do whatever he said, "Greg knew he needed better training. That was my father."

Greg's first order of business after cheated in the first Paz fight was bringing George Chemeres back in. He they are at the gym ready to work (Courtesy of John Chemeres)

Bringing George Chemeres back also meant working with John Chemeres once again. Greg & John taking a break from training before the Paz rematch (Courtesy of John Chemeres).

Greg also added a new member to help him work on conditioning. "I started working with Keith Klevin, who worked with Larry Holmes, to get me in shape," Greg explained. Thanks to the magicianship of Keith's methods, Greg would find himself on weight a week before the fight. "I could eat, I was putting fluids in my body, so I wasn't dehydrated," Greg explained. Klevin's work was well documented, and Keith's methods were elemental in Greg's success. According to Greg, 'Doc Klevin,' was "the smartest dude I ever met in terms of knowing the human body. Each day he would have a goal for my weight, and I would say to him, 'ain't no fucking way I am making that,' but if I did exactly what he said, I would make the goal every time," Greg summarized.

Going into the rematch with Paz, Greg was even stronger because he was not starving himself anymore.

Despite the fact that KO Magazine felt Greg won the first fight and even went so far as to call the decision a robbery, they predicted Vinny Paz to win the fight by a close, 'deserved' fifteen-round unanimous decision in their December 1987 issue. The main reason for the prediction was that Paz, who suffered from diarrhea going into the first battle, will be stronger. Also, KO pointed out that Greg froze during the few times Paz did throw exploding punches in bunches (I did not observe that), and a "faster, more inspired Paz could result in a more tentative, less aggressive Haugen." The KO prediction also suggests that Paz would win the fight due to his "razzle-dazzle" influence on the judges. If indeed a fighter wins a decision by influencing judges of something that did not actually result in scored punches, then how could the decision be a deserved one?

The venue for the rematch had some controversy attached to it. The Convention Center in Atlantic City was the chosen arena for Vinny Paz and Greg Haugen to wage battle for a second time. Greg was not happy about it. "I said what's the difference between Atlantic City and Providence, one-hundred miles and ten thousand dagos. It was another home fight for Vinny. We had an agreement, if I fought in his hometown, then they would come to mine in Vegas or Washington to fight me. But when it was fucking all said and done, Vinny didn't have the balls to do it. He would only fight on the East coast," Greg explained.

161

Kathy Duva could not confirm or deny Greg's claim. "I do not remember. It does sound like something we would agree to. I don't know why it did not go to Vegas. But then again, at that point, the Convention Center had the much greater capacity compared to Vegas. Arum would not have gone to Atlantic City if it wasn't the most lucrative option," Kathy explained. In KO Magazine's prediction write up, they suggested that this rematch had a strong chance of being held in Las Vegas; supporting Greg's claim about the agreement with Vinny and the Duva's.

Even though Greg Haugen had to once again put on his road warrior hat, he explains that he was given some assurances before the fight, "Larry Hazzard was the New Jersey commissioner, and he assured me I would be given a fair shake, and I was. None of that fucking bullshit in that first fight was going to go down." A new referee was also a big difference in the rematch. Veteran referee Tony Perez was given the assignment. Indeed, Tony Perez had a well-deserved reputation for being an inept official. He was the center of attention for the epic Joe Frazier versus Muhammad Ali rematch, for all the wrong reasons. He could have cost Ken Norton his life by letting him take way too many punches against Gerry Cooney, and years later, Tommy Morrison against Ray Mercer. Tony also cost Marvelous Marvin Hagler his no knockdown streak when he called his obvious slip against Juan Roldan a knockdown. Indeed, the fact that Tony Perez kept getting high profile fights is not a good endorsement for the Athletic Commissions who appoint the officials. With that said, nobody was going to accuse Tony Perez of breaking fighters too early. A clear plus for Haugen.

While Greg Haugen was being given assurances about the rematch, Vinny Paz made a very strategical error. "I figured I beat him when I was sick as a dog, I was going to kill this kid when I was right. And for the next fight I just let myself go, I lost thirteen pounds the day before the fight, and I got my ass kicked in the second fight," Vinny Paz admits.

The rematch took place on February 6th, 1988. This time around, the fight was aired on ABC instead of NBC. Greg had one fight before the rematch, a sixth-round stoppage against Derrick McGuire in December. While Vinny remained on the shelf since winning the title in June.

The history of boxing tells a narrative that rematches typically do not equal the second stanza. The truth is that rematches are much more complicated than that. The idea that rematches are dull is grossly overstated. It is well documented that the second fight between Sandy Saddler and Willie Pep was the best, as well as most competitive fight of the series. The second fight between Floyd Patterson and Ingemar Johansson is my favorite of the trilogy. The first fight between Matthew Saad Muhammad-then Matthew Franklin-and Marvin Johnson is an absolute classic. Anyone who saw this fight puts it on their shortlist of the best fights ever. Their rematch was just as fabulous. While there was no footage of the second fight between Greg and Ted Michaliszyn, both fighters confirm the action was much more intense the second time around. Indeed, rematches are a big part of boxing, and its narrative deserves more respect.

Greg Haugen also debunked the moniker that the fighter who wins the first fight wins the rematch. As this fight was a drubbing from start to finish. Greg Haugen dominated Paz, using the best weapon in boxing to regain his title. "In the second fight, I used my jab more and busted him up with it," Greg explained. "Haugen just ate him up with the jab the second time around," Dave Murphy concurs.

Vinny Paz knew he was in trouble going into the rematch. As a result, he called upon the boxing Gods for help, "I have had five 'oh God' fights. When I was walking to the ring, I said, 'Oh God, please let this fucker have a bad night.' I felt terrible, and I knew I needed the other guy to have a bad night if I was even going to have a chance. Haugen two was one of those fights. But of course, they got ready because it was me. They knew it was going to be a war with me," Paz explains.

Pictured are John Chemeres, Roberto Duran, & Alan Lowery, a sparring partner for Greg. Picture was taken during the Paz rematch in Pleasantville (Courtesy of John Chemeres).

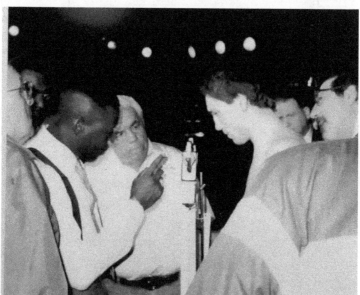

Haugen-Paz 2 Weigh-In. Pictured: George Chemeres, far left, Larry Hazzard, Lou Duva, Greg Haugen on the scale, February 6th, 1987 (Courtesy of John Chemeres).

Greg nailing Paz in their rematch. It was one of the best performances of the decade.
(Courtesy of Greg Haugen).

If Paz was banking on Greg Haugen not to be ready, he picked the wrong night. It was arguably his most polished performance, "That and the Mancini fight were two of my best," Greg recalls. Along with the jab, Haugen's defense was better in the rematch, and referee Tony Perez, as expected, allowed more infighting. All Vinny had was guts, and that was never going to be enough when Greg Haugen is right. Paz even tried to turn southpaw in this fight. Nothing was going to derail the Greg Haugen machine on this day. Round eleven was one of the best of the fight. Paz came out maniacal because Dr. Frank Doggett warned Vinny that the fight was close to being stopped. Always a ton of heart, Paz went for broke and landed haymaker after haymaker. Haugen weathered the storm and countered Vinny with a hard-left hand that hurt the champion. Haugen dominated the rest of the round and the fight. A two-fisted attack behind the jab. A maestro at work. The scorecards read 147-138, 147-138, and 145-140 for the winner and new IBF champion, Greg Haugen. Not a boo could be heard throughout the pro-Vinny Paz crowd. The dominance was undeniable. "I don't think anyone could have scored the second fight for Vinny," Kathy Duva admitted.

Once again, Greg Haugen was champion. Compubox numbers favored Greg in total connects, four-hundred forty-eight to three-hundred fifty-four, as well as jabs, one-hundred sixty to eight-two. The power punches stats were a bit closer but still favored Greg two-hundred eighty-eight to two-hundred seventy-two. The numbers back up the wide score, as round eight was the only round that Paz performed to where you would expect.

Once again Jeff Ryan covered the fight for KO Magazine, and in their June 1988 issue, he wrote that Greg established a stiff jab early, (a tool not used as effectively in their first fight), and dictated the pace with that essential punch for fifteen dominate rounds. Ryan also pointed out how more carefree Greg appeared before the rematch. A combination of Doc Klevin's training regimen and Larry Hazzard's promise that the scoring would be fair could be credited for that behavior.

Ryan also wrote a piece for Boxing '88, KO's sister publication, for this rematch titled, Greg Haugen: More Than Just A Tough Guy. In the piece, Ryan illuminates how Greg has been erroneously dismissed as just a tough guy. Everybody from Showtime Championship Boxing; before the Jimmy Paul fight, as well as all his opponents, failed to recognize the pure boxing skills Haugen showcased. We all saw it, Jeff Ryan scribed it, yet a lot of people still have trouble getting it. What Greg Haugen did get was his lightweight championship back.

Now it was time to defend it.

VINNY PAZIENZA UD 15 GREG HAUGEN
06/07/87 - PROVIDENCE, RI

Total Punches Landed / Thrown															
	1	2	3	4	5	6	7	8	9	10	11	12	13	14	15
PAZIENZA	11/54	10/52	11/46	8/48	15/73	15/68	10/65	12/54	9/64	15/76	14/75	15/80	8/55	26/90	17/91
	20.4%	19.2%	23.9%	16.7%	20.5%	22.1%	15.4%	22.2%	14.1%	19.7%	18.7%	18.8%	14.5%	28.9%	18.7%
HAUGEN	13/57	7/54	12/52	12/46	10/51	14/56	9/50	14/58	12/57	13/61	13/51	13/56	22/92	22/93	28/78
	22.8%	13%	23.1%	26.1%	19.6%	25%	18%	24.1%	21.1%	21.3%	25.5%	23.2%	23.9%	23.7%	35.9%

Jab Landed / Thrown															
	1	2	3	4	5	6	7	8	9	10	11	12	13	14	15
PAZIENZA	6/31	4/27	4/24	2/28	7/39	7/34	2/29	5/21	6/34	3/29	5/39	3/28	2/20	5/25	2/18
	19.4%	14.8%	16.7%	7.1%	17.9%	20.6%	6.9%	23.8%	17.6%	10.3%	12.8%	10.7%	10%	20%	11.1%
HAUGEN	4/24	1/29	4/36	6/25	2/32	4/34	2/25	6/31	3/35	2/26	4/19	2/30	7/34	7/40	5/25
	16.7%	3.4%	11.1%	24%	6.3%	11.8%	8%	19.4%	8.6%	7.7%	21.1%	6.7%	20.6%	17.5%	20%

Power Punches Landed / Thrown															
	1	2	3	4	5	6	7	8	9	10	11	12	13	14	15
PAZIENZA	5/23	6/25	7/22	6/20	8/34	8/34	8/36	7/33	3/30	12/47	9/36	12/52	6/35	21/65	15/73
	21.7%	24%	31.8%	30%	23.5%	23.5%	22.2%	21.2%	10%	25.5%	25%	23.1%	17.1%	32.3%	20.5%
HAUGEN	9/33	6/25	8/16	6/21	8/19	10/22	7/25	8/27	9/22	11/35	9/32	11/26	15/58	15/53	23/53
	27.3%	24%	50%	28.6%	42.1%	45.5%	28%	29.6%	40.9%	31.4%	28.1%	42.3%	25.9%	28.3%	43.4%

Final Punch Stat Report		
Total Punches (Body Landed)	Total Jabs (Body Landed)	Power Punches (Body Landed)
PAZIENZA		
196 (79)/991	63 (21)/426	133 (58)/565
19.8%	14.8%	23.5%
HAUGEN		
214 (90)/912	59 (1)/445	155 (89)/467
23.5%	13.3%	33.2%

Note

Although the decision was widely criticized, this was a legitimately close, tough-to-score fight. After 10 rounds they were tied 116-116 in total connects but it was in the 13th and 15th rounds that Haugen would forge his narrow leads in the raw numbers, for he out-landed Pazienza 50-25 overall and 38-21 power in those rounds and ended with connect leads of 214-196 overall and 155-133 power (Pazienza prevailed 63-59 in landed jabs). While Pazienza led 8-7 in the CompuBox round-by-round breakdown of total connects, 10 of the 15 rounds were decided by three or fewer connects, and, in those rounds, Pazienza led 6-4. Haugen won his rounds by larger connect margins and was more accurate overall (23%-20%) and in power shots (33%-24%). Haugen also prevailed 90-79 in landed body shots. The biggest factor swinging the fight Pazienza's way was the location -- Providence, R.I. -- and the huge vocal support Pazienza received. Had the same fight unfolded in Haugen's adopted hometown of Las Vegas, there might have been a different result. Scoring: 144-141 (3x) P.

167

02/06/88 -

	Total Punches Landed / Thrown														
	1	2	3	4	5	6	7	8	9	10	11	12	13	14	15
HAUGEN	25/54	29/55	25/48	27/58	20/50	19/49	22/60	24/67	33/71	31/62	35/62	26/57	42/69	53/88	37/80
	46.3%	52.7%	52.1%	46.6%	40%	38.8%	36.7%	35.8%	46.5%	50%	56.5%	45.6%	60.9%	60.2%	46.3%
PAZIENZA	23/68	29/74	13/57	21/70	13/48	22/60	21/68	37/69	19/60	38/61	24/69	15/55	26/68	20/62	33/74
	33.8%	39.2%	22.8%	30%	27.1%	36.7%	30.9%	53.6%	31.7%	62.3%	34.8%	27.3%	38.2%	32.3%	44.6%

	Jab Landed / Thrown														
	1	2	3	4	5	6	7	8	9	10	11	12	13	14	15
HAUGEN	12/21	13/19	11/21	11/24	10/25	6/21	11/28	13/38	11/29	8/19	9/14	6/17	13/22	13/21	13/20
	57.1%	68.4%	52.4%	45.8%	40%	28.6%	39.3%	34.2%	37.9%	42.1%	64.3%	35.3%	59.1%	61.9%	65%
PAZIENZA	7/37	6/27	6/36	7/27	3/19	9/25	9/33	11/24	3/19	2/9	1/18	3/15	8/25	5/17	2/6
	18.9%	22.2%	16.7%	25.9%	15.8%	36%	27.3%	45.8%	15.8%	22.2%	5.6%	20%	32%	29.4%	33.3%

	Power Punches Landed / Thrown														
	1	2	3	4	5	6	7	8	9	10	11	12	13	14	15
HAUGEN	13/33	16/36	14/27	16/34	10/25	13/28	11/32	11/29	22/42	23/43	26/48	20/40	29/47	40/67	24/60
	39.4%	44.4%	51.9%	47.1%	40%	46.4%	34.4%	37.9%	52.4%	53.5%	54.2%	50%	61.7%	59.7%	40%
PAZIENZA	16/31	23/47	7/21	14/43	10/29	13/35	12/35	26/45	16/41	36/52	23/51	12/40	18/43	15/45	31/68
	51.6%	48.9%	33.3%	32.6%	34.5%	37.1%	34.3%	57.8%	39%	69.2%	45.1%	30%	41.9%	33.3%	45.6%

	Final Punch Stat Report		
	Total Punches (Body Landed)	Total Jabs (Body Landed)	Power Punches (Body Landed)
HAUGEN	448 (0)/930	160 (0)/339	288 (0)/591
	48.2%	47.2%	48.7%
PAZIENZA	354 (0)/963	82 (0)/337	272 (0)/626
	36.8%	24.3%	43.5%

Chapter Thirteen
Olympic Gold

"I said to myself maybe one day I would be on the Olympic team.
I knew I had to put the work in."

—Pernell Whitaker

When Greg Haugen regained his IBF lightweight title, in a marvelous performance against Vinny Paz, the year was nineteen-hundred eighty-eight.

This year was the last of the Ronald Regan administration. However, when George H.W. Bush thrashed Michael Dukakis in November of 1988, four more years of Republican rule in the United States was guaranteed. Also, in 1988, the Iran-Iraq war came to an end, with the death toll reaching the one million mark. The truce between Iran and Iraq did not equate with peace in the Middle East; however, as 1988 saw the formation of Osama Bin Laden's Al Qaeda.

The world of pop culture was a little bit more encouraging in 1988. Who Framed Roger Rabbit, Coming to America, Beetlejuice, and Big, were creative, refreshing, box-office smashes. On the tube, the sit-coms where front and center with NBC leading the way with The Cosby Show, A Different World, Cheers, The Golden Girls, and Empty Nest. If you were looking for something a little deeper in 1988, Mississippi Burning made you think at the box office. In the world of music, we had a little bit of everything in 1988. Michael Jackson and George Michael both had a bunch of number one hits. Hard to believe they are both dead now. Def Leppard had its greatest success, newcomers Rick Astley and Terence Trent D'Arby provided the pop world with an adrenaline shot. Billy Ocean commanded us to get into his car, and Bobby McFerrin told us to be happy, even if our life was going down the toilet. My favorite pop culture moment in 1988 came from Star Trek, as it often does. It Marh 19th episode title, Heart of Glory, indicated that enslaving animals for food is no longer legal. Today, the exact opposite is true.

As land approximately the size of Africa is used to enslave and slaughter animals. Hoorendous and unacceptable.

In the world of sports, the top stories were about exceptional individual performances, as well as dominant franchises. Doug Williams became the first black quarterback to win the Super Bowl when the Washington Redskins bested the Denver Broncos. Oriel Hershiser had one of the most dominant performances on the baseball mound for the Los Angeles Dodgers, capping it off with a World Series win over the heavily favored Oakland Athletics. In the NBA, the Los Angeles Lakers outlasted the Detroit Pistons in one of the best NBA championship finals ever, going the full seven games. The NHL saw the Edmonton Oilers continue their dominance, and Mats Wilander fell a Wimbledon championship short of tennis' Grand Slam.

In boxing, Mike Tyson continued his dominance with impressive wins over Larry Holmes, Michael Spinks, and Tony Tubbs, in less than seven rounds of boxing. Iran Barkley stunned Thomas Hearns, and Tony The Tiger Lopez, and Rocky Lockridge participated in the fight of the year, with The Tiger winning a close fight.

Similar to 1984, the United States Boxing Olympic Team created headlines in nineteen-hundred eighty-eight. Not often spoken about in the same breath of the 1976 and 1984 teams, the 1988 team was just as epic. The 1988 team produced Hall of Famers Riddick Bowe and Michael Carbajal, future hall of famer Roy Jones Jr. and world champions Ray Mercer and Kennedy McKinney. Unfortunately, the biggest story in all of boxing was the blatant robbery Roy Jones Jr. suffered in the gold medal match against Park Si-Heon. It was the kind of decision that was so disgusting, where corruption could be the only explanation for Jones's hand not being raised in victory.

Greg Haugen not only had a second chance at Vinny Paz in 1988, since he was victorious in the rematch, he also had a chance to successfully defend his lightweight championship that year. Indeed, it is true that most boxing people felt Greg should have gotten the decision against Vinny; however, the only thing that is preserved for all time on record is that Greg Haugen lost his first title defense. It was time to change that. For his new first title defense, Greg chose Miguel Santana. Born in Portugal, Santana resided in Puerto Rico and sported a record of 21-3-1, 11 KO's. Santana was a rugged foe who was given the moniker El Zorro. Santana embraced his nickname as he played it out in full Zorro attire when entering the ring.

Going into his fight with Haugen, Santana had quality wins over Miguel Aguado, Wesley Shuler, Michael Gamble, Rodney Moore, Felix Gonzales, and Philadelphia's Anthony Fletcher. Santana was also on the wrong side of close decisions against Terrence Ali on two occasions. Santana's first fight with Ali was on the undercard on the famed Lloyd Honeyghan upset over Donald Curry. A twelve round war that fit like a glove on that magical year of boxing in 1986. Santana felt he did enough to beat Ali in that first fight, and he gained more in the loss than any of his victories. Bill Mazer, who announced Miguel's first fight with Ali, described Santana as a counter puncher who was a good athlete. Santana was much more than that. Miguel Santana had a facial resemblance to Edwin Rosario, with a body that was a carbon copy of John John Molina, he looked a bit like John John facially as well. Miguel was a boxer who was comfortable and successful with being first. He could lead with a snapping left jab, a stiff left hook, and a thudding overhand right. El Zorro was also an excellent inside fighter, his right uppercut being his Sunday punch. This diverse and eclectic approach made Miguel Santana a tough opponent to prepare for. Up until his first championship fight with Greg, Miguel Santana looked outmatched only against Pernell Whitaker. More of that to come.

Greg Haugen's defense against Miguel Santana had a different narrative than Haugen's previous fights. After his dominant performance against Paz, which should go down as one of the best in lightweight history, Haugen was a clear favorite over El Zorro. It was not a matter of if Greg will win, but how Mutt will successfully defend his title. Another big difference in this fight was that is was scheduled for twelve rounds instead of fifteen. The IBF was the last sanctioning body to schedule world championship fights for fifteen rounds, but even they succumbed to the twelve-round limit in 1988. A decision Greg Haugen protests until this day, "American championships should be twelve rounds (such as the NABF) world championships should be fifteen rounds," Haugen said. Most men who have laced up the boxing gloves agree that the fifteen-round limit in world title fights should have never been circumcised. However, the fighters do not have the power in boxing, for the most part.

Jose Suliman and the WBC had all the power around the time the decision to eliminate the fifteen rounders. 1982 is when Suliman had the juice to put the trend in motion. As a whole, 1982 was not a great year for boxing. The tragic death of Doo Kuo Kim in his fight against Ray Mancini is considered the main reason for the change. However, the aesthetically grueling TKO of Alexis Arguello against Aaron Pryor, a fight that happened the night before the Mancini Kim fight, was also cited as a problem. The negative momentum continued just a couple of short weeks later when Larry Holmes drubbed Randal Tex Cobb over fifteen, one-sided rounds on national television in primetime. In that fight, referee Steve Crosson failed to do what everyone was begging him to do, stop one of the most lopsided affairs in boxing history. Twelve rounds of this catastrophe would have been more manageable, and perhaps would have not chased announcer Howard Cosell away, but fifteen rounds of this was way too much agony for anyone to witness. Jose Suliman knew boxing had to be saved from itself, and the championship rounds of thirteen, fourteen, and fifteen, rounds that have meant so much to the rich history of boxing, had to be snipped to save the troubled sport. That was their explanation anyway. Not everyone in boxing believes this is the real reason for changing championship fights from fifteen to twelve rounds, however.

Perhaps the most significant change in the narrative for Greg Haugen going into the Santana was the fact this fight would take place in Greg's home state of Washington. A move that you would think would have been welcomed and beneficial. However, many boxers have expressed that fighting in their hometown is more of a curse than a blessing. Former world champion Devon Alexander spoke on how fighting so close to where you lay your head could be maladaptive. When Devon Alexander The Great faced Andriy Kotelnik in his birthplace of Saint Louis, he stated that he was distracted by all of the extra attachments that come with fighting at home. Regis Prograis, one of the best pugilists today, also said he felt pressure when he fought in front of his hometown of New Orleans, against Juan Jose Velasco in 2018.

Greg had added pressure, as he had a heavy hand in promoting this championship fight to be held in the Tacoma Dome A dynamic Greg did not embrace. "I was being pulled in ten different directions trying to get this done. That was the first and last time I did that, trying to promote the fight. I like just concentrating on training and being ready. There was a lot more to promoting the fight than I thought, and I wasn't in the shape I needed to be in." Greg said.

Greg Haugen's fight against Miguel Santana is shrouded in mystery, even for boxing. What is certain about this fight is that it went to the scorecards in the eleventh round. A Santana headbutt caused a horrific cut on Greg. By all accounts, it was a heinous cut, J Michael Kenyon, of The News Tribune, quoted George Chemeres as saying to the ringside physician, 'Doc you gotta stop it. It's bad. It's horrible. He's gonna have to go to the hospital.' John Chemeres said, "My dad wanted to stop the fight because of the cut. I told him not to stop the fight, let the referee stop the fight."

Kenyon also reported that Greg had to lose five pounds the night before the fight to make weight and began to fade in round nine, ten, and eleven. Given Chemeres' uncanny reputation, you have to wonder if his plea could be taken at face value. Or, did George realize that his fighter was tiring and wanted to go to the scorecards. Given the nature of the cut and the fact that Santana was initially awarded the victory via TKO, such a theory might be an overreach.

The details get cloudy when the question of who deserved the decision is raised. Bill MacDonald is firm in his belief that "Greg lost that fight. Santana was giving it to Greg. Years later, the IBF gave Santana the belt because they felt he should have been given the victory," MacDonald said.

Greg's version of the fight is as follows, "I was confident I was ahead. I think it was the seventh round, or the ninth round…he was jumping in, he was bending down and he would jump in, leap in on me, he was like a fucking Billy goat, it was just a matter of time. He hit my eyebrow, and it was a bad cut, I think the doctor about passed out when they looked at it, they stopped it immediately." The fight was stopped in the eleventh round due to an intentional headbutt; therefore, the judges scored cards would decide the winner. Miguel Santana would not be the winner via TKO. It gets even more complicated. Miguel Santana was declared the winner initially. However, one of the judges declared that he voted incorrectly, and Haugen was indeed the winner via split decision. Miguel Santana and his team were not accepting the error and launched an investigation into the decision. "It does sound fishy, doesn't it," John Chemeres opined. Eighteen years after the fight, the IBF decided to award him their version of the lightweight championship. Greg Haugen stated he was not aware of that fact. The IBF never returned my inquiry about this manner.

The actual decision still reads in favor of Greg Haugen. So why give Santana the belt, but not the victory? Was it a sympathy gesture? Feeling bad because one judge's score was reversed? Was it because they thought Miguel actually won the fight and wanted to let that be known, even though they could not officially change the result? Or did they discover that the judge's reversal was not genuine, and it was a favor done for the A-side fighter? In boxing, none of these outcomes are farfetched.

On April 12th, 1988, The Olympian features an article from the Associated Press (AP) that reports two of the three judges had Greg ahead, 106-103, while the third judge had the exact same score for Santana. The AP, which has had a solid reputation over the years, had Greg ahead, 106-104.

John Chemeres also felt Greg was ahead in a close fight, "Greg won the first seven rounds, he ran out of gas and was getting his butt kicked in the end, but he was ahead when they stopped it."

William Tuthill covered the fight for The Ring Magazine. His report, which is featured in the August 1988 issue of The Ring, offers more clarity of what took place inside of the squared circle and is worth reading in its entirety:

In a dream-like scenario, IBF lightweight king Greg Haugen, 135, successfully defended his championship belt against contender Miguel Santana, 134 ½, with a bizarre, 11-round technical decision.

On the 11th of the scheduled 15, a clash of heads resulted in a horrid laceration along Greg's right eye. He was cut badly above the left eye as well. Santana wasn't undamaged, having two ugly cuts, above and below the left eye.

After the round referee Jack Cassidy consulted with ringside physician Sam Adams, then halted the bout and awarded the belt to Santana. Twenty minutes later, Jimmy Rondeau, Washington state boxing commissioner and vice president of the IBF, announced to stunned reporters that the cut had been due to an unintentional butt and that, according to IBF rules, the result would depend on the scorecards.

At the time of the stoppage, judges Paul Gibbs of Seattle, and Tom McDonough from Tacoma each had it 106-103 for Haugen, while Portland's Paul Weitzel had the same score, but for Santana. The Ring card favored Santana, 106-104. Thus, Haugen was ruled still titleholder, while the Santana camp raged and pandemonium reigned.

To placate the Santana group, Rondeau will recommend a rematch as soon as possible, but Haugen needed 35 stiches to close his wounds, and it will be at least six months before he can begin sparring again.

Haugen, 22-1, with 10 knockouts, told The Ring, "I thought I won, but I have to think that way. I know my timing was off. I couldn't find my rhythm, my jab wasn't there. I had to lose too much weight too soon. I fought like blep man."

Haugen now makes Las Vegas his home, but this was his hometown and he started quickly in front of his home folks, moving well and peppering the muscular New Yorker, who fell to 20-4-1 with 12 KOs, with crisp combinations. But as early as the fourth round Haugen began running out of gas and Santana began moving in behind lead rights, roughing up Haugen, then moving out of danger.

By the 10th Haugen was fighting on heart alone and in that session powerful lead rights shook Haugen, and it appeared for a moment he might go down for the first time of his career. Only his giant heart and chin of stone prevented a trip to the deck.

-William Tuthill, Ring Magazine

The research suggests that the big question is whether or not Greg Haugen deserved to be ahead at the time of the stoppage. It appears to be evident that Santana did not deserve a TKO victory and going to the scorecards was indeed the correct call. But who was ahead?

The sad reality of this fight is that most of us will never be able to determine for ourselves who the rightful winner should be because there is no footage of this fight. "It seemed like national TV did not want to come up to Washington State. I don't know if I wasn't a good enough draw," Haugen explained. Haugen vs. Santana joins the likes of Ray Leonard vs. Randy Shields and Hector Camacho vs. Freddie Roach, as 'holy grail,' fights that boxing fight collectors dream to one day see. In the case of the Haugen fight, as Camacho v. Roach, we at least know why these fights are gone forever, neither fight was televised. Which is unfathomable, Hector Camacho was one of the biggest stars of the day and on television all the time when he fought Roach, who himself was a television regular. So why was such a fight blacked out?

When Greg fought Santana, he was coming off his best performance in the Vinny Paz rematch and returning home to Washington. How come no television networks picked up this fight? When I asked Greg about it, he said he was not sure because he never dealt with that part of his fights. In the case of Ray Leonard vs. Randy Shields, it cannot even be determined whether this fight was indeed televised. There are conflicting reports. One round of Leonard vs. Shields surfaced on YouTube for a brief period, I believe it was round seven, but the footage came from a camcorder, and not from a television broadcast. The fact that nobody can say for sure this fight was even televised is peculiar, and since all of Ray Leonard's other fights were televised, if this fight was kept off television, what was the reason? Randy Shields was the only man to beat Leonard as an amateur, you would think this would be a television ratings dream, as all of Leonard's fights were. Bizarre, to say the least.

What we do know for sure is that on April 11th, 1988, Greg Haugen officially defended his lightweight title for the first time against a very tough opponent. "He was a pretty good in-fighter for as tall as he was. One of the most awkward fighters I faced," Greg said. It was also the last time as champion that Greg fought so close to his birthplace, "I never even thought about fighting there again. They taxed the shit out of me. Federal tax, county tax, city tax, state tax. It was ridiculous. Mike Trainer, Sugar Ray Leonard's guy, talked me out of fighting here again," Greg offered.

Greg Haugen needed time to heal from the bad cut and waited over six months to defend his title again. "I went to a plastic surgeon after the fight to have it right. That way, I was assured the cut wouldn't open up again. He was a certified plastic surgeon, Dr. Potenza, and he did a great job on it. I was ready to fight a couple of months after that. I was confident that wouldn't happen again," Greg said.

For his second title defense, Greg fought Gert Bo Jacobsen of Denmark. Going into the fight, Jacobsen was undefeated, 26-0, 17 KOs. All of Jacobsen's victories came overseas. The Denmark fighter would not have to travel to the United States to face Greg either, as the champion agreed to travel to Denmark to defend his title. Greg wanted to get as far away from Washington as he could.

Greg Haugen was very confident going into the Gert Bo Jacobsen and was not too worried about fighting in Jacobsen's country, "I watched some tape on him, and I wasn't real impressed with him. I wanted to go in there and show him I wasn't fooling around. Before the fight, I had psyched him out. He was much taller than me, so I kept telling him I was going to break his ribs," Greg said.

Psychological warfare was not the only pre-fight tactic from Haugen, "I had a choice of two officials for the fight. I wanted to make sure I had the referee because he was the only one who was going to be able to stop the fight. So, I had Randy Neuman as an American referee and an American judge. I really didn't think the fight was going to go twelve rounds if I had the right kind of people in there. It worked out for me," Greg explained.

Greg's pride in his country was evident for the Jacobsen fight, as he sang along when the National Anthem was being played in Denmark. Hood of his boxing robe off, right glove on his heart. Greg also made sure the American flag was embroidered on his white boxing trunks for all to see.

Greg outclassed, outworked and outmuscled Gert Bo Jacobsen. As typical, the Haugen jab worked like a charm throughout the bout. Greg's underrated right-hand hurt Bo early in the fight. The Dane fighter showcased beautiful lateral movement in the bout, however, without any effective punches landing as a result of the movement, all a mover is, is pretty to watch. There are no style points in boxing. At least there should not be. When he needed to be, Greg Haugen was a master off cutting of the ring. This fight quelled another myth that Greg was just a counter puncher.

The sequence of punches that ended the fight in the tenth was a beautiful one-two by Haugen, perhaps the best right hand he ever delivered, dropping Jacobsen. It was a knockdown that showcased all that Greg Haugen did well inside the ring. The combination was set up by a subtle feint that Bert Go took, hook line a sinker, but throwing a right hand that left him in a vulnerable position. Greg took a little step back to avoid the power punch but remained in a position to land a stiff jab, followed by a thudding straight right cross. With the amount of punishment Jacobsen endured throughout the fight, he had no chance to stay on his feet. Resistance was futile.

Jacobsen got up after being decked with his punch, but it appeared clear that he was in no shape to continue. Clear to everyone but referee Randy Neuman. Neuman allowed Bert Go to continue, but he did not last long. Neuman must have realized he made a colossal error and jumped in to protect the Dane fighter as soon as Greg jumped on him. Greg's foreshadowing of not needing 'favorable' judges for this fight was spot on, as all three judges, including the one Denmark judge, had Greg ahead by a wide margin at the time of the stoppage.

Jeff Bumpus said he spoke with Gert Bo Jacobsen, and the Dane stated that Greg Haugen was just 'too strong' for him. Jeff Bumpus also said, "Bo was pretty strong himself." Jeff was a common opponent for Greg and Gert, going the distance with Greg and being stopped by the Dane.

Indeed, this fight is another example of how Greg was much stronger than most of his opponents. Given Jacobsen's comments to Bumpus, this fight is also an example of how Haugen's boxing skills are once again overlooked. Strength might have been a factor in the fight, but not a more significant factor than Greg's beautiful boxing skills he showcased in this fight. A boxing clinic as they say. Greg was clicking on all cylinders, his jab, his feints, his ability to cut off the ring, his defense, his power, it was all there that night for him. Greg explained his strategy for success against Jacobsen, "Every time he threw the jab, I went under and threw up top. I basically nullified his jab after a few rounds. He was there to be hit," Greg explained. This fight is another example of Greg's fantastic boxing mind, sizing up his opponent and using what was supposed to be an advantage for him, his height, against him.

The Gert Bo Jacobsen fight was Greg's first fight outside of the United States, and he enjoyed being in Denmark. "It was a lot different. They (people of Denmark) are more laid back. They are not so into the fights. They make different sounds. They cheer different. But I was having fun. The way I saw it, I was getting paid to see the world," Greg said.

Culture shock and world travel are a lot easier to digest when you looked as good as Greg Haugen did in this fight.

The victory was Greg's second title defense in 1988. Making 1988 one of the most successful of Greg Haugen's career. It was Greg's last fight in 1988, and he appeared to be at the top of his game. Just in time to face a high-profile Olympian form the United States.

Ring Magazine covered the fight, and in there March, 1988 issue, they somehow wrote in print that Gert held his own in the first six rounds. False. This fight was a beautiful, dominating performance by Greg Haugen. I say 'they,' because a writer's name does not appear at the end of the report. Go figure.

When the calendar year read 1989, it marked the ninth straight year of having a Republican President, as George H.W. Bush was sworn in as Commander in Chief. Other major news events in 1989 were the end of the Soviet-Afghan War, the release of Salam Rushdie's novel, The Satanic Verses, Oliver North getting off Scott-free for his heinous acts in the Iran-Contra affair, same-sex marriage becoming legal in Denmark; the first country to pass such legislation, and the United States flexed its military muscle by invading Panama to overthrow dictator Manuel Noriega.

1989 was an iconic year in the world of pop culture. The Simpsons made its broadcast debut, Phil Collins asked us to be kinder to the homeless, Madonna made half of America nauseous when she locked lips with black actor Leon, while the other half applauded, and Tim Burton brought the dark, grizzled version of Batman to the big screen, beating out an impressive list of summer blockbusters.

In the world of sports, an earthquake was the big story in a one-sided World Series between the Oakland Athletics and San Francisco Giants. The people of San Francisco were probably still celebrating the dominating season of their beloved 49ers anyway, who crushed the Denver Broncos back in January. The Detroit Pistons crushed the Los Angeles Lakers four games to zero to capture the NBA championship, and Greg LeMond served as the ultimate Cinderella story by winning the Tour de France in the most sensational fashion the world of sports has ever seen. In a year that saw the championships of the team sports be terribly one-sided in the United States, LeMond's come from beyond victory resonated throughout the U.S. and earned him the Sports Illustrated Athlete of the year.

In boxing, 1989 was the final year of Mike Tyson's dominance, as he beat Frank Bruno and Carl Williams. Ray Leonard was still getting gifts from judges, as most people thought Thomas Hearns did more than enough to defeat the 1976 Olympian in their long-awaited rematch. The fight was declared a draw. Rene Jacquot decisioned Donald Curry as the upset of the year, and Roberto Duran decisioned Iran Barkley for the fight of the year.

Was it a coincidence that Greg Haugen suffered from his worst loss in the same year the world of sports suffered from so many lopsided championships?

Pernell Sweet Pea Whitaker was born on January 2nd, 1964 in Virginia. Whitaker explains, "I started boxing when I was seven years old, in the city of Norfolk, Virginia." Pernell fought as an amateur for twelve years, and he shined like a beacon. Whitaker explains that watching the famous 1976 Olympic team on television was "an inspiration for me. I said to myself maybe one day I would be on the Olympic team. I knew I had to put the work in."

Indeed, Pernell put the work in, and he never shortchanged what he had to do.

Just like the 1976 Olympic team, Whitaker was part of an Olympic team in 1984 that was historical, as well a tight-knit bunch of fellows, "All of those guys were like brothers. Everybody got along, we had fun, and we supported one another. That carried over to the professionals," Whitaker said of his 1984 Olympic teammates. However, even amongst a great crop out talent, Sweet Pea shined the brightest, as he was easily the most successful gold medal winner on the team. "I won just about everything the amateur career could offer, and I moved on to a professional career," Whitaker explained.

Pernell made his professional debut on November 14th, 1984, at Madison Square Garden in Manhattan, the world's most famous arena. It was a get together with his other high-profile Olympic teammates, Virgil Hill, Tyrell Biggs, Meldrick Taylor, Mark Breland, and Evander Holyfield. Pernell described his professional debut with his close teammates as a "beautiful moment." Andrew Consolvo, who sparred with Pernell for the Haugen fight, explained that he "first became aware of Pete when I was about 10 or 11 years old at a local boxing club put on by the Norfolk (Va.) Police Dept. My dad was a trainer there. We grew up one neighborhood apart in Norfolk, and both went to Booker T Washington High School, although Pete was about 5 years older than me. We had been in the ring together on several occasions. Usually, not "official" sparring sessions."

Pernell moved up the lightweight rankings fast, his slick southpaw style, sneaky power, and masterful defense were not lost upon the boxing world. "Whitaker was just a nightmare," Greg Haugen said of Pernell. All that talent would have been enough to wreak havoc on the boxing world, but Pernell had another ace in the hole, a great corner. Georgie Benton and Lou Duva were a winning team in the corner for Main Events for a long time, and Pernell was one of their top pupils. "I had one of the greatest trainers in Georgie Benton. He was able to transform me. He taught me to tone it down and tune it up for the professional ranks. He was like a father figure," Whitaker said. Buddy McGirt, an opponent of Pernell's and a Hall of Fame boxer, also spoke highly of Benton. "Most of my losses were against fighters who were trained by Georgie," McGirt explained. Georgie told my wife that if he trained me, I would never lose," McGirt added. After his boxing career was over, Buddy became a world-class trainer, and credits Georgie Benton for his growth as a successful cornerman, "I would sit down with Georgie, and pick his brain, he was the best," McGirt said.

Indeed, Whitaker was in great hands with Benton, but if Pernell needed a little extra boost of motivation, he also had a human adrenaline shot working his corner in Lou Duva, "Lou was one of the greatest motivators, inside and outside of the ring he would stand up for his fighters. George was the technician, but Lou would amp you up for a fight," Pernell explained. "Both Benton and Duva were active, but as Pete's career progressed, Benton was more active than Duva. Like Pete, Benton had a more laid-back demeanor, yet extremely knowledgeable and Pete seemed to respond better to that." Explained Andrew Consolvo.

Benton and Duva were a contrast in personalities, and they excelled at different aspects of training a fighter, but their camaraderie is what made them a winning team for many years, "Georgie and Lou were always on the same page," Whitaker explained.

Going into his first championship fight, Pernell Whitaker had it all: talent, he worked hard, was confident, and had a winning team; Ace Morata was another blue-chip cornerman who dealt with cuts of a fighter. If anyone was lucky enough to touch Pernell square enough to cut him, Ace was there to handle the duties. There was nothing Team Whitaker was not ready for when he challenged Jose

Luis Ramirez for his lightweight title. Nothing legitimate, that is. In boxing, there is no antidote for erroneous scoring, and Pernell Whitaker fell victim of this recurring black eye on boxing.

After twelve rounds of masterful boxing, judges Newton Campos and Louis Michel had the audacity to say Pernell did not do enough to win. Only judge Harry Gibbs of England had a clue that night, calling the fight for Whitaker 117-113. Campos had an incompetent score of 118-113 for JLR, a scorecard that even the world of science fiction could not explain, and Michel had JLR the winner by one point, 116-115.

The loss was a big blow for boxing. Whitaker should have been the WBC lightweight champion. Instead, he had an egregious 'L' on his record. The robbery had to hurt Team Whitaker, but Pernell took it in stride, "The great thing about it is the world got a chance to see it, so they can make up their own minds," Whitaker explained.

Indeed, minds were made up. And the consensus belief is, in a sport saturated with heinous decisions Jose Luis Ramirez' twelve-round spilt decision 'victory' over Pernell Whitaker ranks as one of the worst decisions in boxing history. Newton Campos went on to judge a handful of more high-profile fights, as well as Louis Michel. Fascinating.

There are many reasons why bad decisions still rear their ugly head in boxing, but the fact that such terrible scorecards from judges does not equate to immediate expulsion is one of the greatest factors.

The fight took place in Paris, which was considered Jose Luis Ramirez country, but it did seem odd that a fighter of Pernell's caliber would have to travel there to fight for a world title. Pernell explained, "I guess that is where he was living, so that is where I had to go. It don't matter where the fight is, I will be there."

After the JLR robbery Whitaker fought Antonio Carter, who would be described by any boxing insider as a, 'soft touch', Pernell stopped him in the fourth round. Pernell's next fight would be Greg Haugen's next title defense. This time Sweet Pea would not have to venture that far to win his first official world title, as the fight took place in the cozy confines The Coliseum in Hampton, Virginia.

Having to defend his title against Pernell Whitaker on the road was not a promising prospect for Greg, and not something he was happy about. "I had an idiot for a manager (Wes Wolfee) who would take a little bit more money to fight in their hometown. He let the

Duva's outsmart him and out fucking negotiate him. He wound up taking fifty-grand more to fight in Whitaker's hometown because he thought I liked to fight on the road all the time, which isn't the case, especially against a guy like Whitaker," Greg explained.

There was no doubt Greg knew all about Pernell, "Southpaw, tough, fast, it's a nightmare," Greg described.

Pernell admitted he did not know much about Greg Haugen before their fight, "I didn't know a lot about him, but he was a champion. I knew I had to go in there and do what I had to do."

Pernell explained that he approached the fight with Greg the same way he approached all of his fights, "I never watched film in my career ever. Hitting the road, running, getting in the gym, staying on weight. I fought at the same weight for dam near ten years. What I did worked. I always prepared for everybody the same. I loved training camp, and I am going to work hard." But Pernell did have a specific approach with Greg going into the fight. "My preparation for Greg Haugen was to get in and get my shots off, keep my hands moving and make it as easy as possible," Whitaker explained. Andrew Consolvo adds that when preparing for Greg, he was instructed to, "To cut off the ring on Pete as much as possible." Lou Duva already knew how good Greg was, and Benton was always prepared. Andrew also suggests that Whitaker knew a little bit more about Greg than he led on, "Pete thought Greg was a good, tough fighter, but had ultra-confidence in himself. He felt that way against everybody he fought. Pete never really did a lot of shit-talking to opponents. Duva did that more than Pete."

The repercussions of the JLR robbery was apparent to the boxing observer, as Pernell was much more aggressive in this fight. Pernell stayed in the pocket and sat down on his punches more against Greg. It was a fantastic performance because Whitaker executed this game plan without sacrificing any of his brilliant defense against Haugen. Apart from the first twenty seconds of the fight, Greg could not lay a glove on the challenger. "Greg was a pretty good fighter, I knew I couldn't make any mistakes against him, but my illusiveness and movement were too much for him. It was just one of those nights for me. It was probably one of my easier nights," Whitaker said.

Pernell put on a clinic against Greg. He knocked Greg down for the first time in Greg's career in the sixth round. It was more of a flash knockdown than a damaging blow, but the knockdown was in keeping with the entire fight, never was Greg Haugen so dominated inside the squared circle. The twelfth round was also a product of the JLR fight because Pernell must have known he was way ahead on the cards but came out as aggressive as he had ever been in the final round. Was he going for the knockout? "I don't ever look to try and knock someone out. When the knockout happens, it happens. When you go in there looking for a knockout, it doesn't normally turn out in your favor," Whitaker explained.

When the scorecards were read for the fight, there was no chance of Pernell getting hijacked a second time (at least for this fight). Two judges had Pernell pitching a shutout. Paul Gibbs of Washington managed to find two rounds for Greg Haugen. While Gibbs' scorecard read in favor of the right pugilist, he certainly could have received disciplinary action for such a grave mistake.

Gibbs' blunder aside, Pernell Whitaker was now a world champion and Greg Haugen no longer held that distinction. When describing this fight, all Greg could offer was his great admiration for Whitaker, "He was just a nightmare to fight. There was no doubt about it, Whitaker was the best I ever fought. He was hard to hit. Whitaker was one of those guys you really couldn't hit good more than once, you were not going to lay anything hard on him," Greg explained.

The loss was damaging to Greg's boxing cred. First, he was no longer a champion. The belt he fought so hard to obtain, and rightfully win back, was no longer his. Also, he was humbled by Whitaker. From the age of six, nobody ever handled Greg Haugen inside a boxing ring with such ease as did Whitaker. Not on any level. Such a one-sided loss was bound to be a major blow to Greg's psyche. But Greg Haugen was a different animal. He took the loss in stride. He knew all that he could do was move on, and, under the right circumstances, he felt he had what it took to defeat Pernell Whitaker. He never got that chance.

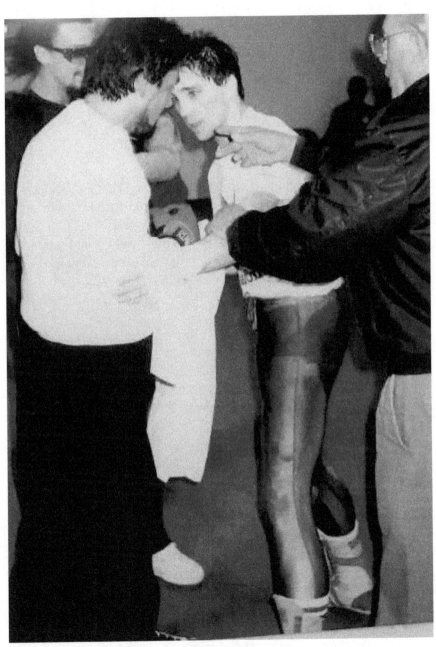

George Chemeres, far right, instructing Roberto Duran & Greg Haugen at
The gym in Pleasantville, New Jersey (Courtesy of John Chemeres).

Chapter Fourteen
Meeting the Devil a Third Time

"Thank god Kevin Rooney came into my life because I was about to die."

—Vinny Paz

Now that he was no longer a champion, Greg Haugen decided to finally take care of a recurring problem, "The last four or five fights I had to go in there knowing my right hand was hurt, so I had to be careful throwing it. I had surgery on my right hand after the Whitaker fight to fix it. It was big fixing it," Greg explained. The surgery contributed to a big layoff for Greg. It was over a year before he got back into the ring, "I chose to get back into it slowly. I did not want to rush it," Greg added.

After the Whitaker loss, Greg returned to Las Vegas for his comeback fight on March tenth, 1990. His opponent was Guillermo Cruz. This fight with Cruz can be seen as one of Greg's most important fights. For starters, fighting Cruz meant putting the 135-pound weight class in the review mirror. Even though stepping up in weight is common practice for most pugilists, there are always a ton of questions attached to the move. Can the fighter bring his power up in weight? Will these bigger fighters be too strong? For Greg Haugen, a fighter who always appeared to have an advantage in strength at lightweight, you had to wonder if would he still have that advantage at a higher weight.

At the time, however, the step up to 140 was temporary, as Greg still had his sights on getting his belt back from Whitaker. With that said, other than insisting on a neutral venue, Greg admits that he was not sure what he could do differently against Pernell, "You weren't going to hit him with too many big shots. If we fought again, I would have tried to put more pressure on him, but he nullifies a lot of that with his ring generalship. He was just a smart fighter." Pernell passed away during the writing of this book, and Greg was taken aback by the tragic news, "It blows my mind that he is not here anymore. I always had great respect for him."

Another reason why Greg's fight with Cruz was crucial was that it meant a return to the ring after being thoroughly dominated. Make no mistake about it, Pernell Whitaker thoroughly beat Greg and proved to the boxing world that there was a tier level in skill that Greg, and most everyone else, was not on. How do you come back from that? On paper, the Whitaker fight was not Greg's first loss, however, after Vinny Paz got the decision in their first fight, more people were calling Haugen the winner, great motivation for Greg and he answered any questions about that fight in the rematch. Against Whitaker, Greg might have won ten seconds of the entire fight. Getting a rematch would be a hard sell.

Guillermo Cruz, Memo, was another tough Mexican fighter who was a tough test for any boxer. If you want to know where you stand in boxing, you match yourself up against a no-nonsense style that is not going to crumble at the first sight of a stiff combination. "Trial-horses," was how Greg referred to fighters of Memo's cloth. It was the kind of style Greg looked for when he was coming up, and it was the kind of style Greg chose for his comeback, "You can get rounds in. Those guys come to fight; they are not just going to lay down. I always wanted to get rounds, and Cruz was the guy they came up with," Greg explained. While only a small percentage of Mexican boxers cross over to the world-class level, compared to the large number of Mexican fighters who compete, such fighters will never struggle to look for work.

Haugen faced Memo Cruz on March 10th, 1990, at the Dunes Hotel in Las Vegas, Nevada. Greg was the headliner- getting beat by Whitaker did not affect his ticket-selling prowess out in the dessert. The fight televised by Sports Channel America's Pro Boxing Tour. In his pre-fight interview with Wallace Matthews, Greg expressed that he was a bit nervous coming back from a lay-off of more than one year and that he was not looking to knock out Memo, whom he described as a "Tough Kid." Haugen also explained that other than his impressive knockout percentage, he knew nothing about Memo Cruz.

The legendary Chuck Hall, decked out in a lavish tuxedo, announced the participants. When both fighters met at the center of the ring to listen to referee Carlos Padilla's pre-fight instructions,

Greg absorbed his opponent with a glaring stare, while Cruz's eyes drifted towards the canvas.

At the opening bell, Greg raced to the center of the ring while Cruz was still navigating around his corner, Cruz flicked out successive jabs in Haugen's direction, while these punches just hit air, it did back Haugen up momentarily. But as is the case when things are going Greg's way, he established himself as the boss of the ring soon after, controlling the pace with his jab and lead left hooks; Greg even tried to hurt Cruz early by launching an unusual lead-left uppercut, "I thought I was able to land it, he had his guard down a little bit, so I decided to try and throw it. But it is a dangerous punch. You can get beat to the punch with a right hand. It not one of those things you are really told to do, you need to be careful when you do throw it."

Greg took the play away from Memo, backing the Mexican fighter up throughout the round. Haugen was first and diverse in round one. It must have felt good to be back, "I was feeling pretty strong, I wasn't sapped for strength," said Greg. Another thing of note in this first round was that Greg looked much thicker carrying 140-pounds, "I had been having a lot of trouble making 135 pounds, and I decided to move up. I did not have to starve and kill myself to make 140. Those five pounds might not seem like much of a difference, but for me, it meant the difference of not starving to death and making weight and staying hydrated. A lot of times at 135, I would make weight, but I did not stay hydrated. I could feel myself getting dehydrated in the fights (at lightweight), and I could feel myself cramping up a bit. Not enough to stop me from fighting, but it just got to the point where it became so hard to make 135 pounds." Greg said of the decision to move up in weight.

In round two, both fighters met at the center of the ring and launched jabs, Greg quickly established distance and managed to back Cruz up. Cruz tried to come forward, with Greg slipping Cruz' jab and attacking the body. Haugen proceeded to score with a left jab, lead right hand and stiff body shots throughout the first minute of this round. The second minute of the round was more of the same, as Greg controlled distance and out jabbed the longer Cruz. Cruz did try to go to the body and scored with a good left hook to the body but soon backed off when Haugen delivered his own right to the body, once again showing off his underrated inside fighting skills.

On the outside, Greg slipped a lazy jab from Cruz and countered with a stiff left hook. Haugen then landed three jabs on the mouth of Memo Cruz, not debilitating punches, but it was the only scoring that was happening. Haugen scored with a solid right counter within the last thirty seconds, the showiest punch of the round up to that point. Greg did not stop and take a picture after that punch, as he sat down more on his shots and appeared to buzz Memo Cruz with a stiff one-two in the last twenty seconds of the round. Greg did not let up and delivered stiff jabs to close out round two. A solid round from Haugen. He appeared sharp, accurate, and elusive, showing no signs of rust after a long layoff.

Greg Haugen put on a clinic for the rest of the fight. His hands never stopped moving, and he never stopped scoring. Greg scored on the inside, from distance, with his jab, to the body. A two-handed attack that confused and wore down the police officer from Mexico City. Memo Cruz did score with a stiff right-uppercut in round four- a punch that indeed got Haugen's attention. Haugen responded to this stiff blow by stepping up his aggression and backing Cruz up soon after, delivering hard power punches with both hands. As Lee Groves said about Greg's fight with Jimmy Paul, he was 'first, last, and always.'

Memo Cruz took a thorough beating in round nine. If Cruz's corner or Padilla, decided the fight should have been stopped after round nine, nobody would have questioned that decision. However, Memo Cruz did come out for round ten, a beaten fighter with swelling around both eyes, looking for a miracle. That miracle seemed even less likely when Greg began round ten tattooing Cruz with every punch thought possible since the inception of the Queensbury Rules of boxing. But Cruz would not fold, which was exactly what Haugen was looking for, and continued to try and land the blow that would turn the tide in his favor. Cruz's last stand should be admired because he was still trying to mix up his punches, hoping that left hook to the body, that he repeatedly threw, would finally hit the sweet spot. Memo Cruz was not winging wild, undisciplined punches in desperation during the first minute of round ten, but they were missing their mark nonetheless, and Haugen was making him pay with tremendous power punches. The fight started to resemble the thrashing that Larry Holmes put on Randall 'Tex'

Cobb in 1982. Carlos Padilla realized this and put a halt to Cruz' inspired, yet futile effort.

Greg Haugen was back on track. Flashing boxing skills that would make every fighter in 1990 not named Pernell Whitaker envious. "Cruz was considered a tune-up, but they are really no tune-up fights. That is the biggest fight he (Memo Cruz) will ever fight. So, I had to be ready and on my best game because it was a chance of a lifetime and I didn't want him to make a name on me," Greg explained. His next fight was with Robert Nunez in June of 1990, another dangerous 'tune-up' fighter looking to strike gold on a big name. Greg stopped Nunez in six rounds.

Greg was happy with his performance in these fights because neither Cruz or Nunez was able to make a name for themselves by besting the former lightweight champion, and all things seemed well with his surgically repaired right hand. "I was able to throw it at will, and it didn't hurt me. So, I had confidence in using my right hand again," explained Haugen.

Now it was time to really test it.

The first two fights between Greg and Vinny were thirty rounds of boxing bliss. Everything you could ask for, skills, guts, animosity, controversy, and brutality. Even with the second find being so one-sided, it was an entertaining gem. Indeed, they needed to give us a third fight.

The third fight between Greg and Vinny took place on August 5th, 1990, at the Trump Plaza Hotel in Atlantic City. Plenty had happened since their second fight. Greg defended and lost his IBF lightweight title, and Vinny was coming off a twelve-round decision loss to Hector Csmscho, where once again, he had weight issues. "To be honest with you, I just could not make that weight. We wanted to make the fight at 147 or a catchweight at 145, and he (Camacho) wouldn't do it. He wouldn't do it. I said, 'come on Hector, don't be a little pussy. It is not like I am asking you to gain twenty pounds', He wouldn't do it," Paz explains. Even though Hector would not meet Paz on the scales, Vinny still has great respect for him, "The late great Hector Camacho. Hector could fight, He was fast as lightning. He beat me. I didn't win that fight. Had we fought at the weight I wanted, I would have knocked his ass out," Paz explains.

Going into the fight with Greg, 140 pounds was also the weight limit. But Vinny had newfound confidence in Kevin Rooney, "Thank god Kevin Rooney came into my life because I was about to die," Paz recalls.

Another big difference in the fight was that it was ten rounds instead of the fifteen rounds Greg and Vinny fought twice before. "You go into a fight like that (10 rounds instead of 15) with a different mindset. You are able to do a lot more stuff, pick and pock, stay away, run...Vinny was able to do that, and he got the decision. It was something I was not happy about, but (I) can't argue with it, and all I could have done was put it behind me and get ready for the next fight," Greg explained.

Often, circumstances before the fight have a big say in what manifested in the ring. For this fight, Greg Haugen explains a situation the day of that fight that affected his mindsight for the fight, "Vinny was with his steroid geek friend Mighty Mike Quinn and this other guy. So, they cornered me in the bathroom and started pushing me around. It took my attention away from the fight because I really wanted to take his head off. I just let the anger get the best of me. I wanted him to fight me, and he just wouldn't fight me. He got introduced to Kevin Rooney and became a track star. I guess they figured if he ran, I wouldn't be able to pound him with the jab. But since I was so angry, I followed him around instead of cutting the ring off. It cost me a ten-round decision."

Meanwhile, Paz was feeling large and in charge, "I think I got to weigh in at 142, and I came in at 152. I felt great, he didn't touch me, he didn't lay a glove on me. It was great. President Trump was in the front row with Evander Holyfield, it was a great day. It wasn't even a hard fight," Paz explains.

There was no doubt the extra size benefitted Paz. "In the third fight, Vinny looked a whole lot bigger than Greg, and he was visibly larger than the 140-pound weight class, and Vinny boxed his way to victory," Lee Groves explains.

The scorecards read 96-94, 98-92, and 97-93 for the Pazmanian Devil. In reality, this was not a close fight. Greg did not look good against Paz, a fighter whom he won a significant number of rounds against in the past two fights. Greg could never get it going in fight three, and Paz showcased beautiful lateral movement. And Paz did enough scoring to secure at least six rounds, probably more. No, he never hurt Greg at all, but sometimes the circumstances of a boxing match do not dictate that kind of opening. Besides, Greg had an iron chin when he was right. The only thing one can question from this fight was whether or not Paz could have kept up that kind of movement in a fifteen-round fight, or even twelve round fight. I asked Vinny if he would have been able to keep that up for more than twelve rounds, he laughed, "Oh sure I could have come on." I asked Vinny if his playful tone when answering meant a wink-wink should be followed by his response, "Just one wink," Vinny laughed. The bottom line for this fight was that Vinny Paz stopped to take a picture over and over again, and not once did Greg make him pay for that ill-advised tactic.

According to John Chemeres, there was a lot going on to attribute to Greg's subpar performance, "There were a lot of distractions. Greg was there with his wife; I was there with my girlfriend. Paz even tried to come into our locker room after the bathroom incident. Trump came in and he caused a lot of distractions, because he wanted it to be about him. It was just different from the second fight."

As with most things in boxing, there is always an alternate point of view, and Dave Murphy had one with this fight, "I thought Greg had a better case for a robbery in the third fight. I thought the harder punches were landed by Haugen. Vinny did a lot of running in that fight. I am not one who scores the stick and move. I did not see Vinny winning that fight," Murphy explained. John Chemeres also felt Greg won, even though he admitted the focus was lacking, "Paz was not even hitting Greg. I thought Greg won."

Indeed, an opinion not held by many. But that is what makes boxing the ultimate Rorschach test. Looking back at the trilogy, there is one comment Dave Murphy made that is easy to subscribe to, "Of the three fights Greg Haugen had the most convincing win with the second fight," Murphy explains. Indeed.

Greg Haugen and Vinny Paz fought forty rounds, "That's a lot of fighting," Paz said. When two fighters share the ring for that many minutes you would expect them to have a fondness for each other all these years later. But that is not the case. Vinny Paz has nothing but disdain for Greg Haugen. Most of the animosity has to do with Greg's feelings about their fights, "After the first fight I won, he cried like a little bitch. After the second fight he won, I gave him all the credit in the world, I said he is a tough kid and he beat me, there is nothing I could do about it. Boom, okay. The third fight, I dust his ass off, he doesn't touch me. I give him a boxing lesson and he cried like a baby again. That is why I am sick of that kid. I am done with him," Paz explains.

Vinny may take solace in reading Greg's comments about their third fight. As Greg all but admits Vinny won that fight. "If Vinny won any of the fights, I thought it was the third one. He outboxed me a little bit, when you are in there you think you won every fight. But I thought Vinny did a better job as a boxer and staying away, not getting hit as much," Greg explained.

Of course, as soon as Vinny reads that, Greg's comments about their first fight is sure to catch his ire again, "The first two fights I beat him up," Greg boasts.

Today, the bad blood remains between Greg Haugen and Vinny Paz. Tony The Tiger Lopez explains how he saw it firsthand, as he fought Greg on the undercard of Vinny's first fight with Roberto Duran, and The Tiger does not comprehend their loathing for one another, "I don't understand it. If I saw an opponent of mine today, I would go over and shake their hand and say, 'let's go have a drink.' If I saw John John Molina, I would invite him to my house, kick back and have a great time. That is where I came from."

Al Bernstein has a theory as to why Greg and Vinny still have bad feelings towards each other, "Both Greg and Vinny have the kind of personality that could get under someone's skin, if they choose to be that way. I found both guys to be engaging guys. Vinny, when he was fighting, could be a little rougher in my opinion because he worked hard at being difficult. Greg could be difficult, but there was that other side of Greg Haugen that most people got a kick out of. You always thought he was kind of putting everyone on. But he very much knew how to get under his opponents' skin. If you put those two personalities together, to me, that is the kind of recipe for two fighters who are going to be annoyed at each other. I am almost not surprised they never kind of figured out how to bury the hatchet."

Kathy Duva describes how unfortunate it is that these two fine pugilists have such animosity. History tells us that this is not the norm when it comes to fighters' relationships after they shared the ring, "I watched Arturo Gatti, and Micky Ward become good friends. I guess if you don't feel like you were treated fairly at some point in the relationship, you harbor grudges. Gatti and Ward ended up loving each other, but neither of them was resentful about judging or where the fights took place, none of that stuff was ever in their heads," Kathy explains. Kathy Duva also suggests that Greg and Vinny might also have some bitterness about how their careers played out. "Gatti and Ward exceeded all expectations of themselves, so maybe they were at peace. I do not get the feeling that Greg and Vinny were. Today Greg and Vinny would be huge stars, I do not think at that time it was possible to be a huge star. At that time, you had heavyweights like Tyson, Lennox Lewis, Holyfield and Bowe. It was not possible that lower weight fighters could be stars like that. The heavyweights just took up all of the energy," Kathy suggested.

The Fab Four of the 1980's also sucked up a lot of the press clippings from Haugen and Paz. Ray Leonard's robbery over Marvelous Marvin Hagler was named Ring Magazine's fight of the year over the classic first battle in Providence. The latter was a much better fight. Indeed, a point that can be debated. "I thought it was a good fight, but I do not think it was better than Hagler versus Leonard. It did not have that same weight," Dave Murphy explained. There is no debate, which was the bigger fight, with more historical significance, but should that be the main criteria when voting for the best contest of the calendar year? Another excellent boxing question to debate.

Had Ray Leonard never decided to challenge Marvelous Marvin Hagler, after he learned that Hagler's desire to fight had all but left him, Greg Haugen and Vinny Paz' first scrap would have been a clear front runner for the fight of the year in 1987, a much weaker year than the previous one. Lee Groves agreed with this point, "Definitely, yes. A pulsating fight with all the toughness you would want in a boxing match," was how Lee described this fabulous first fight.

If Greg Haugen and Vinny Paz could ever get to even a cordial friendship, it would be great for boxing. But do not hold your breath. Paz has a paper trail of not getting along with some of his other opponents. Paz says of Dana Rosenblatt, "I hated him then, and I still kind of hate him now." As far as Greg goes, Paz is the only opponent he does not care for, "Vinny is the only guy that rubs me the wrong way because he still talks shit. He knows he didn't win that fight. He still talks about how he beat me; he knows he didn't. But I respect him. I respect everybody I fought because not everybody has the balls to get in there. Once you climb through those ropes, it's only you. You are the only one that can prevent *you* from getting hurt. Any fight can be your last fight.".

The Haugen-Paz trilogy deserves a place with the great trilogies in boxing history. It generated drama, debate, skill, guts-the kind of memories and discussions only boxing could create. Both men should be proud of what they have given the fans.

Chapter Fifteen
The Comeback Trail
Back On ESPN

"I had like 103 temperature, and they didn't want me to fight, but I don't like canceling fights, so I decided to go with it."

—Greg Haugen

Victor Machado was already a veteran trainer by the time he and Greg Haugen crossed paths in 1990. A lifer. Victor worked with such champions like Jose Napoles, Mike McCallum, Saoul Mamby, Wilfred Benitez and Juan Laporte. To work with such great talent, as Victor puts it, "You have to know what you are doing." It was Juan LaPorte, who was the link between Victor and Greg. "I met Greg in 1990 in downtown Las Vegas. He was working with Juan LaPorte, a fighter I was working with," Victor described.

Even though this was Victor's first encounter with Greg, he was well aware of his talent. "I saw when he beat Jimmy Paul. At that time, according to Gil Clancy, Angelo Dundee, guys like that, Jimmy Paul was the best lightweight in the world. And Greg fought a beautiful fight in Caesar's Palace," Victor added.

For the Jimmy Paul fight, Greg explained how important sparring was to his success. It was sparring, that essential element when preparing for a fight, that got the ball rolling for the Team Haugen-Machado. "When I saw Greg, he was with George Chemeres at the Tocco's gym, and they were looking for sparring. Greg was on the comeback trail, and George asked me if Greg could spar with this young kid I was working with. When they sparred, Greg liked the way the kid was moving. The kid was just starting out, but I had him moving good. Greg Haugen liked Latin fighters. He and Laporte got along real good, he liked LaPorte's style. Latin fighters have special moves. They do things (in the ring) nobody else does. Latin boxers are graceful, they have music in the body," explained Victor. Greg corroborated this admiration by saying, "They always did a lot. All Puerto Ricans were pretty good fighters. Most of the Latin guys I worked with were all quality, quality fighters. They had been taught the right way from the start, and it shows. Those are guys you can learn from. When you are in there with those guys, and you are holding your own, it just makes you feel real good."

It was more than just Greg's admiration for the style of Victor's fighters that gravitated him to the Puerto Rican trainer. "Greg appreciated that I lent him the kid, he had nobody. After the sparring, we started to talk to each other, feel each other out. He kind of liked me, if you do not know Greg, he didn't trust many people. People always told me they didn't understand how I got along with Greg Haugen because he was so hard to get along with. But Greg was always beautiful to me," Victor said.

Victor said it was George Chemeres who asked him if he could work with Greg a little bit for his upcoming fight. "I gave him a couple of rounds with the hand pads, and he liked the way I moved," explained Victor. Greg explains that the word 'like' is an understatement, "Victor was the best mitt guy I ever worked with, I never had someone like that before," Greg said. Victor explained how a fighter hitting the hand pads enhances their accuracy, movement and the overall flow of the punches, "Before that Greg was just hitting the bag," Victor said.

Victor Machada was also known to use a method to improve a fighter body punching that was atypical at that time. "I had a vest you put on your chest for body punching. Body armor, like a baseball catcher's equipment. I had one in Gleason's Gym in New York City. Nobody had them for the fighters back then, and I worked with Greg with the vest. Now you see it all the time," Victor explained.

"Greg already had a great jab, I helped polish it. He would also throw a good right hand to the ribs and come back to the head. Greg was already good. I just helped advance his game," described Victor.

This advancement did not stop in the gym. The very straightforward Chemeres asked Victor if he would help out in the corner for his upcoming fight against Tommy Hanks. Liking what he saw in Greg, Victor Machado jumped on this offer. Against Paz, Greg looked pedestrian, letting an opponent get away with things, and do things to him, that he would never allow during his great run from 1984-1987. How would he look against Hanks?

197

A legitimate question for sure. Fighters at the lighter weights often have a shorter peak. In Greg Haugen's case, it seemed odd that his tank was empty, however. Greg showcased above-average defense in most of his fights. Other than the first fight with Paz and the Pernell Whitaker fight, Greg did not get hit all that much. And in both of those fights, Greg never appeared seriously hurt. When Whitaker dropped Greg, it was a flash knockdown, and in his last loss against Paz, he did not take big, deliberating shots either.

So why did Greg seem to have many miles off his engine by 1990? Greg explains that he probably lost the Paz fight on the scales, "The third Paz fight was at 140, he didn't make weight, and I was not that smart or savvy, I should have made him sweat out that extra pound, but I let him get away with it. It might have cost me a fight."

There are other ways that fighters can empty their tank besides inside the ring. Perhaps too much hard sparring? Maybe too much wear and tear on your body with vices? According to Victor Machado, "Greg liked to run around with the girls and the booze." Behaviors that would erode the skills of any boxer. But in fairness to Greg, these behaviors did not seem to dominate Greg's habits until way after 1990. "When he took a fight seriously, he was hard to beat," Victor also added about Greg.

In 1990, Greg Haugen desperately wanted to return to the championship status. Greg tasted the 'champagne wishes and caviar dreams,' the ultimate status made famous by Robin Leach in the 1980s, and was not about to go back to the taste of average beer and fast food if his fists had anything to say about it.

1990 was the start of a new decade. The landscape of the country was going through many changes. There were many similarities, as well. The Republicans still had a stronghold on the White House, as George H.W. Bush represented the tenth straight year of the Grand 'Ol Party, slowly stripping away the concept of a nation where the separation of church and state meant something, the fairness doctrine was a mere memory now in 1990, the ball was just getting rolling with contrasting views being absent from political opinion. Indeed, 'Daddy Bush,' as he was referred to later in life, was building a legacy that made the religious conservative right, the greedy hand grabbers of Wall Street, and the War Hawks, proud. At the same time, President Bush made great strides on the international front by signing the Chemical Weapons Accord, along with Mikhail

Gorbachev, and caught the ire of many Americans by reneging on his vow for 'no new taxes.' As in boxing, often in politics there is one mistake that there is just no coming back from. The new taxes seemed to be it for Bush. 1990 also saw tensions in the Middle East boiling over, the Smith & Wesson gun had an upgrade, and a huge oil spill occurred on the Gulf of Mexico. Indeed, doom and gloom was the pulse of the nation in 1990.

1990s mixed bag was also prominent in the world of pop culture. In movies: Martin Scorsese gave us Goodfellas, Arnold Schwarzenegger showed us his funny side in Kindergarten Cop, Presumed Innocent was a crackling thriller and a box office smash, Kathy Bates tortured James Caan in Misery, and Ghost topped the box office and is credited as one of the best tear-jerkers of all-time. On the other hand, the horrible film Driving Miss Daisy won the Best Picture Oscar in March of 1990; a terrible choice, I guess the voters could not resist the charm of an obedient black man, Bruce Willis continued to shoot up things in the meaningless Die Hard 2, and Back to the Future III turned us on our heads, almost ruining the merits of the original classic.

In music, George Michael asked us to Listen Without Prejudice; can we ever achieve that goal, Run DMC came Back From Hell, Jon Bon Jovi went solo in a Blaze of Glory, Public Enemy released the classic album Fear of a Black Planet, and Bell Biv Divoe warned us to never trust a big butt and a smile. Indeed, the entire landscape of emotions was prominent within the music of 1990. And I must confess that all were fun to listen to.

In the world of sports, Pete Rose was sent to prison for tax fraud, proving once again there was nothing decent or honest about a hard-nosed baseball player who happened to hit the baseball better than everyone else. Nolan Ryan pitched his sixth career no-hitter, and Jose Rio and the Cincinnati Reds neutralized the Bash Brothers from the Oakland Athletics to capture the World Series in four surprising games.

Also, in 1990, the Detroit Pistons won back to back titles by defeating the Portland Trail Blazers, the San Francisco 49ers destroyed the Denver Broncos in one of the most lackluster and one-sided Super Bowls of all time, the Edmonton Oilers won another Stanley Cup, and veteran Martina Navratilova captured Wimbledon in women's tennis.

However, it was the world of boxing that dominated the sports headlines in 1990. Terry Norris dismantled Ray Leonard, squelching another miracle comeback by Leonard. Pernell Whitaker became the undisputed lightweight champion of the world. Chris Eubank stopped Nigel Benn in nine rounds; in one of the best rivalries, the sport of boxing has ever seen. Julio Caesar Chavez made an unbelievable comeback against Meldrick Taylor in a classic battle that is still debated with passion today. And James Buster Douglas pulled off the biggest upset in sports history by knocking out the perceived unbeatable Iron Mike Tyson. It was an upset that did not shock Greg, he explains, "I had seen Mike training in the gym, and I knew he wasn't in shape. And I knew that Buster could fight a little bit, and if he could get in shape, he was going to have a good chance. It just so happened that Buster's mom died, and it motivated to get in shape, and Mike wasn't ready. That (the upset) didn't really surprise me at all. You can't take anyone light."

Douglas' win put boxing front in center for all the right reasons. A rarity in boxing today, unfortunately. Even more unfortunate was Buster's follow up to his monumental victory. Indeed, later in 1990, Buster all but erased his glory from the Tyson upset when he showed up grossly overweight and unmotivated against Evander The Real Deal Holyfield for his first title defense. All it took was one big right hand from Holyfield to end the improbable championship reign of James Buster Douglas. It was a right hand that was set up by Holyfield by a marvelous feint that baited Douglas into throwing an ill-advised right uppercut from way outside. Undoubtedly a setup from Holyfield that was influenced by the Great George Benton, Holyfield's ace trainer.

One cannot help to look at the ups and downs of 1990 and analyze how much the events of that year mirrored Greg Haugen's 1990 as a boxer. The turmoil in the Middle East can be directly equated to Greg's failure against Paz; as can Driving Miss Daisy's Oscar win, the calamities of Pete Rose, and the failures of Leonard and Buster Douglass, in his first title defense. The absolute worst of the worst.

On the other hand, the Chemical Weapons Accord, Arnold singing Old MacDonald, Chavez' comeback, Buster's upset, Pernell's dominance, Public Enemy's message, Jose Rio' Reds, are all examples of the cream rising to the top, signature moments that will stand the test of time. Greg Haugen's collaboration with Victor Machado could be seen as such a moment as well.

Before Greg Haugen could shock the world one more time, he had to defeat Tommy Hanks. Hanks sported a record of 19-5, 7 KO's, going into the fight with Greg Haugen. Hanks had some appeal to him. A swarming fighter who also had a decent jab. Hanks won the USA Ohio State Lightweight Title in a tough twelve-round decision over Forrest Winchester. He gave a good account of himself against Anthony Jones, before being stopped in the ninth round and went the ten-round distance with Hector Macho Camacho. Hanks fought Camacho when he was a sizzling 34-0, and just coming off his decision victory over Ray Boom Boom Mancini. Main Events was fixing to match the Macho Man against Haugen, so it seemed fitting to pit Haugen up against a fighter who went the distance with Hector.

Greg Haugen faced Tommy Hanks on November 29th, 1990, at the Horizon Casino Resort, in Lake Tahoe Nevada. The fight was scheduled for ten rounds and was the co-feature for a fight that featured the popular television fighter Vince Phillips against the veteran Victorio Belcher, in an ESPN showcase. Indeed, Greg Haugen was once again in front of the ESPN cameras. The network where he made his bones was now at the forefront of a much-needed comeback win.

As the fight started, Tommy Hanks intended to make it a street fight. He charged right at Greg, beating him to the center of the ring, not often done against Greg, and backing him up. Greg did not appear deterred by Hanks's aggression and flicked a jab in Hanks's direction, showing he was intent on participating in a boxing match. Hanks slipped the jab and fired off a wide left hook, followed by an even wider right hook. The latter punch did touch Haugen's chin but had virtually nothing behind it. After the amateurish punches, Hanks seemed to settle down and staring firing stiff jabs in Haugen's direction. Haugen remained relaxed, even though some of these jabs were landing. Greg attacked the body with forceful punches and came back upstairs with a straight, stiff jab. This sequence of punches established the real estate Haugen needed and showed the spectators who had the superior pedigree. The rest of round one saw Greg control the pace from distance. As often, when he is going right, he is first and diverse. With less than a minute left in the round, Greg pinned Hanks against the ropes and landed stiff headshots. The cherry on top was a beautiful one-two that landed on Hanks' face at the twenty second mark of round one. It was a sizzling combination that was set up by a jab that was thrown, not with the intent to land stiff but to distract Hanks from the hard-right hand that followed.

Diversity is what often separates the champions from the contenders. In particular, how a fighter throws a jab. There are many ways a fighter can deliver a jab and with many purposes. To disturb rhythm, as a range finder, to keep an opponent at range, to land a hard punch with your lead hand, to serve as a distraction for a follow-up power shot...the creativity has endless possibilities, and Greg Haugen showcased such creativity quite often in this first round against Tommy Hanks.

Rounds two and three were more of the same. Greg Haugen was dictating the pace and keeping Hanks at distance with his jab. When Hanks did get in close, he paid for it with those hard body shots Haugen's often deliveries with effective debilitation. Indeed, Victor Machada's influence was oozing through as Greg Haugen's jab appeared to be more polished and was clocking in a lot of minutes. As round three ended, the television audience was treated to its first glimpse at Haugen's new corner. Stan Tischler was gone, "I just think I needed some new blood in my corner. I wanted to work with Victor, he was a good guy, a smart guy and the best mitt guy I ever saw," Greg said of the decision to remove Stan. George Chemeres was now served as the head trainer, with Victor by his side and the father figure of Jim Montgomery serving as the calming, consistent symbol in Greg's life. But it was Victor Machada that would take on the responsibility of cut man, a role Stan Tischler took on with impeccable competence. A transition that Greg had full confidence in, "Victor was one of the best cut men as well," Greg explained.

When Greg returned to the corner after round three, the new team immediately went to work. Machada's voice was first heard as he encouraged Greg that he hurt his opponent to the body. Machada then began to massage the arms of 'Mutt.' Chemeres then chimed in by telling Greg he was doing well, but he wanted Greg to get closer. Perhaps to land more of those painful body shots. With Greg being such a maestro at distance with his jab, it was a curious piece of instruction from Chemeres to want Greg to get closer, as that would appear to give Hanks' style the best chance to do well.

When round four began, Greg delivered successive jabs that flowed like fine wine, preventing his adversary from getting set to deliver his own debilitating blows. The remainder of round four saw Greg Haugen make more of a conscious effort to get inside, as Chemeres requested. The results saw Greg more in Hanks's chest and scoring more solid combinations. This tactic also gave more opportunities for Hanks to land some hard stuff, however, and, indeed, Hanks did catch Greg with more power punches in round four. The best Hanks looked was with about a minute left in the round. He pinned Greg against the ropes and landed some wide, yet hard punches. Greg smirked at this work from Hanks but also showed the wherewithal to get off the ropes and proceed to throw rapid-fire jabs at distance, indicating the work from Hanks was felt and put on notice. The round still belonged to Greg Haugen, but Tommy Hanks was shaping up to be a tough customer who had no plans of leaving early. Which could have proven to be problematic, as Greg was suffering from the flu. "I had like 103 temperature, and they didn't want me to fight, but I don't like canceling fights, so I decided to go with it," Greg explained.

Which turned out to be a wise decision because Greg owned the ring that night. He was first and diverse. Keeping distance, working his jab overtime, and stopping Hanks in his tracks with a stiff right hand when need be. When Hanks did manage to close distance and get inside, Greg was clever enough to tie Hanks up and let referee Mills Lane lay down the law of the Queensberry Rules. As the punches kept landing on Hanks, his eyes became the visual, residual effects of Haugen's work. By the time round eight began, the spunk and hope that was once pronounced on Hanks' face was drained away. All that remained for this kid from Cleveland was the heart and guts that only a fighter knows.

Ring announcer Barry Tompkins said it was desperation time for Tommy Hanks at the start of round eight. Probably true. But what everyone needed to realize was that desperation time stared for Greg Haugen at the start of round one. Another loss for Haugen at this point would have proven disastrous for Haugen; it probably would have meant retirement. Only a win, and an impressive win, would answer those questions in Haugen's favor.

Greg Haugen was not equipped to go back to fighting on small, non-televised club shows, his success and skills were too far removed to go back to those basics. Either he had enough to continue the television/championship level, or he did not. "I would have retired if I couldn't beat Hanks," Greg admitted. However, a loss to Tommy Hanks did not mean Greg would not be seen on television again, it just meant he would longer be seen as a prizefighter anymore. Greg's act two, had he lost this fight, was to be a television commentator. A position Greg was more than qualified to do. But would that have filled the void of fighting? Probably not. That sensation of punching somebody in the face, as well as getting punched in the face yourself, is often addictive and hard to give up. Greg did not want to give that up in 1990.

Indeed, Tommy Hanks was desperate for a win too. However, he had not reached the pinnacle that Haugen did, so going back to the small clubs would have been natural for Hanks, and quite honestly probably inevitable. With such pressure on Greg, as well as battling with the flu for this fight, the fact that Greg defeated Tommy Hanks with such perfection should not go unnoticed. Another clutch performance from a guy who always seemed to have the odds against him.

In round ten, when Tommy Hanks's only chance for a win was to stop 'Mutt,' Greg was at his absolute best. Greg knew when he needed to be first, when he needed to neutralize the desperate, rushing Hanks, and when he needed to use the ring to kill time. Not by running, but by being where he needed to be. With about 1:23 left in round ten, Hanks did find some success in his aggressive posture. But Greg turned it back on in a blink of an eye, and slugged Hanks with a hard-left hook upstairs. The hardest left hook he threw all fight. Simply fantastic and just when Greg needed to be. Greg must have felt his oats with that punch because he went into more of a brawling mode the rest of the round, "I thought I hurt him pretty good, so I tried to finish him off," Greg admitted. When the bell sounded to end the fight Greg Haugen and Tommy Hanks embraced, as is often the case between two boxers after a hard-fought battle. Tommy Hanks was a little extra when the bell sounded, however, and proceeded to lift Greg Haugen by the waist and carry him around in a celebratory fashion. "I had a couple of guys do that to me, I guess they were just happy to be in there with me," Greg chuckled when asked about this incident.

There was no doubt that Greg Haugen responded to the pressure and lived to fight another day. Michael Buffer confirmed this belief when he read the official scorecards. 100-90, twice, and 99-91, all in favor of the winner Greg Haugen. Somehow judge Burt Clements found a round to give Tommy Hanks. Perhaps the only person in the entire universe with such a thought.

Such injustice was not about to get in the way of Greg Hagen's dominating victory, however. Greg was fixing to fight again in less than a month, and he needed to be focused.

Kelcie Banks, a tall, lanky southpaw, was rumored to be Haugen's next opponent had he got passed Tommy Hanks, for December 20th. Instead, Greg squared off against Billy Young, and Banks faced Ben Lopez at Bally's Casino in Las Vegas.

Billy Young fought out of Michigan and sported a record of 29-5-1, 22 KO's. He was a hard-punching lightweight who had a victory over Tommy Hanks, Haugen's last opponent, and impressed the ESPN cameras with his knockout victory over Roland Commings. Young fit the mold of fighter that ESPN and Top Rank Boxing wanted to feature at that time; a good-looking white kid who could fight a little bit. Same as guys of the past like Freddie Roach, Charlie 'White Lightning' Brown, Chris Calvin, Ted Michalizsyn, and, of course, Greg Haugen, up until now, the best of them all.

Like the formula of the 1980s, these white fighters, with the matinee idol looks, were going to be matched tough, to see what they were made off. Well, Billy Young was already matched tough going into his fight with Greg as he found himself on the losing end against guys like Frankie Mitchell, Frankie Rhodes, Vinnie Burgese, and Sharmba Mitchell, but gave a credible account of himself. Good enough to land the ESPN main event against the former lightweight champion. Young was certainly matched good enough to be ready for Greg Haugen, but as Victor Machada said, "Greg might look easy to beat when watching him, but he is very tough once you get in there with him."

Once again, the ESPN lights and camera were focused on that kid from Auburn, Washington. A ten-round affair that held the upmost importance to Haugen. Indeed, Haugen looked spectacular his last time out against Hanks. But what was equally true was a loss to a

Billy Young could put an end to his comeback. Once again, a poor performance might mean the television networks go dark on him, all but erasing his chance to be a world champion once more.

As referee Carlos Padilla gave his pre-fight instruction, Greg was focused on nothing but Billy Young. After all, it was indeed Young who had more of a say on his future than anyone else. Except, of course, for himself.

When the bell sounded for round one action, it was Greg Haugen who reached the center of the ring first, a contrast to his previous fight with Tommy Hanks. Bouncing on his toes, Greg was winning the battle of the jabs early on. Haugen was owning the real estate and controlling the pace in the first minute of round one. 'Mutts' defense was also on display during this first minute of the fight, as the former lightweight champion stymied an aggressive moment form Young when he slipped three straight jabs and a right hand thrown by the lanky pugilist from Michigan, with relative ease by using subtle movement. Vintage Haugen. The second minute of round one saw Greg continue to make Young miss; however, he was not landing any meaningful shots in return. A grazing, but showy left uppercut landed from Young at the two-minute mark of the round. It was not a damaging enough punch to mitigate the superior ring generalship and defense Greg was showcasing, but it was the kind of punch that can trick the judges into favoring Young; in this case, the judges were Chuck Giampa, Patricia Morse Jarmen, and Paul Smith. There was one thing that was for sure, the winner of the round was still in the balance for the final minute of the first stanza.

In that final minute, Haugen bounced on his toes, feinted, and tried to deliver a stiff right hand to the body of Young. The Haugen body shot found its mark, but with very little starch. Young countered with an equally underwhelming combination. Who gets the advantage during that sequence? In the final forty-four seconds of the round, Greg did slightly more landing and made Young miss a lot of punches by a wide margin. But for some reason, both Barry Thompkins and Al Bernstein, the ESPN television announcers, voiced round one as a good one for Young. Looking at this round through a critical lens, it should be a round scored for Greg Haugen. With no clear advantage in punches landed, and no hard blows landed by either pugilist, Greg's superior defense, as well as his ring generalship should have been the deciding factors to score the round in Greg's favor. Albeit, it was not one of his more effective opening rounds.

When Greg returned to his corner after round one, it was lifelong father figure Jim Montgomery who took center stage. Providing Greg with salient instructions as George Chemeres crept through the ropes on Haugen's right. Victor Machada was also in Greg's corner but was not in the view of the camera. In his previous fight, it was Chemeres, who was the lead guy. The reason for the switch? "Jim had been with me since day one, it was important for me to get him in there and make him the head guy and let him know he was in charge," explained Greg. The main focus of Jim's instructions to Greg was to counter the Young jab. Victor Machada could be seen toweling Greg off towards the end of the one-minute break.

Round two saw Greg begin by backing up Young and trying to find a rhythm with his jab. Billy Young looked comfortable in the role of the matador, as he sat back, poised, content to counter Greg's leads. Young was indeed delivering these counters, but they were not landing with any authority. During the second minute of the round, Young decided to give the role of the bull a try and started coming forward more. Well, only the best of the world-class fighters can lead against Greg Haugen and be effective. The rest of the lot, as is where Billy Young falls, soon find out that Greg is a very elusive target when he is at his best, and sooner or later he is going to make you pay for leading. This moment came at the 1:29 mark of round two when Greg countered Young with a hard-left hook to the jaw. This punched stopped Young in his tracks, and he soon went back to the role of the matador. Haugen made a strategic mistake at this point because he did not jump on Young. Instead, he stopped to take a picture. Haugen was not firing, this allowed Billy Young to get brave and lead again. Young's decision paid off as he landed a showy combination. The follow up left hand to Haugen's face was one of the best punches of the round. Young went back to be the matador and appeared to have Greg confused a bit, as he was only throwing one punch at a time in the direction of the herkie jerky motion Billy Young was showcasing. As this was occurring, Young would pick his spots to rush in and throw combinations. While Greg was savvy enough to evade the brunt of the blows, he was not making Young pay for rushing in, in such a careless manner. Very uncharacteristic to the fighting style of Greg Haugen. At around the

:29 mark, Young threw a combination that missed bad, and all Greg offered in return was one last jab. With under twenty seconds to go in the round, Greg finally resembled himself and landed a few stiff jabs. Barry Thompkins seemed to think it was a more even round. It was one of the worst tactical rounds Greg Haugen fought.

During the first minute of round three, Haugen went back to the basics with his jab. He fired it with more authority and rapid-fire precision, and he kept making Young look silly when he fired and missed with his power punches. Haugen was in command during the second minute of round two as well. Leading with his jab and making Young miss. Greg did try to lead once with a right to the body, but it was exclusively jabs the rest of the time. The final minute of round three saw Greg continue to be economical with his jab, but it was landing with accuracy, as Young missed with virtually every power punch he threw. With less than ten seconds to go in the round, Greg opened up with more power punches and scored well. Putting an exclamation point on the first easy round to score in the fight.

In between rounds, the ESPN cameras captured just how special a fighter Greg Haugen was. In slow motion, we see Billy Young throw a right hook, Greg just took a subtle step back and was still in position to counter with a stiff left hook. There is only a small percentage of pugilists in the history of boxing who could execute such a move with such fluidity, and Greg Haugen performed such movements regularly. Most great defensive fighters do not stay in the pocket, make their opponent miss, and still be in a position to throw a hard shot of their own. Indeed, more than just a ToughMan.

Billy Young looked like a beaten man as he was set for round four action. Greg once again got to the center of the ring first and started popping his jab. Young was wasting a lot of energy by swaying from side to side, but he also managed to back Haugen into the ropes with his aggression. Haugen stood calm, made Young miss, and found his way off the ropes. Once Greg got set again, he landed two nice jabs. Young danced around a bit, then ate three or four more Haugen jabs. At the 2:08 mark, Young ducked and leaned forward, exposing himself to Greg. Haugen, always the savvy veteran, took advantage of this vulnerable position and slugged a left hook to Young's head, then came back upstairs, with a stiff right hand. The best power-punching sequence by Greg so far. Haugen put on a clinic the rest of the round with his jab and superior defense. For the most post. Billy Young was much more aggressive the rest of the round, probably trying to get back those power punches from Greg and did get in a strong left hook and a straight right hand during the stanza. But it was not nearly enough work to sway the judges.

Greg Haugen was bouncing with confidence and purpose in round five. He even tried his famous right lead to the body early on. But it was the consistency of the Haugen jab that won him the round. Billy gave a better account of himself in this round compared to the previous two, countering well in spots, which is why it was odd that he decided to turn southpaw for the first time in the fight, with about a minute left in the round. All Young's surprise diversity did was cause him to eat more leather. Greg has often said that fighting a southpaw is a nightmare, but in this case, he looked much more comfortable staring down Billy Young from the southpaw stance, "He wasn't your typical southpaw. He did it to try and confuse me, and it didn't. It is different when you are fighting a seasoned, polished southpaw. When somebody starts switching up on you (who is not experienced), it doesn't really affect you," Greg added. When the bell sounded to end round five, Young's frustrations seemed to seep over, and for a moment, it appeared as if Young was going to take a swipe at Greg after the bell. Young quickly put on his cooler head and short-armed the punch.

Greg walked back to his corner after round five and looked confident. Montgomery, Chemeres, and Machada all knew their role and did their part effectively. This trio had not been in Greg's corner much as a team, but they were all boxing lifers, and it showed.

When round six began, Billy Young took his chances with an overhand right, he was countered with a more effective left hook for his efforts. A steady diet of jabs and savvy defense put Haugen in control once again. During the second minute of round two, however, Greg decided to open up more and throw a hard-right hand behind his jab. While the tactic work, it left Greg more vulnerable, which was significant because Young was throwing power punches overtime in this round. During this sequence, Young managed to trap Greg in the corner and land hard power shots. Haugen's attention was gotten, as he was in a dangerous position for the first time in the fight. Greg's experience seeped through, however, and he managed to counter with stiff left hooks and then tied the surging Young up when the right moment came. A lesser skilled fighter probably would have continued with the carnage, but Greg Haugen was too smart for that. Being so comfortable in a boxing ring since the age of six, Haugen put out a potential fire. A moment in boxing history that has probably gone unnoticed and underappreciated up until now. The rest of the round, Haugen went back and forth from matador to bull. With his left jab being the key to all the action. With under a minute left, Billy Young suffered a bad cut on his left eye. Young seemed to think the cut opened from a Haugen elbow. The ESPN cameras showed a replay of a stiff one-two combination from Haugen that might have opened the eye. The only truth that was certain is Greg Haugen won another round.

Greg Haugen began round seven by working and scoring with his jab. What else? He also started talking to Young, "A round or two before that he was telling me 'you got nothing' so, after I started tagging him pretty good, I started saying 'how's that,' reiterating to him I was going to be in charge. There was one boss, and it was going to be me," Greg explained the nature of the chatter. The rest of the round, Greg dominated with his jab, as Billy Young fought more in a survival mode, protecting the cut, looking for an opening that would never come. The reason being Haugen kept strictly to his jab and threw very few other punches, giving Young virtually no chance to counter. Haugen was smart enough to realize the fight was his and was not about to open with power shots when he did not have to. The same way a smart football team is not going to try and throw the ball downfield when they are sitting on a big lead. Greg Haugen was also very good at what gamers who played the Madden Video Game called 'clock balling.' Indeed, Greg Haugen's version of 'killing the clock' was much more painful than that of a gamer.

After round seven, the ESPN television cameras showed the accidental elbow that landed that might have caused the cut above Young's left eye. However, it was not conclusive evidence.

Greg Haugen must have been bored with the 'clock balling' tactic in round seven because, in round eight, he was his most aggressive. It was clear he was set out to knock Billy The Kid out. The knockout did not come for Greg, but it was not due to a lack of trying or accuracy. Young hung in there and still tried, but he was blocking more punches with his face now. Which is not where any fighter ever wants to be. But Greg Haugen in his prime had a knack for making things happen in his favor.

Rounds nine and ten were clear indications that Billy The Kid Young had all the heart in the world. But lacked the necessary skill to ever compete at this level. And he never did again. But The Kid was game. Greg Haugen was back at the level he needed to be. His jab, accuracy, and defense carried him through, doing what he does best. Win rounds. It was only against Pernell Whitaker and in the third fight against Paz that Greg Haugen convincingly lost more than four rounds in a prizefight. The scorecards for the Billy Young fight, of course, read heavily in his favor, 98-92 and 97-93 twice. The three rounds, both Chuck Giampa and Patricia Morse Jarmen gave Young were questionable. As it was hard to find any rounds for Billy Young save for the first two. As the Paul Smith card accurately dictated. Greg put on back to back boxing clinics on ESPN and was now ready for a big title shot on a premium cable network. Just like in the old days. Greg was focused on the donut rather than the donut hole. Meaning he was going to be a handful for whoever was next.

Chapter Sixteen
Macho Time

"Greg was best prepared for Hector Camacho."
—Trainer Victor Machada.

Hector Macho Camacho was one of the greatest thoroughbreds in boxing history. The flashy southpaw grew up in Manhattan, New York City. He resided in the Johnson Houses, or el barrio, as it was more famously known as. Hector turned professional at the famed Felt Forum in New York City (the small arena outside of Madison Square Garden), winning a four-round decision over David Brown. Right out of the gate, the boxing world knew Hector was going to be special. His fluent movement made him look like a graceful ballerina, contributing to his incredible defensive prowess. Camacho also had stop and drop power in his early days. The total package.

Victor Machada describes Camacho as a "machine gun." Vinny Paz described him as extremely "hard to hit." Lee Groves said of Camacho, "The first time I remember seeing him was in his national television debut against Louis Loy, and he was something. He had extremely fast hands, terrific mobility, but he had a mean streak about him. This kid from Spanish Harlem fought with a chip on his shoulder. He was just too fast. He threw punches that few people could see coming. And on top of everything else, he was left-handed."

Adding to Hector's impressive skill set, he was also the consummate showdown. Always dressed in flamboyant garb, which was bound to catch the ire of grizzled boxing scribes of the day, such as John Condon and Dick Young. Hector always captured the attention of the audience before he even threw his first punch. And the fans ate it up. He would shout the emphatic question, 'What time is it,' and the crowd would always reply, 'Macho Time!' When Hector Mach Camacho burst on the scene, boxing had not quite seen anything like this. Sure, Muhammad Ali was a great showman, who had the great gift of gab, but Camacho would have fired Ali's fashion designer on site. "Hector Camacho was the best self-promoter I ever saw," Craig Houk added.

Nobody could have competed with Camacho if boxing ever held a catwalk competition, with his gold nameplate of Macho hanging around his neck when he trained, Hector was even lavish when the outfits were off. Indeed, Hector was 'extra' before the term even existed. But his career would only have legs if Hector could indeed fight. You see, Hector came around at a time where dazzling defense was not enough. If you did not engage in the pocket and hurt your opponent, your act would grow stale quickly. The early returns showed that Hector could fight.; making quick work of veterans like Rafael Lopez and Refugio Rojas, beating up the undefeated Louis Loy on CBS, and beating formidable opponents like Melvin Paul and Greg Coverson soundly.

But Hector also had discipline issues and would scrimp on training when he felt he can get away with it. Machada knew that Greg would fit that criterion for Camacho. "Greg felt he could beat Camacho but wanted to know what I thought. Greg knew that I knew Hector a long time, he was Puerto Rican, I am Puerto Rican. I told Greg, Hector Camacho is the type of guy that if we prepare properly, we can win. Because I knew with a guy like Greg, Hector wouldn't take seriously. And Greg listened. Greg was best prepared for Hector Camacho," Victor said.

Leading up to this fight, Hector had been in there with some of boxing's best and appeared to take them most seriously. He was impressive when he beat the undefeated Irleis 'Cubanito' Perez. For his first title shot against Rafael 'Bazooka' Limon, Camacho was at his very best, stopping Bazooka in the fifth round. Once Camacho became champion, his zenith really arrived. He now had some impressive hardware to go along with his lavish outfits. Camacho was just brilliant when he dominated the rugged Jose Louis Ramirez, "He was as accurate and as impressive as you can be. He was brilliant," Lee Groves said of Hector's performance against Ramirez. After that victory, he virtually shut out Freddie Roach.

By the time 1986 arrived, Hector was one of the biggest stars in boxing. His showdown with Edwin Rosario for the WBC lightweight title was an all Puerto Rican showdown that took place in the main arena at Madison Square Garden in New York City. Hector had progressed immensely since his debut at the Felt Forum. His fight with Rosario was an instant classic that still is a hot topic of debate amongst boxing fans today. There are enough golden nuggets in this fight to write an entire book. The short summary of Camacho vs. Rosario is that Hector indeed flirted with disaster but controlled most of the early rounds in the fight, where Edwin spent too much time posing. As a result, a narrow win for Camacho was more than warranted. The official result was a split decision win for the Macho Man. "I thought he (Camacho), edged it seven rounds to five. I thought Hector did enough. It was razor thin though," was boxing matchmaker and promotor's Mike Acri's take on this classic fight.

Since that close call with Rosario, Camacho remained undefeated. Facing formidable competition such as Cornelius Boza-Edwards, Howard Davis Jr., Reyes Antonio Cruz, which marked the first time Camacho was knocked down, (he managed to stay on his feet, despite being badly rocked, against Rosario). However, Hector no longer was that fierce fighter who can take you out at any moment. The Rosario left hook that rocked his world transformed him, "Hector invested the speed in his legs in defense, instead of offense," Lee Groves explained of the transformation.

Transformation or not, Hector continued his winning ways and was still a draw. Leading to the much-delayed fight against Ray Boom Boom Mancini. Hector versus Ray was a fight on top of most boxing fans' wish list many years before it actually took place in March of 1989. Sound familiar boxing fans? By now, Camacho fully embraced his role as the villain, a heel is how such characters are referred to in professional wrestling.

Boom Boom had not had a fight in four years when he squared off against Camacho. But that layoff did not deter the fight from being a big one. Ray fit the role of good guy like a glove.

His fight with Mancini would be the first time Camacho would headline a pay per view fight. As with Rosario, Camacho won a debated split decision. Mancini appeared to do enough to earn the decision. Hector did more holding than punching, but two out of the three judges felt Camacho won.

After that fight, Ray went back to retirement, and Camacho would have two tune-up fights, against Tommy Hanks and Raul Torres, en route to another pay per view extravaganza against Vinny Paz. A solid card that featured lightweight champion, Pernell Whitaker, defending his title against the dangerous Fred Pendleton and light heavyweight slugger Michael Moorer defend his WBO light heavyweight title against the undefeated Marcellus Allen. Camacho was defending the WBO version of the 140-pound title, a belt he won by defeating Mancini for the vacant title.

Unlike against Rosario and Mancini, all three scorecards were in favor of Camacho, against Vinny Paz. One score was razor-thin, 117-116, while the other two were a bit more comfortable for Hector, 115-112, and 119-109. In this fight, Paz was all over the place, just like the scorecards. He just could not get it going against Hector and often resorted to dirty tactics to get some play go his way. There should be little doubt Hector won, but there are some who have suggested otherwise. Vinny Paz is not one of those people who suggested he should have won, "A lot of people say I won the Camacho fight, I did not win the Camacho fight. I couldn't make the weight, and he was too tough to hit," Paz explained.

After two big wins on pay per view, Camacho returned to HBO to face the competent Tony Baltazar. This card also featured Meldrick Taylor and saw Pernell Whitaker unify the lightweight title against Juan Nazario-Nazario, who won his version of the lightweight title against Edwin Rosario, it was the second time Rosario and Nazario locked horns for the lightweight title, with Edwin winning the first time and Juan earning a victory in the rematch.

Pernell Whitaker, Hector Camacho, and Meldrick Taylor all in action on the same card. What a gift for boxing fans. A showcase of great hand speed, lateral movement, and superior defense on display. Indeed, it was Hector who stole the show with his boxing skills. Whitaker made quick work of Nazario, dispatching of him in the first round, one of the few times Sweet Pea performed as if the meter was running.

Conversely, Camacho took all twelve rounds to defend his 140-pound title against Tony Baltazar, and he was spectacular. He gave the veteran Baltazar a boxing lesson, willing to stand and trade, showing us that excellent hand speed that made him so 'Macho.' It was easily Hector's best showing since the Ramirez fight in 1985.

In the post-fight interview, Camacho was not his usual brash, caricature-like self. He spoke in a more tranquil emotional tone. It was if Hector knew he was on the other side of his career and still needed to build his legacy.

That legacy was set to continue on HBO against the Mexican-born Louie Lomeli. But in December of 1990, Lomeli was knocked out in the first round against Ramon Zavala. A tune-up fight gone wrong. Examining this circumstance reveals a striking difference to boxing's tolerance of losses in tune-up fights just a few years later. Lomeli's loss meant he had no chance to face Camacho, HBO would not accept such a fight.

In contrast, when Zab Judah lost his tune-up fight against Carlo Baldomir, he still was able to face Floyd Mayweather Jr, in a pay per view extravaganza in his next fight, in 2006. In 2010, Roy Jones Jr and Bernard Hopkins' dreadful rematch still went on as scheduled, even though Jones was blown away in one round against Danny Green in his tune-up fight. In the early '90s, boxing was not as generous, and Camacho needed to find a replacement fighter.

Greg Haugen's name was on that shortlist.

1991 was a watershed year for the United States, as it was for Greg Haugen. In January of that year, just when Greg was preparing for Hector Macho Camacho, the Gulf War began. Operation Desert Storm jump-started the U.S.' dismantling of Iraq, which led to a swift declaration of victory for President Bush. The Gulf War might not have been lengthy, but its repercussions still resonate today. Also, in 1991, William Kennedy Smith was accused of sexual assault, Governor William Jefferson Clinton declared he will seek the Democrats Presidential nomination. David Duke of the Ku Klux Klan ran for Governor in Louisiana. He lost. Clarence Thomas was confirmed to the Supreme Court. And a bunch of republics seceded from the Soviet Union, which officially dissolved in December of 1991.

The world of cinema also experienced a watershed year. Terminator 2: Judgement Day, knocked out all the competition and forever changed the scope of special effects for a film. Oliver Stone told a bunch of lies in the still entertaining JFK, Robert DeNiro chewed off a woman's cheek in Cape Fear. New Jack City saw proclaimed cop killer, ICE T, portray a cop onscreen. Spike Lee combined a strangle tale of interracial affairs and drug addiction in Jungle Fever. Boyz n the Hood was an instant classic, and Anthony Hopkins showed us that a lot of screen time is not necessary to win the best actor Oscar, as Hannibal Lector in Silence of the Lambs.

Hopkins had less than thirty minutes of screen time, but still walked away as the Best Actor of 1991.

In music, bands like Nirvana, Pearl Jam, and Soundgarden shook up the music industry. Queens Bohemian Rhapsody once again became a hit. Tupac Shakur's made his solo debut, with the classic 2Pacalypse Now. Janet Jackson informed us that we are all a part of a Rhythm Nation; I had no idea. And rock n' roll legends Paul Simon and George Harrison performed iconic concerts at separate locations, Simon at Central Park in New York City, Harrison in Japan, his first concert since 1974.

The world of sports was also impactful in 1991. The New York Football Giants won an emotional Super Bowl over the Buffalo Bills, that started with a haunting performance of the National Anthem by Whitney Houston. In baseball, Nolan Ryan tossed his seventh career no-hitter, and the Minnesota Twins beat the Atlanta Braves in a seven-game World Series classic. The NBA finals saw Michael Jordan's Bull face off against Magic Johnson's Lakers, with Chi-Town proving to be too much for Showtime. The NHL had a new star in 1991, Mario Lemieux, he and his Pittsburgh Penguins captured Lord Stanley's Cup four games to two over the Minnesota North Stars, and Monica Seles fell a Wimbledon short of capturing the Grand Slam and tennis.

There were plenty of chills and thrills in sports during 1991. However, it can be argued that boxing outperformed all sports in 1991. Mike Tyson fought Donavan Razor Ruddock twice, and on both occasions, the fans held their collective breaths, as one-punch could have ended it for both men. George Foreman almost came all the way back to win the world heavyweight title but fell just a bit short against Evander The Real Deal Holyfield. Thomas 'The Hitman' Hearns defeated future hall of famer Virgil Hill for the light-heavyweight championship, it was an amazing accomplishment, as Hearns began his career as a welterweight. Terrible Terry Norris made a considerable impact in 1991, by dominating Ray Leonard and knocking out Donald Curry. James Light Out Toney also had a breakout year, knocking out heavily favored Michael Nunn. The fight out the year was Robert Quiroga's unanimous decision victory over Kid Akeem Anifowoshe. The fact that neither of these fighters was household names, and fought in the obscure super flyweight division, did not deter the voters from giving this brutal classic its rightful place in history. It would be Kid Akeem's last fight, as the brutality of the action caused a blood cut to form in his brain. An unfortunate circumstance for such a proud warrior.

In 1991, Julio Cesar Chavez was the top dog at the 140-pound division and, perhaps, in all of boxing. JC Superstar was still riding high from his miracle win over Meldrick Taylor, and Camacho had his sights set on JC Superstar. A fight against Haugen was just seen as a bridge to get there. The oddsmakers agreed with this sentiment because Greg Haugen was a sizable underdog against Macho Time.

However, there were tells that should have tipped some people that this fight was not going to be easy. "Camacho did have problems making weight. He reported he had to lose three or four pounds the day before the weigh-in," Lee Groves explained. Also, "The fight was in Vegas, which was Greg's adopted hometown," Groves added. There was also some older evidence that Greg Haugen would prove to be difficult in this fight. Greg and Hector crossed paths in 1983. Camacho was in Anchorage, Alaska, preparing for his fight with John Montes, and was looking for sparring. The ToughMan from Alaska was willing to oblige, as always. "I was aware of how he fought. Hector came up to Alaska (in 1983). They told him he was going to do some sparring, and they got him the Alaskan lightweight champion. He (Camacho) thought I was some hillbilly from Alaska, so we started sparring, and he tried to start dropping bombs on me. So, I said, okay, 'you want to drop bombs on me I am going to drop bombs back,' so I started to drop bombs back. I bloodied his nose and mouth up a little bit. So, he knew who I was," Greg explained. Greg's declaration of what happened in their sparring sessions makes you wonder why Hector chose to take Greg lightly.

Hector's documented struggles to make weight provides substantial evidence that Hector did not put much stock in his sparring session with Greg. A mistake against such a cerebral fighter like Greg. When Greg Haugen was right, he would always do his due diligence to look for any edge against his opponent prior to a fight. Hector Camacho was no exception. Mutt was not about to rest on the laurels of 1983. "I studied him. I knew that he would always walk behind the referee when the referee said break, this would give him another twenty or thirty seconds (an old school trick taught by most savvy trainers), he would hold, he didn't like to fight. He basically liked to fight one minute of each round. My philosophy was to go out there and bang him for three minutes and make him keep fighting for three minutes of each round. By the sixth, seventh round, he would be tired," Greg explained.

Greg was also placing the proper seeds to get under his opponent's skin prior to the fight. A skill Haugen was so good at, and often paid huge dividends if done correctly. Greg explained that during the press promotions for the fight, he would remind Hector of the plasma he drew from his flesh during their sparring session.

The donut, not the donut hole.

The first fight between Greg and Hector took place on February 23rd, 1991. Hector entered the ring wearing an army helmet and full army attire. This outfit was Hector's attempt to honor the American troops who were risking their lives in the Middle East, in the Gulf War. Hector also had a championship strap draped over both shoulders, as well as one around his waist. Once both fighters were inside the ring, Michael Buffer introduced them. By now, Michael was his own attraction as a ring announcer, with his patented phrase that always rocked the house. When Buffer announced Greg, the Vegas crowd cheered in appreciation. Haugen looked fit and confident. Greg's classic boyish grin trying to sneak through his stoic look. When Buffer sounded off Hector's credentials, the champion was shadow boxing and looked to be all business. The combination of knowing he was going to be fighting a guy much better than the 7-1 odds suggested, the trouble he had making weight, and the fact that the desired fight with Chavez lurked in the shadows, all but erased the boyish, circus-like, antics often associated with Camacho right before the bell sounded for action.

When the pugilists met at the center of the ring for the pre-fight instructions, Haugen was focused right on Camacho. The champion was making every effort to look away from Haugen.

The first round was a stellar one, not in the sense that it was a nonstop brawl, but high-level skills were on display. Most of the round took place at the center of the ring, and there was no holding. Hector did try and circle away and use lateral movement in spots, but for the most part, he was right in front of Greg, on his toes, trying to establish his jab. Most of these jabs caught air, however, and Greg won the round courtesy of landing more often. Haugen found Hector's body with stiff punches and was even successful with some right hand leads upstairs. As Lee Groves put it, "It was pretty apparent that it wasn't the uneven match a lot of the oddsmakers figured it to be. Haugen was getting off quicker in the first round and was more efficient with his punches." The three official judges were not in agreement with this opening round, Bill McConkey scored the round for Camacho, while Dalby Shirley and Art Lurie were in accord with scoring the round for Mutt.

In round two, Hector upped his work rate and had more success, but Greg was still getting home with what appeared to be the harder punches. Such a fight is a conundrum for the judges. What takes precedent? The higher volume, or the efficiency? Given Camacho's reputation, it would appear the kid from Spanish Harlem would be awarded round two. All three judges scored the round for Camacho.

Hector won round three by scoring the only knockdown of this 24-round fight series. Macho caught Greg off balance during an exchange with a compact, right hook to the jaw. It was more of a flash knockdown than a damaging blow, but it also secured a 10-8 round for Camacho, nonetheless, as all three officials scored the round as such. Since the bell rang to end the round as soon as Padilla wipes Haugen's gloves off, Hector did not have an opportunity to indeed see if Haugen was stunned at all.

When Greg went back to the corner, his very competent team went to work. Jim Montgomery instructed Greg to stay inside during such exchanges, and that if he pulls back carelessly, as Greg did, a consummate pro like Camacho will take advantage.

Early in round four, Greg was more aggressive, and it paid off. A three-punch combination, where Greg landed a right upstairs, followed up by a hard left-right to the body backed Camacho up. Greg moved forward and landed a classic one-two on Camacho's chin. Round four was also the first time Greg trapped Hector against the ropes, landing solid body shots. Indeed, Greg was fulfilling his game plan of making Camacho fight for the full three-minute stanza of every round. He was dictating the pace and setting the tone for the second half of the fight. "Haugen was really banking on Camacho tiring in the later rounds," explained Lee Groves. Already, in round four, the Haugen pressure was taking its toll on Camacho. For the first time in the fight, Camacho clinched and began to back up more. More running than fighting was what Camacho was doing. But

Haugen was having none of it and kept pressing, not giving Hector a chance to rest. At the end of round four, Haugen really roughed Hector up along the ropes, with short, robust body shots. A brilliant round, especially after he was put on his ass in the prior round. All three official judges were in agreement with Haugen's mastery in the fourth round.

Hector Camacho fought virtually all of round five in retreat, with Greg pressing the entire time. Haugen cut off the ring as well as one can expect against such a slick mover like Camacho. It was clear that Greg won two rounds in a row, after dropping a 10-8 round in round three. Perhaps even more critical, Haugen's game plan was working like a charm. Haugen's pressure was well-timed, and he avoided most of Hector's forced clinches. Not giving Hector that chance to get that extra rest by staying behind the referee after a break. Hector was expending a lot of energy avoiding a fight but was still getting hit. Once again, Haugen swept the round on all three officials scorecards. So far, this was not a difficult fight to score, save for round one, the judges were in one-hundred percent agreement. And they were getting it correct.

Haugen was still stalking in round six, forcing an unbelievable pace. Hector look drained, but, to his credit, did a little more fighting than the previous two rounds. However, most exchanges were started and finished by Greg, and he continued to make Camacho pay to the body. A closer round, but a round that Greg Haugen should have won on the scorecards. Indeed, the sixth round was the third straight round Haugen swept on the scorecards.

Hector Camacho had more success with his combinations in round seven and probably won it. All three official judges thought so. But Haugen was still landing to the body and making Hector work for three-minutes, Haugen's work rate in round seven lessened, however, and Camacho was flashier. But Hector seemed drained, and Haugen noticed. "Haugen was very perceptive. He would take peeks at Camacho's corner in-between rounds. After the 8th round, he noticed that Camacho's trainer was rubbing down Camacho's legs. Haugen really picked up on that and picked up the pace," Lee Groves observed.

Haugen appeared to do the better work in the second half of the fight. With round nine being the only round you could claim for Camacho. "I actually had Haugen winning four of the last five rounds, 8.10.11 and 12," Lee Groves concurred. The official judges' cards were a bit more complicated. Camacho swept round eight, not sure how. McConkey favored Haugen in round nine, Shirley liked Camacho's work, and Lurie scored round nine even. Round ten was a sweep for Haugen. Round eleven saw Camacho winning on the Shirley card, while McConkey and Lurie disagreed with their peer on round eleven, thankfully. Shirley must have taken that round off.

Greg Haugen was also aware of his success, and he was feeling it, "I was talking to him the whole fight, calling him names," Haugen explained. Haugen was also fighting and had a very good eleventh round. So much so that when Greg went back into his corner, they already were in a celebratory mood. Victor Machada and Jim Montgomery expressed in jubilant fashion that their fighter was just three minutes away from being a champion. Greg howled in agreement. But there was a lot more to be determined.

The beginning of the twelfth is where most observers point to as the telling point of this fight. Greg explained that because of the nature of the fight, "I didn't want to touch gloves at the end of the fight," Greg explained. Carlos Padilla, however, had other plans. Before coming to the center of the ring, both Greg and Hector were raising their arms in victory. Padilla did not acknowledge this and was adamant that they had to touch gloves before fighting the last round. Neither fighter seemed interested in doing so, however. Rather than forgetting about it, Padilla was insisting that the fighter's touch gloves. As a result, Camacho offered his right glove for Greg to touch, but the sly dog from Tacoma, Washington, did not offer his glove in return, and instead appeared to say something to Camacho. Hector, tired of the posturing, proceeded to throw punches at Greg. Padilla did not take a liking to this behavior and took a very crucial point away for the champion.

Greg said of the moment, "I goaded him into losing a point."

Did Padilla overreach by first insisting the fighter's touch 'em up before round twelve and then deducting the point? By Greg's own admission, there is no rule where you must touch gloves at the start of the last round. Of the point deduction, Mike Acri said, "I thought it was cheesy, Hector thought it was bullshit. Some guys have so much disdain for each other during the fight that they just cannot bring themselves to do it" Lee Groves offered a more in-depth explanation of the situation. On the insistence on touching gloves,

Groves said that is boxing protocol, and protocol often trumps the actual rules, "Lots of referees were very insistent on the protocols of boxing being followed. He (Padilla) did what other referees did." On the point deduction, Lee admitted that it was "Very unusual," but at the same time, Lee explained that, "Considering Camacho was throwing punches at Haugen, who's hands were at his side, it could be determined to be an un-sportsmen like act."

If boxing protocol creates the kind of confusion that occurred between the fighters as a result of Padilla's insistence, thus manifesting in a point deduction that wound up deciding the outcome, then perhaps protocol should be scrapped. Often referees infuse themselves into the snapshot of a fight. Instead of hardly being recognized, they become grandiose. Their job is to protect the fighters and ensure any breaking of the rules is addressed. Touching gloves before the start of the final round is not a rule. It is a suggestion. A suggestion Greg and Hector obviously did not want to take. It should have been over with. If only Carlos Padilla was as insistent in the Thrilla in Manilla, the classic third fight between Muhammad Ali and Joe Frazier. In that fight, Padilla let Ali continuously get away with holding Frazier behind the head. A tactic that is illegal and such a tactic, when done as effectively as Ali did, saps your energy. Padilla gave minimal warnings to Ali, but in essence, did nothing to stop it.

Of course, in boxing, there are so many layers, if indeed Padilla took the proper course of actions, no point would have been deducted, and the fight would have been scored a draw. Creating a travesty on the scorecards. Regardless of where your opinion lies on Padilla's actions, there is no question that it was the deciding factor in the fight. Without the point deduction, Greg's split decision victory would have instead been a draw, allowing Camacho to retain his title. Art Lurie's scorecard of 114-113 in favor of Haugen, was the deciding score, but without the point deduction, Lurie's score would have been 114-114 apiece. Greg would have been the winner on only one scorecard, judge Bill McConkey.

Dalby Shirley's score of 114-112 in favor of Camacho would have read 115-112 in favor of Hector without the penalty. A three-point victory for Camacho indeed seems erroneous. The most fantastic thing about this fight that is seldom discussed is how the official judges scored the last round. It what should have been a clear

10-8 round for Greg Haugen, with the point deduction, only official judge Bill McConkey scored the final round this way; Dalby Shirley and Art Lurie both scored round twelve for Camacho, making it a 9-9 round on the scorecards. It is hard to fathom how Art Lurie could justify giving this round for Camacho, considering he gave Greg rounds nine, ten, and eleven. Dalby Shirley gave round eleven to Camacho, and had Camacho winning overall, so, at least there is some consistency there with Shirley's philosophy. Albeit a philosophy that is not proportionate with reality.

Dalby Shirley was a judge based out of Las Vegas who was no stranger to Greg Haugen fights. He scored Haugen's matches against Edwin Curet and Ernie Landeros, correctly scoring in favor of Haugen by a comfortable margin. Shirley also worked Greg stoppage wins over Charlie Brown and Memo Cruz. But Dalby Shirley dropped the ball on Greg's fight with Camacho. In fairness to Shirley, he had a respectable reputation for the most part as a judge during his career. When you have such a flashy competition as Camacho, illusions are sure to abound.

The other big story attached with Haugen vs. Camacho 1 was that Greg tested positive for marijuana after the fight. Knowing that a super fight with Camacho and Chavez was now in jeopardy, as we were still in an era did that did not for such fights following a loss, the powers that be tried to get the Camacho loss overturned because of Haugen's failed drug test. The incredible thing about this drug test was that such performance enhancers, like steroids, were not tested and not illegal. "If I tested posted for steroids instead of weed at the time, nothing would have happened," Greg explained.

Despite the calamity with the failed test, everyone know Mach Time had been had. "Don King was talking about Camacho fighting Chavez in the battle of the undefeated, but it didn't really work out that way. They tried to do everything they can to protest the fight and wanted Nevada to overturn the victory. The state of Nevada wouldn't do it because it wasn't a performance-enhancing drug," Greg explained.

Indeed, Haugen's victory over Camacho was upheld, but he was stripped of his title. The fact that the WBO took the title away Greg did not hold as much importance as the fact that, once again, Greg won a fight where he was a big underdog and will go down in history as the first fighter to defeat Hector Camacho.

Mike Acri put Hector's thoughts on the loss in perspective, according to Mike, "Hector thought he won, but he didn't take the loss badly. He said, 'the pressure is off, I am now 38-1, and I am going to fight again.'"

Besides being stripped of his title, Greg was fined by the Nevada State Athletic Commission for the failed drug test, was ordered to do 200 hours of community service, and had to fight Hector in an immediate rematch for the vacant WBO 140-pound title.

Greg Haugen vs. Hector Camacho II took place a little less than three months later. This time the fight took place in Reno, and all three judges were replaced. Carlos Padilla was also replaced by Robert Ferrara out of Arizona. Once Michael Buffer announced the participants in front of a raucous Reno crowd. They were expecting fireworks. Since the title was now vacated, Camacho was the A-side fighter and had the privilege to be announced by Buffer last. However, if the fight were to be decided based on fan approval when the fighters were announced, Haugen would have won by a score of 120-108.

When Haugen and Camacho met at the center of the ring for prefight instructions, Hector seemed more focused, more willing to look at Greg, compared to the first fight. When Ferrara completed his instructions and asked fighters to shake hands, Greg was willing to comply; in keeping with his mindset that you must do so before a fight. Camacho, on the other hand, turned his back on his opponent as he half-heartedly offered his left glove in Haugen's direction.

The opening round of the rematch was fought at a high level. Both combatants were trying to work their jab and establish dominance at the center of the ring. Hector landed a good straight left at the onset, but Haugen did not blink A scoring blow, nonetheless. The rest of the first round was fought on an even keel. Both fighters could make a claim to have won it. Camacho appeared to land more non-jabs over the course of the three minutes. But Greg had a solid last-minute of round one. His crisp one-two-jab, straight right- was perhaps the showiest punches landed in the round. Indeed, round one was the kind of round that is a nightmare for a judge to score. It was also a beautiful round of boxing where there was not one clinch. The only work, Arizona referee Robert Ferrara, had to do in round one was rule a slip when Haugen's knee feel down to the canvas. The professionals did the rest. The official judges did not agree on this round. Doug Tucker and Burt Clements favored Haugen, while Dave Moretti scored this opening round for the Macho Man a questionable choice that would prove crucial to the decision.

The second round was perhaps Camacho's best round against Haugen up until now. The Macho Man boxed beautifully for three minutes, using all the ring and being consistently first. Greg manage to land a few stiff jabs to Camacho's face, but he was out landed by his Puerto Rican foe. Ferrara also had some more work to do in round two. He had to warn Hector for holding the back of Greg's head with his right, as he delivered punches with his left, and there were also two clinches in round two, one forced by Greg, one by Hector. All three judges correctly scored the round for Camacho.

Rounds three, four, and five were hard rounds to score. Give and take rounds. Hector could claim the edge in defense, ring generalship, and was very effective landing his left hand. Haugen could claim the harder, thudding blows, but none in combination. A slight edge to Camacho is probably the slightly better option. In round five, there was an odd moment. Robert Ferrara decided to call time to address the slightly loose tape on Camacho's gloves. This took time because Camacho's corner had to repair both gloves, and they did not appear to be ready for the unexpected labor. It was a peculiar moment to call time by the referee because the action was at a high level. No, the fighters were not going toe to toe, but the octane level was high from both fighters at that moment. The last thing there was, was a lull in the action. Besides, it was not like the tape was dangling in a demonstrative manner. It is hard to conclude what fighter benefited more than the other from Ferrara's overreach. If any at all. With that said, this moment once again showed how savvy Greg Haugen is. As Camacho's corner worked feverishly to repair the gloves, Haugen took on the role of cheerleader and got the crowd cheering, "HOW-GUN, HOW-GUN," empathically. Just another moment inside the ring where Haugen separates himself from most everyone else who laced up the boxing gloves. Perhaps these rounds were not as difficult to score as it was perceived to be because the judges were in one-hundred percent agreement with their scores, all three judges gave Camacho rounds three and five, while Haugen swept round four on all three official scorecards.

It can be argued that Haugen's Ali moment also provided much-needed fuel in Mutt's momentum tank because round six was his best round of the fight. In this round, Greg got back to the basics. He was first, harder to hit, and landed combinations. Greg even found Camacho's body with stiff blows. Punches that were a staple to Haugen's success, but were hard to come by against the fluid Camacho. When round six ended, Haugen started jawing at Camacho before he walked back to his corner. The confidence was back, and Hector did not appear to be as confident. The spring was now gone from Hector's body and face. Camacho was sucking wind as he sat in his corner. All three judges correctly scored round six for Greg.

Camacho dug down and began round seven by throwing a lead left, tripling up on his jab, and a stiffer straight left behind the rapid-fire jabs. This sequence of punches did not hurt Greg, but it was sure to get the attention of the judges. Now it was Greg's turn. Haugen backed Camacho up by throwing a lead right hand, followed by a two-handed body attack. Again, no damaging punches, but it took the play away from Hector, who was now trapped on the ropes, where Greg slugged him with a swift right hand. However, Camacho has one of the highest boxing IQ's the sport has ever seen, so he was quickly able to work his way off the ropes, knowing that was no place he needed to be.

Camacho was now tentative to lead (he must have felt that right hand) and tried to feint Haugen into to committing so he could counter. A tactic Haugen was a master at. So much so, he did not take the bait. Greg was too good for that. Instead, he faked out Camacho's feints by subtly backing up and then throwing a left hook that was not meant to land, followed by a feint with his right hand. This sequence made Camacho back up, allowing Greg to swiftly close distance and land a digging left hook to the body. Such boxing brilliance may go unnoticed by some observers, but it is boxing on its highest level. A level Haugen could have never reached if he was just a mere Tough Guy. The rest of round seven belonged to Haugen. He stalked Camacho and took his time setting up stiff body and head shots-as Greg always does when he is going well- to a now visibly fatigued pugilist. Round seven was a round were the judges did not agree with each other. Doug Tucker gave it to Camacho. While Clements and Moretti favored Haugen. This is a round that shows some inconsistency in the judge's philosophy. How could Doug Tucker explain favoring Haugen in round one, but not in round seven? Conversely, Dave Moretti scored the opening round for Camacho, yet favored Haugen in round seven. These are the kinds of moments were judges should be put to the test, but in most cases are not.

Camacho was probably slightly ahead when the eighth round began, but it was clear he was approaching empty on the gas tank. Bad news for a fighter who depends on his legs and his flash to bank rounds. Even worse for Hector, while competitive, he has not appeared to be able to hurt Haugen in the nineteen rounds they have fought up until now-the knockdown Hector enjoyed early in their first fight was of the flash variety, not physically damaging in any way. With still fifteen minutes of boxing left, might as well be four hours to a drained fighter, how would Hector Macho Camacho pull this fight out and get his title back? How would Greg Haugen take advantage of his fortunes, build on his momentum, and take back what he feels was unjustly stripped from him? As a boxing fan, when you have such deep questions to be answered, all you have to do is sit back and enjoy. On the official scorecards, Dan Tucker and Dave Moretti scorecard's read 68-65 in favor of Camacho, Burt Clements had Camacho ahead 67-66 going into the eighth round.

Camacho started off the eighth round well. He was more aggressive, scoring with a hard, straight left behind a sequence of jabs. Hector then circled to Haugen's right, which is typically a tactical error against a right-handed fighter. But Greg might have been confused by this movement because he posed rather than punched, and Camacho landed a stiff one-two combination to the head. Hector then escaped the pocket unscathed, and Haugen tried to chase him down. Greg turned up his work rate and tried to land to the body and head, he did so with mild success, but Hector was doing a good job of keeping Greg off with his jab. Greg kept the pressure on in round eight, as he knew this is when Hector typically gets fatigued, as in their first fight, however, Hector secured the round by being elusive and landed enough hard left hands, often in counters, throughout the round. Greg failed to win his third straight round. Camacho felt this way as well, as he celebrated by wiping his right arm in celebration. Haugen did the same. Camacho swept the rounds on all three official scorecards.

Round nine began as a jabbing contest that Hector edged by getting in a hard left behind his jab. Hector landed a stiff jab upstairs shortly after, as well as a short left. Camacho then snaked two half-hearted jabs, not the hard ones he started the round throwing with but managed to avoid a straight right that Greg tried to throw over the lazy jab. Good start for Macho. But this impressive work did nothing to slow Greg down, as he started bulling his way in the close distance. Greg wanted to land something hard on Hector. While Greg succeeded in closing distance, he did not really land any telling blows at this point in the round. Which would be a problem on the scorecards. Greg was indeed having success draining Hector but was getting hit more in this rematch and was not as accurate going into the ninth round. By no means was round nine a go away round for Hector Camacho, however. What Greg did do well was cut off the ring. So, even though he did not land many meaningful punches, he was coming forward the whole round and closing the distance on Hector, which could have been enough to impress the judges. Haugen swept the round on the judges' scorecards. Greg needed to get back into the fight, and he responded in clutch fashion.

Round ten saw a much clearer winner, and that was the Kid from Auburn, Washington. Greg was more successful scoring at distance and was still cutting off the ring. All Hector could offer in return was shoeshine punches, which look flashy, but should not be counted as effective punches, or hold. There were very few clinches in both fights between Greg and Hector prior to round ten of the rematch. Hector started to employ this strategy because he was drained and could no longer keep Greg off him with his jab and straight left. Unfortunately, judge Doug Tucker did not acknowledge the excessive holding from Camacho in round ten and somehow gave him the round. Burt Clements and Dave Moretti did find the excessive holding detrimental and gave the round for Haugen, however.

Hector Camacho began round eleven by throwing a hard lead left hand. This aggressive move from Camacho took Haugen by surprise. Greg would typically be ready to counter a non-jab as a lead punch, but in a fight where he needed to muster up all the points he could, he just mugged at Camacho after he was hit. Not very Haugen-like. Greg's imposter soon dissipated, however, and the real Greg Haugen went to work. Scoring with stiff jabs, straight rights, and hard body shots with both hands. Camacho shoeshined Greg when he was trapped on the ropes, and Greg momentarily backed up. But Hector did not follow Greg. Instead, he retreated, and Greg once again closed distance. Camacho clinched to prevent Greg from scoring. When Robert Ferrara broke the fighters, the sly Macho Man backed up behind him to buy more time. Back in the center of the ring, Haugen landed a decent right hand behind his jab and followed this sequence up by landing a left upstairs and a clubbing right that found the middle of Hector's face. Hector tried to clinch Greg again, but this time Haugen did an excellent job fighting him off; however, Camacho succeeded in the sense that he bought more time and made Greg use his energy in a way that was not beneficial for him.

Camacho threw another lead left that Haugen failed to counter. Camacho then swallowed up Haugen with his arms, Ferrara broke them, and Hector crept behind the referee on the break. Once Haugen found space, he scored with a quick one-two. Haugen also landed a straight right that backed Hector up. But Hector did survival mode well and reeled Greg in close to his body when Greg got inside. Hector also did a good job of sneaking sharp left hands in on Greg at the end of the round. Making it a difficult one to score. Another telling moment in round eleven occurred when Hector swallowed Greg up and walked him back on two occasions. It bought Hector more time and showed that Hector was strong enough to move Greg around the ring. An element not often done on Greg, as he was always the strongest guy inside the ring when he fought.

Camacho's grappling really got out of hand in the final seconds of round eleven. As the Kid from Spanish Harlem emulated the moves required for a guillotine choke. Haugen landed a showy, looping right hand after the break, but Hector was once again able to force another clinch. On this break, Hector was in a good position to attack but opted to walk to the other side of the ring. Haugen chased him down and managed to score while Hector was on the ropes. But Hector shoeshined, then forced another clinch. As the bell sounded to end round eleven, Hector was in a familiar position, holding onto Greg. The pattern for the last few rounds for Camacho was to fight in spurts and do his best impression of Pete Carril.

It can be argued that Hector did enough to win round eleven. But the counter, more effective, point of view, is that Macho held way too much to earn ten points in that round. Greg was the one who was trying to make the fight in round eleven. He was able to close the gap on Hector and landed enough punches to be awarded that round. All three judges saw this point of view and gave Haugen the round. It was a crucial moment in the fight because when the bell rang to end round eleven, Haugen and Camacho went forehead to forehead, jawing at each other. Robert Ferrara then grabbed Haugen, who was closer to him, and while Greg could not defend himself, Camacho took a swipe at Greg with his left hand, that connected on Haugen's right cheek. It was not a hard blow, but it was considered an unsportsmanlike act, once again, Camacho's actions cost him a one-point deduction in the final stages against Greg Haugen in a close fight. It gave Greg Haugen a 10-8 round on all three scorecards.

Realizing he could not afford to give away any points in a fight of this nature, with the crowd against him, Hector was visibly upset when the point was taken from him. But he could not take his foolish foul back. Greg was more demonstrative and practically celebrating before the start of round twelve as a result of the point deduction. He appeared to still have plenty left in the tank-a clear indication he trained hard for this fight-had another free point, and the capacity crowd at the Reno-Sparks Convention Center were on his side. Going ballistic in anticipation of the final three minutes, and another Haugen victory.

Going into round twelve, Haugen was behind 105-103 on the Tucker scorecard, was ahead 105-103 on the Clements scorecard, and things were all even on the Moretti scorecard 104-104. As with their first fight, Greg Haugen and Hector Camacho's fight still hung in the balance.

Camacho came out aggressive in the final round and started off well. He even forced Greg to initiate a clinch to ward him off. This flash of the old Camacho went away as quickly as it came, as he subsequentially reverted back to his holding tactics and meaningless shoeshine punches. Greg's best work came in the second half of the round, as he never relented. A good left hook landed late in round twelve forced Camacho back into the ropes. Camacho was too slippery to get caught with a severely hard shot and held Greg when he closed distance, making it more of a round of frustration for Haugen, rather than a round of good, clean work. With that said, round twelve should have been a round Greg won, as Hector spent more time avoiding a fight than committing to meaningful punches. No pugilist should ever be awarded a round performing in such a manner. Unfortunately, both Dave Moretti and Doug Tucker did indeed award Hector Camacho the round for his counterproductive actions.

When the bell rang to end the fight, Greg seemed more interested in congratulating Camacho than celebrating. A moment that showed just how good a sportsman Greg can be. After twenty-four hard rounds with one of the greatest fighters of his day, Greg wanted to embrace with his foe, and secure the forever lasting bond that was created inside the ring. The kind of bond only participants of combat sports can relate to. Haugen's attempted gesture does not suggest he was conceding defeat to The Macho Man. Just the opposite was true. Greg said of the rematch, "I thought I beat him easier in the second one." Camacho was not in a sportsmanlike mood when the fight ended, and he rejected Haugen's gesture by turning his back on him and walking into the arms of his cornermen.

What Hector Camacho did next could suggest he conceded the contest to Greg. He walked out of the ring before Michael Buffer read the results of the decision. As Buffer began to articulate that the result of the fight was a split decision, Hector was storming off like a disappointed schoolboy. At the same time, the crowd groaned with disapproval, and Greg was visibly upset. Indeed, there were very unsatisfied people in the arena at that moment.

The first score Buffer read was in favor of Haugen 115-112, the Burt Clements card. That score was followed by the Doug Tucker scorecard, which was the identical score to Clements, but flipped for Camacho. Dave Moretti held the deciding scorecard, and it read 114-113, for the winner by split decision...Hector Macho Camacho. As Buffer read his name as the winner, Camacho was making his way back into the ring. When he got there, he was chastised by Dan Duva, the late Main Events promoter. Camacho's actions were telling, "He knows he lost; that is why he left the ring," Greg explains.

After the fight, Camacho told HBO announcer Larry Merchant that he would be willing to fight Haugen a third time. That was not to be. "He (Camacho) told me, no way," Greg Haugen, when asked why there was not a rubber match. Haugen expressed to Merchant that he felt the referee did a poor job, as he let Hector get away with his constant holding. Therefore, neither pugilist was happy with the referee's performance.

When the smoke cleared, it was another tough loss for Greg Haugen. A loss that can be, and still is, disputed. Unlike the second Paz fight, many people thought the loss was justified against Camacho in the rematch, however.

Mike Acri said, "I thought Camacho won the fight." Historian Lee Groves offered this take on the fight, "It was clear that Camacho was better prepared for the rematch, both physically and strategically. His body appeared trimmer yet stronger, and he was determined to fight more assertively and to put more weight behind his punches. His jab also worked better, and his accuracy was better. As for Greg, he stuck with his plan, and he proved that he could still get under Camacho's skin because, at the end of the 11th, he got into Hector's face, spewed some invective, and got Camacho to punch him as the referee stepped between them, a move that earned Camacho a rightful point penalty. Remembering what happened to him in fight one, Camacho fought with better urgency in the 12th and helped secure the split decision win. In my eyes, Camacho won the fight in the early rounds by getting off to a much better start and by properly responding to the late-fight adversity."

The story of scoring this fight lies with the question of the constant holding Hector did in the later rounds. At what point do you take away a fighter's ability to win a round if they make a strong effort to avoid a fight? Which is what excessive holding does. Boxers are supposed to be awarded for making the action, not nullifying it. The sweet science rule of hit and not get hit cannot be executed by either fighter if one is continually holding. Indeed, holding is a skill inside the boxing ring, and sometimes necessary, but it should never be a factor in winning a round. The exact opposite effect should hold true.

In 1964, referee Arthur Mercante took a round away from Ernie Terrell, in his fight against Bob Foster, for excessive holding. That fight was scored on the rounds system, not the ten-point must system Haugen vs. Camacho II was scored on. Terrell got the message and stepped up his aggression and stopped Foster in the seventh round. Subsequently, years later, Floyd Mayweather Jr. is giving credit for having a dominating win over Manny Pacquiao. The brutal truth of that fight is that Mayweather Jr. did as much holding as he did scoring and should have been penalized for it. But referee Kenny Bayless had no interest in penalizing Mayweather Jr. In fact, he was quite content in letting the hug-fest from Mayweather persist. Quite the opposite tactic was employed by Bayless in Mayweather's previous fight, the rematch against Marcos Maidana. In that fight, Bayless was so quick to break the fighters, he sometimes stepped in to break up the fighters before a clinch even took place. When there is such inconsistency with officials, there should be a hard inquiry. No such thing has taken place in the case of Bayless as he continued to be Floyd's personal bodyguard...I mean, referee. Kenny is otherwise a very comepetent offcial, and a geniue nice guy, so the apprenhension to criticize him on the aforementioed inconsistencies is somewhat understandable. However, if you do not address them, you cannot say your love for the sport of boxing comes first before all else. And many people who are mute on criticizing on such situations try and present themselves as such.

There were also inconsistencies with the official scoring in Haugen vs. Camacho II. It defies logic and common sense for Dave Moretti to score round twelve for Hector Camacho after scoring rounds nine, ten, and eleven for Haugen. It is just that simple. Dave Moretti's gross inconsistency was the deciding factor in the fight. Had Moretti been consistent with his philosophy and gave round twelve to Haugen, he would have retained his title. Doug Tucker was all over the place in the final four rounds, literally flip-flopping each round from nine to twelve. You are scoring a critical title fight, Mr. Tucker, not giving out cookies. Only Burt Clements produced a consistent scorecard. He was consistent with two of the tougher rounds to score, the first and the seventh, giving both rounds to Haugen, and he did not award Camacho any of the rounds where he held excessively.

The official Compubox numbers also proved telling in this fight. Total connects favored Camacho 305 to 223, but you have to take into consideration that most of Camacho's lead was built up because he out landed Greg by a large margin in the rounds he clearly won: 2,3,5 and 8. Also, Compubox counts the pitty-pat shoeshine punches that Camacho threw plenty of, which a judge should not count, which is why rounds 9, 10 and 11 were close in connects, with Hector out landing Greg in rounds 10, and 11. Also, Compubox cannot account for all of the holding that Hector did in these rounds, where a competent judge can indeed penalize a fighter for such actions by not scoring the round for them. With that said, Compubox does indeed annunciate the egregious error of not scoring the twelfth round for Greg Haugen. According to Compubox, Greg out landed Hector in round twelve 33-25, threw 73 punches to Hector's 58, and enjoyed a better connection percentage 45.2% to 43.1%. Add the fact that Hector held excessively, and Dave Moretti scored the previous three rounds for Greg Haugen, a major investigation should have been conducted by the Nevada State Athletic Commission on the scoring of this deciding round.

Instead, Hector Camacho went on to have a tune-up fight with Eddie Van Kirk before securing his super fight with Julio Cesar Chavez. A fight in which he was thoroughly drubbed but managed to finish on his feet. Greg Haugen now had two very questionable losses on his record. Both in title fights with significant consequences attached to them. Both with questionable, inconsistent judging.

Haugen was given what can be perceived as a soft touch as a follow-up, in the form of Alfonso Perez, who went into the fight with a paltry record of 0-4. Perez managed to take Greg into the eighth round before he was stopped. A very familiar position for Perez, who etched out a forgettable record of 0-13-1. To add some gloss to such an inferior opponent, Greg was the first opponent to stop Perez, and Perez was only stopped two other times and lost a bunch of close decisions.

But if Greg Haugen was going to stay relevant as a fighter, the Alfonso Perez's of the world had to be in his rearview mirror. This was indeed the case, as one of boxing's biggest icons soon echoed the ToughMan from Alaska, a big challenge and a tremendous opportunity.

05/18/91 -

Total Punches Landed / Thrown

	1	2	3	4	5	6	7	8	9	10	11	12
HAUGEN	13/31	12/38	17/47	21/49	16/45	15/51	19/59	15/55	20/64	21/62	21/60	33/73
	41.9%	31.6%	36.2%	42.9%	35.6%	29.4%	32.2%	27.3%	31.3%	33.9%	35%	45.2%
CAMACHO	11/62	25/68	27/59	23/66	30/69	32/67	27/65	32/61	20/54	26/62	27/67	25/58
	17.7%	36.8%	45.8%	34.8%	43.5%	47.8%	41.5%	52.5%	37%	41.9%	40.3%	43.1%

Jab Landed / Thrown

	1	2	3	4	5	6	7	8	9	10	11	12
HAUGEN	10/25	9/21	7/20	10/20	7/19	5/19	10/30	7/23	10/34	10/29	5/18	9/20
	40%	42.9%	35%	50%	36.8%	26.3%	33.3%	30.4%	29.4%	34.5%	27.8%	45%
CAMACHO	2/40	12/43	7/28	7/37	12/35	10/30	7/37	15/36	12/36	9/36	6/29	3/13
	5%	27.9%	25%	18.9%	34.3%	33.3%	18.9%	41.7%	33.3%	25%	20.7%	23.1%

Power Punches Landed / Thrown

	1	2	3	4	5	6	7	8	9	10	11	12
HAUGEN	3/6	3/17	10/27	11/29	9/26	10/32	9/29	8/32	10/30	11/33	16/42	24/53
	50%	17.6%	37%	37.9%	34.6%	31.3%	31%	25%	33.3%	33.3%	38.1%	45.3%
CAMACHO	9/22	13/25	20/31	16/29	18/34	22/37	20/28	17/25	8/18	17/26	21/38	22/45
	40.9%	52%	64.5%	55.2%	52.9%	59.5%	71.4%	68%	44.4%	65.4%	55.3%	48.9%

Final Punch Stat Report

	Total Punches (Body Landed)	Total Jabs (Body Landed)	Power Punches (Body Landed)
HAUGEN	223 (0)/634	99 (0)/278	124 (0)/356
	35.2%	35.6%	34.8%
CAMACHO	305 (0)/758	102 (0)/400	203 (0)/358
	40.2%	25.5%	56.7%

Chapter Seventeen
Sparring A Legend

"Every round was a war. It was just what I needed for my fight with
Nelson."

—Jeff Fenech

Sparring, good, solid sparring is the equivalent to breathing air for a
boxer. 'Good sparring' could mean the difference between a win or a
loss for a pugilist. One can only imagine how different Chris
Calvin's career would have been if the proper investment would
have been made in him, and good sparring was present in his
training camps.

Greg has undoubtedly had good sparring, which has helped him in
some of his biggest fights. Freddie Roach said he witnessed a lot the
sparring sessions between Greg and Roger Mayweather and that they
were something to behold. Gym wars, that, according to Roach,
Roger typically got the better of it. Such information might be
neither here nor there at this point, but what is relevant is that Greg
benefited from sparring with Roger, as he was his main sparring
partner for the Jimmy Paul fight, as well as the Paz rematch.

Some years later, Greg had the chance to spar a boxing legend,
Jeff Fenech. Jeff is a member of the International Boxing Hall of
Fame, who had one of the most crowd-pleasing styles in boxing
history; proving that you could be a legend without having a ton of
fights. Brittle hands prevented Fenech from having a lengthy career,
but quality over quantity has never been more evident when
examining the onion of Jeff Fenech. Jeff captured the bantamweight
title in just his seventh fight, the super bantamweight title in his
sixteenth fight, and the featherweight title in his twentieth fight. A
three-time world champion in three different weight classes by his
twentieth professional fight. Ironically, Jeff explains that boxing was
never his passion, "I got into boxing by accident. I never wanted to
be a boxer, I wanted to be a rugby player. I went to a youth club, I
saw a boxing gym there, and a friend of mine was boxing. So, I got

in there, it didn't go very well, but the trainer said it went very well for someone who has never been in there before. I went back the next day and slowly gave up boxing." Not a bad career for someone who fell into this brutal sport by 'accident.'

It was Jeff's quest for the super featherweight title where he and Greg Haugen crossed paths. Fenech won a tough twelve round decision over Mario Martinez in November of 1989 in a WBC title eliminator. But brittle hands put Jeff's career on hold, and some thought finished for good. Jeff did not fight again until 1991, where he stopped John Kalbhenn in four rounds. That victory led to the biggest fight in Jeff's career.

Azumah Nelson was the WBC super featherweight champion and a rising star. Promoted by Don King, at a time when it had its perks, Nelson was scheduled to defend his title in June of 1991, the co-feature for the Mike Tyson vs. Razor Ruddock rematch. Jeff Fenech was the chosen opponent for the pugilist they referred to as The Professor. A significant fight for Fenech for many reasons, one being this would be his first fight in the United States. In comes the guy they call Mutt.

" I was getting ready to fight Azumah Nelson in Vegas, and Greg approached me, asked me if I needed sparring. I told him I would love to spar. A couple of days later, we booked a few rounds, and we slowly, slowly built it up. He helped me a great deal for the fight," Jeff explained. After they 'built it up,' both Jeff and Greg describe sparring sessions that should have been recorded and preserved for all time. The kind of sparring Greg fed on, "When you spar against world champions and hold your own, more than hold your own, that is brain food, that tells me I can do it," Greg explains. And Jeff Fenech attests to Greg's claim that he more than held his own in their sparring sessions, "Every round was a war. It was just what I needed for my fight with Nelson. Greg was one of the toughest guys I sparred."

Where Greg separated himself from Jeff, besides starting his boxing career very young, was his thrill-seeking attitude outside of the ring. Jeff told of a story of how He, Greg, and a bunch of Jeff's Australian buddies went golfing. While on the golf course, Greg kept messing with Jeff and his buddies, saying that there were snakes all over the course. Knowing Jeff and his gang was weary, Greg found one of these snakes, wrapped it around his neck, and ran around the golf course, dangling the snake to and fro. "Crazy fucker," Jeff said of Greg. Greg corroborated the story, as it was his way of passing the time.

What was even crazier than Greg's antics on the golf course, was the judge's scorecards for Jeff's fight with Azumah Nelson. On a grand night at The Mirage Hotel & Casino in Las Vegas, Fenech flourished against Nelson in a classic action fight, Fenech's kind of fight. Fenech came close to stopping fellow Hall of Famer Nelson in the twelfth round. When the fight was over, there was no question Jeff Fenech won his fourth world title in his fourth different weight class. However, in boxing...

What other sport would get it so wrong? How could it be that only one of the paid professionals, Jerry Roth, scored the fight correctly for Fenech? Dave Moretti scored the fight level at 114-144; indeed, Super Dave strikes again with glaring incompetence. Yet, he still gets the big fights today. As astonishingly wrong as that score was, Miguel Donate scored the fight for Nelson 116-112. Meaning Jeff only won four rounds. A farce for sure. "I won at least nine rounds, but I didn't get the decision, that is boxing," Fenech said. Why is that boxing? Why is such a blatant heist job accepted? Why can it not be any other way for such a great sport?

One of the things that hurt Jeff going into the fight was that, unlike Greg Haugen, he was still unknown to much of the American audience, "Greg had a great name, he had a lot of respect at that time (in 1991). I was trying to make a name for myself. Even though I was a three-time world champion, I fought out of Australia," which is another way of saying that Jeff might as well have been invisible in the mainstream sports section of The United States of America.

However, everyone knew who Jeff was after that robbery. Unfortunately, Jeff never reached the heights of his greatness after that fight. Azumah Nelson blitzed him in the rematch, The Ring Magazine called that fight the upset of the year in 1992, and he was knocked out in brutal fashion against Calvin Grove in 1993. Fenech's hands also kept getting worse as well. With that said, Jeff's early greatness was noticed and was more than enough to get him voted into the International Boxing Hall of Fame in 2002. The draw with Azumah Nelson is baked in the cake as one of the most embarrassing decisions in boxing and is not the only time Jeff was shafted. He also was the victim of wretched foul play in the 1984

Olympics. Fenech was initially scored the winner in his quarter-final bout against Redzep Redzepovski; that decision was mysteriously overturned by the Olympic Boxing Committee. When asked if Jeff was given a reason for the overturned decision, Jeff replied, "They never give you an explanation." Jeff competed in the flyweight division at the '84 Olympics, Steve McCrory of the United States was the eventual Gold Medal winner. Fenech defended his bantamweight title against McCrory in 1986, stopping the Gold Medalist in the fourteenth round.

Despite the disappointments that Jeff Fenech had no control over, his greatness is secured. What is also secure, is Jeff's admiration for Greg, "Greg Haugen was one of those guys who made people want to go to fights. He made memorable fights, gave people what they paid for. I will always be proud to say I shared the same ring as Greg Haugen."

Chapter Eighteen
Battle of the 'Tough Guys'

"I told Ray the best acting job he ever did was acting like he was going to beat me."

—Greg Haugen.

When 1992 began, Greg Haugen was not a world champion. All his hard work over the years; his initial run on ESPN, his excellent performance against Jimmy Paul, his redemption against Paz, his two successful title defenses, his second run on ESPN after the Whitaker disappointment, being the first man ever beat Hector Macho Camacho, was now in his rearview mirror. Greg was without a strap. With that said, Greg was not planning on going anywhere, he felt that his only legitimate loss was against Whitaker; indeed, there is a solid argument for that sentiment, and he still had the desire to build his legacy, as well as his bank account. Just how much was left in the tank for Greg to set forth with his new goals?

Greg's status was in keeping with the changing of the guard that was the year 1992. Things that were baked in the cake dissipated and replaced by other entities that changed the fabric of the country. William Jefferson Clinton won the Presidential election in 1992, beating incumbent George H.W. Bush. Putting an end to twelve years of Republican power in the White House. The country read Bush's lips and was tired of the same old story. However, before 'Daddy Bush' left office, he made sure six national security advisors that were implicated of wrongdoing in the Iran-Contra debacle were pardoned. The shift of politicians protecting their own, instead of working for the people, took shape, and is now prominent in our culture.

In pop culture, Bruce Springsteen released two albums in one day. While Human Touch and Lucky Town were far from commercial disasters, they both failed to reach the coveted number one spot that Springsteen was getting accustomed to. Part of the reason why could be attributed to the new sound of alternative rock. Bands like

Nirvana and Peral Jam were in full swing and changing the way youth behaved and shopped. The movies of 1992 were a mixed bag, as the animated feature Aladdin topped the box office, the sweet sound of Whitney Houston helped carried the Bodyguard near the top, and everyone wanted to get a glimpse of Sharon Stone's snatch in Basic Instinct. Sharon was a working actress before 1992 but became a household name overnight by unknowingly showing her vagina onscreen, and murdering men with an icepick. Indeed, what was once seen as trash, was now the top class of movies and copied plenty over time. Although with the Me-Too movement of today, the way Paul Verhoeven tricked Stone into showing her glory would not have been received well today.

In sports, the Washington Redskins ignored claims of their supposedly offensive name and capped off their dominating season with a Super Bowl trophy. In baseball, the Toronto Blue Jays took the World Series championship across the border for the first time, the Chicago Bulls won a second NBA championship, the Pittsburgh Penguins captured Lord Stanley's Cup and Monica Seles, and her grunting style dominated the tennis circuit, falling a Wimbledon short of a Grand Slam.

In boxing, the heavyweights were the story. Riddick Bowe captured the heavyweight title over Evander Holyfield in an all-time classic fight, Michael Moorer and Bert Cooper waged war, and Larry Holmes upset the rugged Ray Mercer, earning a title shot against Holyfield. Another heavyweight of sorts, Oscar DeLahoya, also became a household name in 1992 when he captured the lone Gold Medal for the United States in 1992. A significant shift from years past, as the 1976, 1984, and 1998 USA teams all had multiple Gold Medalists, a disturbing trend that has worsened over the years.

When 1992 began for Greg Haugen, his fate would be determined by a fighter who was believed to have seen his best years go by, but he still had the kind of star power that would generate interest.

Ray 'Boom Boom' Mancini turned professional in 1979 and captured the WBA world lightweight title in 1982. Mancini's journey to get to the title, and the tragedy that haunted him while champion, has been well documented. Not enough has been said, however, about what a big star the kid from Youngstown, Ohio was in the early '80s. Very few pugilists ever reached the zenith of popularity that Ray enjoyed. His star power was rivaled only by the likes of Dempsey, Louis, Ali, Tyson, Leonard, and perhaps a few others. But it is a small group that Mancini was a legitimate member of at his zenith. Ray walked away from the limelight after he lost his rematch to Livingstone Bramble in 1985. He was just twenty-four years old. It was believed that a combination of never being able to get over the Deuk-Koo Kim tragedy, and the harsh reality that the kind of style and skill set Ray possessed did not have a long shelf life, contributed to the early retirement.

However, as with most boxers, retirement usually does not last. Mancini returned to the ring again in 1989, where he faced Hector Macho Camacho in a matchup that was way overdue. Ray dropped a tough split decision and looked good. But after the disappointing loss, he once again walked away. Mancini was trying to fill the void with an acting career. He appeared on the hit television show, Who's the Boss, as well as the TV movie, The Dirty Dozen: The Fatal Mission and played Mr. Black in the theatrical science fiction drama, Timebomb. Mancini also performed off -Broadway. Ray's boxing juices flowed once more in 1992. The desire to be a leading man once again, and to be paid handsomely for doing so, were the leading causes for the rabbit hole Ray was about to dive into headfirst.

Mancini chose Greg Haugen as his supporting actor. The fight was billed as Tough Guys Don't Dance for April 3rd, 1992.

Ray made the same mistake many people made. He equated the lack of razzle-dazzle and panache Greg Haugen had, to him not being a brilliant pugilist. Which is what Mutt was when he was right. Haugen's brilliance was hard to spot, as well as respect if you did not have the keenest of an eye. Even after all his fights and victories, Greg Haugen was still being mistaken for an easy fight. "They picked Greg to come back against because Boom Boom thought he was easy," Victor Machado said, laughing. There were, however, some people connected to Mancini who did see the danger that Greg presented. Mike Acri recalls, "When Ray was set to fight Haugen, I remember saying to him, 'why are you taking this fight, this guy ain't that far gone?' and I remember Ray saying, 'Oh, he comes right at you, he is perfect.'"

By then, Mike knew Greg well and began developing a liking to him, as he understood Haugen's crass approach. Mike recalls that Greg would often call him and bust his chops about working with Camacho, "Haugen use to call me and leave messages, 'Mike, quit sucking Hector's dick and give me a call,'" Mike laughed. And unlike Mancini, Mike Acri recognized that Haugen possessed excellent boxing ability, and was a tough out for anyone, especially a fighter who had only one fight in the last six-plus years, as was the case with Mancini. Actor and Mancini's friend, Ed O'Neil, also thought the decision to jump in against someone with Haugen's ability was a red flag. O'Neil, a fellow Youngstown native, was an avid boxing fan and trained in Brazilian Ju-Jitsu; he now has a black belt in that discipline, cited Haugen's jab as a significant concern. Mancini's response to O'Neil was the same he gave to Acri, dismissive of Haugen's ability. Not even the suggestion of a tune-up first interested Ray. According to Craig Houk, his name was mentioned as a tune-up fight for Ray, but Ray was not having it, "He thought he was on a higher level. But I would have been a perfect opponent for him. Every once in a while, I'll see Ray and I'll say to him, 'you should have took me man.' He does not like that. He still cannot let that fight go." Ray opted not to contribute to this book.

Despite his warnings, Mike Acri still thought Ray had a chance until he saw Ray in training camp that is, "I saw Ray sparring in Vegas, and I said, 'oh boy.' I wasn't shocked that Haugen drilled him after I saw that," Mike explained.

With that said, Victor Machada explains that things were not clicking on all cylinders in the Haugen camp either, in fact, there were times where it became downright frustrating, "We were training for the Ray Mancini fight, and the sparring was not working out, nothing good was coming from the sparring. Greg was getting hit, and he wasn't avoiding punches. The press was there because this was a big fight. Greg became nasty, and in the middle of sparring, he took off his gloves with his teeth and said he wasn't sparring anymore more, and he went back to his hotel room." Despite not being sharp in sparring, Victor still liked Greg's chances.

Before the fight, Greg and Ray did not get along, the bad blood remains today. At least for Ray. Greg said he has no ill feelings towards Ray, and although he does not consider him a friend, he resepcts him. Ray is not as outspoken as Vinny Paz about his disdain for Greg, so some people might not realize that. "Ray hates Haugen," Mike Acri stated, and many others have made this same declaration.

245

When Greg wants to, he can trash talk with the best of them, holding a Ph.D. in getting under his opponents' skin. With Mancini, he pushed all the right buttons. "Ray was trying to be an actor. I guess since he thought he beat Hector, he was going to beat me. I told Ray the best acting job he ever did was acting like he was going to beat me. He didn't like that." Mancini also did not seem to like what needed to be done to get ready for a big fight. Reports of his lack of desire and focus for this fight has been well documented. Family distractions, in particular, the desire to enjoy time with his newborn son, were running rapidly. Mancini was still expected to handle Greg Haugen. The same way Ted Michaliszyn, Freddie Roach, Chris Calvin, Charlie White Lightning Brown, Jimmy Paul, Vinny Paz, and Hector Camacho were all expected to handle him.

Besides being a sizable payday for both fighters, this fight also had the golden carrot of a potential fight with Julio Cesar Chavez waiting in the wings. A big score was to be settled on April 3rd, 1992, and dancing shoes were to be left at the door.

The bell and whistles were shining bright and piping loud for the Tough Guys Don't Dance promotion at the Reno-Sparks Convention Center in Nevada. The undercard featured the sideshow carnival act that was Mark Gastineau. The former New York Jets defensive end was 8-0, 8 KO's and set to face Lon Liebergen, 5-5, 4 KO's. Lon was stopped in the first round and never fought again, the exciting lightweight Rafael Ruelas also enjoyed a first-round stoppage, against a fighter named Francisco Lopez. Lopez was 0-7, losing all seven of his bouts by knockout. Lopez finished his career with a record of 1-19, and all of his fights ended via stoppage. A young phenomenon named Roy Jones Jr. was also featured on the undercard. Roy was well known for being robbed at the 1988 Summer Olympics and was climbing up the ladder. On this night he was 16-0, 16 KO's, and squared off against Art Serwano, who had a respectable record of 17-4-1, 9 KO's, albeit not against top tier competition. Serwano's most recognizable name on his record was against Irish Bret Lally, who stopped Serwano in four rounds; Jones bettered that result and finished Serwano in one round. Jones was undoubtedly destined for greatness. Spoiler alert, he indeed reached that mountain.

While Greg Haugen could call Las Vegas a second home, Reno was no doubt Mancini country. Boom Boom entered the ring first and did so too grand applause. Greg Haugen followed Mancini into the ring and did so to resounding boos. Mancini still had the heart of the crowd. Bert Sugar, who provided the analysis for this fight on the pay per view telecast, indicated that a fan through some kind of an object at Greg just before the singing of the National Anthem. Of course, Greg threw it back. Al Bernstein explains that Greg was just playing the role that he felt was fleshed out for him with this fight, "Greg knew he was supposed to be the bad guy because everyone loved Ray. Greg was kind of a dick before that fight. And I think he justifiably realized that was the way he was supposed to be before the fight. Mancini's the wonderful guy… Greg probably took it to a place it did not need to be taken. I don't necessarily see that as Greg being a bad guy. I look at him calculating that, but maybe not having the nuance to do it in the way without being so over the top. He was playing the role of villain to the hill," Bernstein said.

Greg Haugen enjoyed the perk of entering the ring last; however, he was announced first by ring announcer Jimmy Lennon Jr. Often, when a fight has no precise A-side fighter, such a compromise is made where one fighter enjoys the A-side treatment of entering the ring last, and the other opponent enjoys the A-side treatment of being the last to be announced. The fact that Greg Haugen earned the right to split up this intangible pie that comes with a prize fight with a pugilist of Mancini's cloth spoke volumes of how far he had come.

When both fighters met at the center of the ring to listen to referee Mills Lane's final instructions, the foreshadowing of the fight was obvious. Boom Boom was looking down at the canvas and appeared distracted, while Haugen was focused and relaxed; he even leaned into Mancini, with the classic Haugen smirk, and said something to Ray as Lane was finishing up. It is important to note that the fighters chose not to touch gloves, and Mills Lane did not make an issue out of their decision.

When the bell rang for round one, both fighters rushed right out to the center of the ring. With the soles of both of their boots bouncing on the very distracting Budweiser logo. They both tried to establish their jabs, flicking it at one another and missing. Greg even tried to land his patented right hand to the body, but Mancini managed to avoid it. Mancini managed to back Greg up early in the round but save for a light jab, did not do much landing. Haugen was giving Mancini his well-earned respect and was looking for openings and ways to set traps. At around the 1:25 mark of the first round, Haugen landed the showiest punch of the round, a short right cross, but Mancini appeared to take it well. The rest of the round played out primarily as a jabbing contest, with Haugen getting the better of it. Greg also scored with two short, stiff right hands with under fifteen seconds to go in the round; much crisper punches than the right hand earlier in the round. When the round was over, it should have been clear that the round belonged to Haugen. Compubox numbers indicated that Haugen had the advantage in connects, 35-25. Mancini was far from being out of this fight, however. All things considered, the long layoff, Mancini did not look terrible in this first round. His jab was getting close, and he took Greg's hard shots well. Mancini also had a target as Greg suffered a cut along his left eyebrow, apparently from a clash of heads. The blood was not anywhere near severe, but it was the kind of target that a fighter cut from the Mancini cloth would find insatiable.

Round two was not as kind to Boom Boom. He started off missing badly, winging telegraphed punches that Haugen could slip in his sleep. Greg, on the other hand, did a beautiful job of shorting up his punches, and they were finding their mark. Early in the round, a very angry mouse shown below Mancini's left eye. At around the 2:06 mark of the round, Greg hurt and backed up Mancini with a sequence of short, bludgeoning right hands. Greg tattooed Mancini's face with another crisp right cross at around the 1:19 mark of the round. Greg was in full control and staring jawing at Mancini. Greg's confidence was growing and even threw an ill-advised right uppercut from distance. When you feel the man in front of you poses no threat, you tend to get a little reckless. After all, if you know your opponent cannot possibly come back with something to hurt you, why not attempt a little razzle-dazzle for the fans? Was that not part of what made boxers Muhammad Ali-Greg's favorite-Ray Leonard, and Roy Jones Jr. so revered?

When the second round came to a close, it was clear Mancini was done. He was getting tagged with clean, stiff punches, his own punches were too slow, and Greg was too good to be caught by them. Somehow Compubox reported that Mancini landed twenty punches in round two, with ten of those connects being power punches, better described as non-jabs based on the Compubox criteria. Even if that number was accurate, whatever punches

Mancini was given credit for as a statistic, did little in the sense of turning the tide of the fight. Also, Greg was credited with thirty connects in round two, sixteen falling under the power punch criteria of Compubox. Pedro Fernandez served as the unofficial scorer for the pay per view telecast and awarded Greg with a 10-8 round in round two.

Indeed, save for Greg Haugen slipping on a banana peel, Ray Mancini had no chance to win this fight. The only question now is, how long with Greg's dominance continue. How much of a beating was Mancini willing to take? Ray's heart and will was the size of Warren Buffet's bank account, so the answer was that he had the will to take a lot. More than the average bear would be willing to take. Therefore, it would become a question of how far would referee Mills Lane let a fight that was anticipated to be an even brawl, which was now manifesting into a one-sided slugging, go?

Five more rounds would be the answer. The mastery for Haugen, as well as the agony for Mancini, went on until round seven. Greg hurt Ray in round four-the fight probably would have been stopped during and/or after that round had it been held today-and once again unofficial scorer Pedro Fernandez credited Haugen with a 10-8 round. Mancini had a decent round five, where he was actually given credit for landing more punches from Compubox, 31 to 29. This surprising success woke the now docile crowd up, as chants of BOOM BOOM, BOOM BOOM, began to bellow inside the Spark Convention Center. One last rally cry in hopes of getting their beloved son back on track. But it was all for not. Mancini did very little meaningful work in round six, doing more grabbing and mauling than clean punching. Round six was another questionable one from Compubox, as Mancini was credited with 32 connects to Haugen's 40. Ray should have only been credited with around 20 connects, with zero of them having any impact on Greg or the fight. With fifty seconds to go in round seven, Mancini walked into a colossal Greg Haugen right hand that sent him crumbling down; his knees on the canvas, with his body dangling on the ropes from the waist up. Always a warrior, Mancini got up at around the count of six, as he instinctively used the ropes for leverage to help him get back to his feet. Ray nodded his head that he wanted to continue when Mills Lane finished his mandatory eight count. But had Lane let Mancini continue he would have faced criminal charges, as there was no possible way to allow this fight to go on. Mancini's desire to fight on was grossly disproportionate to his ability and physical well-being at that point.

As Lane waved the fight off, Greg raised his arms in victory, then bent low to do an arm pump in celebration. Haugen then made sure he covered every real estate of the ring to taunt the pro-Mancini crowd. While Greg was a master at riling people up, he also should be credited with often displaying solid sportsmanship. As with the case with Jimmy Paul and many others, Greg made sure he embraced Mancini and raised his hand as if he were victorious. After he caught the ire of the crowd, of course. Greg did this to show that indeed Mancini was a champion in life, even though he fell short on this particular night.

The night belonged to Greg Haugen. He trained his ass off, sparring with the likes of the Ruelas brothers and Hector Pena. Greg's conditioning was impeccable as well, as he was all in on Keith Klevin's regimen; Doc Klevin helped work Haugen's corner for this fight. Ray presented a unique challenge for Greg in the sense that Ray was lower to the canvas than Greg. Greg was accustomed to fighter taller fighters and would bludgeon their readily available midsection throughout the fight. With the shorter Mancini, Haugen's work rate to the body decreased exponentially, as he only managed to sprinkle body shots in here and there during the fight. Despite having a crucial weapon compromised, Haugen still managed to dominate and pick apart his opponent. "The Mancini fight was a great, dominant performance," Al Bernstein summarized.

What also made this victory so lucrative for Greg, was that he goaded Mancini into betting 100,000 for the fight. There was even a giant check made out to the Mancini vs. Haugen winner revealed at the press conference, the promotion took the winnings out of Mancini's purse to pay Haugen.

Ray Mancini still came away with a handsome payday, much more so than his acting gigs were paying, albeit it was a harrowing way to earn his coin. An embarrassing beating at the hands of someone you felt was inferior to you, as well as the realization that you no longer could do what once you did so well. While the latter is a valuable lesson when looking at the grand scheme of things, it had to be depressing existentially.

In boxing, the question is always raised when a fighter loses when their career has seen better day; what would have happened had Ray and Greg fought when Ray was at his peak? Ray was a very versatile fighter when he needed to be. His virtuoso performance against Jose Luis Ramirez takes a back step to very few performances in lightweight history, and he was very competitive against the masterful Alexis Arguello. A fight against Greg, when Ray was at his peak, would have been special. "I thought he was easy to hit. I wish we would have fought back then," was Greg's take on an earlier fight against Mancini.

Greg's performance against Mancini established him as one of the top 140-pound boxers and put him in the catbird seat for some lucrative fights. Greg kind of had an idea of who he wanted next. But there were existential threats outside of the ring that the Mutt from Auburn would have to deal with.

Total Punches Landed / Thrown

	1	2	3	4	5	6	7	8	9	10	11	12
MANCINI	25/74	20/59	22/54	27/57	31/60	32/63	24/37	-/-	-/-	-/-	-/-	-/-
	33.8%	33.9%	40.7%	47.4%	51.7%	50.8%	64.9%	-	-	-	-	-
HAUGEN	35/73	30/61	36/75	40/81	29/71	40/76	31/51	-/-	-/-	-/-	-/-	-/-
	47.9%	49.2%	48%	49.4%	40.8%	52.6%	60.8%	-	-	-	-	-

Jab Landed / Thrown

	1	2	3	4	5	6	7	8	9	10	11	12
MANCINI	14/39	10/22	10/23	10/21	15/26	18/28	12/19	-/-	-/-	-/-	-/-	-/-
	35.9%	45.5%	43.5%	47.6%	57.7%	64.3%	63.2%	-	-	-	-	-
HAUGEN	23/48	14/30	18/35	17/37	15/37	22/39	19/28	-/-	-/-	-/-	-/-	-/-
	47.9%	46.7%	51.4%	45.9%	40.5%	56.4%	67.9%	-	-	-	-	-

Power Punches Landed / Thrown

	1	2	3	4	5	6	7	8	9	10	11	12
MANCINI	11/35	10/37	12/31	17/36	16/34	14/35	12/18	-/-	-/-	-/-	-/-	-/-
	31.4%	27%	38.7%	47.2%	47.1%	40%	66.7%	-	-	-	-	-
HAUGEN	12/25	16/31	18/40	23/44	14/34	18/37	12/23	-/-	-/-	-/-	-/-	-/-
	48%	51.6%	45%	52.3%	41.2%	48.6%	52.2%	-	-	-	-	-

Final Punch Stat Report

	Total Punches (Body Landed)	Total Jabs (Body Landed)	Power Punches (Body Landed)
MANCINI	181 (0)/404	89 (0)/178	92 (0)/226
	44.8%	50%	40.7%
HAUGEN	241 (0)/488	128 (0)/254	113 (0)/234
	49.4%	50.4%	48.3%

Chapter Nineteen
An Arduous Tune Up: Or Was It?

"I didn't have a whole lot, but I used my skill, my old wits."
—Greg Haugen

A fight between Greg Haugen and Julio Cesar Chavez had been talked about years before 1993. After he recaptured his lightweight championship, Jeff Ryan alluded to it in his Greg Haugen: More Than Just A Tough Guy article. In that piece, boxing trainer and TV analyst Gil Clancy began handicapping Greg against the top lightweights at the time. According to Clancy, Greg proved that he is a much better fighter than Paz, would have a good chance against Rosario, would beat Bramble easily, and had a good chance against Pernell Whitaker; because according to Clancy, Sweet Pea was still a bit green circa 1988. But against J.C. Superstar? Clancy advised that Greg should forget about that fight because he would not stand a chance.

Despite Clancy's analysis, a fight with Julio was a big money fight, and on Team Haugen's mind. Greg's manager Wes Wolfe expressed in the article that Chavez was where the money was. Greg wanted the match as well. But told Jeff Ryan that he wanted to defend his title a couple of times first. Greg did indeed defend his title twice, but of course lost his title to Whitaker in 1989, as Chavez was competing in the 140-pound division by then, winning his third world title in as many weight classes against the defending champion, as well as consummate Greg Haugen sparring partner, Roger Mayweather. Also, Chavez did not hold the IBF, the title Greg held, in high regard.

With that said, a paper trail exists of matching Greg with J.C. Superstar before February of 1993. Greg dropped out of their scheduled bout on September 14th, 1991. Greg cited perplexing negotiations with Chavez promoter Don King as the reason for pulling out. According to Greg, King's dishonesty and doubletalk were not worth the 400,000-dollar payday he would be getting for the fight. Greg was replaced by Lightning Lonnie Smith, a solid boxer with a professional record of 28-3-1, 14 KO's when he faced Chavez. However, Chavez was on a different planet at this time and dominated Smith over twelve rounds. This card also lost the much-anticipated welterweight showdown between Simon Brown and Buddy McGirt due to an injury sustained by Brown. That fight was rescheduled in November. McGirt dominated Brown and personally told me that the extra time due to the postponement made all the difference.

Haugen and Chavez were once again scheduled to meet on December 5th, 1992. But in October of 1992, Don King decided to cancel their pay per view card, which would have also featured Terry Norris against Simon Brown (Brown wound up fighting McGirt in November) and Michael Nunn against Victor Cordoba. Don did not want to put an important card up against an HBO telecast that featured Roy Jones, Jr., James Toney, and Iran Barkley in separate bouts; Toney and Barkley fought against each other on February 13th, 1993. Lights Out sliced up The Blade in one of his signature performances; Roy Jones, Jr. also fought on this pay per card, blitzing Glenn Wolfe (no relation to Wes) in one round. It was February 20th of 1993, when Greg and Julio would finally meet, in one of the most ambitious pay per view productions of Don King's career.

Before that February date, however, King constructed a card of tune-ups on December 13th, 1992, televised by Showtime Championship Boxing. Greg was matched up against Armando Campas of Mexico, Julio was set to take on Marty Jakubowski. Going into these tune-up fights, Greg already caught the ire of Chavez by making his infamous 'Tijuana Taxi Drivers' comment in October, during a press conference in New York. This December card was also thick in talent, as Hall of Famer Terry Norris (who was fixing to get his own fight with Chavez) Tony Tucker, Hall of Famer Julian Jackson, Oliver McCall, and Greg Page were all scheduled to fight.

But precisely who were they fighting was a salient question, that did not have an appetizing answer. The press ridiculed this card for being mismatch central and were right to do so. Armando Campas had a record of 0-6-1, despite his 37-0 record, nobody believed Jakubowski belonged in the same ring as Chavez, the same could be said of Pat Lawlor, the opponent of Terry Norris. Tony Tucker was scheduled to fight Frankie Swindell, who was at best a decent light heavyweight. Eddie Hall, Julian Jackson's opponent, had a victory over Iran Barkley in 1984, but by 1992 Hall was previously stopped by Reggie Johnson, Tony Thornton, in one round, and Dave Tiberi, and no longer seen as competitive.

Don King conjured up a card that was indeed star-studded but wreaked of abysmal match ups. Marc Ratner, the Nevada State Athletic Commissioner at the time, was taken to task for sanctioning these fights but defended his actions. Ratner reported that he turned refused about thirteen or fourteen other fighters that Don King Promotions tried to get on the card-one can only imagine who they were-before accepting these names.

The only reason to tune in on December 11th, 1992, was to see how both Greg and Julio looked in anticipation for their February showdown. What kind of a mood was Chavez going to be in given Greg's comments about his great record? It is never a good thing when the story outside of the ring gets more attention than inside the ring. But since everyone decided to fixate on Greg's slight, let us look at his words, 'The way I see it, sixty of the guys he fought were just Tijuana cab drivers that my mother could beat...I am not taking him light, but I am not taking him as unbeatable either.' Greg's comments were a response to a question he was asked if he was indeed intimated by Chavez's incredible record of 82-0 record. Another way Greg could have made his point was to say, no I am not intimated because not all eighty-two of his opponents were world-class fighters, so 82-0 is not as scary as it looks, I have fought top guys as well, and while I respect him, I do not think his record reflects as someone who cannot be beaten. Or something of that nature. But what fun would that be? Greg wanted to help sell tickets and get under his opponents' skin, a tactic that had worked for Greg in the past, and many other top fighters such as Muhammad Ali and Bernard Hopkins.

Was what Greg said that bad compared to what they did? Ali ridiculed Joe Frazier, calling him an Uncle Tom, as well as an ugly gorilla. Hopkins violated the Puerto Rican flag prior to his showdown with Felix Trinidad and taunted Joe Calzaghe by calling him a 'white boy' in the buildup for their fight.

Deep down, I think Greg knew that this was his biggest moment, both in terms of making money, as well as facing a boxing great. Even though Chavez's 82-0 record might have been a bit padded I think anyone who would try and dispute his greatness is not in keeping with reality, he was no doubt one of the two or three best fighters in the world at that time. Mike Tyson lost to Buster Douglas. Marvelous Marvin Hagler was gone, and Pernell Whitaker had not yet reached that status yet. Chavez destroyed the formidable Edwin Rosario, handled the capable Roger Mayweather twice, made the comeback of all comebacks against Meldrick Taylor, and beat up Hector Camacho. Along the way, he also had solid wins against Rocky Lockridge, Juan LaPorte, Jose Luis Ramirez, Sammy Fuentes, and Angel Hernandez. His skills were without question. But what was his mental makeup like? Greg decided to test it by making comments he knew would sting, and nobody else would have the audacity to say. Of course, Greg went even a step further when he insulted the people of Mexico by suggesting there was no way 130,000 Mexicans can afford to buy a ticket to see their fight. One must understand, however distasteful as that may sound, Greg made those comments in tongue and cheek and has no ill will or malicious feelings towards people of different races or cultures.

Armando Campas might not have been much on a threat on paper. But fights are not decided on paper. To some degree, all fights are tough. Considering that, and the fact that Greg was battling the flu and could not get any sparring for this fight, some ambitious gamblers might have wanted to take a chance on Campas, a 17-1 underdog. This fight was not easy.

Showtime Championship Boxing aired the card, the same network that carried Greg's fight with Jimmy Paul was now airing a fight that nobody thought much of in terms of being competitive. But that is why they fight because you never know what can happen. The card was Showtime's first-ever Sunday night telecast. The beginning of the telecast was dominated by news connected to the Mike Tyson/Desire Washington rape trial, as well as the legal conflict between Don King and Tim Witherspoon, where King won a major battle in that conflict. Steve Albert, Showtimes blow by blow announcer, went on to recap the undercard fights that featured Julian Jackson, Tony Tucker and Greg Page. All three men won their fights by stoppage, although Tucker's stoppage victory was induced by a hand injury by Frankie Swindell. Steve Farhood went on to interview Tony Tucker about benefiting from the WBC's apparent decision to strip Riddick Bowe from the heavyweight title and awarding the title to Lennox Lewis, with Tucker facing Lewis for the WBC title. The very next day, Riddick Bowe held a press conference and proceeded to throw the WBC belt in a trash can. Lewis was awarded the belt and defended it against Tony Tucker via a 12-round decision.

After Tucker's interview, where he made sure to thank Don King by name in closing, Showtime focused on Greg Haugen, as his fight with Campas was the first to be televised. The first statement made about Greg was how he had come a long way from fighting tough man contests in Alaska; when you have a hit, it is hard to let it go. The telecast went on to say how Greg is a master of verbal blows, mentioning nothing about his boxing skills and what they have gotten him so far. Showtime's piece on Greg went on to highlight his trilogy against Paz, not the boxing skills that were showcased during their forty rounds, but their war of words. It should be noted that Greg stated in the piece that he and Paz were now friends, and Paz was pound for pound one of the toughest guys in boxing. The focus of the piece then shifted to Greg's rivalry with Camacho, where Greg stated the bad blood with the Macho Man still existed. Showtime then showed highlights of his fight with Jimmy Paul, where they finally gave him credit for being a skillful boxer.

The piece then focused on Greg's quest to fight Chavez. This is where Greg went after Chavez's resume, here is what Greg told the Showtime cameras, "I think I am just as tough as anyone out there. I got that reputation from fighting in Alaska in the tough guys contests. I fought up there twenty-four times and won twenty-four times. Basically, I could be close to Julio's record right now if I was to take all the patty cakes that I fought up there. But I chose not to pad my record like he has. The way I see it, sixty of the guys he fought were just Tijuana cab drivers that my mother could have knocked out. But the other twenty guys, or twenty-two guys were good fighters. So, I'm not taking him light, but I am not taking him as he is unbeatable either." When reading Greg's comment in full, the Tijuana cab drivers' comment does not have as much bit or insult to it. It is just Greg's honest evaluation of Chavez's standout record at the time. If you listen to the monotone delivery when Haugen speaks to the camera, the statement becomes even more analytical than insulting. But such an observation does not stir the pot or sell tickets, and one cannot blame Julio for being fixated on the insulting part of Greg's analysis.

Showtime then focused on the announcing crew and their analysis of Greg Haugen. Ferdie Pacheco said Greg's career was one of, "Unrelenting aggressiveness. He just comes out to attack" The Fight Doctor went on to say, "For a guy with a Baby Face, he is such a mean guy. He has hard hands and an even harder jaw. And the biggest thing about this little guy is his heart. He will not quit; he will not admit defeat…" Indeed, Pacheco's analysis is flattering, but it falls way short of the complete boxer Greg Haugen was up until that fight. Steve Albert went on to inform the audience that Greg was suffering from the flu and had difficulty getting motivated to fight Armando Campas. Such elements of a fight are often kept under wraps, but Greg has always been brutally honest. When Bobby Czyz joined the discussion, the topic of conversation centered around the fact that Greg was looking passed Campas. After all, a big payday against a great fighter loomed in the wings.

Armando Camps previously fought to a draw against Ray Beltran, no not that Ray Beltran, a Ray Beltran who finished with a career record of 5-4-1, 4 KO's, and entered the ring to the Rocky theme song. A win over Greg would have been the first of his professional career. Despite being winless, Campas looked relaxed and focused. When Greg was set for his ring walk, he looked pale and peaked, but Steve Albert stated that Greg promised a first-round knockout. Greg's music for this fight was Pearl Jam's Alive, opting for the new alternative rock music of the time, over the classic rock sound Greg was so fond of. Greg came in heavy, one-hundred forty-six pounds, and had a distinct disadvantage in reach, 65 ½ to Campas's 70.

At the start of the introductions, Jimmy Lennon Jr. informed the crowd that Don King was dedicating the card to the incarcerated Mike Tyson; today, Tyson loathes King. Greg might have been sick and unmotivated to fight Campas, but when referee Toby Gibson gave the prefight instructions at the center of the ring, Greg was visually fixated on his opponent.

Greg enjoyed a solid first round. He worked behind a stiff jab, threw crisp combinations, and invested in the body. He really tried to make good on his prediction of a one-round stoppage. However,

Campas did not appear as if he was going anywhere. The corner of Jim Montgomery, Victor Machado, and Keith Kleven, who served as Greg's cutman, immediately went to work on their fighter after round one. Jim advised Greg to double up the jab and work his right hand, he also warned Greg that he was backing straight out with his chin high. Solid council.

Campas mixed it up more in round two, bloodying Greg's nose in the process. But Greg won the round by being more accurate and diverse. He established his jab and kept making deposits to the body. But he did not appear to be his typical strong self, as Campas was able to bull him to the ropes during the round. When Greg sat down after the round, Doc Klevin went to work on Greg's bloody nose, shoving two Q-tips up Greg's right nostril, which went it snow white, and came out crimson red. It must have been cumbersome to absorb any of Montgomery and Machado's instruction when having to deal with a leaky nose in a sick condition. Once again, the astute Montgomery warned Greg to keep his chin down when backing out, and Machado instructed him to drive his right to the body and come back with a hook to the head of Campas.

Round three saw some conflicting commentary between Pacheco and Czyz. Ferdie said of Haugen, "This guy is a barroom fighter, he wants to get in close. He wants to punish a guy in close." Czyz immediately followed by stating that, "Haugen has a much shorter reach, but yet, he out jabs Campas every time he tries to." It was clear that Czyz, a light heavyweight and cruiserweight champion of the world, was accurately assessing what he was watching. Greg's jab was working from round one, a mere barroom fighter would not have been able to pull that off. Indeed, while laborious, Greg should have been considered the winner of round three. He was more accurate and slipped or blocked most of Campas's incoming leather. Haugen scored the best punch of the fight up until that point as well under the thirty-second mark of the round, a stiff right hand from long range.

After round three, the Showtime cameras went into the dressing room of Chavez. JC Superstar was getting his hands wrapped for his fight, was also focused on the action at hand. There was also a glimpse of a youngster from the back, perhaps it was Julio Cesar Chavez Junior. By now, Greg's bloody nose did not appear to be a factor, but Greg looked extremely sick before going out for round four.

The start of round four saw more inside fighting, with both fighters scoring to the body, Haugen, even in his apparent weakened state, was able to walk Campas back, however. This action speaks to the Haugen strength most of his opponents have cited, as well as experienced. Greg went on to have a good fourth round. He let his hands go the entire three minutes, was much more accurate than Camapas, and landed the sharper punches. Including some effective one-two's from long range, putting his superior boxing IQ on display, Greg also eliminated any further body attack from Camapas the rest of the round. Campas earned cheers from the pro-Mexican crowd. But, he in no way earned the round. The Showtime cameras went to the dressing room of the WBC 154-pound champion Terry Norris in between rounds. Terry was a rising star at the time, and a potential fight against the winner of Chavez and Haugen was already in the air. On this night, Terry was preparing for the game but severely outmatched Pat Lawlor, in a non-title match. A tune-up fight for his upcoming title fight against Maurice Blocker that was scheduled to take place in Mexico City.

Round five was another productive one for Mutt. He was first and diverse. While Campas' best feature in the round was his ability to take a punch. In somewhat odd fashion, the Showtime television crew of Steve Albert, Bobby Czyz, and Ferdie Pacheco presented the action as much closer than it actually was. Whatever flurries Campas through had very little behind them and did minimal scoring. Up until now, it was a hard fight for Greg in the sense that he was laboring because he was so sick, and Campas was being resistant, but it was not a tough fight in the sense that he was winning every round. For whatever reason, the veteran television crew was not relaying that narrative to their audience. Bias crowd noise has been said to influence judges, perhaps the crowd, who was overreacting to every move Armando Campas made, was also influencing the television crew.

In between rounds, Team Haugen asked for more right hands. In round six, Haugen once Haugen began with solid work behind his jab, and Steve Albert wrongly called it a competitive fight. Ferdie Paceho then made a salient point, as he pointed out Doc Kelvin's brilliant work of stopping Greg's bloody nose. But soon after, Ferdie went back to reporting fake news, as he said it was remarkable that there was no more bleeding because he was getting hammered there all night. Not true. Campas landed very few substantial shots on Greg's face since the nose began to bleed. Shortly after that erroneous comment from the Fight Doctor, Campas did have some of his best moments of the fight, as he opened up on Greg with a barrage of right hooks, but these shots were stiffer than the majority of leather he was slinging, and they were landing clean; a right uppercut being the showiest punch landed. But Greg came right back with a solid one-two that stopped his adversary in his tracks.

Greg then took over with subtle boxing skills the crew did not acknowledge. He feinted going forward and then took a step back as Campas took the bait, and Greg proceeded to land with a double-left-hook, then came back with a left hook to the body and then a right hook to the body. Now, this four-piece from Greg did not land with any kind of power; Greg really appeared to be weakening at this point, but the punches did find their mark, as well as show superior ring generalship form Haugen. Which is supposed to be an essential element of judging. Shortly after that beautiful piece of boxing from Greg, he was able to push Campas back, measuring him for another one-two that landed. Campas.

As round six continued, the Showtime crew kept over-selling the competitive nature of the fight and hyping up Campas as if he were slice bread. With under thirty seconds to go in the round, Pacheco stated that there was nothing on Greg's punches. Seconds later, Greg landed a strong right hand that snapped Camaps's head back like a Pez-dispenser. To his credit, Campas answered right back with a flurry, but only one punch landed in a scoring zone, and that punch had nothing on it. An argument can be made that the volume of punches Campas threw made round six closer than most. But Greg was the clear leader in ring generalship, even during Armando's best moment, Greg stood poised and made sure his chin was tucked in tight to his body, and Haugen also landed the cleaner punches from long range.

Round seven began with Steve Albert stating that if Greg loses this fight, his huge payday with Chavez was, 'very much in jeopardy.' The Fight Doctor then stated that Haugen was up by a mere point, 58-57 because Campas won the last two rounds. Now some people could have been deceived into think Campas edged out round six, but to score round five for him is just not in keeping with any reality. The first half of round seven was a strong showing for Greg, although you would not know that if you depended on the Showtime crew. Greg was working his jab and scoring one-two combinations, as well as some nice left hooks upstairs. He was also walking Campas back to set him up at long range. Campas was still game, and slinging leather, but he had very little success, even less than in round five, in terms of landing anything in the scoring zones. During this time, the Showtime crew was pointing out how Greg was not doing enough after landing a one-two, never mentioning the fact that Greg was doing virtually all the landing, as well as controlling the ring.

The second half of round seven was more of the same, but Campas did get off a flurry of six punches that woke up the crowd and elated Pacheco, but in reality only one of the punches landed in the scoring zone, the rest either missed the intended target or were blocked. After round seven, it would be generous to give Armando Campas two rounds, but the Showtime crew was painting a much different narrative. Showtime went into the dressing of Chavez after round seven. There, Julio had a very young Julio Cesar Chavez Jr. in his lap, and Steve Farhood sat next to him with a microphone. Farhood did all of the talking, as he related that JC Superstar had not taken his eyes off the action and that he thought Greg Haugen was very 'malo,' which means bad in Spanish.

Haugen won the first half of round eight, and even Ferdie Pacheco acknowledged as much, but Albert will still trying to sell Campas to us. Haugen's work at long range was the difference. At the 1:30 mark Campas tied Haugen up and the supposedly weaker Haugen (Because of the flu) managed to walk his opponent back to set him up from distance after the break. With less than a minute to go in the round, Campas landed his best punch of the fight, a short right hand upstairs that clearly got Haugen's attention. But Greg kept his poise and was soon working his jab at range. Under the twenty-second mark, Greg muscled Campas against the ropes and pinned him there. Referee Toby Gibson elected not to break the fighters and instructed to work out of the clinch. Campas did manage to get off the ropes, but the cagey Haugen was the fighter who scored when they eventually broke their clinch. As the round ended, Ferdie Pacheo stated that Greg won the round, but it was only because Campas, 'quit fighting.' The ultimate back-handed compliment. It would have been nice if, just once, the television crew would have acknowledged how impressive it was that Greg, a guy laboring and suffering from the flu, was able to constantly use his strength to walk and push Campas around. And how could Pacheco, a veteran announcer, make a claim that a guy quit fighting when he landed his best punch of the fight in that round?

Toby Gibson put a momentary halt to round nine as he took Campas back to his corner and instructed his trainer to take some of the Vaseline off his face. Pacheco objected to the command, as he seemed to be okay with the clump of white gook on the left cheek of Campas. As round nine resumed, Greg continued to labor behind his jab. You could tell it was becoming tougher for Greg to tap into that tank and throw relevant punches. This dynamic is always the case in the later rounds, but the extra caveat of being sick must have raised the problem exponentially. But Greg was still throwing and scoring from long range. Campas did more work than in the previous round, but not enough to make a reasonable claim for it.

Going into the tenth round, the fight still stood in the balance in the sense that Campas was still strong, and slinging leather with bad intentions. However, any claim other than all Greg had to do to win was finish the fight on his feet would have made Twilight Zone creator Rod Serling proud.

Jim Montgomery seemed to know Greg just had to last the round to win. He instructed Greg to kill the clock, so to speak, by holding Campas inside and walk him around when the opportunity arose, Victor Machado reinforced Jim's instructions by saying, "take him for a walk, take him for a walk, that's all." Somehow Steve Albert missed that point and related to the television audience that Greg's corner was, "pleading with Haugen in the corner, 'come on you're a world champion,' they were saying, 'look like one.'" The quote that Albert was trying to paraphrase was, "Come on, you're a world champion, get him." But that statement of urgency was not uttered by Jim Montgomery or Victor Machado, the boxing men in corner of Haugen. The statement did not even appear to come from Doc Klevin, his head was to the television camera, so it was hard to

263

determine. But it did not appear that Klevin's mouth was moving because his head was completely still; the statement of urgency appeared to come from someone who was not on the ring apron, as only three members of a boxing team are allowed on the apron, yet there is often more members of the team on the ringside floor. Whoever said it, Steve Albert changed the narrative from Greg's boxing men instructing their fighter to talk Campas for a work, because they knew he had the fight won, and there was no need to take any other chances with this guy, to their corner being in urgent ra-rah mode because they felt they desperately needed the round to win. Disingenuous. But what narrative had a better chance of keeping their viewers?

As the final round began, Toby Gibson was going to make sure there was going to be no calamity with the ceremonial touching of the gloves at the start of the round, and forcibly took Haugen's left glove and made him touch Campas' right glove. Greg did not need any assistance throwing punches once the round began, however, as he immediately began to throw his jab, albeit with much less snap than typical of Mutt. But the tactic did have the desired effect in the sense that it kept Campas on the defensive. Greg tried to sprinkle in a right to the body, but it was a weak punched and led to a clinch. There Greg proceeded to follow his corner's instructions and tried to walk Camapas around, but referee Gibson broke the fighters up fast. On the break, Campas did more posing than attacking, which is precisely what Greg wanted to happen, and it happened because Campas was still trying to figure out that jab, even in its weakened state it was winning the fight for Greg.

The remainder of round ten saw Greg try to work his jab and clinch when he can, but Tony Gibson was very quick to break up the clinches in this round. Campas continued to try and land the kind of punches that would drop Greg, but that did not happen. Campas did do some scoring but did not land with the game-changing effect that he needed. Yet, the Showtime crew still tried to sell the point that Greg could still lose a decision. In the closing minute, Pacheco touted, "here he comes," as Campas was landing successive rabbit punches, and Steve Albert gave Campas credit for landing a left hook that Greg clearly blocked. Campas did score with a good right hand at around the :11 mark, but it was not a crunching punch, and Greg responded with two consecutive right hooks. Campas retaliated with a seven-punch flurry, but only one of those punches should have been counting as landing in the scoring zone, and it did not land solidly.

Ferdie Pacecho certified the round for Campas and said, "he did his job here (round 10), now let's see what the judges say." Since Greg did not land with his jab as much as he would have liked, Campas could make a claim to win round ten based on his work rate, but he missed an awful lot with his wild punches.

When the bell rang to end the fight, as is typically the case, Greg was at his sportsmanship best and immediately sought out to hug Campas. The Fight Doctor stated that he had Greg the winner by a mere point but indicated that he would not be surprised if it went the other way. Bobby Czyz, after seemingly giving a lot of crucial rounds to Campas, also had Greg winning by a point, 96-95.

When Jimmy Lennon Jr. began to read the judges' scorecards, he indicated that it was a unanimous decision. Dalby Shirley's card was announced first, 99-91, then it was 97-93 for Bill Graham, and finally Davey Pearl, who was no stranger to Greg as a referee, rendered a scorecard of 99-93, all in favor of Greg Haugen. It was refreshing to see that the judges watched a much different fight than the Showtime crew. To give Campas three rounds is questionable, anything more than that would have been criminal, and indeed, the judges got this one right.

It is unclear why the Showtime crew was way off in depicting what was actually happening to their television audience. While I was never a big fan of Ferdie Pacheco, I will never suggest he lacks boxing knowledge, he was a more than competent matchmaker for the NBC network in the early eighties, and he must have learned something after being so close to Angelo Dundee for years. Bobby Czyz is an accomplished world champion. To suggest he does not know boxing would be foolish. As far as Steve Albert goes, there is no doubt that he landed such a prestigious job more for his golden tonsils than his boxing knowledge, but that is the case with all blow by blow announcers; some just understand boxing more than others. I would not put Steve at the top of the list of knowledgeable blow by blow men, but I would not place him at the bottom either.

So why did these three accomplished men mislead their audience for ten rounds? Perhaps they were expecting Greg to blow away Campas with ease, and when he did not, their eyes played incredible tricks on them. Or maybe they saw an opportunity to make a fight sound closer than it was in an attempt to keep and/or even grow their audience. Someone who actually believed what they were saying might have called up a buddy and said, 'man you gotta turn on Showtime, Haugen might lose this fight!' I raise these questions because these announcers are too experienced to just chalk up their erroneous telecast as incompetence. Steve Albert did not do himself any favors, however, when he voiced disapproval for the scorecards.

Whatever the case may be, Showtime now had one piece of their gargantuan extravaganza set for Mexico City. After the fight, Greg once again showed class that he rarely gets credit for and congratulated Campas for a good fight and raised both of their arms up in the air. Ferdie Pacheco interviewed Greg after the fight, with Don King standing on Greg's right. Pacheco told Greg that he had him winning only by one point. Greg responded in a voice that exuded poor health. So much so that both King and Pacheco had to be worried they would catch what Greg had. Haugen stated that he considered pulling out of the fight, but he said pulling out of fights was not a behavior that he liked. He went on to give Campas credit for being tough and was happy that he was able to get ten rounds in "for Julio." Greg also said that he hurt his right hand in the third round, and admitted, "I didn't have a whole lot, but I used my skill, my old wits…," Pacheco cut Haugen off mid-sentence to tell Greg that Julio was watching the fight from his dressing room and he is probably not very worried about what he just watched, Haugen replied, "He is probably feasting off this, but it will be a different show come February 20th… He can guarantee that I'll be ready."

All that was left to find out if indeed Greg would perform better against Chavez was for Chavez to take care of business against Marty Jakubowski, from Whiting, Indiana. Marty was undefeated in thirty-seven contests entering his fight with Chavez. He defeated the likes of Rocky Berg, Mark Brannon, and Craig Houk on two occasions. But nobody felt he was in the same class as Chavez. Not even Julio believed as much. He stated that he did not want to hurt Marty too bad when talking about this fight. Such a claim can be made by a boxer only if they feel far superior to their opponent; indeed, there may be other elements connected to such a remark, but one cannot have a chance to show such restraint against someone they feel is a formidable challenge. As a result of Chavez not wanting to hit the accelerator against Jakubowski, it took him six rounds to take the tough kid from Whiting out. When the fight was over, all attention was focused on February 20th.

Greg met Haugen in the ring after the fight, and it was clear Chavez had pure disdain for Greg. Greg, who appeared to be regaining some strength, was in full promotion mode as he said to Julio, "take it easy, take it easy," in a mocking tone. Everybody got what they wanted on this night. The fans were treated to better than expected fights. Don King saw both Chavez and Haugen become victorious and unscathed, putting operation Mexico City in full throttle, Julio Cesar Chavez was going to get the chance to legally assault a man who he hated, in front of his beloved Mexican people, and Greg Haugen was set to earn his biggest payday, with the chance to once again be the first man to defeat a boxing legend.

February 20th ,1992, was the date where all those involved had a chance to fulfill their wildest dreams.

Chapter Twenty
Mexico City

"I never watched that fight because I knew Greg was going to lose.
And I never will."

—Pamela Balding.

All parties involved passed their tests on December 13th, and regardless of what you thought of the matchups, the performances, or the scorecards, the night served its purpose. Fans were uttering those magic words that, according to Don King, all promotors want to hear, "When is the next? When you hear those words being said, you know that you have done your job as a promoter," King said. Indeed, the boxing world was inquiring about Chavez and Haugen. Don King was in his comfort zone, and he was prepared to answer those questions for the fans in the most grandiose way.

As was the norm for a Don King Production, he brought the kitchen sink to the undercard. It was a simple formula that was ensured the paying public the best bang for the buck and ensure that something magical would occur inside the ring for a Don King Production. "The most important thing is the attraction. You had to put on a great show, you had to put on a great card. I try and make most of my fights the main event in case the main event doesn't turn out to be the main event," King explained. And whatever else is said about Don King today, most boxing fans still rave about the kinds of dense cards he would provide for the public. On this night, many of the fights did not give the fans much drama, as they were one-sided and quick in nature, Felix Trinidad, Michael Nunn, and Terry Norris all had quick nights. Only Azumah Nelson's majority decision over Gabriel Ruelas provided any real memories on the undercard. Does a promoter cringe when their fights pan out this way, Don King said its part of what happens, and you cannot help what happens, you cannot, "tell them to put on a show for fuckery."

Despite trying to warm up the fans for the main event in his typical fashion, King also knew the only thing that mattered on

February 20th was Julio, Greg, and the frantic people of Mexico City. Everything else was academic. And it was the people that King really focused on. "You have to promote the people. You want to preach a sermon, to bring the people together. Make it a standard. And for this fight, they got it on the grapevine. When you get it on the grapevine, it is the essence of truth. Mexico was incredible, and agitation from this Gringo made it maddening," explained King. Of course, Greg believes that Don King increased the agitation, "The only thing I said was about the taxi drivers, all that other shit was instigated by Don King," Greg stated. While King might have overblown Greg's feelings about the people of Mexico, "King made sure the people hated Greg Haugen," Victor Machado stated, Greg did also insult the people of Mexico by saying that they could never afford to fill Azteca Stadium. Not only did over 132,000 people fill the arena, a record crowd for a boxing match that still stands today, but Don King also stated that "We had to put a closed-circuit TV outside of the arena so thousands more could see it."

Don King was focused and on his game. The people of Mexico were focused and on their game. There was very little doubt that Chavez was focused and on his game. Not only did he want to beat Greg, but he also wanted to beat him up, slowly and thoroughly. There was no way his mind was going to be occupied with anything else.

Meanwhile, on the other side of the pond, life was turbulent for Greg, and he just could not focus on the task at hand. For the Chavez training camp, Haugen's behavior made Gypsy Joe Harris's training methods look stable. According to Jim Montgomery, "Greg would say he was going to get a newspaper, and I would not see him for a week. I tried to get his head straight, I told him 'come on Greg, you are fighting for one of the biggest championships there ever was.' In fact, Dan Gossen, who had Terry Norris, told me he will offer the winner of this fight ten million dollars. I said, 'Greg, you are blowing it. Do you know what kind of money that is?'" No amount of money could get Greg focused.

"When he fought Chavez, he was partying up a storm. His personal life crawled into his professional life," explained Bill McDonald. "For the Chavez fight, nobody knew where he was. He got back to camp five days before the fight and was seven pounds overweight. So now it was all about making the weight so we can get

269

that money. He did," Montgomery added. Of course, if all your time is spent on making weight, training camp has to be chalked up to be a failure. "We did not prepare properly for Chavez. We made the weight, but we did not put many rounds of sparring in. Greg was doing all kinds of shit. He was smoking weed, drinking every night. Greg was down." Victor Machado corroborated.

Why did Greg Haugen choose such a critical time in his boxing career to slack off? Karen Haugen, Greg's wife, was at the root of the problem. "He was going through a separation with his wife," explained Machado. Their relationship was more combustible than ever, and it caught the ire of his family. "With Karen, there was always turmoil. I never wanted him to marry her. She was mad as a fucking hatter," was how Lee Haugen described her, as well as her relationship with his son. Greg's sister, Pam, described Karen as having a "manipulative mind...she played with his head. She was not the best supporter of his career. She was always bringing him down." The turmoil that Lee described took on a more tangible meaning that was devasting for Greg. He found out that Karen was sleeping with a good friend of his, as a result a divorce from what Greg thought was the love of his life, was inevitable. For those reasons, Greg said he did not have it in him to properly prepare for the biggest fight of his life. "She was my childhood sweetheart, the mother of three of my kids, it is not something you easily get over," Greg explained.

There is no question that Karen's actions had a significant impact on Greg's career. But Lee Haugen felt it was more than just that which led to his demise in Mexico City, roots that went back to his biggest success, "Once Greg got the title, he kind of slacked off, as though the title was going to carry him through. He has a circle of friends, hangers-on and none of them did him any good. Groupies that he somehow came to know. I told him one day he was going to need some real friends, and these assholes ain't going to be around. But he never paid any attention to what I said. He never listened too much to anybody." Victor Machado backs up Lee's observation, as he said if he ever tried to tell Greg about his lousy behavior he would just say, "Mind your fucking business." John Chemeres added, "When Greg became champion, he became lethargic and was not as focused. Karen was a big part of that. He did not care about learning anymore."

Indeed, Greg was listening to somebody, those demons inside his head. Demons that were loud and violators of peace. Only partying would get the noise out of his head. Whether Karen was solely responsible for Greg's bad behavior, or there were some other triggers after he became a world champion, did not matter much now. Because Greg was self-destructing at a time when he needed stability and focus. Making weight for the Chavez fight was indeed a titanic miracle. But no miracle has ever beat a fighter of Chavez's caliber.

Before anyone even know about Greg issues in training, the harsh reality is not many gave him a real chance to beat JC Superstar. There were exceptions. Don King believed in Haugen. "Greg's talking made him great, he was an instigator, but he also had ability. With his talking, he showed the eloquence and genius to capitalize on his fighting ability," King described. And his issues with Chavez were just a part of boxing accruing to King, "It is like the wild west. Everyone is a gunslinger. Everyone wants to call you out. There is no such thing as an easy victory," King said.

Those closest to Greg felt he had what it took to beat Chavez, which made his behavior even more frustrating, "I thought if the right Greg showed up, he had a fair chance of whipping Chavez," stated Lee Haugen. "If we properly prepared, Greg had the tools to beat Chavez, I am telling you. He only lost because he did not take care of himself," Victor Machado added. "I thought the fight with Chavez was going to be very close," explained Jeff Fenech. Despite all of the issues Greg faced leading up to the fight with Chavez, the marital strife, the lack of training, Greg presented as a very confident fighter. Joe Hipp recalls running into to Greg at the airport on his way to Mexico City, Joe was preparing to travel for his own fight in a different location, "Talking to him, he had the confidence that you needed. He was saying that he (Chavez) is just a cab driver. I was thinking, 'man, he is going into a hornet's nest down there,' he just didn't care. He came to fight. It did not matter who he was fighting."

The referee chosen for the fight was veteran Joe Cortez, which was important because this was going to be a very intense battle, and the Mexican fans had the potential to be a dangerous backdrop. A very dangerous backdrop. Pamela Badling explained, "Greg did not let us go that fight because it was too dangerous. In fact, I never watched that fight because I knew Greg was going to lose (Because of his lack of training). And I never will." Jim Montgomery was in Mexico City, and he spoke of how he felt their lives were always dependent on the Mexican law enforcement and some dumb luck, "Greg wanted to go get pizza, we had guys protecting us with uzis (two cars worth of protection). We park the car to go get pizza. We go in without our protection. When we came back out, our car and the two cars protecting us are gone," Jim explained. Only a story so sensational and concerning would trump the concern over why in the world was Greg eating pizza while he was supposed to be getting ready for Chavez.

Joe was a veteran referee who was based out of Nevada but was born in Harlem, New York. His first assignment as a referee was in 1979 at the Felt Forum-also known as the small theater at Madison Square Garden- in New York City. The bout Joe officiated was Gerald Hayes' first-round knockout over Jose Nieto; a historic fight card that featured a first-round victory for Mark Medal, a split decision victory for Mike Ayala over Enrique Solis, and the tragic fight between Wilfred Scypion and Willie Classen; Willie died from the punishment he sustained in this fight.

Cortez went on to referee many world title fights, his first being Aaron Pryor's title defense against Miguel Montilla in 1982. Cortez was the third man in the ring when Mike Tyson went the distance for the first time against James "Quick" Tillis, Roberto Duran's fight of the year victory over Iran Barkley, the controversial draw between Jeff Fenech and Azumah Nelson, and the epic first bout between Riddick Bowe and Evander Holyfield. He had seen all shapes and sizes, but never officiated a Greg Haugen fight. Although he was the referee for many of Greg's opponents, including Vinny Paz, Jimmy Paul, Pernell Whitaker, and Hector Camacho.

Joe Cortez knew about all the concerns and bad blood attached to the fight. "When I got assigned for the fight, they told me it was going to be in Azteca Stadium. I knew what that meant. But it did not change my duty. My duty as a referee is to first and foremost protect the fighters. I am there to enforce the rules," Cortez explained.

Cortez did not think Haugen's comments prior to the fight were all that unique. He categorized them as old hat in boxing, "Like all fighters, he was trying to hype up the fight. Mike Tyson would tell Lennox Lewis I am going to eat up your children," Joe also explained this tactic is also strategic in nature, "You figure as a fighter, you get your opponent upset, he goes to the ring mad, when they go in their mad they are not focused, and you hope they make mistakes. They all do that for that reason."

While Don King described Mexico City as a sermon, a beautiful gathering of people who were "God-inspired," and "having closed circuit parties," his description of the people gathering just to witness the event, and see Chavez, "expend his hostility in the ring," was not in keeping with the feelings of the Mexican people who were there because they wanted to get a piece of Haugen's hide. As Don King said, "Greg incensed Julio, the idol of Mexico," so being spectators was just not going to be enough.

Victor Machado first describes what happened to Team Haugen on the limousine ride to the stadium, "The Mexican people are crazy. What Greg said made Chavez feel low, like a piece of shit and the people wanted to beat the Gringo. Going to the fight in the limousine, they saw us and said, 'there goes the Gringo,' and they started rocking the limousine. They wanted to knock us over. I stuck my head out of the top window of the limousine to try and talk to them in Spanish, and they said, 'we are going to kill you too, you fucking Puerto Rican.' The police had to come with the hoses to get us inside."

Once Greg got inside, he had to deal with what he thought was a dishonest Don King. "I made him put a million dollars in my bank account before I went to fight. And I told him that if he didn't, he would have to explain to all of these people that there was not going to be a fight." King made good on the money. While Greg was waiting for that hefty deposit, he received the prefight instructions from Joe Cortez, "I gave the instructions in the dressing room, and Haugen was confident of what he can do (was that before or after the deposit?) And I knew Chavez wanted to tear him apart," Cortez observed.

When Greg set forth to walk down the aisle he was the biggest villain in boxing history; Don King says of a typical boxing match, "some people are for you some are against you," well the only people that were for Greg in that stadium was his cornermen. During this moment, Greg infuriated the Mexican crowd further, "Greg came in playing the Bruce Springsteen song, Born in America, Born in America. He was walking in with the American flag with that song playing," explained Victor Machado. The actual name of the song is Born in the USA, and Bruce Springsteen never intended the song to be one of American pride; although Bruce has a great deal of American pride, and would not have approved of the context Greg put it in. But those details did not matter much in the moment, Greg got his desired effect. Greg's actions probably made the fluids the Mexican people slung at Greg's people even more satisfying. "They were throwing piss and beer at us. I got hit in the head," Machado described. "We were soaked with pee by the time we got inside the ring," added Montgomery.

Besides getting drenched with God knows who's bodily fluids, Greg Haugen made it to the ring relatively unscathed, as well as a million dollars richer. The good news ends there, however. All the words were spoken, all the theatrics were over. Now it was time to fight. Don King said, Greg, "Stirred up havoc. Greg insulted the fighters, people, and culture of Mexico, and Chavez came out of the swamps, incensed, to get the Gringo." King's description may be viewed as a bit over the top, but what was true was that this fight was not business as usual for Julio. It was more than money, belts, or even pride. It was a chance to literally try and hurt a man as bad as you possibly can with your fists and not get in trouble for it. Greg was not prepared for the onslaught that was coming, and there were no Federale's with uzi machine guns there to protect him this time.

The noise from the record-breaking crowd was deafening as the fight came closer to fruition, "The crowd was so loud I never heard a crowd so loud when Chavez was entering the ring. I really had to cover my ears, that is how loud it was," described Joe Cortez. However, Joe had to remove his hands from his ears because he had a job to do that required some heavy lifting. The atmosphere was indeed different from most boxing matches, and the size of the crowd was not the only element, "When I came to the arena I saw all these police, they had rifles, they came prepared in case anything breaks out," Cortez added.

As Joe Cortez was giving the prefight instructions at the center of the ring, Chavez did not seem interested in listening or even being in the center next to Greg and Joe. Instead, Chavez was bouncing up and down like he was on a pogo stick, inching his way back to his corner. When Cortez was close to finishing his instructions, he grabbed Chavez by the right wrist in anticipation to touch gloves with Greg before the fight. As Cortez anticipated, Julio was reluctant to touch them up and pulled away from Cortez empathetically, shook his head 'no,' and went back to his corner. But Joe Cortez was not having any of that, and he swiftly went to Chavez's corner, grabbed Julio by his right wrist, and brought him over to Haugen to touch gloves.

Cortez's actions can be seen as an overreach of power. Afterall, as Randy Gordon, the former New York State Athletic Commissioner, can attest, there is no official rule which states fighters have to touch gloves in peace mode before the fight. With that said, Joe Cortez had a valid motive for his actions, "Chavez was so upset with Haugen. So, he was like I ain't going to touch your goddam gloves, I am going to kick your ass. That was the impression he gave me He wanted to show that he was in control, he was the boss. I was like, 'uh uh,' you are going to touch gloves.' As the referee, I felt I had to take control." A bold move from Joe, considering that over 130,000 people with access to beer and piss were not going to be pleased with his showing up of JC Superstar. But Cortez explains, "You cannot be a referee if you are going to be intimidated."

No one would ever accuse Greg Haugen of being intimated either, but he was obviously in over his head on this night. As Cortez, the man who was closest to the action, put it, "Chavez was dying to tear him apart. He started tagging Haugen and put him down in the first round, and I said to myself it looks like it is going to be a short night."

Greg had tasted the canvas before; however, this time around, it was much different. Against both Whitaker and Camacho, they were flash knockdowns, and both of those men wanted to box, Chavez wanted to obliterate Haugen, and he had the right toolbox and circumstances to do so, "I worked over 176 championship fights, and Chavez was in the top two or three of those fighters," was how good Joe Cortez thought Chavez was, "and Chavez was on the top of his game that night," Cortez added.

When Greg arose from the knockdown, he actually fought back, would you expect anything else? Greg threw a short right behind a double jab, then he threw a left hook to the body, a right hook to the body, then he came back upstairs with a short chopping right hand, the only punch that actually landed and appeared to have some kind of an impact. While Greg was trying to silence the record-breaking crowd with this offensive surge, Chavez was holding a good defensive posture and was waiting for an opening. When the time came, Chavez uncoiled a thudding left hook upstairs that had more effect than anything Greg was dishing out.

That was the pattern of the round for the next minute or so. Greg put forth a valiant effort trying to fight with Julio, but Julio shots were exponentially more impactful, especially to the body. At the 1:10 mark, the round became less competitive, however. Greg spent a lot of that time on the ropes taking had shots from Chavez. A controlled, two-fisted attacked that was doing damage. All Greg had to defend himself was his boxing moxie and savvy; he actually turned Chavez at one point. But those elements would never be enough to be competitive against one of the most celebrated pugilists of all-time. Only a Greg Haugen in the best shape and at the top of his game could have been competitive against such a unique force. That version of Greg was on Pluto this night.

When Greg went back to his corner, Jim Montgomery urged his fighter to get off the ropes. He then advised him to "throw something" when he got down underneath. Victor Machado held an ice pack to the back of Greg's neck, and Joe Cortez came over and ask Greg how he was doing.

Chavez looked focused for carnage as he awaited the start of round two, he opted to stand during the minute rest. The two pugilists met at the center of the ring, and Greg tried to take the lead with his jab. But Chavez's defense was just as subtle as Greg's was, and he avoided these punches. Julio would continue to uncoil thudding left hooks to the head and the body. Impressive shots because they did not come from behind a jab, and they landed with force. Greg tried to stay competitive and did score with some straight right hands, but Ferdie Pacheco analyzed of these shots, "The problem is Haugen ain't got that big a punch," but just one fight prior the Fight Doctor erroneously described Greg as a fighter who resembled that of a slugger. But he was right in the sense that these shots did not come off as crisp as when Greg was successful. Part of that was because of the shape he was in, and because Chavez had a super tough chin.

Chavez continued to be methodical and land hard shots when he saw an opening. And make no mistake about it, Chavez could punch. Jeff Bumpus described that when Chavez hits you, you could feel his knuckles through the gloves. But it was also apparent that Julio was taking his time with Greg. A big tell that Julio was not in a rush to get the fight over, came at around the 1:22 mark of round two, as after a sequence of unanswered hard shots, Chavez took a step back. The end of round two was particularly unkind to Greg, as he appeared helpless on the ropes, eating a sequence of head and body shots. Once again, Chavez chose to stand during the one-minute rest.

Before Chavez could resume his legal battering in round three, Joe Cortez sent both fighters to a neutral corner because a Corona sign that was on the blue corner fell off; you would think that for the biggest boxing event of all time they would have done a better tape job. What made matters worse were that Joe shouted, "come on tape, we need tape," yet nobody came over to repair the malfunction, and Joe began working on the problem himself. Finally, a worker came over to help, and Pacheco could not resist this window of opportunity to try his hand at stand-up comedy, "Now here is our Showtime people, using our Showtime tape, we are gonna have to charge them for that," Ferdie poked. Caroline's Comedy Club did not call.

Unfortunately, listening to the Fight Doctor's terrible attempt at humor was not the most excruciating part of the night for Greg Haugen fans. Greg continued to take a battering from Julio. A methodical battering that Chavez seemed quite content to sustain for the long haul, a tactic that was not missed by the veteran eye of Joe Cortez, "I could see Chavez was not going full blast. He did not go into that second gear, third gear, I said okay I could see this coming," explained Joe. In the fifth round, Cortez observed that Julio, "started to pick it up," this was probably because Chavez had a $100,000.00 bet with Don King that the voice of the judges would not be heard on this night.

In the first minute of that fifth round, Chavez landed a crunching right on Greg's jaw that caused his legs to buckle and saw his eyes roll to the back of his head. Greg's only defense was to fall back on the ropes to keep from falling. Chavez attacked, but Greg survived. With still over two minutes left in the round, Greg was soon back to throwing punches. Indeed, these punches had no effect, and few landed at all, but with this sequence did show was what Greg Haugen was made of. Not enough has been said about the valiant effort from Greg to remain on his feet in this fight. It would have been much easier to find a way out. But such a path did not exist for Greg Haugen Jeff Fenech knew this of Greg, "He was all heart. Even in the Chavez fight, he never wanted to quit."

There was no quit in Greg, and Chavez was in no rush, "He is playing with him, he could have put him away," Showtime blow by blow man Steve Albert observed in round five. Indeed, it was going to be the responsibility of the third man in the ring to end this massacre, "I think he was past his prime when he fought Chavez, I knew he was not at his peak, so I had to be a little more cautious of him taking too much of a pounding." In prize fights, when the best are willing to exchange, there are going to be shifts in momentum. During these shifts, fighters take punishment and they come back to give punishment, "It is essential to come back from punishment, it has to be reciprocal," Don King said of what it takes to survive inside the boxing ring. In Mexico City, the punishment was a one-way street because Greg was not at the top of his game.

Joe Cortez decided that Greg took all the pounding he could absorb with just under a minute to go in the fifth round. Once again, Greg tasted the canvas, but he got up and nodded that he was willing to continue. Soon after, Cortez intervened to save the man they call Mutt from himself, "I gave him an opportunity. I saw him taking a few too many, and I said, 'this is it,' and I waved it off." A decision that was not very popular, "I could see Chavez was getting upset because he wanted to hurt him a little bit more," explained Cortez. However, any decision to let Chavez continue to batter Greg would have been reckless and interpreted as playing right into the hands of Chavez and the crowd, "I knew I would be under the microscope. As a referee, you are under the microscope at all times. For this fight, I knew I had to be at my best." It should have been apparent to those that were looking under that microscope that Joe Cortez made the right call.

When the fight ended, Chavez and Haugen did embrace and share words, if there was a money line on that happening after this fight, the bookies would have made a killing. Perhaps Don King would have bet in favor of this moment, however, as he said of the bad blood that is built up for boxing matches, "Hostility and threats are the only communication (before a fight), but that hostility gets expended in the ring, then the hostility is gone." This might have been the case for Greg and Julio, but the people of Mexico City were still fixing to get a piece of the Gringo, according to Victor Machado, "After the fight, we had to stay in the stadium because they were waiting outside. They wanted to kill us. It was Saturday night, they were drunk, smoking weed, and they wanted to whip us. They wanted to kill us because this Gringo talked bad about Chavez." Even after Greg admitted that he was wrong about Chavez's opponents, the hostility remained for the fans.

What remains for Greg on this fight is regret, "That's my only regret of all my fights, not being in the kind of shape I could have been. My mind wasn't into it. I had no desire to do anything because I was going through an ugly time. I was basically fighting with a broken heart. I didn't want to train; I didn't want to do anything. I wasn't in any kind of shape, and it took me out of my game. He kicked my ass, and it was an embarrassment."

Indeed, Greg had a lot on his plate going into the Chavez fight. But one might ask how a man who had to digest a pretty big emotional burger all his life could not preserve and do the things he needed to do to give himself the best chance to win in the biggest fight of his life. Greg was bullied as a kid, came from a poor home where he was fatherless for most of it, his father was replaced by an abusive slob, he had turmoil with George Chemeres-a fellow with plenty of clout- yet still managed to focus and be ready come fight time. So why now, when the stakes where at the highest it could possibly be in boxing, did he decide to fold his hand and succumb to bad behavior? Anyone who has had strife with the love of their life knows the answer.

We also have to consider that Greg not only cheated himself out of the best chance to beat JC Superstar, he also cheated the fans who paid money to see it. Another anomaly for Greg, as he always wanted to perform for the paying public in the past.

What makes this fight most frustrating is that I am one who believes Greg Haugen at his best could have given Chavez all he could handle. He had the right style and makeup to do so. We saw elements of how Greg could work his right hand behind his jab on Julio, and a Haugen who sparred and been in shape would have had a better defense. And an in-shape Greg, as he explained it to me, would have had the legs that he needed to absorb crippling blows form an all-time great thudder and be able to recover. Greg said his legs never recovered in this fight because he did not train. Of course, this does not mean I am suggesting Greg would have won. It would have still been the toughest fight of his life where it was unlikely Greg could have scored a victory on the scorecards, even in a fight that he might have deserved. With that said, there is no doubt in my mind a close contest against Chavez that went the distance would have earned Greg a slot on the International Boxing Hall of Fame ballot. An upset over Julio would have guaranteed Greg a plaque in Canastota. It would have been the cherry on top of an already impressive sundae, non-dairy of course.

We will never know what might have happened had Greg Haugen trained for this fight the same way he did for his ESPN fights, Jimmy Paul, Paz II, Camacho, and Mancini, but I would rather speculate on that than fantasy fights with boxers who fought decades and decades apart from one another.

What we do know is Mexico City is nothing but a black eye for Greg during a turbulent time in his life.

There would be more storms to come.

JULIO-CESAR CHAVEZ TKO 5 GREG HAUGEN
02/20/93 - MEXICO CITY

Total Punches Landed / Thrown

	1	2	3	4	5	6	7	8	9	10	11	12
CHAVEZ	33/73	29/56	32/69	43/89	30/80	-/-	-/-	-/-	-/-	-/-	-/-	-/-
	45.2%	51.8%	46.4%	48.3%	37.5%	-	-	-	-	-	-	-
HAUGEN	15/95	15/81	19/107	19/101	4/46	-/-	-/-	-/-	-/-	-/-	-/-	-/-
	15.8%	18.5%	17.8%	18.8%	8.7%	-	-	-	-	-	-	-

Jab Landed / Thrown

	1	2	3	4	5	6	7	8	9	10	11	12
CHAVEZ	6/21	8/22	10/22	6/19	11/33	-/-	-/-	-/-	-/-	-/-	-/-	-/-
	28.6%	36.4%	45.5%	31.6%	33.3%	-	-	-	-	-	-	-
HAUGEN	4/62	7/61	6/67	4/47	2/38	-/-	-/-	-/-	-/-	-/-	-/-	-/-
	6.5%	11.5%	9%	8.5%	5.3%	-	-	-	-	-	-	-

Power Punches Landed / Thrown

	1	2	3	4	5	6	7	8	9	10	11	12
CHAVEZ	27/52	21/34	22/47	37/70	19/47	-/-	-/-	-/-	-/-	-/-	-/-	-/-
	51.9%	61.8%	46.8%	52.9%	40.4%	-	-	-	-	-	-	-
HAUGEN	11/33	8/20	13/40	15/54	2/8	-/-	-/-	-/-	-/-	-/-	-/-	-/-
	33.3%	40%	32.5%	27.8%	25%	-	-	-	-	-	-	-

Final Punch Stat Report

	Total Punches (Body Landed)	Total Jabs (Body Landed)	Power Punches (Body Landed)
CHAVEZ	167 (47)/367	41 (0)/117	126 (47)/250
	45.5%	35%	50.4%
HAUGEN	72 (11)/430	23 (0)/275	49 (11)/155
	16.7%	8.4%	31.6%

Note

Before a record crowd of 136,274 in Mexico City Chavez acted as an avenging angel for the Mexican people by not only pounding Haugen but also punishing him for comments Haugen made (and didn't make) during the build-up. Chavez produced an unusually active first round as he went 33 of 73 overall and 27 of 52 power while Haugen had no time to do anything but react and absorb. Chavez scored a knockdown with a right hand seconds into the fight to establish dominance, then sustained it by beating him up to the point of a knockout before laying back and letting Haugen recover. Meanwhile Haugen, to his credit, tried to fight back but while he maintained a hefty work rate (91.9 per round) his punches didn't register at all with Chavez. The Mexican legend was accurate (46% overall, 35% jabs, 50% power), proficient with the jab (8.8 connects per round) and defensively effective (17% overall, 8% jabs, 32% power) as he solidified his claim as the best pound-for-pound boxer on Earth. To add insult to injury: Chavez's assault was mostly to the head (only 47 of 126 power connects and 47 of 167 total connects).

Chapter Twenty-One
Fighting Without Gloves

There is no doubt that Greg Haugen had a problematic life. Growing up poor and different from those rich white kids is detrimental to those who you would not think to be minorities. Greg was indeed that. Along with financial hardship, the broken home, and the bullying, Greg Haugen was also exposed to domestic violence as a kid. Lee Haugen, Greg's dad, was far removed from the house, but Greg's mother still had the desires of the flesh and companionship that most of us have. Bob was Greg's mother's candidate to fulfill those human needs. According to Greg, Bob was a sweetheart of a man when he was not drinking. However, when influenced by alcohol, Bob turned into a violent demon.

When individuals drink, their real self often appears. There is the happy drunk, the obnoxious drunk, and those with thirst for violence showing their true colors. Usually, those violent types do not choose a fair fight and beat on someone who is not their equal. For Bob, Greg's mother was the victim. Greg was around eleven years old and could not stand to see his mother be the victim of domestic violence. And even though he was flourishing as a young pugilist, Greg was young and terrified at what was happening. He did not yet have the confidence to take matters in his own hands. Or better put, he was ,not sure he could use his maturing fists to fix the situation.

Therefore, Greg did what many Americans do when they feel threatened. He invested in hard steel security. Greg had a 12-gage shotgun and knew how to use it. Fed up with his beloved mother being using for fistic target practice, Greg loaded up a couple of shells in his security blanket and ordered Bob out of the Haugen home. But Bob was as loaded as Greg's steel comfort, probably more so, and did not take the future world champion seriously. So, Greg fired off a round in Bob's vicinity, but nothing close to reaching its mark. A warning shot. A round fired in your direction is indeed more sobering than a pot of coffee. Especially if the belief is that the next round will undoubtedly make contact. Bob hightailed it out of the Haugen home. Not the most diplomatic way to settle a dispute, but not everything can be fixed with a Coke and a smile. As far as Greg was concerned: Mission Accomplished.

Imagine Greg's shock when his mother took Bob back. He could not believe his mother could make such a poor choice. How could such a strong woman allow herself to be subject to such abuse? But Greg also knew that his mother felt that she was deeply in love with Bob, and love has not always had the best relationship with common sense. If Greg saw how charming Bob could be, those feelings probably grew exponentially in his mother's heart. Psyche is also an essential element when examining relationship decisions that make little sense. Greg's mother was no doubt fractured by the departure of Lee. When someone has experienced such personal rejection, it is not so easy to throw the attention you are now getting to the curb. And what can be said about Bob's affections towards Sandy? For him to want to come back after looking down the barrel of a shotgun is telling. Indeed, it is easy to dismiss him as an abuser with no feelings, but the unfortunate part of life is human being's often feel the need to control and batter those they have the strongest feelings for. Many individuals label such people as 'animals,' but no animal acts in such a way. Only human beings.

Even the simplest of the simple-minded could have predicted that the beatings continued. Once again, Greg could not stand by and do nothing. Not interested in eating a murder charge, Greg did not go back to his 12-gage and instead opted to try and solve this dilemma with his improved fistic prowess. Often, when someone has endured a tough life, and frustrations have built up to the point of having a physical and mental effect on you when the opportunity occurs to take out those frustrations on one person, you pounce on that opportunity. Sometimes the victim of your frustrations did not deserve the retaliation. Punishment does not fit the crime. But in Bob's case, it was absolutely warranted. Greg always hated bullies, and Bob was the biggest bully of all. It was time for Bob to square off against a formidable threat. Greg Haugen, the adolescent, got the assignment. Was it fair matchmaking? No one would question it, given the circumstances. But it was evident early on that Bob was no match for Greg. Haugen used his fists to pounce on Bob. Protecting his mother's honor, he did not hold back. When it was apparent that

Bob was outclassed, there was no referee to intervene, and Greg did not show any mercy, save for the fact that he stopped short of killing Bob with his bare hands. Greg ended his night with a warning. If Bob was going to continue to include hitting his mother as a daily routine, Greg would continue testing out the strength of his hands, on Bob's face.

Unlike his boxing career, where Greg had to constantly prove that he was indeed worthy of the highest level, night after night, fight after fight, Greg only needed one showing to straighten Bob out. As Bob sat at the breakfast table the next morning, he looked at his scrambled eggs through eyes that looked more like walnuts. Bob could not manage to scoff down anything harder than lose eggs when he did manage to raise his fork. According to Greg, Bob never tried to raise his hands to his mother again. If only every story of domestic violence could end so amicably. But often it does not.

It is often said that children who grow up in a home where domestic violence rears its ugly head, that child either plays the bully or becomes the victim himself. For Greg Haugen, his marriage was no different.

Karen was the person Greg chose for his companion. While he thought she was the love of his life, his family had reservations from the start. Lee Haugen claims that he told his son she was a problem, but when a person is in love…Greg and Karen's marriage crumbled just when Greg was at the peak of his boxing career, and making the kind of money Greg and Karen never saw before in their lives. Money can buy fancy cars, but they cannot compensate for fractured psyches. For whatever reason, Greg and Karen were not suitable for each other. It is easy for Greg and his family to attribute the problems to Karen's mental issues, and that very well be the cause of it all. With that said, when it gets to the point where it reached for the Haugen's, one variable to blame is unlikely. Indeed, Greg's heart was fractured right in half when he learned of Karen's infidelity with a good friend of his. For men, that is an action that is impossible to come back from. By April of 1994, Greg's marriage was over. But there was the matter of the children. Greg wanted to desperately see his kids, but Karen was being vindictive and not being compliant.

At this time, Greg was still financially well off and used his impressive bank account as ammunition in his version of the Battle of the Roses. Greg canceled Karen's credit cards and cut off any pipeline to fancy living that did not involve putting clothes on his kids backs, or food on their table. But Greg could not stay away and kept trying to see his children. Never one to be told what to do, Greg showed up at his estranged wife's home in Henderson, Nevada, to try and see his kids. He just wanted to see the kids. But Karen was livid that Greg hurt her in the wallet. Fuel by hatred and revenge, Karen got into her BMW, a gift from Greg, and tried to run him over outside of the home. Greg, who never given credit to be nimble on his feet as a boxer, erased any doubt by dodging the raging vehicle operated by Karen. Karen's red rage saw her crash the vehicle into the broken Haugen home. Which was now literally a broken home.

Crashing your car into the side of your house would bring most individuals back to some sort of normalcy, but Karen was pretty far gone by now, and heavily influenced by drugs. Therefore, plugging some lead bullets into the father of her children was her plan B. She grabbed the gun that was inside the car. Greg knew if Karen had the chance, she would use it, so he made sure she did not get that chance. He wrestled the gun away. By now, the Henderson police were on the scene and took charge. Even though Karen just tried to take his life, Greg did not like how aggressive the Henderson police were with Karen and voiced his anger towards their aggression. Telling the cops what to do is not a good idea. The same way Greg did not like people telling him what to do, the police snarled at such an approach. It was of no surprise that the police were now trying to restrain Greg. Greg's pride as a fighter took over, and he made sure that the multiple police officers who were trying to take Greg to the ground were not going to be successful. Greg knew he was in trouble but refused to let the gang of cops take him to the ground. A level-headed police officer who was familiar with Greg and Karen took control of the situation and managed to get Greg to agree to be handcuffed, but he was not going to go down for them.

A horrible night for sure. But in the end, Greg won full custody of his children. Something that did not happen in Nevada at that time.

This incident shows just how in control Greg Haugen could be. He just wanted to see his kids and was of sound enough mindset not to hurt his fractured, soon to be, ex-wife. A situation like that could have easily gone the other way, with Karen Haugen ending up in a body bag. After all, she gave her body to another man, Greg's good friend, and was using their children as a pawn in their awful split.

Actions that are combustible all on their own. Then Karen tries to literally try and kill Greg. In most situations, one of them would have ended up dead. The only reason why it did not end up that way is Greg is great under pressure and has a special kind of heart. I am not sure he gets enough credit for that.

As a boxer, it should be clear how well he could perform under pressure. Even when Greg was at his trash-talking best, he always went out of his way to congratulate his opponent at the end of their fights. Often, he would go so far as to raise their hand in victory, even after he defeated them. How many other boxers have done this? Greg Haugen was never perfect, but he certainly was much more compassionate than he is given credit for.

Chapter Twenty-Two
Greg On The Comeback Trail:
Trying To Tame A Tiger

"No one ever said a fight with Greg Haugen was going to be easy"
—The Tiger Lopez

After the beating he took from Chavez, Greg got back to work. The year was 1994, designated as "The Year of the Family," which seemed kind of out of whack for Greg Haugen. It was the second year of the Clinton Administration, and Bubba was having all sorts of issues with Somalia. Republicans took control of both the House of Representatives and the Senate for the first time in forty years, and they made sure they flexed their muscles. No, there was no sense of family on either side of the aisle. It was also the year we found out that Ronal Regan had Alzheimer's disease, and George W. Bush was elected Governor of Texas. 1994 also marked the year both Richard M. Nixon and Jaqueline Kennedy Onassis passed away. These events certainly changed the Regan, Bush, Clinton, and Kennedy families forever. One bright spot on the world stage was when Nelson Mandela was inaugurated as the President of South Africa. The first black individual to do so.

In entertainment, 1994 saw Nine Inch Nails have a Downward Spiral, Kurt Kobain blow his head off, Michael Jackson married Elvis Presley's daughter, and Woodstock returned. Indeed, game-changers across the board. In movies, The Lion King and Forrest Gump dominated the boxed office, Schwarzenegger got away with some True Lies, Christian Slater had An Interview With A Vampire. Some of these successes were used with the same old formula, especially with True Lies, but all were done with great success. Just like when Greg Haugen was at his best. If it ain't broke, just tweak it. With that said, ground was broken in the film industry in 1994. Quentin Tarantino's Pulp Fiction was a masterpiece that changed the way films were made in so many ways.

Television saw Seinfeld and ER dominate the ratings, Bill Cosby returned to television with Mysteries, and Claire Daines broke ground with her So Called Life. There was also a gamechanger with a hot new show, as NYPD Blue showed they could along just fine without David Caruso.

Along with the disappearance of John Kelly, Major Leagues Baseball's World Series had a disappearing act. As Greg Haugen's other favorite sport saw a work stoppage jeopardize their Fall Classic. Baseball picked the wrong time to go dark because not only did it turn the lights out on great seasons being had by the New York Yankees, their first in a long time, and the Montreal Expos, an excellent novelty team that no longer exists, the other team sports indeed had banner years. The NBA saw the Houston Rockets outlast the New York Knicks in a dramatic seven-game series to capture the NBA Championship. New York saw a better outcome in hockey, as the NHL had one of its best years of all time. First, the New York Rangers outlasted the New Jersey Devils in a conference final that had it all. Then, the New York Rangers won Lord Stanley's Cup for the first time since 1940 by defeating the Vancouver Canucks in a somewhat forgotten series that went seven games. Indeed, these sports helped fill the baseball void wonderfully.

Richard Steele, Tony The Tiger Lopez & Greg Haugen. This was one of the toughest
fights of Greg's career (Courtesy of Greg Haugen

Boxing also had a banner year in 1994. For starters, Frankie Randall upset Julio Cesar Chavez, Oliver McCall upset Lennox Lewis, Michael Moorer upset Evander Holyfield, and Moorer was then flattened by George Foreman in one of the most improbable boxing comebacks. Foreman was once again a world champion at the age of 45. Roy Jones, Jr. was the fighter of the year, as he dominated James Toney in their super fight, and Jorge Castro snatched victory out of the hands of defeat when he knocked out John David Jackson in a fight, he thoroughly dominated in before the knockout blow.

1994 was a year to remember, but perhaps the biggest story of the year was the white Bronco. O.J. Simpson's dysfunction made even the horror's going on in the Haugen household seem timid. But Greg's mind was not on the white Bronco or the double murder that horrified the nation. Or the lost baseball season. Or hockey. Or David Caruso's terrible decision to leave a hit television show. Or a box of chocolates. Or the great happenings in his own sport. Or Karen Haugen for that matter. Other than his kids, the only thoughts that occupied Greg's cranium were getting back in the ring so he could wipe away the terrible feelings of Mexico City.

Greg's first fight back was against Darren Brennan. While he won all his fights by knockout, Brennan had a losing record and had nobody on his record that was the caliber of a Greg Haugen. It was a clear example of getting back in the ring against somebody you are supposed to look good against, but Greg also had to be careful because of Darren's knockout percentage. Haugen and Brennan fought a good scrap, both fighters were letting their hands go from the onset. Greg's championship pedigree was the difference, as he threw and landed punches behind an educated jab. While active, Greg made sure he controlled distance and threw straight punches, it was apparent he was trying to tire his man out before he would taste his power.

Greg kept tagging Brennan with a straight right hand behind the jab. An effective jab from Darren Brennan did not exist. This deficiency prevented Brennan from landed anything substantial despite being very active. Greg dropped Darren in round four and had him hurt and on rubbery legs when he got up. But Brennan was a tough customer and survived the round. Brennan managed to test Haugen's chin in round five with a crunching straight right hand at long range, but Greg barley blinked when it landed and otherwise dominated the round. When a fighter lands their Sunday punch, and their opponent reacts as if it's a holiday, that must be discouraging, especially when the name of your game is power. It should have been no surprise that the end of the fight was soon near. Greg was now comfortable getting closer to Brennan and throwing more high-risk shots. Such as a crippling right uppercut that set up Brennan for a crunching finish. Greg stopped Brennan in six, high energy rounds.

Greg then knocked out Ray Garcia, a fighter who was of the same ilk as Brennan, once again in six rounds, Garcia did face some recognizable names such as Kelice Banks and Vernon Forrest and was a knockout victim of both. Greg was Garica's last fight.

After fighting twelve rounds against, at best, mediocre competition, it was decided that Greg would get another big fight. He was set to face the formidable Tony "The Tiger" Lopez on June 25th, 1994, at the MGM Grand in Las Vegas. The fight would be the co-feature for the main event between Vinny Paz and Roberto Duran for the vacant IBC super middleweight title; it was the second meeting between Paz and Duran-who were now both competing at thirty-eight pounds above lightweight, the weight class that put both boxers on the map. Greg would face the Tiger at welterweight, a weight class he was feeling out against Brennan and Garcia.

Tony "The Tiger" was a kid from Sacramento who turned professional in 1983, at slightly over 130 pounds. Entering the fight with Greg, Tony had a record of 44-4-1, 31 KO's. Lopez had two victories over Rocky Lockridge, including a 12-round decision in 1988 in The Ring Magazine's Fight of the Year. He also defeated robust competition in Tony Pep, Tyrone Jackson, Jorge Paez, and Joey Gamache. His trilogy against John John Molina is one of the best of the late '80s/early'90s. Tony won two of three of those wars. Lopez also fought Hall of Famer Brian Mitchell to a draw in 1991. Lopez would be the first to tell you he was not a boxer. The Tiger was a fighter. Tony's boxing curriculum consisted of making sure you hit your opponent back much harder if he tagged you. Indeed, if Greg was going to beat a fighter the caliber of Lopez, he would have to be on his P's and Q's. His attitude would have to change exponentially from the Chavez fight. But with all the drama with Karen in 1994, how could it?

Besides the raw emotions from home, Greg was having issues in training camp for this fight. Greg was indeed present in the gym this time, but some of the training was not ideal. "For the Tony Lopez fight, we could not get sparring. So, we were sparring guys one-hundred ninety pounds. Greg got his nose busted in sparring," explained Victor Machado. Greg did have some checkmarks in his corner going into the fight. For one, Greg was a perfect 14-0 in Las Vegas. When Mutt did experience home cooking of some sort, he indeed performed well. Also, Greg had some newfound motivation because he had a promotional contract with the MGM Grand. A victory over a fighter the caliber of Tony meant a bigger bank account.

Tony Lopez was riding a two-fight win streak going into the fight with Greg, and he was the betting favorite in the fight. He stopped Larry LaCoursiere and Amancio Castro in a combined seven rounds of boxing. Prior to those fights, Tony had back to back twelve round lightweight title fights with Dingaan Thobela, winning the first fight, and losing the rematch. Lopez had double trouble when assessing Greg. Of course, he was aware of the skill set, but was also concerned about the trash talking, "I remember going into the fight, Greg was known as kind of a smack talker, and I am not much of a smack talker. I do not get into that. "

Tony saw firsthand the kind of verbal warfare Greg and Vinny Paz got into, and he was bothered by it, "I was at one of the press conferences with him and Vinny Paz, and I was like, 'oh my God,' these guys were going off on each other. Every F word, every cuss word. They were talking about your mama's, daddy's, cousins, and sisters, it was terrible. If someone was talking to me like that, we would have been slugging. I do not know how these guys were doing it without swinging. I was shocked." Tony was so taken aback by Greg and Vinny's rhetoric he questioned whether or not what he was witnessing was indeed genuine, "When I left, I wanted to know if these guys were for real or where they playing? It did look one hundred percent genuine to me. I did not like it. I never had an opponent do that to me, and I never did it to anyone I fought," Tony added.

Would Greg be the first one to test Tony's ability to hold his aggression until fight time? Much to Tony's pleasure, he was not. "I was hoping he did not do that to me, and he did not. He was actually a very nice respectable guy. He did not pop off. I guess he liked me because I did not say anything to him." Greg felt there was no need to talk trash to Tony, "He didn't do it to me, so I felt there was no need to do it to him. The only time I did it is if they did it to me. Like with Vinny, he talked shit, and I'd have to talk back. I wasn't going to let anyone talk shit to me."

Where Greg could not afford to be a gentle person was inside the ring, and Tony was expecting the same old Greg Haugen there, "No one said a fight with Greg Haugen was going to be easy. You either have to toughen yourself up to be tougher and better than him, or you are going to get your ass kicked. It is that simple." Tony also knew that along with a great skill set, Greg Haugen had a great resume, but Tony had an answer for that, "I knew Greg fought a lot of great fighters. But, as a fighter, for me, I don't care. He has never beaten me. And that was my attitude going into every fight."

Part of what shaped Tony's mindset that way is, once again, the very crucial aspect of sparring for most pugilists, and pointed out an error in judgment from Greg, "I always went in confident because I was Bobby Chacon's main sparring partner for the first three years of my career. Bobby was no joke. He had sledgehammers for hands. Sparring with Bobby for so long, you get used to getting hit hard. Greg thought since I was moving up from 130 that I never faced anyone who hit as hard as him. But in reality, I was doing it every day," Tony offered. With that said, Tony had no delusions that his rite of passage with sparring a legend would be enough to win, "I knew it was going to be tough. I knew Greg Haugen was not going to be a pushover. And that night, he wasn't."

Both men weighed in at the contracted weight of one-hundred-forty-two pounds. Greg had the honor of coming into the ring last, but Tony was announced last, much like the Mancini fight. When Greg was coming into the ring, his gloves rested proudly on the shoulders of Victor Machado, Victor was pumping Greg up by chanting that Greg never lost in the town of Las Vegas. Tony Lopez sported trunks that showed half of the American flag and half of the Mexican flag. The judges for the fight were Duane Ford, Bill Graham, and Paul Smith. Richard Steele was the third man in the ring.

When round one began for that fight, both men tried to get their jab working; even though Tony did not see himself as a boxer, he did indeed work behind the jab quite often, Greg's jab was also his go-to punch when he was successful. Haugen took the early advantage by landing a stiff straight right hand behind the jab on Tony's face. Greg had Tony backing up, but he did not appear to be losing focus. Tony was calm and looking to set traps as Greg gained confidence. Halfway through the round, Greg dug a nice left hook to Tony's body. Greg continued to work a beautiful jab in round one. Doubling and tripling it up on Lopez's face. Tony was content to throw one punch at a time and let Greg control the real estate of the ring. But he did not appear to get frustrated at all, and he was taking Greg's power shots well. Tony became more aggressive in the last twenty-five seconds of the round, but Greg put the cherry on top with an outstanding right hand that appeared to shake Tony up for the first time and the very end of the round. All three judges scored the round for Greg Haugen.

Round two was a better one for Tony. He stood his ground more and landed good power shots. A right hand at the midway point of the round got Greg's attention and caused Greg to initiate a rare clinch. A big right uppercut at the end of the round really buzzed Haugen. Tony's attack was boxing 101 for a guy who wants to attack in the pocket. Ray Mancini, who was calling the fight for TVKO, referred to Tony as a technician. Greg had some good moments in the round as well. His jab was sufficient, and a bruise was beginning to develop under Tony's left eye. A good boxer always welcomes such an enticing target. All three judges scored the round for Lopez.

Round three was a beautiful to watch. Both men stood in the center of the ring and pounded each other with hard shots behind their jab. Haugen appeared to have a slight advantage by landing a few more power right hands and backed Tony up momentarily when the leather was flying. But it was the type of round that creates the results we saw from the three judges, one judge went one way, Duane Ford scored it for Tony Lopez, while the other two judges went the other way and gave it to Greg.

In between rounds, Jim Montgomery and Victor Machado went to work. Jim served as the lead trainer and went inside the ring, Jim told Greg, "Only fools rush in," then repeated that warning one more time. Jim enforced to his fighter the dangers of rushing in, and then incorrectly told him he won all three rounds. Greg won two of the three rounds on two of the judges' scorecards. But was down a point on the Duane Ford scorecard going into round four.

Tony came out firing lead right hands in round four and scored well. Greg retaliated by popping his jab, creating more space, and slipping Tony's power shots. But this was not Greg's best showing as a defensive fighter. Despite being committed to a jab, he fought Tony's fight. But that does not mean he was not doing well. Greg could always handle himself in a fight and swept round four on all three scorecards.

Round five was even on Duane Ford's card. But both Graham and Smith awarded the round to Tony. Lopez was landing hard right hands at long range early in the round, and Greg appeared to look tired. With that said, Greg bounced back and used his jab to score well. But Tony was still getting in those thudding right hands at range, and in close, that was taking a noticeable toll on Greg. Tony landed a short, chopping, left hook at the twenty second mark that physically moved the three-time world champion. Greg came back with about nineteen unanswered punches that started with a double jab. Not all the blows landed, but enough did to make it a close enough round that not all the judges agreed on.

Indeed, the fight was still up for grabs after five rounds. One could even make an argument that Greg was slightly ahead. However, circumstances were occurring that were not in favor of Greg. First, he was fighting Tony's fight and getting hit a lot. Tony did not lose many fights where they were on his terms. Also, Tony appeared to be the much fresher fighter. When Greg sat down after round five, he looked peaked, while Tony had bounce to his step and was enjoying the ferocious combat. But the fight belonged to Tony after round five. He dropped Greg in round six, and the fight was stopped in the tenth round.

Part of the reason why Greg was sapped was from the power punches he was eating. Lopez was economical and accurate. Most of his landed power punches were actual power shots. But Greg was also suffering from an ailment that was sucking his stamina. Even in training, Greg spoke of how he found it odd that he kept tiring a lot sooner than usual. He was training hard but found himself having to rest often. Greg just thought he was getting old. It was not until after the fight that he found the root of the cause, "I had some abscess teeth. Normally I start warming up after the first five rounds, that fight I started fading after five rounds because the infection set in, it hit me hard. I had five teeth pulled out the next day. The doctor was surprised I could even walk, let alone fight."

A simple trip to the dentist before the fight would have certainly taken care of the infection. His mouth was bothering him, but he ignored those signs for a good reason. Greg's exposure to dentists as a kid led to his decision to stay far away from dentists, "I was deathly afraid of dentists because when we were kids, we were on welfare. When I would go in, I don't think they ever used Novocain, so they were drilling on my teeth, and the pain about sent me through the roof. I just thought that was the way it was every time you went to the dentist. So, I did not go for a long time." It was easier for Greg to accept that the reason why he was always tired because he was getting old, rather than see if the pain in his mouth had a connection. Since Greg was not yet thirty-four when he faced Tony, his thought process is telling. Despite his condition, Greg gives nothing but credit to Lopez, "Tony was a great fighter."

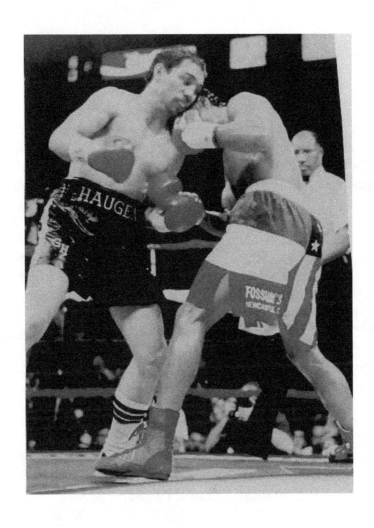

Mutt & The Tiger In Close Quarters (Courtesy of Greg Haugen).

Chapter Twenty-Three
The Twilight Is Here

"I never been hit that hard. It felt like bones were breaking in my face"

— Grover Wiley

After the disappointing loss to Tony Lopez, Greg fought the rest of his career against lower-tier competition. Fighters not at the world-class championship level that he was used to. Good fighters, nonetheless, but not prime stars. The second tier, if you will. Greg Haugen was still a better-skilled pugilist than virtually all these fighters, but he was not exactly fit for the championship level anymore. It is an odd, and sometimes frustrating fork in the road to be at for a boxer. A grey area where there is no real home for you. But Greg needed money, and fighting was the best way he knew how. Greg also still had great belief in his ability that he would indeed fight at the top level once again.

First up for Greg in this quest was Mark Brannon, a classic club fighter from Indiana who faced the likes of recognizable names such as Reggie Strickland, Tommy Hanks, Joey Gamache, Mart Jakubowski, Todd Foster, Kenny Willis, Karl Willis, and Eric Jakubowski. Mark became as successful and recognizable as a man with his skillset can hope for. Mark was like so many other fighters of his ilk and had to make a living working another profession. For "The Cannon," it was cutting lumber. Greg fought him on January 1st, 1995. The card was aired by ESPN and notable for the fact that Alexis Arguello lost a ten-round decision to Scott Walker on that night. It was the explosive thin man's last fight. Greg's fight with Brannon was the co-feature and called by Al Bernstein and Dave Bontempo. ESPN began the telecast paying homage to the Star Wars scroll while telling the comeback story of Arguello. Then Al Bernstein showed he was a science fiction novice by referring to himself as Jean-Luc Bernstein! If you did not identify Al's blunder, perhaps you are a victim of watching too much boxing as well.

For the prefight interview on ESPN, Greg looked healthy and optimistic. Sporting a goatee and cropped hair, he spoke about the disappointment that was the Lopez loss and his initial thoughts to retire. But Greg said he felt great since he fixed his nose and teeth and was ready to please his fans with a vintage Haugen performance. Michael Buffer was not the superrich big shot he is now, so he had the announcing duties for the undercard fight. The referee for this contest was Mitch Halpern, who earned a pretty solid reputation as a referee with a ton of integrity, but sadly took his own life at just thirty-three years old.

When Buffer introduced Greg, he had already worked up a good sweat and stared Brannon down at the center of the ring. Brannon opted to look down to the canvas. The fight began with Greg stalking the boxer Brannon, who decided right away he wanted to inspect every square inch of the ring. The bad news for Brannon was the ring was not that spacious, probably at the request of the star attraction Arguello. Greg found Brannon's body early and began to soften him up with solid blows to the midsection. To Brannon's credit, he did stop and pop while showcasing lateral movement. Mark's success with this tactic allowed him to get brave and play right into the scientific Haugen's plan. Greg began setting traps allowing his opponent to get brave. By the end of round one, Greg had Brannon missing with power shots and making him vulnerable for solid counters.

In round two, both fighters took turns leading, both had good moments. Greg landed a solid one-two from range that sounded a lot better than the other punches landed up until that point and got the attention of the crowd. Brannon's best shot was a right uppercut on the inside. In the second half of the round, Greg started to work a more consistent jab. Brannon was becoming left-hook happy, continually throwing that power shot as a lead punch, Greg either slipped or blocked virtually all of them. By the end of the round, Brannon was letting his hands go and outworking Greg by a large margin. But Greg was measuring his attack and managed to avoid getting hit with solid combinations. To showcase this kind of defense while staying in the pocket is not easily done, Greg made a living doing this when he was on.

The start of round three saw Greg working behind his jab with more urgency, as such an economical game plan might not be in keeping with winning rounds, and most judges fail to score defense and ring generalship when the other fighter is throwing many more punches. Greg wanted to keep the fight at range, as he now figured out how to work his jab on a taller man with a longer reach, who was a mover. More boxing 101 that Greg does not get enough credit for. At range, Greg nailed Brannon with a solid left hook that sent him to the canvas. Brannon barely beat the count of ten. When the action continued, Haugen stalked his hurt opponent but was smart enough to stay at distance because Brannon was winging away with dangerous shots. So, Greg back off and let his defense go to work. Brannon was exerting more energy by missing big power shots.

When Mark slowed down, Greg dug a hard-right hand to Brannon's body, then came back upstairs, doubling up on his jab, followed by a strong right and left hook. An impressive five-piece. Brannon tried to respond to the attack by winging another wild left hook that Greg avoided with ease. Greg went on the attack again behind a good jab and had Brannon in trouble on the ropes. Two consecutive right hands dropped Brannon for a second time with under forty seconds to go in the round. Brannon got up around the count of six this time, Halpern asked him if he was okay, Mark quickly said 'yeah,' had his gloves wiped off and went back to defend himself. With twenty-five seconds to go in round three, Brannon did his best Jesse Owens and tried to keep Greg away with wild shots when Mutt got close. It was enough for Brannon to survive the round, but it was a massive round for Greg in many ways. The former champion's patience paid off, and he now knew he could hurt his opponent.

Brannon came out on his bicycle in round four, but Greg literally stopped him in his tracks with a thudding lead right hand. Greg proceeded to land hard rights behind his jab, and Brannon was visibly hurt. Halpern was keeping a close eye on a man whose health he was responsible for. Greg's typical strength advantage was now apparent as well because he was able to push Brannon backward; indeed, the punishment Mark was absorbing certainly weakened his condition, but Greg seemed like the stronger puncher from the onset. Mark was also spitting out blood as he tried to avoid Greg's attack. Brannon was trying to buy time with his legs, but Greg was too good at cutting off the ring and was very accurate with his punches, so he kept forcing Brannon to fight back, which just made Brannon an easier target for Greg. With under a minute to go, Greg hurt Brannon with a lunging right hand, trapped on the ropes, Brannon slumped down to the canvas from an onslaught of short little, stiff shots from Greg. Brannon just beat the count, and emphatically raised his arms above his head when he got up, but Mitch Halpern did not like what he saw and waved the fight off.

It was the last time Greg Haugen won a boxing match with a stoppage.

ESPN was planning on building up a potential fight between Greg and Arguello. But Arguello's surprise decision loss to Scott Walker on that night put a halt to those plans. It was a welcomed circumstance as far as Greg was concerned. He had developed a friendship with Alexis over the years and was not keen on fighting the Nicaraguan legend, "I sparred him a bunch of times after he fought Mancini. They were talking about him fighting Ray again, and Alexis thought I fought like Ray. We sparred a couple of hundred rounds over a few months at Johnny Tocco's gym. We became pretty good friends. I told Bob Arum I was not crazy about fighting him. I was stronger than him and knew I could beat him, but I did not want to do that because I respected him so much. I was not happy that he got beat, but I was happy that that kind of squashed the thoughts of me and him fighting," Greg said.

Greg then dropped a ten-round majority decision against Oscar Gabriel Gonzalez in December of 1995 on a card in the Sundome in Yakima, Washington. Greg weighed in at one-hundred fifty-six pounds for this fight. The heaviest of his career. Joe Hipp was also on that card and said, "It was a hell of a good fight." Greg not only bought his fighting spirit, he also helped sell quite a few tickets, "He brought in a lot of people. They all wanted to come out and see Greg fight. You usually don't see that caliber of fighter in the smaller towns. He was able to pack the crowd in," Joe added.

Greg did not have a fight in 1996. He resumed his boxing career in 1997 and got off to a winning start against Jesus Mayorga. A veteran of over thirty fights, Mayorga was stopped by Vernon Forrest in one round. Greg won a comfortable ten-round decision against him in the Tacoma Dome. Greg was the headliner, and the Tacoma Dome was packed with Haugen fans. Todd Miles, of The News Tribune, described a great action fight where Mayorga had a big fifth round where he had Greg in serious trouble, but the

301

ToughMan from Auburn rallied back to the pleasure of the rabid Tacoma Dome fans. Les Carpenter covered the fight for the Seattle Times and described how Greg hurt Mayorga with the very first punch that connected. Carpenter went on to declare that, at thirty-six years old, the championship level Haugen was indeed in the review mirror, but he could still win a good old-fashioned street fight. Greg weighed one-hundred fifty-four pounds for this fight.

It was only a natural that Greg's next fight would once again be at the Tacoma Dome. The returns for the fight were fabulous, and the match delivered on a high-octane level. Greg headlined the card against Greg "Cool 'n' Deadly" Johnson. Johnson was a Cool 'n' Deadly 8-4, 2 KO's going into the fight. He lost a six-round decision to Bronco McKart. The bout ended in a ten-round draw. Greg suffered a cut on his nose from a headbutt early in the fight. Susan Wade, of the Seattle Times, reported that Greg conceded to losing the final two rounds of the battle, but felt he won the other eight rounds to secure a comfortable win, and that Greg was happy as he was more defensive in this fight. A victory, however, was not to be, and this draw was a mild setback for Greg because he had his sights set on the welterweight championship.

Greg finished out 1997 by at The Emerald Queen Casino in Tacoma. His opponent was Mark Fernandez in a scheduled ten-round bout. Mark fought out of Denver and went by the nickname "King Cobra." He was a veteran of forty-eight fights, winning over sixty-five percent of his fights when he fought Greg. He lost a ten-round decision to Jesse James Leija and a twelve-round decision against Stevie Johnston for the NABF lightweight title in 1996. Mark was very capable and was fighting much more frequently than Greg was. Greg weighed in just under the one hundred forty-seven-pound limit, indicating that he was prepping for a big fight at that weight. A win against a Mark Fernandez would be essential for that wish to bear any fruit. Greg won a ten-round decision and secured another title fight.

The World Boxing Federation (WBF) was founded in 1988 and has had a shaky reputation in terms of name recognition. Even the hardcore boxing fans would be hard-pressed to run off names of pugilists who won world titles under the WBF umbrella; considering the shady history of most of the very recognizable sanctioning bodies, morals and integrity is probably not the main reason why the

WBF has not been able to secure a reputation saturated with credibility.

One of the most significant fights the WBF had ever occurred in 1998 when Greg Haugen and Paul Nave fought for the vacant WBF welterweight title. It was a major attraction that was televised on ESPN 2. The fight took place in San Rafael, California, and was promoted by Howes Entertainment. Nave was a resident of San Rafael and was garnering a reputation as a credible ticket seller. Boxing is dictated by the business side of it. Therefore, sometimes your ability as a ticket seller takes precedent over your boxing skills. Boxing skills are essential to fight at the highest level, but the ability to sell tickets for a promotion will always secure a fight. Which equates to food on the table.

Peter Howes was the man in charge of Howes Entertainment, and he came with an impeccable reputation. Tony The Tiger Lopez spoke very highly of Mr. Howes, stating he was one of the few men in boxing that he dealt with who always did what he said he was going to do. And treated all fighters with great respect. Peter has the luxurious distinction of promoting a card that featured Floyd Mayweather, Jr. and Manny Pacquiao on separate bouts on November 10th, 2001, for HBO boxing. Mr. Howe's accomplished this by constantly pushing the legitimacy of his promotions to HBO. When the opportunity came for HBO to do something with Peter, they entrusted in him the two greatest boxing stars of their generation. Peter said the promotion was so successful that Bob Arum, who had Mayweather Jr. at the time, told him that he "under promised and over delivered on all levels." Music to a local promoter's ears. Peter's promotional prowess, combined with Nave's matinee idol treatment, was a dream spot for the WBF. Greg Haugen was the final piece of the puzzle.

Back in 1998, Peter saw an exceptional quality in Paul Nave and knew that he was selling tickets in San Rafael, "I wanted to promote Paul and help him go to another level," Peter explained. Howes resources combined with Paul's charisma became a perfect match, "Paul is a unique guy to promote because he doesn't just show up, he is very hands-on. It was like Paul was running for mayor, and the community was behind him. I never had a fighter before or since that had such a community commitment. And Paul was great at selling sponsorship," Peter added.

From the onset, Peter and Paul (minus Mary) had a specific plan, "Paul and I were talking about what we might do to bring some excitement to the area, so we started looking up opponents that we could bring in that might encourage ESPN to get interested. Because when you get television involved in a promotion, that brings in a lot more money. We wanted to get a television date, and Paul was popular, but we needed to get someone with a name cache to goose up the TV interest. Greg's name came up, and Paul went to watch Greg fight, and he thought he could win." The fight that Paul saw was his ten-round decision over Mark Fernandez. "I went to see Greg fight Mark Fernandez live, and I thought he deserved the win, but I was confident I could do well against him," Paul Nave explained.

Peter Howes was the man that had to get the fight secured for the lucrative ESPN date. That meant going over the specifics with Greg, Peter has fond memories of working with Greg to get that fight, "We spend a whole day together getting his stuff straightened out for the fight, and I really enjoyed it," Peter recalls. Peter also knew he had great pieces to promote, "I liked Greg's edgy nature and thought he would be great to promote. When Paul tried to be cordial and shake his hand for a television spot, Greg got in his face and said, 'I am going to kick your ass.' Paul was a gentleman and didn't like Greg's edginess too much, but I thought it was great for the promotion. I had two perfect guys," Peter remembers.

With that said, Peter remembers that there were some circumstances connected with Greg that he could have done without, "I picked up Greg myself. I didn't send somebody to do it, I picked him up. Greg was my main event fighter for a television fight, and he was a big shot, I was not going to let anyone else pick him up. So, I drop him off at the hotel, and he goes AWOL. Disappears. He went out and partied with Pat Lawlor, and he was hanging out with all these other characters that were filling his head with nonsense about how Nave was going to be a walkover." Paul figured Greg was going to take him lightly because even his closest friends did not think he stood much of a chance. Paul joked that Greg probably also read a piece in the SF Weekly that was written prior to the fight entitled, The Great White Nope, a less than flattering piece that gave Paul little chance against a fighter of Greg's caliber.

Paul was quite content having the doubters pile up against him. He watched Greg up close and was confident that he could win. If Paul turned out to be correct, he would be a world welterweight champion. The fact that it was a WBF world title did not mean any less to Paul, or Greg for that matter, "none of the press said a thing about any alphabet, or which one (sanctioning body) was better. They were just delighted that a local guy was fighting for a world title," Peter Howes indicated.

The other potential problem going into the fight was the issue of back child support that Greg owed. Peter indicated that such an issue could have prevented Greg from fighting. But Peter was determined to see this promotion through, and negotiated with social services with Greg's approval, "Greg said that he wanted the kids to have the money and was glad to have an opportunity to make money. So, we worked out a deal where the child support was paid right after the fight."

When the time came, Greg showed up at the weigh-in and made weight, as did Paul. Everything else fell in place, "Promotionally, it came together beautifully," Peter declared.

ESPN 2 was now featuring boxing and carried the fight. Bob Papa called the action, while Al Bernstein provided the color commentary. In the pre-fight interviews, Paul expressed his desire to try and outbox Greg, who he felt was a pressure fighter. Al pointed out that the promotion chose the wrong ring for their hometown fighter if boxing was indeed their strategy, as the eighteen foot ring was more in keeping for a telephone booth affair. Peter Howes took exception to that criticism, "That was the ring that we could get. We were not in the position to make a specific request for the size of the ring. When Floyd Mayweather, Jr. came to us, he had ring requirements, but we were not big enough for this fight," Peter explained.

If boxing was what Paul Nave wanted to do in this fight, his plans were quickly derailed courtesy of a hammer right hand from Haugen. "At first, I did not know I was knocked down. That is how hard he hit me. The next thing I knew, the referee was counting, and I did not know why. I saw Haugen in a neutral corner I figured I must have been down. My body just automatically got up, and I did not even know I was down. That never happened to me before," Paul explained. "Going into the fight, I liked Paul's chances because he watched Greg fight and believed he could beat him. Paul is the kind of guy you take at his word. But he dam near got knocked out in that first round," added Peter Howes. Greg tried to jump on Nave after the knockdown but had a hard time getting to him. Paul was very unorthodox, throwing wild overhand rights that upset Greg's timing. Nevertheless, Greg had a big round one with the knockdown.

But the knockdown came at a cost, "When Nave went down, my arm got tangled up with his, and it just blew my shoulder out," Greg explained. Paul has heard this explanation from Greg and replied, "What a bunch of bullshit, watch the fight he keeps throwing the right." The ESPN 2 replay corroborates Greg's story of getting tangled up and having his right arm twisted as Paul went down. Greg did not visibly appear hurt, and the team of Papa and Bernstein did not address it. But it was clear Greg stopped throwing his right hand in round one. There were also rumors before the fight that Greg had a shoulder injury.

Round two once again supported Greg's claim of injury as he rarely threw his right hand and showcased his jab almost exclusively. He did a good job of making Nave miss his power shots but landed nothing of substance himself. Paul did land with a decent right hand at the end of the round, that would make a case for him winning it. But it was by no means a slam dunk round for Paul, Greg clearly had the edge in defense and ring generalship and the numbers gave him the edge in connects nine to seven. There was still no mention of the absence of Greg's right hand, the punch that dropped Nave, from the television announcers. In fact, Al Bernstein pointed out that Greg was probably not working his jab as much as he would like.

The third round was a clear one for Nave. With that said, it was also clear that Greg was hindered by his right hand. He could not throw it. Bob Papa asked Al Bernstein why he felt Greg fought so defensive in round two, and Al answered by not answering, "That is a good question. I would have expected that he would come out a little more aggressive in round two, especially after knocking Nave down. Haugen has not used his jab as much as I think he might." While it is understandable that Bob and Al did not see how the injury occurred, but up until this point, they had not even acknowledged that Greg stopped throwing his effective right hand.

Round four was another blatant example of a one-handed fighter facing a two-fisted attack. It was a closer round, where Greg appeared to land the heavier punches. He caught Nave with a nice, short, lead left hook. Greg tried that punch again, albeit he threw it much wider, but Nave slipped it. Late in the round, Greg once again scored well with a left to the head and came back with a hard left to the body. Greg's power shots, combined with his ability to make Nave miss, should have given Greg the round. If Paul indeed won the round, it was only because he had a higher work rate. But one would be hard-pressed to call it effective aggression.

Paul had a clear advantage after four rounds because he was able to use a two-fistic attack. But things became a little dicey for the hometown hero, as he was cut above his left eye towards the end of round four, "I missed him with the hook, but as soon as I miss him, I started to come straight forward with the right hand, he leaned in and bang, we cracked heads," was how Paul described the cut. The replay does not support Paul's claim that Greg caused the clash of heads. Instead, it was Nave who led with his head that caused the clash.

Despite having the nuisance of what was becoming a severe cut, Paul had a little more success landing his power punches in round five. Greg tried to throw his right more in this round, but there was no extension or snap on it. Greg failed to take advantage of the flowing plasma above Nave's left eye.

Paul Nave fought more technical in round six. He stood tight behind his defense and worked primarily off his jab. It was apparent he was trying to protect the horrific cut, but he also did his best scoring of the fight. Greg just could not keep up with Paul without the use of his right hand. Greg had a better round seven. He used the ring more and kept a consistent jab in Nave's face. Nave was not nearly as effective and appeared to be getting tired. Greg's left stick seemed to be enough to win round eight as well. The seesaw nature of this fight continued, as Nave had a good round nine. He took Greg's jab way from him with sheer determination and bullish aggression. Not even the kitchen sink was spared as Paul let it all hang out. He managed to trapped Greg on the ropes, revealing what Paul felt was an important element of this matchup, "Greg is usually stronger than his opponents, but I was a three-time league wrestling champion and was just as strong as him. Maybe stronger." Paul also felt that he had no choice but to turn on the burner, "The cut was so bad I thought they were going to stop the fight. So, if you think they

307

are going to stop the fight, what do you do? You try and win every round."

Round ten was uneventful, and Paul did most of the throwing but missed badly. Greg could not get his jab going the way he did when he was winning rounds. Nave's work rate probably won him the round. Greg's jab was the most consistent punch for most of round eleven. Paul landed good power shots with under twenty seconds to go in the round, but Haugen was more accurate for the majority of the round.

The crowd was on their feet for the start of round twelve. For the second time in the fight, Paul Nave improved his technique and delivered short, accurate punches in the first minute of the final round. Greg did not get going in this round and did not do enough to take away from the early lead Paul had. To give away a vital round like this was crucial. Conversely, Paul stepped up and took a round that he knew was precious.

However, in the end, the twelfth round was not as important as one might think because the scorecards were grossly wide in favor of Paul Nave. Scorecards read 117-110 two times, and 118-109 in favor of Paul Nave. After the fight, Greg told Al Bernstein about the injury and said he was "done" boxing. Of course, Greg did continue to fight on.

This fight raises a fascinating boxing question, how much weight does punches thrown have when scoring a fight? When is defense worth more? There is no question Paul Nave pressed more and threw more punches in every round. Greg was clearly the better ring technician and made Paul miss badly, but very few times did he make him pay. Defense or work rate?

Peter Howes stated that it was a "great fight," but he could not declare who he felt won because of his role as a promoter, "I was a small local promoter, and I was pretty hands-on. Running around all over the place making sure stuff was being done properly. I did not watch close enough to say who I think won." A promoter has a plethora of stressful tasks fight night, but Peter had an added attachment that not every promoter can say they experienced, "James Lester was fighting on the undercard, and he had a warrant out for his arrest." Law enforcement wanted to put the bracelets on Lester before he fought. Peter had to pull out all of his negotiating chops to not let that happen, "I told them, 'he's not going anywhere let him have his fight. I am not going to alert him. And when the fight is over you, can do whatever you have the legal right to do.' They let him fight and then they arrested him. So, I was also dealing with that."

None of these unexpected roller coasters deterred from Peter's memories of this night, "It was a beautiful night," were Peter's final thoughts on Haugen versus Nave I.

It was so beautiful for all involved that they decided to do it again. The rematch was not precisely the same, however. First, there was no television for the fight. Peter felt that the lack of television for the rematch was not because of a lack of interest in the fight. He just thought that the rematch fell victim of boxing and the television business, and there were no open dates to air the fight, "They (television) usually fill up their que pretty well in advance with fights, they probably was just no room in the que for it," was Peter's explanation. Also, this time around, Greg Haugen won a decision. Greg felt he won the first fight and was delighted to secure a split decision victory over twelve rounds this time around. Greg won the WBF world welterweight title. When Paul Nave was asked about the rematch, he said that Greg, "fought better because he moved more. But I think it should have been a draw." When a fighter states that he should have earned a draw, it can be interpreted as an admittance that they did not win the fight without saying that they lost. Paul could not claim victory as he did with the first fight. Telling.

What was also telling was that Haugen and Nave were all tied up at one apiece. "They both won a fight, let's get a final solution," was how Peter Howes saw it. According to Peter, that final solution was protected within the contract, "For the rematch, we had it in the contract that if Paul had a loss or a draw, we would have an immediate third fight. Greg went off and fought four times instead. He didn't even take our calls. He went off and did what he wanted to do, and that is the way Greg is." Peter decided not to take action against Greg, "We all have to pick our fights in life, and that was a fight I didn't want to pick," Peter explained. "I really enjoyed working with Greg and left it at that."

The four fights Greg had after the Nave rematch had mixed results. He won back to back decisions against solid competition in Rudy Lovato and Grover Wiley, eight and ten rounds, respectively.

The fight with Rudy Lovato saw Greg return to the Emerald Queen Casino in Tacoma and has some controversy attached to it. Lovato was a tough customer who knew how to fight. His 12-13 record does not begin to tell the story of how difficult he is as an opponent. "I watched Greg fight on TV and knew about him from the tough man contests when I had a chance to fight him, I thought it was great," Lovato stated. Knowing the kind of luster Greg's name had, especially in that area, Rudy stated that he felt a little different than his other fights, "I was nervous, that was my first big fight with somebody with a name. To have an opportunity was exciting." Rudy made sure his cardio was better than ever before, and that he worked on his defense. These were the areas that he and his team felt needed to be enhanced to have a chance against a Greg Haugen. As far as Rudy is concerned, the training worked, "I learned a lot. I think I outboxed him. But the main point was that I learned a lot." Bill MacDonald was also in attendance watching the fight, and he felt that the decision in Greg's favor was erroneous. According to Rudy, most observers of the fight felt the same way. He even suspects Greg knew he was given a gift, "You know Greg is not too friendly a person, after the fight, he said, 'good fight,' and offered to buy me dinner and a beer. He was never going to admit he lost, but that offer was his admittance." Greg does not share the same sentiment on the fight, "Rudy showed up and definitely held his own, but I think I did enough to win."

There is no known footage of this fight to make a determination who deserved the decision. However, one thing is clear, both fighters took a liking to each other afterward, and Greg liked Rudy as a fighter, "I started fighting regularly at the Emerald Queen, I got to know Greg pretty good after a while. He gave me instructions in the gym, and he would always support me during my fights. He was always close to my corner." Rudy also speaks highly of Greg's skill set, "He punched harder than Yory Boy Campas. He was probably the best puncher I faced. He came forward and was aggressive in a championship way. That was the first time I fought somebody like that." Since Greg and Rudy have spent so much time together, you might think they have spoken about their fight with each other, "No, never," Rudy laughed when asked that question. Rudy explained that he knows he won the fight but understood that was how boxing went, "I was disappointed, but it was a hometown decision. If you do not beat up a four-time champion convincingly, they are not going to give it to you," Rudy expressed.

After beating Rudy, Greg went to Portland to fight Grover Wiley in April of 1999. Grover was a solid second-tier fighter who had a record of 13-2-1, 6 KO's. He went on to stop Julio Cesar Chavez, Sr. in his one-hundred fourteenth fight, and became a key sparring partner for a young kid named Terence "Bud" Crawford. "I was always a fan of Greg, and then they called me to fight him. I got in great shape to fight him," Grover explains. In preparation for the fight, Grover and his team were focused on the same weapon that dropped Paul Nave, but the preparation was fruitless. "We knew he had that sledgehammer for a right hand. We trained for that. During the fight, I can hear my trainer yelling, 'he's setting you up for the right hand,' then, bam, I got dropped in the second round. I never been hit that hard. It felt like bones were breaking in my face," Grover described. Greg went on to win a ten-round decision. Similar to Greg's fight with Rudy, no known footage exists of this fight, Grover claims there was footage of the fight, but was not surprised how illusive it is to obtain, "When you cannot find the fight footage, that usually means the hometown guy did not fair too well," Grover explained. Greg was happy with his performance in this fight and thought highly of Grover, "Grover Wiley was a good little boxer. He was a tough kid. He came to win. I just outboxed him. He definitely was no pushover, but I thought I handled him pretty decent and won the decision."

It was Greg Haugen's last official victory.

After the victory in Portland, Greg traveled to Verona, New York, to fight Henry Hughes in a ten-round bout. The fight took place in June at the Turning Stone Casino during The International Boxing Hall of Fame weekend. The fight was a disappointing decision loss. Dave Murphy was at the contest and thought Greg looked like a "shot fighter." "I saw him the next day on the grounds, he was eating a hot dog, and was wearing sunglasses to hide his bruises. He was friendly enough, but very quiet." Greg admits he was not in shape for the fight. "I took the fight on short notice because it was for Hall of Fame weekend. Like a dipshit, I took the fight when I shouldn't have. I knew nothing about Henry. I come to find out after I fought him that he was a pretty good amateur fighter," Greg offered. As a professional, Hughes fought Eddie Van Kirk to a draw and lost to

Meldrick Taylor and Felix Trinidad before facing Greg in 1999. "He had pretty good hand speed. A slick boxer. He was very hard to hit. I wish I did not take that fight." explained Greg.

Greg went on to face Thomas Damgaard in September of 1999 in Denmark. Damgaard was a respected undefeated prospect at the time, with a record of 14-0, 12 KO's. Adding to the complications, Daamgard was also a southpaw. A victory against this caliber of fighter would propel Greg in a good position for bigger money fights. For that to happen, Greg would have to churn out a great performance on the road. A position he was all too familiar with.

Greg worked up a good sweat before the fight. His hairline was now reciting, and a bald spot was visible on the top of his dome. Conversely, Damgaard looked like he still could be carded. Greg started the fight looking confident and dug a good left hook into Damgaard's body. He proceeded to try and work his jab and got in some right hands to Damgarrd's face. Scoring blows, but nothing debilitating. Damgaard seemed content to let Greg get off, as he was feeling out the four-time champion. The first hard shot Damgarrd committed to were left hooks to Greg's body. He came back with a hard left hook upstairs, but Greg deflected it nicely. Those shots must have gotten Greg's attention because he fought off his back foot the rest of the round.

In round two, Greg allowed his opponent to be the boss. It was the first time Greg fought in an entirely defensive mode. The jab was not there, the slick counters after making his opponent missed seized to exist. The diversity when leading disappeared. If there was a question of Greg being shot before this fight, round two provided resounding evidence that Greg's glory days were now in a time capsule. On sheer heart and championship makeup, Greg lasted until the sixth round against Damgaard.

Many people felt Greg should have stepped down after this fight. But he decided to fight the rubber match with Paul Nave instead. That fight ended in a draw, that was eventually ruled a no contest because of a failed drug test from Greg. After three matches and thirty-six rounds between Haugen and Nave, Peter Howes jokes, "It is still not settled. But I would highly advise against a fourth fight at this point."

Greg Haugen never again laced up the boxing gloves as a professional.

The year was 1999, and Greg's boxing career was over. 1999 was indeed a special year, even if it was not memorable for Greg. It was the year before the so-called Y2K, and individuals were in a panic. How could the planet continue with so many zeroes in the calendar? Everything will come to a halt...right? As silly as it seems now, the fear of our precious technology breaking down when the year turned 2000 provided genuine anxiety. People were taking their savings out of banks and stuffing them into their mattresses.

As panic began to set in, 1999 trucked along quite well otherwise. President Bill Clinton was acquitted by the Senate in his impeachment hearings, and he went on to run the country quite moderately. Yugoslavia and NATO signed a treaty to end their hostilities during the Kosovo War, and The United States turned over the Panama Canal to the Panamanian Government. Also, in 1999, Prime Minister Vladimir Putin became President of Russia after Boris Yelstin's resignation. Famous people who were born in Greg's final year of boxing include Colin Sexton, Vladimir Guerrero, Jr., Chandler Riggs, Ja Morant, Jaren Jackson, Jr., and Little Nas X.

1999 was also an excellent year for pop culture in the United States. Lauryn Hill won a bunch of Grammys, Eminem released his epic The Slim Shady LP, Christina Aguilera let the Gennie out of the bottle, Santana, with the help of Rob Thomas, became so Smooth, and Brittany Spears teamed up with NSYNC at the MTV Movie Awards for a memorable performance. Some may say the quality of music had eroded like Haugen's boxing skills, but there is no denying their popularity.

Television and film enjoyed a terrific 1999. In television, Family Guy, Batman Beyond, SpongeBob SquarePants, The West Wing, and The Sopranos debuted. Regis Philbin wanted to know who wanted to be a millionaire, ER, Friends, The Practice, Frasier, and Touched by an Angel provided quality programming for television viewers. And Everybody Loved Raymond. Quality films were also in abundance in 1999. The Matrix, American Pie, Eyes Wide Shut, The Sixth Sense, Fight Club, Boys Don't Cry, Being John Malkovich, The Insider, The Green Mile, The Cider House Rules, and American Beauty were all released and became instant classics. Angelina Jolie enjoyed her breakout role in Girl, Interrupted. Jamie Foxx showed off his acting chops as Willie Beamen in the very underrated Any Given Sunday, and Hurricane was released amid substantial controversy in the boxing community. Indeed, Denzel Washington was fabulous as the incarcerated Rubin Carter, but maybe people felt there were many inaccuracies with the truth.

The world of sports in 1999 saw the Denver Broncos win their second straight Super Bowl, The New York Yankees also repeated as champions by sweeping the Atlanta Braves. New York could not secure a second championship, however, as the New York Knicks lost the NBA finals to the San Antonio Spurs, and the Dallas Stars defeated the Buffalo Sabres to capture Lord Stanley's Cup. In boxing, the sport suffered a major embarrassment when Lennox Lewis's dominating performance over Evander Holyfield was ruled a draw. Lennox was victorious in the rematch later that year, but the draw spoke volumes about how the stench of boxing can really cost them their fans. Paulie Ayala's twelve-round victory over Johnny Tapia was Ring Magazine's fight of the year. Ayala was also named fighter of the year, as he also defeated David Vasquez and Anupong Srisuk in 1999.

Indeed, there was a lot to keep people occupied as Y2K crept upon them. But when the clock struck midnight on December 31st, 1999, absolutely nothing happened. All the fear manifested by the media bore zero fruit. But for Greg Haugen, it was different. 2000 was not going to be a great year for him, as the craft that put food on the table was indeed shut down. He had no pension and received no severance pay. What was he to do now?

Chapter Twenty-Four
Retirement

"He was the first person to believe in me. He made me think that I
could do it."

—Thomas Migneault

Not being able to box anymore was a harsh reality for Greg. But it
was a reality that he had no illusions about, "I knew if I couldn't stop
a guy like Nave that I just did not have it anymore. So, I chose to get
away from it before it took a toll on me. You can't hang around and
be mediocre as a fighter, it just is not going to work out for you."
While Greg knew it was over, the boxing bloodsuckers wanted to
keep earning coin off a fighter than was past their prime, "I had a
bunch of offers, but they were all as an opponent. I chose not to take
them. I just didn't think I had it anymore and did not want to be an
opponent for anybody," Greg offered.

Greg's realism about his boxing career being it over did not make
it any easier to cope with the fact he was no longer fighting for a
living, "I was lost for a few years. Boxing was all I knew. I knew I
was too old to do it, but I was only forty fucking years old. As an
athlete, you are only given so much time." That time probably would
have been easier to manage if Greg had the benefit of enjoying some
of his fortunes from boxing. But just like his ability to work off his
jab, Greg's money was virtually all gone. Ill-advised investments
and a deviant accountant wiped out Greg's funds, "I was not paying
attention. By the time I noticed, I was fucked. Everything I worked
for my kid's future was gone."

What could Greg fall back on? Greg's knowledge of boxing was a
strong resource for him to utilize. But in what capacity? Haugen had
the right makeup to make a living in boxing in some capacity other
than delivering punches. His mind was a proverbial sponge when it
came to boxing knowledge. And, from most people's account, was a
very caring person. The Muckleshoot Boxing Gym in Auburn,
Washington, provided an opportunity for Greg's kindness to shine.

Thomas Migneault explains, "This had to be about 2007. I was a little ghetto kid. Bad. My neighbor brought me to a big barn in the middle of the reservation an introduced me to Greg. I was one of the youngest there. I was the most out of shape. I was clueless and had the biggest attitude. That attitude dissipated within the second week. Greg's response to me was to shake his head, then he would tell me to go run with the others. At the gym, he was never too far away. He used to pick up a lot of us in his big van to go to the gym. He made me work harder than ever before. He made me keep going through the sweat, the burning pain, and the puke. He was the first person to believe in me. He made me think that I could do it."

Greg defiantly wanted to train kids. To pass his knowledge on to an inspired youngster. To find that next world champions. But the dynamic of a world-class champion becoming a trainer is a peculiar one. Hall of Famers like Emile Griffith and Eddie Mustafa Muhammad have indeed proved competent as trainers. Buddy McGirt is a Hall of Fame boxer who should reach that same accomplishment as a trainer one day. But they are considered to be on a shortlist. The men considered to be the greatest trainers did not become world champions when they were fighting. Greg never materialized as a boxing trainer either. Greg said it was because the boxing scene in Washington was bleak, and he found most of the kids to be "lazy."

Greg had a huge opportunity to teach young kids the tricks of the trade through a contact he made with Chris Cates Lopez. Lopez is a Washington native who has the interest of Seattle in his bones. His christening into boxing was watching old fight films of boxing greats like Archie Moore with his grandfather. Ironically, when he met Greg, Vinny Paz was one of his favorite fighters, "I do not remember who introduced us, but I remember we got along right away," Chris offers. At the time of their meeting, Chris was developing a program on Rainer Street in Seattle, Washington, called the Your House Boxing & Community Club (YHBCC). Rainer was a hotbed for youth violence, and Chris Cates Lopez was cut from the kind of cloth that prevented him from standing by and doing nothing. The YHBCC was an athletic outlet to help kids on the right path and find a productive way to get out their aggression.

Boxing is a lifesaver for many people. All over the world, troubled and poor individuals walk into boxing gyms, lace up the boxing gloves, and hope they are half as good as Sugar Ray Robinson; such an attribute would be good enough for a professional career. And while only a small percentage of these hopefuls actually reach the championship level in boxing, boxing has indeed been a game-changer for individuals in ways that might not be as obvious. When Chris heard that Greg Haugen wanted to teach these kids boxing, he immediately hired him as a coach.

Greg was the only coach at YHBCC with any professional boxing experience at the time. The marriage was a culture shock for both Greg and the kids. For the kids, on the positive side, having a multiple world champion instructing them added a sense of realism to the program. But it was also very intimidating for them. According to Chris, Greg's drills were repetitive, rigorous, and stealth. Chris likened the drills to the training that Daniel LaRusso had to endure in The Karate Kid. Like Daniel, not all the youth of Seattle understood the benefit of such methods right away. And according to Chris, Greg did not have the kind of patience and understanding of Mr. Myagi. "I think Greg had a really hard time relating to the younger generation," Chris offered.

Greg also had a hard time embracing the working conditions of YHBCC. Inadequate funding did not allow for a boxing ring, and Greg despised that dynamic. Also, the respective mission statements for YHBCC differed drastically for both Chris and Greg. Chris's mission was to get these kids to stop shooting each other, while Greg was hell-bent on making a fighter, finding a world champion. Part of the YHBCC program required kids to do their homework. Greg wanted no part of that. You wonder why Chris offered Greg a job knowing their philosophies on such different ends of the spectrum. Chris explains, "It is not like I did not want to develop fighters. I wanted that too, but I know that was years down the road. Greg just lost interest before we could get there." John Chemeres was not at the YHBCC at the same time as Greg Haugen, he ventured down there after reading that Andre Ward visited the club. John stood around and began working with the kids on the fundamentals of boxing, such as footwork. But like Greg, John was frustrated with the skimpy budget of the YHBCC. John also had no interest in helping kids with their homework. John was not surprised that Greg had issues working under such conditions.

Regardless of the split, Chris explains he treasures his time with Greg, and he learned so much from him about boxing. Chris learned great techniques, such as using a penny to improve your footwork and using your body correctly when throwing punches, as well as the mental aspect of boxing. Chris brags that he is now an excellent mitt man thanks to Greg Haugen's tutelage. Being able to works the mitts effectively was always very important to Greg Haugen, it is what lured Greg to Victor Machado, and he passed that skill on to Chris Cates Lopez.

With that said, Chris explains that another frustrating dynamic for Greg during his YHBCC days was the inability to fully work the mitts because he only had use of one arm. According to Chris, Greg always offered to wear the body shield when training with the kids. Something that Chris himself hated to do.

Greg also tried to parlay his exceptional knowledge of the sweet science into a productive career color analyst. Indeed, Greg did work various fights behind the microphone and was very effective. But he is currently not working in such a capacity. Greg was told a few years back that he would be hired as a color guy during the time boxing was trying to make its way back to network television. But that plan crumbled once Al Haymon and the PBC began to make deals to crowd the networks. This is peculiar because Greg indeed fits the mold of what Mr. Haymon wants behind the mic-a former fighter who is knowledgeable and outspoken.

Currently, Greg Haugen is not working in any capacity today. He is dependent on social security, which amounts to about nine-hundred dollars a month, "It is not fun," Greg offered. But Greg is also very thankful that he wakes up every day, as he often states that waking up is not a guarantee for a guy his age. Greg is happiest when he is spending time with his children and grandchildren. And when he is talking boxing.

The career of Greg Haugen was a great one. For whatever reason, it is not always perceived to be as such. Maybe too much attention is put on the Chavez fiasco. Perhaps too many people associate him as an overachieving ToughMan. Both reasons are unfair. In retirement, Greg Haugen has received proper recognition in certain circles. He has been inducted into The Northwest Boxing Hall of Fame, and The World Boxing Hall of Fame. Both honors were appreciated and embraced by Greg, "They were some of my biggest moments being recognized as a decent fighter. You do not go into a boxing career thinking you are going to the Hall of Fame," Greg explained.

Indeed, Greg Haugen was much more than a decent fighter. More consideration should be given to be put on the ballot for The International Boxing Hall of Fame (IBHOF). The IBHOF is located in Canastota, New York, and is considered the gold standard. Looking at Greg's career, he should no doubt be on the ballot for consideration. No, he does not have the longevity of some boxers, but he was undoubtedly quality over quantity. No, he does not have a high number of title defenses, which is a typical tangible to get fighters inducted, but who knows how many more title defense Greg would have had if the first fight with Vinny Paz was scored in his favor? Since the majority of observers felt he won that fight, it should not be dismissed as an empty question.

What is that you say, what-ifs are not enough to warrant being on the ballot? Well, Greg's career, as is, is worth consideration. Greg defeated a highly experienced, highly rated fighter, in his first two professional fights. In his third fight he went ten rounds. Time and time again, he defeated very good fighters who were favored against him because they had more experience, Ted Michaliszyn, Freddie Roach, Chris Calvin, Charlie White Lightning Brown. Each time Greg proved them wrong. Not because he was tougher than them, although that always helped, but because he showcased better boxing skills than his experienced foes. Then he pulled off two monumental upsets against Jimmy Paul and Hector Camacho for the same reasons. Ray Mancini was also supposed to make easy work of Greg Haugen in his comeback fight.

Lee Groves is a boxing historian and BWAA member. He has gone on record saying one of his measures when considering voting for a fighter who is on the ballot is if that fighter was superior in a particular skill set than that of his contemporaries (which is why Arturo Gatti is worthy of induction because nobody provided the blood and guts drama better than he did at the time; that is my summation, not Lee's). But if you spend time watching Greg Haugen fight, you will identify a fighter who was much better than his peers in many areas. He was one of the best fighters in those early days of the Top Rank Boxing series on ESPN. Without question, one of the most effective jabs of the eighties and early nineties was attached to Greg Haugen's body, a fellow who stood 5'6, with a 67-inch reach.

Greg used subtle moves in the pocket that you hardly see anymore. Time and time again, he would evade an attack from his opponent and still be in the position to punch. His performance in Paz II was one of the great boxing clinics of the decade. I challenge everyone to find five better performances at lightweight during the 80s. Perhaps the only fighters to do it better than Greg in that weight class at the time was Pernell Whitaker and Julio Cesar Chavez, but if we are going to measure fighters against those two, the IBHOF would not have as many members as they do.

And this is not a plea to put Greg in the IBHOF. It is a plea to get his name on the ballot for consideration. Indeed, there is a case to be made for that action. Greg Haugen was not born with impressive physical attributes or superb athletic ability. Growing up, he had no financial advantages either. Indeed, everything he accomplished was built from the ground up. With that said, when he did turn pro, his complexion certainly did help him land fights on ESPN. But such a cache existed for plenty of pale fighters on the young network, and Greg Haugen proved to be better than them all with his superior boxing skills.

If that does not warrant checkmark consideration...

Greg & The Greatest, 1986. 'Nuff said (Courtesy of Greg Haugen).

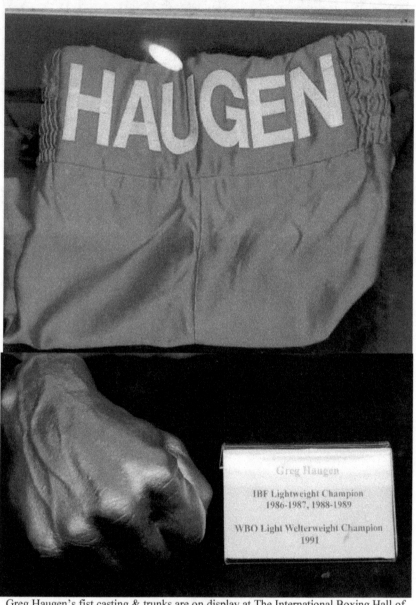

Greg Haugen's fist casting & trunks are on display at The International Boxing Hall of Fame
Museum in Canastota, New York. Will he ever get on the Hall of Fame Voting Ballot?
(Photos
By Anthony "Zute" George.

Chapter Twenty-Five
Rubbing Elbows

While Greg Haugen's great career might have been compromised financially because of the star power of the Fab Four in the 1980s, and later the heavyweights of the '90's, Greg still enjoyed certain perks that most aspiring boxers never get to experience. One of these perks is getting to rub elbows with the biggest names in boxing, as well as other pop culture icons. Greg recalls meeting some of these individuals while he was at the top of the sweet science. Greg describes some of these moments as bliss, while other encounters were equivalent to the feeling one gets when they throw up in their mouth.

Donald Trump: "Donald was going through one of his problems, and he had to file for bankruptcy. He went from a billionaire to a mere millionaire. And my buddy asked him if he can get a picture with him. Donald goes, 'sure'. So, after they take the picture, my buddy goes, 'hey thanks a billion,' Donald didn't think that was too funny. I got a couple of pictures with him, I was looking at some, and I said, 'Oh shit, I got a couple of pictures with me and a fucking idiot President. I didn't really have anything against the guy then. The only time I would see him was right before the fight. He would come in and say, 'good luck, there is a good crowd out there, have a good fight.' There really wasn't much mingling with Donald. I never would have thought he would be President, but he got a lot of suckers to buy into that 'let's make America great again' crap. Now he embraces the country every time he opens his mouth."

Marvelous Marvin Hagler: "I like Marvin. He was no-nonsense; he came to fight. He was robbed against Leonard. He liked me too. He saw my fight with Edwin Curet and was impressed. I cannot say I was inspired by too many guys, but Marvin was impressive."

Bob Arum: "Bob was a no-nonsense guy. I don't think he had much of a personality. Toward the end of my dealings with him, he had his fucking son-in-law come in, Todd DeBouff, who was a fucking duffess who didn't know shit about boxing. He tried to run the business, but he fucking didn't know anything. Bob promised to give me ten thousand dollars for my training. Well, being young and dumb, I called him a cheap-ass Jew bag (when he did not give the ten thousand dollars.) He released me the next day (laughing.) I never got my money.

Mr. T: "He was friends with Dan Goossen. Dan promoted my fights towards the end of my career, and he would come around all the time to watch the fights. He was just a good guy. He didn't say much to people (when watching the fights), but if you got him in a room after the fights he would open up and crack jokes, he was a funny guy to be around. He didn't like crowds of people, he wanted to be left alone, kind of like how I was. After the fight, we would just hang out and have a good time."

Mike Tyson: "I saw Mike at the gym all the time. We got along pretty well. He thought I was a crazy white boy. I was always getting into it with one of his cronies. One time, they threatened to tow my BMW when it was parked outside the gym, I told them, 'You touch that fucking car you're gonna get your ass kicked.' I wasn't taking their shit. I would tell them, 'Go get a fucking job, you're licking Mike's boots, and you're telling me to move the car.' You see Mike would hire out the entire gym, Johnny Tocos gym. He would hire it out from like noon to three PM, Mike would be the only one who could go in there. He would be in the process of beating up one of his sparring partners, if your car was not moved in time, they would cause a bunch of bullshit, and I would be like, 'Shut the fuck up and get out of here.' Mike would just laugh and would finally tell some of these guys to lighten up. I had a lot of interaction action with them because they didn't like my music. I would blast my rock n' roll music, fucking Led Zepplin, Metallica, and they would say, 'I don't like your music,' and I would say, 'Well I don't fucking like your music either, if you listen to my shit you would become a champion.' (laughing).

Muhammad Ali: "The best person I ever met was Muhammad. I got some pictures with me and Muhammad. He was at a party in Vegas at Cesars Palace. He was sitting on a couch, and I asked if I could get a picture with him. He knew who I was, and that just blew me away. We were talking about I fight I just had, and he said he was pretty impressed with me…I think it was the Jimmy Paul fight. I still have the pictures. It is one of the greatest things I cherish from boxing. In my mind, he was the greatest fighter that had ever lived."

When an athlete is young and enjoys fame and fortune, they tend to make some bad choices, especially when they come from nothing, like Greg. It is hard to be humble at times. To be brass and cocky is what carries a lot of boxers. The more success you have, the more you feel like King Kong. When going down memory lane with Greg and his "celebritiness', as he phrased it, Greg speaks of some regret with his dealing with promoter Bob Arum: "Bob Arum was the most trustworthy guy I dealt with in the boxing business. Up until the time we had the problem with the training expense money, Bob had done everything he said he was ever going to do as far as promoting me. I screwed up there. 'til this day, that was one of my only regrets in boxing. I didn't have enough sense to keep my mouth shut and not insult somebody and their religion. It was one of the dumbest things I ever could have done because Bob was at the top of his game back then, he still is! Free boxing on ESPN, still putting some of the best fights together. Bob's got it going on at 85 (Bob Arum is 87 years old). It is unfortunate Bob is going to leave the business to Todd DeBuff. Maybe Todd has learned something from being around Bob all these years. He should have. You got to hand it to Bob, he is doing something right"

Indeed, Greg Haugen made mistakes, and it has taken him a long time to admit he was wrong with some of his behavior. But when he was on top of his game, he was just right. A kind soul who stood up to bullies. A great father who fought to see his kids. A passionate man who was willing to always give credit to his rivals. And he could fight a little bit too.

Greg Haugen, much more than just a ToughMan.

George Chemeres, far right, looks on as Greg greets Donald Trump. Even before he became President, Trump always craved the spotlight, here he is checking to see if Greg is ready to fight Paz (Courtesy of Greg Haugen).

Greg's Official Score Cards: Courtesy of the Nevada Athletic Commission

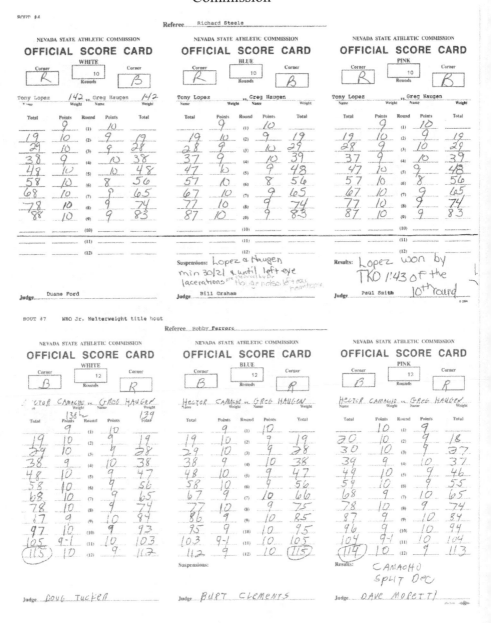

BOUT #4

Referee   Richard Steele

| NEVADA STATE ATHLETIC COMMISSION |
| OFFICIAL SCORE CARD |

WHITE

Corner R   10 Rounds   Corner B

Tony Lopez 142 vs. Greg Haugen 142

Total	Points	Round	Points	Total
	9	(1)	10	
19	10	(2)	9	19
29	10	(3)	9	28
38	9	(4)	10	38
48	10	(5)	10	48
58	10	(6)	8	56
68	10	(7)	9	65
78	10	(8)	9	74
88	10	(9)	9	83
		(10)		
		(11)		
		(12)		

Judge   Duane Ford

| NEVADA STATE ATHLETIC COMMISSION |
| OFFICIAL SCORE CARD |

BLUE

Corner R   10 Rounds   Corner B

Tony Lopez vs. Greg Haugen

Total	Points	Round	Points	Total
	9	(1)	10	
19	10	(2)	9	19
28	9	(3)	10	29
37	9	(4)	10	39
47	10	(5)	9	48
57	10	(6)	8	56
67	10	(7)	9	65
77	10	(8)	9	74
87	10	(9)	9	83
		(10)		
		(11)		
		(12)		

Suspensions: Lopez & Haugen
min 30/21 & until left eye
lacerations are directly by Dr.
Flores not also left eye hematoma.

Judge   Bill Graham

| NEVADA STATE ATHLETIC COMMISSION |
| OFFICIAL SCORE CARD |

PINK

Corner R   10 Rounds   Corner B

Tony Lopez vs. Greg Haugen

Total	Points	Round	Points	Total
	9	(1)	10	
19	10	(2)	9	19
28	9	(3)	10	29
37	9	(4)	10	39
47	10	(5)	9	48
57	10	(6)	8	56
67	10	(7)	9	65
77	10	(8)	9	74
87	10	(9)	9	83
		(10)		
		(11)		
		(12)		

Results: Lopez won by
TKO 1:43 of the
10th round

Judge   Paul Smith

BOUT #7   WBO Jr. Welterweight title bout

Referee   Bobby Ferrara

| NEVADA STATE ATHLETIC COMMISSION |
| OFFICIAL SCORE CARD |

WHITE

Corner B   12 Rounds   Corner R

HECTOR CAMACHO vs. GREG HAUGEN

136½   139

Total	Points	Round	Points	Total
	9	(1)	10	
19	10	(2)	9	19
29	10	(3)	9	28
38	9	(4)	10	38
48	10	(5)	9	47
58	10	(6)	9	56
68	10	(7)	9	65
78	10	(8)	9	74
87	9	(9)	10	84
97	10	(10)	9	93
105	9-1	(11)	10	103
115	10	(12)	9	112

Judge   DOUG TUCKER

| NEVADA STATE ATHLETIC COMMISSION |
| OFFICIAL SCORE CARD |

BLUE

Corner B   12 Rounds   Corner R

HECTOR CAMACHO vs. GREG HAUGEN

Total	Points	Round	Points	Total
	9	(1)	10	
19	10	(2)	9	19
29	10	(3)	9	28
38	9	(4)	10	38
48	10	(5)	9	47
58	10	(6)	9	56
67	9	(7)	10	66
77	10	(8)	9	75
86	9	(9)	10	85
95	9	(10)	10	95
103	9-1	(11)	10	105
112	9	(12)	10	115

Suspensions:

Judge   BURT CLEMENTS

| NEVADA STATE ATHLETIC COMMISSION |
| OFFICIAL SCORE CARD |

PINK

Corner B   12 Rounds   Corner R

HECTOR CAMACHO vs. GREG HAUGEN

Total	Points	Round	Points	Total
	10	(1)	9	
20	10	(2)	9	18
30	10	(3)	9	27
39	9	(4)	10	37
49	10	(5)	9	46
59	10	(6)	9	55
68	9	(7)	10	65
78	10	(8)	9	74
87	9	(9)	10	84
96	9	(10)	10	94
104	9-1	(11)	10	104
114	10	(12)	9	113

Results: CAMACHO
SPLIT DEC

Judge   DAVE MORETTI

BOUT # 4   WBO Super Lightweight title

Referee Carlos Padilla

NEVADA STATE ATHLETIC COMMISSION	NEVADA STATE ATHLETIC COMMISSION	NEVADA STATE ATHLETIC COMMISSION
OFFICIAL SCORE CARD	**OFFICIAL SCORE CARD**	**OFFICIAL SCORE CARD**
WHITE	BLUE	PINK

Corner R — 12 Rounds — Corner B

Hector Camacho MO vs. Greg Haugen 139

Total	Points	Round	Points	Total
	10	(1)	9	
20	10	(2)	9	18
30	10	(3)	8	26
39	9	(4)	10	36
48	9	(5)	10	46
57	9	(6)	10	56
67	10	(7)	9	65
77	10	(8)	9	74
86	9	(9)	10	84
95	9	(10)	10	94
104	9	(11)	10	104
113	9-1	(12)	10	(114)

Judge BILL Mc CONREY

Corner R — 12 Rounds — Corner B

Hector Camacho vs. Greg Haugen

Total	Points	Round	Points	Total
	9	(1)	10	
19	10	(2)	9	19
29	10	(3)	8	27
38	9	(4)	10	37
47	9	(5)	10	47
56	9	(6)	10	57
66	10	(7)	9	66
76	10	(8)	9	75
86	10	(9)	9	84
95	9	(10)	10	94
105	10	(11)	9	103
114	10-1	(12)	9	112

Suspensions:

Judge DALBY SHIRLEY

Carlos Rd. 114

Corner R — 12 Rounds — Corner B

Hector Camacho vs. Greg Haugen

Total	Points	Round	Points	Total
	9	(1)	10	
19	10	(2)	9	19
29	10	(3)	8	27
38	9	(4)	10	37
47	9	(5)	10	47
56	9	(6)	10	57
66	10	(7)	9	66
76	10	(8)	9	75
86	10	(9)	10	85
95	9	(10)	10	95
104	9	(11)	10	105
113	10-1	(12)	9	(114)

Results: HAUGEN SPLIT DEC

Judge ART LURIE

---

②

NEVADA STATE ATHLETIC COMMISSION	NEVADA STATE ATHLETIC COMMISSION	NEVADA STATE ATHLETIC COMMISSION
OFFICIAL SCORE CARD	**OFFICIAL SCORE CARD**	**OFFICIAL SCORE CARD**
WHITE	BLUE	PINK

Corner G — 12 Rounds — Corner C

Greg Haugen 135½ vs. Edwin Curet 134

Total	Points	Round	Points	Total
	10	(1)	9	
19	9	(2)	10	19
29	10	(3)	9	28
39	10	(4)	9	37
49	10	(5)	9	46
59	10	(6)	10	56
68	9	(7)	9	65
78	10	(8)	9	74
88	10	(9)	9	83
98	10	(10)	9	92
108	10	(11)	9	101
(118)	10	(12)	9	110

WINNER: Dave Moretti

Corner G — 12 Rounds — Corner C

Greg Haugen vs. Edwin Curet

Total	Points	Round	Points	Total
	9	(1)	10	
19	9	(2)	10	20
28	10	(3)	9	29
38	10	(4)	9	38
48	10	(5)	9	47
57	9	(6)	10	57
67	10	(7)	9	66
77	10	(8)	9	75
87	10	(9)	9	84
97	10	(10)	9	93
107	10	(11)	9	102
(116)	9	(12)	10	114

Suspension: Haugen (X Ray Right Hand - three Rounds)

WINNER: Dalby Shirley

Corner R — 12 Rounds — Corner R

Greg Haugen vs. Edwin Curet

Total	Points	Round	Points	Total
	9	(1)	10	
19	10	(2)	9	19
29	10	(3)	10	29
37	9	(4)	10	39
47	10	(5)	9	48
57	10	(6)	9	57
67	10	(7)	9	66
77	10	(8)	9	75
87	10	(9)	9	84
97	10	(10)	10	94
(107)	10	(11)	9	103
(116)	9	(12)	10	113

Winner: Haugen

WINNER: Terry Smith

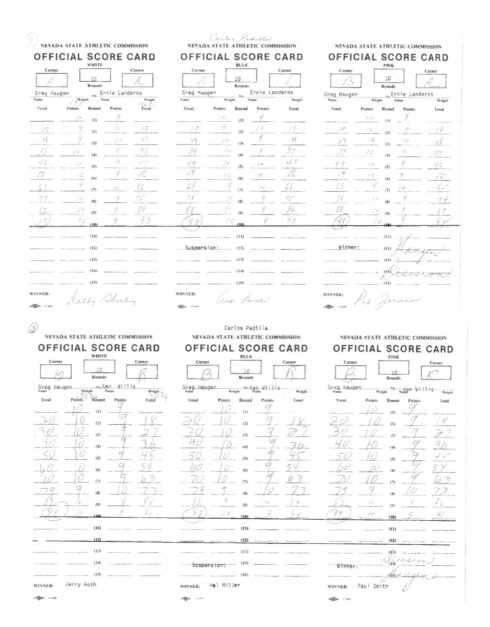

329

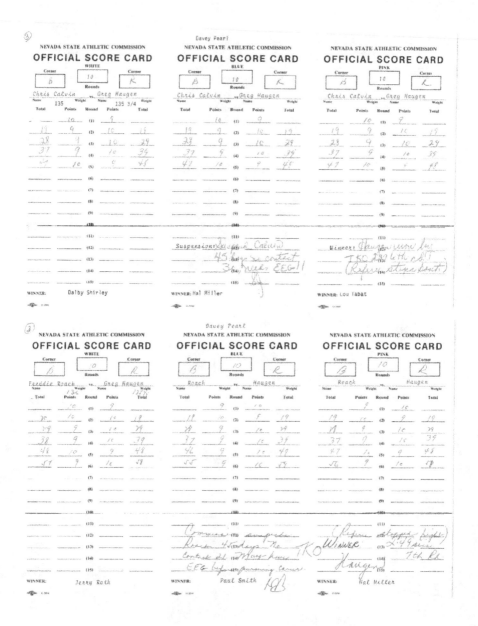

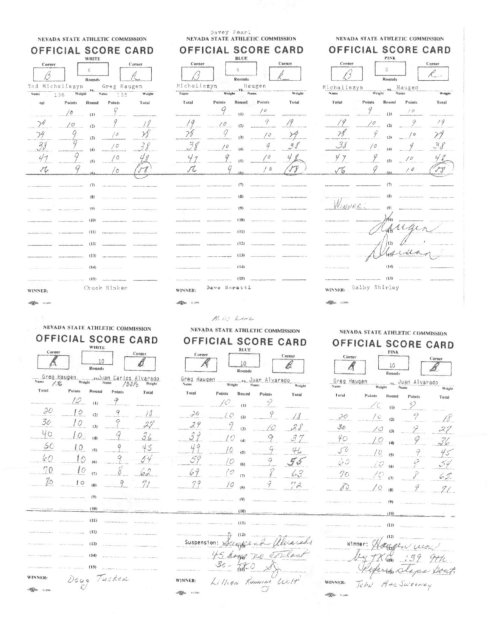

M. H. Lane

NEVADA STATE ATHLETIC COMMISSION

OFFICIAL SCORE CARD

WHITE

| Corner | | 10 | Corner | |
| R | | Rounds | B | |

Greg Haugen _132_ vs. Juan Carlos Alvarado _132½_
Name   Weight   Name   Weight

Total	Points	Round	Points	Total
	10	(1)	9	
20	10	(2)	9	18
30	10	(3)	9	27
40	10	(4)	9	36
50	10	(5)	9	45
60	10	(6)	9	54
70	10	(7)	8	62
80	10	(8)	9	71
		(9)		
		(10)		
		(11)		
		(12)		
		(13)		
		(14)		
		(15)		

WINNER: _Doug Tucker_

NEVADA STATE ATHLETIC COMMISSION

OFFICIAL SCORE CARD

BLUE

| Corner | | 10 | Corner | |
| R | | Rounds | B | |

Greg Haugen _____ vs. Juan Alvarado _____
Name   Weight   Name   Weight

Total	Points	Round	Points	Total
	10	(1)	9	
20	10	(2)	9	18
29	9	(3)	10	28
39	10	(4)	9	37
49	10	(5)	9	46
59	10	(6)	9	55
69	10	(7)	8	63
79	10	(8)	9	72
		(9)		
		(10)		
		(11)		
		(12)		

Suspension: _Haugen and Alvarado_
45 days no contact
30 - TKO

WINNER: _Lillian Running Wolf_

NEVADA STATE ATHLETIC COMMISSION

OFFICIAL SCORE CARD

PINK

| Corner | | 10 | Corner | |
| R | | Rounds | B | |

Greg Haugen _____ vs. Juan Alvarado _____
Name   Weight   Name   Weight

Total	Points	Round	Points	Total
	10	(1)	9	
20	10	(2)	9	18
30	10	(3)	9	27
40	10	(4)	9	36
50	10	(5)	9	45
60	10	(6)	9	54
70	10	(7)	8	62
80	10	(8)	9	71
		(9)		
		(10)		
		(11)		
		(12)		

Winner: _Haugen won_
by TKO :39 4th
Referee stops bout

WINNER: _John MacSweeney_

BOUT #1   Referee   Mitch Halpern

NEVADA STATE ATHLETIC COMMISSION

OFFICIAL SCORE CARD

WHITE

| Corner | | 10 | Corner | |
| B | | Rounds | R | |

Greg Haugen _148_ vs. Mark Brannon _143½_
Name   Weight   Name   Weight

Total	Points	Round	Points	Total
		(1)	13	
19	10	(2)	9	19
29	10	(3)	7	26
		(4)		
		(5)		
		(6)		
		(7)		
		(8)		
		(9)		
		(10)		
		(11)		
		(12)		

Judge   Dalby Shirley

NEVADA STATE ATHLETIC COMMISSION

OFFICIAL SCORE CARD

BLUE

| Corner | | 10 | Corner | |
| | | Rounds | | |

Greg Haugen _____ vs. Mark Brannon _____
Name   Weight   Name   Weight

Total	Points	Round	Points	Total
	10	(1)	9	
19	9	(2)	10	19
29	10	(3)	7	26
		(4)		
		(5)		
		(6)		
		(7)		
		(8)		
		(9)		
		(10)		
		(11)		
		(12)		

Suspensions: _Brannon Cut over Eye_
30 days no fight
21 days no contact

Judge   Al Siciliano

NEVADA STATE ATHLETIC COMMISSION

OFFICIAL SCORE CARD

PINK

| Corner | | 10 | Corner | |
| | | Rounds | | |

Greg Haugen _____ vs. Mark Brannon _____
Name   Weight   Name   Weigh

Total	Points	Round	Points	Total
	10	(1)	9	
19	9	(2)	10	19
29	10	(3)	7	26
		(4)		
		(5)		
		(6)		
		(7)		
		(8)		
		(9)		
		(10)		
		(11)		
		(12)		

Results: _Haugen win by_
TKO 4th Rd

Judge   Dick Houck

332

Referee Mills Lane

NEVADA STATE ATHLETIC COMMISSION
OFFICIAL SCORE CARD
WHITE

Corner		Corner
B	10	R
	Rounds	

Greg Haugen vs. Tommy Hanks

Name	Weight 139	Name	Weight 138

Total	Points	Round	Points	Total
	10	(1)	9	
20	10	(2)	9	18
30	10	(3)	9	27
40	10	(4)	9	36
50	10	(5)	9	45
60	10	(6)	9	54
70	10	(7)	9	63
80	10	(8)	9	72
90	10	(9)	8	81
99	10	(10)	10	91
		(11)		
		(12)		

Judge Burt Clements

NEVADA STATE ATHLETIC COMMISSION
OFFICIAL SCORE CARD
BLUE

Corner		Corner
B	10	R
	Rounds	

Greg Haugen vs. Tommy Hanks

Total	Points	Round	Points	Total
	10	(1)	9	
20	10	(2)	9	18
30	10	(3)	9	27
40	10	(4)	9	36
50	10	(5)	9	45
60	10	(6)	9	54
70	10	(7)	9	63
80	10	(8)	9	72
90	10	(9)	9	81
100	10	(10)	9	90
		(11)		
		(12)		

Suspensions: HANKS CUT AT EYE NEEDS SUTURES - SUSPENDED TILL CLEARED BY PHYSICIAN

Judge Keith Macdonald

NEVADA STATE ATHLETIC COMMISSION
OFFICIAL SCORE CARD
PINK

Corner		Corner
B	10	R
	Rounds	

Greg Haugen vs. Tommy Hanks

Total	Points	Round	Points	Total
	10	(1)	9	
20	10	(2)	9	18
30	10	(3)	9	27
40	10	(4)	9	36
50	10	(5)	9	45
60	10	(6)	9	54
70	10	(7)	9	63
80	10	(8)	9	72
90	10	(9)	9	81
100	10	(10)	9	90
		(11)		
		(12)		

Results: HAUGIN UNAN DEC

Judge Doug Tucker

7:00 pm bout

MILLS LANE

NEVADA STATE ATHLETIC COMMISSION
OFFICIAL SCORE CARD
WHITE

Corner		Corner
B	10	R
	Rounds	

Greg Haugen vs. Bobby Nunez

Name	Weight 140	Name	Weight 139

Total	Points	Round	Points	Total
	10	(1)	9	
20	10	(2)	9	18
30	10	(3)	9	27
40	10	(4)	9	36
50	10	(5)	9	45
60	10	(6)	9	54
		(7)		
		(8)		
		(9)		
		(10)		
		(11)		
		(12)		
		(13)		
		(14)		
		(15)		

WINNER:

Keith Macdonald

NEVADA STATE ATHLETIC COMMISSION
OFFICIAL SCORE CARD
BLUE

Corner		Corner
B	10	R
	Rounds	

Greg Haugen vs. Bobby Nunez

Total	Points	Round	Points	Total
	10	(1)	9	
20	10	(2)	9	18
30	10	(3)	9	27
40	10	(4)	9	36
50	10	(5)	9	45
60	10	(6)	8	53
		(7)		
		(8)		
		(9)		
		(10)		
		(11)		
		(12)		
		(13)		
		(14)		
		(15)		

SUSPENSIONS: NUNEZ - SUS INJUR. LACERATION UNDER LEFT eye until cleared by dents

WINNER:

Doug Tucker

NEVADA STATE ATHLETIC COMMISSION
OFFICIAL SCORE CARD
PINK

Corner		Corner
B	10	R
	Rounds	

Greg Haugen vs. Bobby Nunez

Total	Points	Round	Points	Total
	10	(1)	9	
20	10	(2)	9	18
30	10	(3)	8	26
40	10	(4)	9	35
50	10	(5)	9	44
60	10	(6)	9	53
		(7)		
		(8)		
		(9)		
		(10)		
		(11)		
		(12)		
		(13)		
		(14)		
		(15)		

WINNER: HAUGEN TKO 6th RD - NUNEZ DOES NO ANSWER BELL FOR 7TH

John McSweeney

BOUT #4

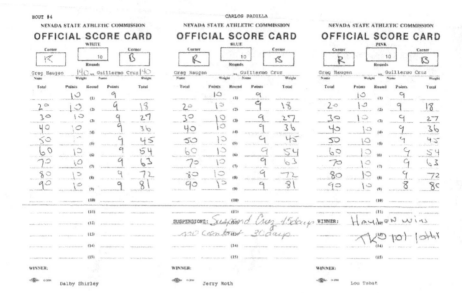

NEVADA STATE ATHLETIC COMMISSION	NEVADA STATE ATHLETIC COMMISSION	NEVADA STATE ATHLETIC COMMISSION
OFFICIAL SCORE CARD	**OFFICIAL SCORE CARD**	**OFFICIAL SCORE CARD**

WHITE / BLUE / PINK

Corner: R — 10 Rounds — Corner: B (all three cards)

Greg Haugen 140 vs. Guillermo Cruz 140

WHITE

Total	Points	Round	Points	Total
	10	(1)	9	
20	10	(2)	9	18
30	10	(3)	9	27
40	10	(4)	9	36
50	10	(5)	9	45
60	10	(6)	9	54
70	10	(7)	9	63
80	10	(8)	9	72
90	10	(9)	9	81

WINNER:
Dalby Shirley

BLUE

Total	Points	Round	Points	Total
	10	(1)	9	
20	10	(2)	9	18
30	10	(3)	9	27
40	10	(4)	9	36
50	10	(5)	9	45
60	10	(6)	9	54
70	10	(7)	9	63
80	10	(8)	9	72
90	10	(9)	9	81

SUSPENSIONS: Suspend Cruz 45days
no combat 30 days

WINNER:
Jerry Roth

PINK

Total	Points	Round	Points	Total
	10	(1)	9	
20	10	(2)	9	18
30	10	(3)	9	27
40	10	(4)	9	36
50	10	(5)	9	45
60	10	(6)	9	54
70	10	(7)	9	63
80	10	(8)	9	72
90	10	(9)	8	80

WINNER: Haugen wins
TKO 10† 10thr

WINNER:
Lou Tabat

About the Author

Anthony "Zute" George was born in the Bronx, New York. His first boxing memory was when Leon Spinks upset Muhammad Ali on national television in 1978. He has hosted Zutes Boxing Talk since 2010. The show can be heard on BlogTalk Radio, AnthonyGeorgeRadio on iTunes, and Google Play. He also currently the Lead Writer for Ringside Report.com. His Twitter handle is @zutesboxingtalk.

Acknowledgements

This book would not have been written without the great career of Greg Haugen. Greg put his trust in me, and I hope I did his great career justice. I also want to give a special thanks to Bruce Springsteen and The E Street Band, as they were with me during a significant part of this journey.

A very special thanks to John Chemeres for allowing me to use such great pictures. CompuBox Stats are courtesy of Bob Canobio & Lee Groves. CompuBox: Every Punch Counts. Established 1985.

Special thanks to the Nevada Athletic Commission for sending the official scorecards of Greg's fights.

I also want to thank all of the people I interviewed for this book, the names appear in no particular order: Jeff Bumpus, Tony The Tiger Lopez, Kathy Duva, Jeff Fenech, Jimmy Paul, Juan Carlos Alvarado, Freddie Roach, Don King, Bill McDonald, Pernell Whitaker, Joe Belinc, Bret Summers, Troy Summers, Victor Machado, Leeonzer Barber, Jim Montgomery, Pamela Balding, Livingstone Bramble, Chris Calvin, Ted Michaliszyn, Paul Nave, Edwin Curet, Al Bernstein, Lee Groves, Dave Murphy, Bob Howard, Thomas Migneault, Chris Cates, Zac Pomilio, Randy Gordon, Bob Howard, Robert Jarvis, Paul Nave, Grover Wiley, Rudy Lovato, Peter Howes, Mike Acri, Joe Hipp, Joe Cortez, John Chemeres, Shelly Vincent*, Robert Brant*, Christian Guidice*, Devon Alexander*, Regis Prograis*, Pinklon Thomas*, James Hagler*, Tim Witherspoon*, Buddy McGirt*, Donny Lalonde*, Vinny Paz*.

On a personal note, I want to give some thanks to those who mean a lot to me and have been either a great support, or inspiration in some way when writing this book, and in my life: Dawn George, Eric Scalise, Jason Rios, Dave Wilcox, Rick Glaser, Ron Christian, Bad Brad Berkwitt, Debbie Edwards, Richard Chirico, Marvelous Marvin Hagler, Michael Spinks, Kim Scalise, Roberta Greatheart, Ashley Bridgett, Jasmine Medina, Richard George SR., Ana George,

Theresann George, George Kimball, Sirin Thomas, Dominic Mo, George Chuvalo, Nigel Collins, Jerry Fitch, Paul Daley, Orlando Canizales, Bert Cooper, Tommy Forte, Crazy Al Rivera, Lou Garcia, John Garcia, Phil Garcia, Robert DeNiro, Bob Dylan, Dan Cuoco, Carol Meyer, Rocky Marciano, Leonardo DiCaprio, Chazz Lent, Joaquin Phoenix, Pat & Goody Petronelli, Mark Too Sharp Johnson, Jorge Arce, Chiquita Gonzalez, Teofimo Lopez, Tony Luis, Larry Fryers, Stanley Kubrick, Paul Newman, John Lennon, Micky Ward, Arturo Gatti, Dicky Ecklund, Spike Lee, Phil Collins, Floyd Patterson, Joe Frazier, Tony Thornton, Sean O' Grady, President Jimmy Carter, John Adams, Harriet Tubman, Fredrick Douglass, John Brown, Martin Luther King, JR , Rosa Parks, Make It Plain With Mark Thompson, Howard Zinn, Michael Eric Dyson, David F. Walker, Frank Miller, Marv Wolfman, Gene Colan, Neil Adams, Jackie Robinson, Dave Bontempo, Henry Jones, James Toney, Steve USS Cunningham, Charles Foster, and The Madden League.

There are so many more. But who has time to read them all? Anyone who has come on Zutes Boxing Talk will always have a special place in my heart. Even those fighters who stopped coming on after they got big.

*These contributions are taken from interviews conducted on Zutes Boxing Talk. All other interviews were conducted directly for this book. Pernell Whitaker was interviewed directly for this book, but some of his quotes were taken from his interview on Zutes Boxing talk.

References

BoxRec Encyclopedia.

"Kirkman Boasts Every Essential For Heavy Title, Hurley Insists," by Nat Loubet, THE RING, June 1968, p. 10.

"Haugen Wins Unanimous Decision," by Craig Smith, The Seattle Times, Wednesday, April 27th, 1983, F-2.

"New Faces: Greg Haugen," by Jack Welsh, THE RING, April 1986, p. 11.

"Ringside Reports: Haugen-Curet," by Jack Welsh, THE RING, August 1986, p. 30.

"KO Closeup: A Thumbnail Sketch of Greg Haugen," KO: The Knockout Boxing Magazine, June 1987, p. 35.

"Letter: Judges View," by Clark Sammartino, Sports Illustrated, July 6th, 1987.

"Vinny Pazienza Bedevils Greg Haugen: A Raucous Rumble In Rhode Island," by Jeff Ryan, KO: The Knockout Boxing Magazine, October 1987, p. 26.

"Between Rounds: Robbery!!!," Letters from L. Bruce De Oilers & John A. Serpe, KO: The Knockout Boxing Magazine, November 1987, P.26. Editors Note p. 27.

"Fight Report: Vinny Pazienza vs. Greg Haugen," by Jay N. Miller, THE RING, October 1987.

"The Devils Dilemma: Vinny Paz Wins IBF Title In Controversial Call…But Can He Hold It?" by Wes Moon, THE RING, October 1987, p. 8.

"The Predictor: Vinny Pazienza vs. Greg Haugen," KO: The Knockout Boxing Magazine, December 1987, p. 31.

"KO Achievement '87," KO: The Knockout Boxing Magazine, March 1988, p. 46.

"Vinny Pazienza & Greg Haugen Go For Each Others Throats," KO: The Knockout Boxing Magazine, February 1988, p. 32.

"Haugen Retains IBF Title," by J Michael Kenyon, The News Tribune, April 12th, 1988.

"Haugen keep title despite 'losing' fight," Tacoma AP, April 12th, 1988, Section D.

"Greg Haugen: More Than Just A Tough Guy," by Jeff Ryan, Boxing 88, June 1988, p. 30.

"Haugen Defeats Pazienza And This Time The Judges Agree," by Jeff Ryan, KO: The Knockout Boxing Magazine, June 1988, p. 24.

"Ringside Reports: Haugen-Santana," by William Tuthill, THE RING, August 1988, p. 24.

"Ringside Reports: Haugen-Jacobsen," THE RING, March 1989, p. 23.

From the rough streets of Auburn, Washington, to the amateur circuit, the bars of Alaska, to the professional ranks, and the championship level, Greg Haugen has excelled in pugilism. For the first time, hear his own words about his boxing career. Anyone who has ever know Greg has respected him immensely as a boxer, even those who hate him. Read the testimonies of Hall of Famers Jeff Fenech, Al Bernstein, Kathy Duva, Don King, and Pernell Whitaker. Opponents Jeff Bumpus, Freddie Roach, Chris Calvin, Edwin Curet, Tony The Tiger Lopez, and Jimmy Paul, all give their stories of what it was like to fight against Greg. Tough Man: The Greg Haugen Story, peels the intriguing onion of the man they called, 'Mutt," boxings career.